After Mandela

Alec Russell is World News Editor of the *Financial Times* and was formerly their Johannesburg bureau chief. He has been a foreign correspondent since arriving in Romania aged 23, ten days after the 1989 Christmas Revolution, to start his career in journalism. He previously covered the wars in the former Yugoslavia and the end of apartheid for the *Daily Telegraph*, where he was Foreign Editor from 2001 to 2003. He has won several prizes and commendations in the annual British Press Awards. His writing from southern Africa earned him a prestigious award for the best published feature on Africa in 2007. He is the author of two previous books. He is married, has two sons and lives in London.

Praise for *After Mandela*

'Excellent and disquieting. Russell offers balanced portraits of the three postapartheid presidents, the policy successes and failures of the successive governments, and the emergence of a black elite . . . Russell leavens his pessimism with inspiring tales of individual courage and virtue . . .'

Foreign Affairs

'A sweeping, up-to-date account . . . A compelling, bracing chronicle. Russell offers an acute look at the remarkable period when apartheid unraveled and a new political system under the African National Congress (ANC) took shape . . . Russell's timely book makes vividly clear that many hopes, both for political freedom and social justice, still hang in the balance'

Washington Post

'A clear-sighted, nuanced portrayal of a country lurching towards its greatest challenges since the end of white rule . . . His sympathetic account is hard but fair – and very readable'

Metro

'It is a relief to view South Africa's past two decades through Alec Russell's gentler, insightful, sometimes humorous, sometimes bleak, but always kaleidoscopic prism. He robustly addresses the doleful issues of governance . . . But his portrait of South Africa, alive with delicious vignettes across a range of humanity, is more nuanced – and more readable'

Economist

'An engaging chronicle of the post-apartheid years . . . nuanced'

Matthew Kaminski, *Wall Street Journal*

'A vivid portrait of post-apartheid South Africa, briskly depicting the dramas of a young nation and the telling threats to its future'

Peter Godwin, author of *When a Crocodile Eats the Sun*

'*After Mandela* is one of the most incisive, balanced, accurate books you're likely to read on the history of our [South Africa's] past couple of decades by an author of any nationality'

Cape Times

'*After Mandela* breaks the mould [of foreign accounts of South Africa]. It is pacy and well-written but more vitally rooted in real research among real people. Moreover it is authoritative . . . Paints a potted history of post-apartheid South Africa . . . He knows how to link the big themes to the small people'

Mail & Guardian, Johannesburg

'Readable and accessible . . . Reflects the complexity of the development process and the political transition from dictatorship to democracy'

Prospect, August 2009

'A cogent study of the political perils ensnaring South Africa since the fall of apartheid . . . An important dispatch from a journalist in the trenches'

Kirkus

'In open, journalistic style, Russell looks in depth and detail at the stalled dream of peace and reconciliation . . . This is exciting contemporary history, a must for anyone concerned with what is happening now'

Booklist

'Alec Russell does not pull punches in describing the widespread disillusionment among blacks and the disasters of the Mbeki years. But he does seek to put the ruling party's shortcomings in context and recognises that life is better for many South Africans than it was . . . Russell maps out [the power struggle in the ANC] and asks what path South Africa will now follow.'

Observer

'In *After Mandela*, Alec Russell provides an absorbing account of the transition [from apartheid]'

Mail on Sunday, 4 star review

'Scrupulously reported . . . damning [about the ANC's record] and hilarious insights'

Sunday Times, Christmas Books of 2009

'Intensely researched and highly readable examination . . . Unflinchingly honest . . . For anyone anxious to understand almost everything of any importance about the country (even rugby) Russell's book is a must: it is hugely thorough and written with lucidity and humanity'

Natal Witness

'Fast paced and thoughtful account . . . has immediacy and relevance'

The Herald, Port Elizabeth

'Nuanced explanatory account . . . made human by anecdotes involving a range of people of different backgrounds and walks of life. Going beyond the politics to look at important issues such as land and crime . . . it brings a broader frame of reference, comparing South Africa to Eastern European countries after the fall of communism . . . This kind of perspective is sorely needed'

International Institute for Strategic Studies, August 2009

After Mandela

The Battle for the Soul of South Africa

ALEC RUSSELL

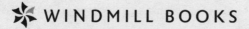

✴ WINDMILL BOOKS

Published by Windmill Books 2010

2 4 6 8 10 9 7 5 3

Copyright © Alec Russell 2009

Alec Russell has asserted his right under the Copyright, Designs and Patents Act,
1988 to be identified as the author of this work.

First published in Great Britain in 2009 by Hutchinson

Windmill Books
The Random House Group Limited
20 Vauxhall Bridge Road, London, SW1V 2SA

Addresses for companies within The Random House Group Limited can be found at:
www.randomhouse.co.uk/offices.htm

The Random House Group Limited Reg. No. 954009

www.rbooks.co.uk

A CIP catalogue record for this book
is available from the British Library

ISBN 9780099534020

The Random House Group Limited supports The Forest Stewardship
Council (FSC), the leading international forest certification organisation. All our titles
that are printed on Greenpeace approved FSC certified paper carry the FSC logo.
Our paper procurement policy can be found at:
www.rbooks.co.uk/environment

Mixed Sources
Product group from well-managed
forests and other controlled sources
www.fsc.org Cert no. TT-COC-2139
© 1996 Forest Stewardship Council

Printed and bound in Great Britain by
CPI Cox & Wyman, Reading, RG1 8EX

*To Sophie and that irrepressible duo, Mungo and Ned,
with my undying love*

CONTENTS

Chronology   xi
Map of South Africa   xiii
Introduction: The New Struggle   xv

CHAPTER 1   Succeeding a Saint   1

CHAPTER 2   The Other Side of the Rainbow   25

CHAPTER 3   Liberation Movements Have a Habit
of Not Ageing Gracefully   53

CHAPTER 4   The Difficulties of Delivery   81

CHAPTER 5   A City Under Siege   107

CHAPTER 6   The White Africans   133

CHAPTER 7   The New Randlords   157

CHAPTER 8   The Graves of the Ancestors   181

CHAPTER 9   The AIDS Betrayal   201

CHAPTER 10   The 100 Per Cent Zulu Boy   231

CHAPTER 11   The Shadow of Zimbabwe   261

CHAPTER 12   Beijing and Beyond   277

Acknowledgements   291
Notes   295
Select Bibliography   311
Index   313

CHRONOLOGY

1652 First Dutch settlement founded at the Cape by Jan van Riebeeck

1836 Start of the Great Trek by Afrikaners from the Cape

1886 Discovery of gold on Witwatersrand

1899–1902 Anglo-Boer War

1910 Union of South Africa founded with the merging of the Boer Republics of the Orange Free State and the Transvaal and the British colonies of the Cape and Natal

1912 Foundation of the African National Congress in Bloemfontein

1913 Native Land Act restricts blacks to reservations, depriving millions of their birthright

1918 Nelson Mandela born in the Eastern Cape

1948 National Party comes to power on platform of separating races

1955 Congress of the People adopts the Freedom Charter

1959 Pan-Africanist Congress (PAC) breaks away from ANC

1960 Sharpeville Massacre: 69 protesters killed by police; ANC and PAC banned

1962 Nelson Mandela arrested

1964 Nelson Mandela and other ANC leaders sentenced to life imprisonment

1976 Soweto student uprising

1977 Steve Biko dies in police custody

1989 F. W. de Klerk takes over leadership of National Party

1990 F. W. de Klerk unbans the ANC and PAC and releases Mandela from prison

1994 First democratic election; inauguration of Mandela as president

1999 Thabo Mbeki inaugurated as president after ANC wins increased majority

2004 Mbeki wins second term with even larger majority for ANC

2005 Jacob Zuma fired as deputy president and charged with corruption

2006 Jacob Zuma acquitted of charge of raping the daughter of a family friend; corruption case thrown out of court on a technicality

2007 Zuma defeats Mbeki in election for leadership of the ANC; Zuma charged again with corruption, fraud, racketeering, money laundering and tax evasion

2008 ANC deposes Mbeki as national president after a judge throws out Zuma's corruption case on a technicality

2009 Zuma elected president of South Africa

INTRODUCTION:
THE NEW STRUGGLE

There is no short cut to the country of our dreams.

— NELSON MANDELA,
ON THE FIRST ANNIVERSARY
OF THE FIRST ALL-RACE ELECTIONS

The history of countries throwing off tyrannical regimes tends to follow a pattern. In the immediate aftermath there is euphoria, accompanied by utopian pledges for the future. Then the new rulers find the business of governing more difficult and messier than they could ever have imagined. They also find that it is far harder to overcome their own past than they had appreciated as they plotted their takeover in prison or in exile. It is in this second stage that the true meaning and trajectory of a revolution unfold.

In Eastern Europe after the fall of the Berlin Wall, the jubilation at the overthrow of communism soon gave way to distress at the hardship of the shift to free-market economics and to agonising over how to exorcise the past. Africa had a yet harder experience in the second half of the twentieth century, when the continent celebrated as colonial flags were struck down, only to see the promise of the new era swiftly implode. The new states were betrayed by the colonising powers, which had equipped them with only a handful of graduates to run their governments. They were betrayed by Moscow and Washington, who used them as proxy battlefields of the Cold War. Most of all they were betrayed by their own leaders, many of whom did little but bask in personality cults and fill foreign bank accounts while beggaring their people. These new states inherited a complex set of challenges, not least how to take a largely undeveloped society into the modern world. The task would have challenged any new political cast, however brilliant. South Africa, the continent's unofficial superpower, is no different.

For a few years after the end of white rule in 1994, Nelson Mandela's visionary leadership encouraged the hazy belief that a political miracle had occurred and that a new South Africa had been born, exorcised of the torment of the past. For many years it had been widely assumed that South Africa's fight for liberation from apartheid would end in a race war. Instead, the tall, dignified leader of the African National Congress emerged from twenty-seven years in prison preaching forgiveness. Together with the last white president, F. W. de Klerk, a more flawed but also brave leader, Mandela steered their troubled land to peace. South Africa's negotiated transition from white rule to democracy was one of the wonders of the late twentieth century. But it was only the first chapter of the post-liberation narrative.

The ANC made a steady start in tackling the legacy of white rule. It swiftly introduced a liberal constitution supported by independent courts that guaranteed rights long denied under apartheid. It revived the economy. It established South Africa as a presence on the world stage. But after fifteen years in power, the ANC is losing its way. It has catastrophically failed its two greatest challenges, AIDS and the collapse of Zimbabwe on its border. Now it is fighting to escape the shadow of so many other liberation movements that came to office with great dreams only to see them founder under the weight of unfulfillable expectations and against the backdrop of corruption, infighting and misrule. South Africa's second 'struggle' is under way.

When I first came to South Africa in April 1993, the struggle against apartheid was reaching a dramatic climax. Mandela had been released from prison and the ANC unbanned three years earlier, but white extremists and Zulu irredentists threatened to secede and plunge the country into chaos. While the worst of the apartheid laws had been repealed, travelling across the country was still like stepping back in time. Outside the major cities the only black people in sight in the areas traditionally set aside for whites worked at gas stations and cafes or waited at the side of the road for transport home to their township. The presenters on state radio had the same homely tones – and fruity 1950s BBC intonation – that had comforted white South Africans through the long years of white rule. The news was unremittingly bleak: mediation talks between the ANC and the government were stalling; pylons had been blown up by right-wing extremists; the townships east of Johannesburg were engulfed in fighting. It all sounded depressingly familiar.

I had come to South Africa from Bosnia after eighteen months' reporting on Yugoslavia's descent into civil war. There I had learned to despair of the cynicism of politicians who whipped up ancient ethnic animosities for their own ends. There were grim parallels with the situation in South Africa. Just as shadowy paramilitaries stoked tensions in the Bosnian hinterland in the countdown to the war, death squads were at work in South Africa, running through early-morning trains in the sprawling townships of Soweto randomly killing commuters and fomenting the fighting in the townships. Then, of course, there were the maps.

Under apartheid the domestic maps of South Africa had resembled giant blotting pads, reflecting the borders that the Nationalists drew up for the tribal 'homelands' to ensure that whites rather than blacks had most of the prime agricultural land. Now right-wingers were once again plotting another unjust carve-up, this time of a white rather than a black homeland that would keep them safe from the 'horrors' of majority rule. Their proposals bore no relation to demographics or political reality. They reminded me of the maps that Bosnian Serb warlords had sketched out for me over endless glasses of plum brandy, ludicrously justifying their annexation of most of Bosnia. In those uncertain months of the southern autumn and winter, I learned to dread the moment when during an interview an Afrikaner would announce it was time to look at the map.

Robert Van Tonder was the ultimate *bittereinder* (from South African history, an Afrikaner who refused to surrender to the British). A short, silver-haired man with a military bearing and bright red cheeks, he favoured a blazer and tie rather than the long socks and khaki shorts that were once the signature of white African farmers. The impression was more country club than Afrikaner patriarch, but his clipped sardonic tones espoused the Old Testament certainties and white supremacist convictions of the early Afrikaners who had settled in South Africa in the seventeenth century.

Van Tonder's father had been one of the diehards who wanted to fight the imperial British troops to the last in the Anglo-Boer war at the start of the twentieth century. His mother had spent years in a British concentration camp. In his fevered imagination he would lead the followers of his tiny *Boer-estaat* (Afrikaner homeland) party into the grave rather than submit to the 'communistic' [sic] ANC. I met him in June 1993, in the last turbulent year of white rule. He stood as if to attention, gazing out over the gum trees that lined his farm. There had been no rain for two months. A chill wind sweeping over the veld rippled through his maize. It also seemed to prime his doom-laden rhetoric. His voice rose. The dismal history of post-colonial Africa would be repeated in South Africa. F. W. de Klerk, the then president negotiating a settlement with the ANC, was a traitor and a fool. Civil war would follow if there were not a white homeland.

'I was in the desert a long time, but now they say I am a prophet . . .' he said. 'De Klerk is trying to reconstruct the Tower of Babel. He's trying to do the impossible. How in the hell will he succeed? They will say, "Van Tonder, you are raving in calling for a separate Afrikaner state." But if they don't agree, they will have a Lebanon situation.'[1] He stopped abruptly and led me into his farmhouse. There he reached for a map of South Africa from the mid-nineteenth century, when the short-lived Boer Republics of the Transvaal, Northern Natal and the Orange Free State were just taking shape. As we sat looking out over the veld, I knew I was in for a long afternoon. There is something about irredentists and maps.

'General de Gaulle said every fifty years the world goes mad,' he said as his stubby fingers jabbed at his chart. 'The nonsense the ANC tells people. The resistance of the *Boerestaat* is as inevitable as the sun coming up in the morning.' He took me outside. Under the thin wintry sun we gazed out over his farm, stretching into the empty veld. He saluted under the *vierkleur* (the old Boer Republic flag) for a photograph. Then, unsmiling, he waved me away.

Van Tonder's defiance and racist rancour appeared unbending. But the elections of April 1994 swept away his dreams of stopping the clock and exposed his party as little more than a few right-wingers with a fax machine. A dozen or so kindred spirits detonated bombs, killing more than twenty people on the eve of the elections. The dull boom echoed across Johannesburg one sunny Sunday morning, as the most deadly of these bombs exploded outside a hotel in the centre of the city. But there was no third Boer War. The bombers were swiftly arrested, tried and convicted. Van Tonder repaired to his farm in mutinous isolation.

For the next four years I chronicled the fairy-tale ending of apartheid and marvelled with the world at Mandela's reconciliatory wizardry and South Africa's transformation from a pariah state to a moral authority. I never saw Van Tonder again. He sounded off in public, decrying the new order once a year on what was known under apartheid as the Day of the Covenant, the anniversary of the 1838 annihilation of a Zulu army by a few hundred Boers. These annual diatribes, handwritten in spidery script, would chug through my fax machine in my office in Johannesburg. I could translate only a few words of the Afrikaans, but the apocalyptic gist was clear from the exclamation marks. Then, almost fourteen years after my first visit to his farm, I had an extraordinary flashback to the old dinosaur. I was keen to write about the phenomenon of the new black middle class bursting out of the townships and had been told to head for Cosmo City, one of the new glitzy housing estates booming on Johannesburg's outskirts.

Themba Molefe, a diminutive figure with square thick-rimmed glasses reminiscent of the style sported by the late Zairean dictator Mobutu Sese Seko, was one of the doughty journalists who in the old era sought to expose the abuses of apartheid. In the final months of white rule we had celebrated together until dawn, after the white government and the ANC reached a peace settlement. Fourteen years later, he was the first to highlight that where Van Tonder's crops once swayed in the winter wind, there was now a smart new housing estate for blacks. The giant gum trees that fringed Van Tonder's home were still standing. But most of the right-winger's farm tracks were hidden beneath tarmac. Where his faded 'old' South African flag once fluttered defiantly at his gatepost was a billboard advertising special deals. In the final insult to his memory, his thatched farmhouse had become the site headquarters. The nerve centre of the *Boerestaat* had become Cosmo City, a temple to black middle-class bling – in an extraordinary twist,

Hans, Van Tonder's son, took up residence there and declared proudly that he was the one white face among nine thousand black ones.[2]

Van Tonder never lived to see the bulldozers turning his hectares into swanky black housing; he died in 1999 after a long fight against cancer, railing to the last against the advent of democracy. But there is one aspect of post-apartheid South Africa that would unquestionably have surprised him: the ANC embraced capitalism with a relish unthinkable when its leaders returned from exile and prison in 1990, talking of nationalising the commanding heights of the economy. With its fancy mock-Tuscan homes with fake campaniles and pastel-shaded villas behind giant engraved bronze gates, the United States of America Boulevard was a solid symbol of the vanquishing of the old order. Cosmo City was the fruit of a partnership between private developers and the authorities. It offered three categories of houses, including state-subsidised low-cost homes for people from a nearby shanty town. It was tangible evidence of the success of the new order. Under apartheid black people had had to reside in drab dormitory townships deprived of all but basic amenities. Now they could glory in the best the free market had to offer.

In the old days, when radical politics held sway in anti-apartheid circles, Castro Street or Guevara Avenue would have been the address of choice. The profusion of American street names in the wealthier area of Cosmo City, including Tennessee Street and Las Vegas Crescent, reflected how a more globalised view of the world had taken hold of the ANC.

The ANC has proved a reliable steward of sub-Saharan Africa's largest economy, embracing orthodox fiscal and monetary policies and handling the nation's finances far more steadily than the Afrikaner Nationalists in the last years of apartheid. A decade after the end of white rule, South Africa enjoyed its most concerted period of economic growth since the Second World War. Between 2004 and 2007 the economy grew at an average of 5 per cent a year. If someone had suggested to me on my arrival in South Africa in the last year of white rule that the big economic argument a decade later would be how to move from 5 to 6 per cent growth, I would have dismissed the idea as absurd.

In April 1993 I had rented a furnished flat next door to a tiny Johannesburg shopping centre. Most nights I would repair to La Via, a homely pasta house run by Bertha, an Italian expatriate. I was usually the only customer. Bertha and her

Swiss waiter, Pierre, would share predictions of gloom over carafes of red wine. She was obsessed with the idea that the ANC would impose a Marxist state.

'Look at them – they will be like Russians,' she said, marching round the empty restaurant in a mock totalitarian goose-step.

Instead, like Van Tonder's farm, La Via and its humdrum neighbouring shops have long since vanished. The shopping centre houses Assaggi, one of the smartest restaurants in town, where members of the new black business elite meet to discuss deals with executives from the old white-run companies. For once in South Africa's history, it was not just white people who were prospering. When I started a second stint as a correspondent in South Africa in January 2007, consumer confidence was at a twenty-five-year high; the Johannesburg Stock Exchange was up nearly 250 per cent over the previous three years; house prices were up over 125 per cent in the previous four years; new car sales had soared year after year by nearly 16 per cent. In a continent where, in the second half of the twentieth century, incoming liberation movements time and again destroyed their countries' economies, these were powerful signs of how the ANC had confounded the sceptics.

And yet I started to fret that I had been too easily seduced by the outward signs of change: the cranes and building sites testifying to an infrastructure boom, the flashy cars on the roads and the emerging black middle class. When Thabo Mbeki succeeded Mandela in 1999, there was a sense in and outside South Africa that his leadership was just what the country needed. I was among his cheerleaders. For five myth-making years the great humanitarian had worked his magic to forge a new nation. His shrewd successor would be the technocrat to consolidate the country's democratic foundations. But long before Mbeki was ignominiously ousted from the presidency in 2008, a more complex and troubled picture was emerging of the new society and of the ANC.

The ANC was quick to label exposés of conflicts of interest as counter-revolutionary, but like so many dominant political parties across the world, it was losing sight of the distinction between itself and the state. It had, in short, been corrupted. What, I pondered soon after my return, was I to make of the engaging party member who gossiped about how he introduced some American investors to officials in the presidency to prove to them that he had the right political credentials so he could have his share of a big deal? How was I to square that with the statistics that showed South Africa still had one of the starkest divides between rich and poor in the world? At the policy conference of the ANC in June 2007, several thousand delegates had assembled from across the country sporting baseball caps and T-shirts with old liberation slogans. The sessions resounded with Marxist–Leninist pledges and calls for the ANC to remember that it should be 'pro-poor'. I stopped in the car park to count the number of limousines and convertibles lined up alongside the buses that had brought humbler delegates from across the country. I gave up when I had reached two hundred.

In the colonial era the white mining magnates who made fortunes from gold and diamonds were known as the Randlords. They lunched at the panelled Rand Club in central Johannesburg, shot francolin and guinea fowl in country estates, and presided over mansions a few miles from the city centre. A decade into majority rule a new class of Randlords had emerged. They were black, super-rich courtesy of the ANC's policies to reverse the financial injustices of white rule, and as well connected to the government as the Randlords had been to the colonial authorities. The new tycoons argued correctly that some of the same commentators who liked to criticise them had for years prophesied the ANC would impose a Marxist state. And yet it was Archbishop Desmond Tutu's lament to me – that too many in the ANC were focused on self-enrichment – that was more resonant.

Life in the townships improved markedly, but with unemployment at around 30 per cent it was hardly the 'promised land' blacks had hoped for at the end of white rule. In 2008, nearly fourteen years to the day after I had reported on the burning of a suspected apartheid stooge, I found myself chronicling such appalling scenes again – only this time the targets were not alleged informers but immigrants accused of taking jobs from impoverished South Africans.

Against this backdrop the 'rainbow nation' has long since lost its sparkle. A casual brutality casts a shadow over society. There were more than nineteen thousand murders in 2007 and over fifty thousand reported rapes. Beyond the small multiracial elite, South Africa is a country of polite polarisation. Fearful of crime, resentful of affirmative action, wary of the pricklier stance of Mandela's successor and still imbued with prejudice, many whites live all but cut off from their black compatriots, in what amounts to a privatisation of apartheid.

Onto the stage of this vulnerable young country balanced between potentially disastrous challenges has stepped the larger-than-life figure of Jacob Zuma.

On a rain-swept day shortly before Christmas 2007, Zuma skipped onto a stage in a large tent outside the northern town of Polokwane. He moved with the grace of a boxer in his prime. Before him were several thousand ecstatic delegates of the ANC, tooting on horns, blowing on whistles, and swaying back and forth to old anti-apartheid tunes. Their man was thickset, in his mid-sixties, with a shining bald head, an easy smile, and a magnificent, deep, rich voice. He delivered a rousing speech. Then he paused for effect as a smile flitted across his face. Opening his shoulders, he swivelled his hips, and the word *mshini* rolled from his mouth. Then his right fist was in the air, and he exploded into the stirring strains of his signature anthem, the old struggle song 'Lethu Mshini Wami' (Bring Me My Machine Gun).

Zuma had just been elected leader of the ANC. Some of the more illustrious names in twentieth-century political history preceded him, including Chief Albert Luthuli, the first of the anti-apartheid movement's three Nobel peace laureates; Oliver Tambo; and of course, Mandela. He offered the electorate the invigorating crowd-pleasing politics that had been sorely lacking under his aloof predecessor, Thabo Mbeki. His election was a seismic event. For a liberation movement to unseat a leader after just ten years in his position was unprecedented in southern Africa. It heralded a potential renewal for the ANC as it emerged from under the shadow of the increasingly autocratic Mbeki. Zuma had cracked the monolith of a hegemonic ruling party, setting a welcome post-apartheid precedent that leaders who erred could expect to be dismissed. The former freedom fighter had a heroic past and formidable political skills. He promised to tackle crime, AIDS, poverty and Zimbabwe, and to bring back the reconciliatory ethos of Mandela's era. But that was not the whole story. The man who saw himself as the country's saviour had no formal education, at least twenty children, a penchant for populism and a history of scandal. He was embroiled in a corruption probe relating to his ties with his former financial adviser, who was in prison for procuring a bribe for him from an arms dealer. He had been tried for the rape of the HIV-positive daughter of a family friend. While he was acquitted, his testimony further clouded his reputation.[3] Less than a year into his presidency South Africa was given an acute reminder of the potential national embarrassment of his personal life when it emerged that he had had a love child with a woman 28 years his junior. The revelation, which came even as the ANC prepared to launch a 'one partner' campaign to combat AIDS, coincided with the celebrations marking the 20th anniversary of Mandela's release from prison. It served only to underline the contrast between the self-sacrifice and moral authority associated with Mandela and Zuma's more compromised record.

The first battle, against the old South Africa of Van Tonder, has been convincingly won. Wonderfully he and his kind shuffled out of South Africa's story without much of a fight. Since then life has improved for most South Africans. But now a new battle for the soul and future of the new nation is under way. It is this drama that this book explores. It is a story of leadership, inspirational and flawed. It is the story of the near impossibility of overcoming the nightmarish legacy of an abhorrent system. It is the story of divided races seeking a common course on the same land. It is also the story of a once-lionised liberation movement learning that it is hard to buck the trend of so many revolutionary movements that have ended up losing sight of their ideals and spending more time on infighting and making money than leading the people. At its heart is the question of whether the ANC can avoid the atrophy that has enveloped other African liberation movements that had such high hopes at independence.

The hopes of a continent rest on South Africa. If it succeeds, it will be a model for the continent. If South Africa, of all places, fails despite all its advantages and the inspiration of Mandela to lead it to liberation, its failure will not just be the end of a dream nurtured for generations but a betrayal.

Chapter 1

SUCCEEDING A SAINT

I have always been unhappy with my depiction as a demigod.

— NELSON MANDELA

I say things very foolishly I shouldn't. Then a debate begins about what is wrong and what is right.

— THABO MBEKI

It was never going to be easy succeeding Mandela. When he emerged from prison in 1990, he embodied the world's hopes of a new optimistic era. He had been imprisoned since 1962 for his opposition to racist oppression. His speech from the dock when he was on trial for his life had been one of *the* political addresses of the century. With his release it was clear that the end of the last white minority regime in Africa was in sight and that South Africa, for so many years a global pariah, would soon assume its rightful place in the world. Just three months after the fall of the Berlin Wall and the collapse of tyranny in Eastern Europe, it was a time of dreams.

As the day of his release drew near, critics inside and outside the anti-apartheid movement feared that after twenty-seven years in captivity, he would be out of touch. Comrades in the African National Congress (ANC) were outraged that he had been negotiating with the apartheid rulers and agonised over whether he had gone soft. Business people and Western officials fretted that the seventy-one-year-old would be a Rip Van Winkle figure clinging to the outdated economic philosophy he had espoused before being imprisoned. Some nervously recalled that as a politician he had had a reputation for being a hothead.

The doubters were spectacularly wrong. Far from embittering or ossifying him, captivity – he made clear – had schooled him for the challenges ahead. Mandela was to be even more remarkable a leader than the ANC propagandists had suggested. His history as a freedom fighter and political prisoner proved merely the warm-up act to his greatest role of all, as a symbol of moral authority and as an apostle of peace.

In the frenetic days before and after the April 1994 election that ended white rule, Mandela was an itinerant prophet of reconciliation, touring the country delivering homily after homily to bind his divided nation together. In August 1993 in Katlehong, an urban wasteland of tin-roofed bungalows and shacks, after five days of fighting in which scores had died, ten thousand ANC supporters were packed into a ramshackle stadium chanting for weapons to fight their enemies from the Inkatha Freedom Party, a Zulu nationalist movement then vying for control of the township. Half a mile away the Natalspruit Hospital was treating the wounded from the latest street battles. The crowd was howling for revenge, yet Mandela gave no ground.

'If you have no discipline, you are not freedom fighters, and we do not want you in our organisation,' he said in his distinctive reedy tones. 'If you are going to kill innocent people and old men, you do not belong in the ANC. I am your leader. If you don't want me, tell me to go and rest. As long as I am your leader, I will tell you where you are wrong. Your task is reconciliation.'[1] He stared his angry supporters down. They shuffled out abashed.

He delivered hundreds of such speeches, often impromptu, and frequently displaying a moral clarity that few dared to question. One of his bravest and most poignant, given on a sweaty Friday morning in January 1994, has been all but forgotten.[2] The first all-race elections were just three months away, and the second annual conference of the ANC Youth League was starting late. 'Comrades' were still pouring into the giant community hall in the centre of Soweto, minutes after Mandela had walked stiffly to the podium. The 'old man', as he was known affectionately in the ANC, was clearly deeply irritated. His lips were pursed, his head held high, his Olympian gaze stony. When he finally started speaking, his words were even more clipped than usual. This was not an irrational or emotional fury. Rather, it was the admonitory wrath of a headmaster.

He was wearing a patterned flowing African shirt in a relaxed style that was to become his sartorial trademark. There was nothing informal, however, about his mien. Intrinsic to Mandela's genius as a leader was his protean persona. One day he would come across in public as an old-fashioned aristocrat, another day as a revolutionary leader, and the third as a world statesman. While, like any experienced politician, he knew how to play an audience, unlike with so many modern leaders in the age of televisual politics there was nothing artificial about his many guises. Rather, they were rooted in his extraordinary life. On this occasion his genes as the scion of a line of chiefs of the Tembus, a rural clan from the Eastern Cape, were to the fore. It was as if he were upbraiding a rowdy village assembly, as his forefathers must have done so often in the past.

He opened as ever with a formulaic courtesy – this was after all a man who was to say on meeting the Spice Girls, a sassy British pop band, that they were his 'heroes'.[3] But he swiftly warmed to his theme: members of the Youth League had to improve their act and quickly if a democratic South Africa was to have a chance.

Ever since his release from prison nearly four years earlier, he had shown a particular concern for the lot of the youth. In 1993 he had suggested that the voting age be dropped to fourteen. This time, however, he thought the youth needed some home truths, in particular about time keeping. He launched into an anecdote about his recent trip to China.

'One of the things I found out was the extent they are disciplined,' he recalled. 'If the meeting is to start at seven, then everyone is there at seven, and their functions are very brief. The main ceremony lasted one hour, unlike here, where they can last three hours. They do not arrive late because to be late for any engagement is the sign of utter irresponsibility. It is the sign of disrespect. They are a disciplined society, and that is why they are an educated society.'

And so his lecture continued. His audience should return to their classes, beware the 'drug boys coming with their suitcases with false bottoms full of drugs', prepare for a long slog to achieve the right results at school, embrace his policy of reconciliation and take on the *tsotsis* (gangsters) in their midst. 'You are going to interact not only with white counterparts but with the rest of the world. You are going to be our ambassadors.' His audience listened in near silence. Then he cleared his throat and embarked on the most sensitive topic of all: AIDS. It threatened to 'destroy' society, he said. It would ravage the economically active section of the population and 'cripple' the economy. Without pausing he moved on to condoms.

'In our society we face a problem because we do not talk about sex. When a little child asks, "Mummy, where do I come from?" the next thing is a slap in the face.'

Coming from a seventy-five-year-old African patriarch this was astonishing. His frankness flew in the face of all he had been taught in his home village of Qunu, where African elders would never discuss sexual issues in public. He did not, however, stop there. Even as angry muttering started in the crowd, he went on to recall a furore two years earlier, after he raised the same topic at a school on the country's eastern border.

He had prefaced his remarks cautiously and conceded that in 'our society' people did not talk about sex in public. But he had then spoken to them about how to engage in safe sex. After the meeting some of his audience came to him and said, 'Mr President, how can you talk in that way? Do you want our girls to go and sleep with those boys?'

Mandela went on to tell the Youth League of another rally where he had courted controversy by lecturing an audience on AIDS. The principal of a school in the town of Bloemfontein, a woman in her fifties, had said to him bluntly, 'I would advise you to keep away from this.' He had given the same response and talked of the need to take precautions, and he received the same hostile reaction. 'I was heavily criticised by the parents, and of course the young people were jubilant,' he told the Soweto gathering. As he gave this account, the muttering continued, but he persevered to the end.

Appearing next on the stage was Peter Mokaba, the league's bantam-cock of a leader. Mandela looked on tight-lipped as Mokaba fired up the crowd with a burst of revolutionary rhetoric accompanied by the *toyi toyi*, the high-kicking liberation dance. The 'old man' had repeatedly rebuked Mokaba over his inflammatory 'Kill the Boer, the farmer' slogan.[4] He once cut Mokaba off mid-flow at a meeting of the ANC's national executive committee. 'He drummed his fists on the table,' a committee member recalled. 'He said, "Enough. You clearly like the sound of your own voice. Sit down." '[5]

Mandela's speech to the Youth League received barely a mention in the next day's newspapers. They were dominated by the launch of the ANC's election manifesto. When I unearthed my notes on the speech and the reaction of the crowd more than a decade later, his advisers were intrigued. They had no record of his speaking out about AIDS before 1997. It was a terrible omission for which he berated himself many times after he stepped down from office. Much later he conceded that people had warned him that the ANC would lose votes if he pressed people to change their lifestyles and use condoms. It was a reminder that even a politician held by his many admirers to be a living saint had to make political choices. But his failure to deal with AIDS when he was president should not obscure the fact that he did speak his mind about the subject several times in the face of deep hostility from his supporters, before his presidency began. It was typical of his unwavering style of leadership that led so many to regard him as little short of a modern Gandhi. It was a description that Mandela modestly declined but hardly objected to, and an image that made him a nightmare to follow as a head of state.

Desmond Tutu, his friend and fellow Nobel peace laureate, is one of the first to bemoan the world's hero-worship of Mandela. He appreciated long before it became a commonplace that the rapture would blind people to the many colossal problems facing South Africa. The risk was, he said, that the country's challenges would seem all the more daunting once Mandela stepped down from office and his attendant aura of magic disappeared. 'He is only one pebble on the beach, one of thousands,' he said halfway through Mandela's term in office. 'Not an insignificant pebble, I'll grant you that, but a pebble all the same.'[6]

Tutu was right. The other-worldly image of Mandela may have been what South Africa and the world wanted to believe, but great humanitarian as he was, he was always foremost a politician. Reconciliation was not a spontaneous miracle as some liked to imagine, emanating from the magnificence of Mandela's soul. Rather, the seduction of the Afrikaners was carefully plotted in Mandela's cell as a way to win and then retain power. Mandela saw his long imprisonment as giving him the luxury of time to reflect on how he should lead if he were released. He had urged his fellow prisoners to learn Afrikaans on the theory that you could only defeat your enemy if you spoke their language. They had realised soon after arriving on Robben Island that apartheid would collapse under its own contradictions, said Raymond Mhlaba, one of his fellow prisoners.[7] Then it was just a question of putting aside their anger at the racism and injustice of their oppressors and plotting how to win over the Afrikaners.

'I knew that people expected me to harbor anger towards whites,' Mandela said, recalling the morning after his release. 'But I had none. In prison my anger towards whites decreased, but my hatred for the system grew.'[8]

He was brilliant at exploiting the world's infatuation with him. He would unashamedly telephone heads of state to ask for their support on policy, or even just to raise funds for the ANC. His seduction routine was masterful. Drawing on the precepts he learned as a child growing up in a chief's household, and also from his British missionary teachers, he had a courtly Old World charm that never failed to dazzle. He could be a stickler for protocol. He chided MPs in the German Bundestag for not wearing ties. Yet he tempered this with an abhorrence of pomposity and an appreciation of the art of the gentle tease. Who else could telephone the queen and call her Elizabeth?

The ability to make people like you is of course merely the first lesson for aspiring politicians. But even so, Mandela had a particular genius for the gladhanding side of politics, primarily because his warmth seemed genuinely uncontrived. A scene from towards the end of his presidency is particularly telling. One day in December 1997 outside the Carlton Hotel in central Johannesburg, the driver of a black Mercedes paused to allow traffic to pass along the busy street before drawing up in front of the entrance. A tall, silver-haired man emerged, almost colliding with a group of schoolchildren in trim black-and-white uniforms as he manoeuvred his way on to the pavement. They hurried past, chattering to themselves. Then one of them glanced back. She looked away and then stared again. There had been no fanfare, no outriders, no flashing lights, no fenced-off streets. 'It couldn't be the world's best-loved leader, could it?' she seemed to be saying. And yet it was.

The girl's confusion was understandable, given the typical behaviour of the post-colonial African 'Big Man' leader. I had just returned from interviewing Daniel arap Moi, Kenya's then president, who was a classic example. He closed down streets of the capital for his motorcade and kept visitors waiting for days as a matter of course. I had had to wait for two days in his antechamber for a brief audience with the 'chief'. With Mandela, however, it was a point of honour to set a different tone and – as he had told the ANC Youth League – always to be on time. With a flash of his dazzling smile he beckoned the schoolgirls to his side.

'So what do you want to do when you grow up?' he asked. 'Do you want to be a politician?'

'Oh no,' one of them gasped. 'That is too much hard work.'[9]

He laughed as if it were the funniest thing he had heard all day. He delivered a brief lesson on the importance of going to school. Then he moved back to the doorway of the Carlton to greet the hotel's manager with the warmth most of us reserve for a long-lost friend.

Mandela had come to have lunch with a group of foreign correspondents. As he settled down with his customary glasses of Perrier and sweet white wine, he launched into a series of anecdotes, taking the group from his home village in the Transkei to a state visit in India, where the opening ceremony went on so long he never had time to make his speech. He then embarked on a long and confusing tale of a dispute over a chicken in which he ended up playing the role of Solomon. Long before the end the journalists were putty in his hands. Halfway to the door at the end of lunch he stopped in front of a tall female television producer. Ever the lady's man, he looked her up and down with an approving glance.

'You must play sport. Do you play basketball?' he asked the astonished young woman. As she spluttered that swimming was her only exercise, he did the closest thing to a presidential wink. Then the great seducer pottered on to the door with a broad smile.

His presidency was not a golden age, as his friends are the first to concede. He had an autocratic streak. He neglected key areas of policy, most critically the fight against AIDS. He was also overly loyal to underperforming ministers. One of the principal conclusions he had reached over the long days on Robben Island was that when in power he should adopt the consensual politics of his forebears' royal household. 'One of the marks of a great chief is the ability to keep together all sections of his people, the traditionalists and reformers, conservatives and liberals,' he recalled later.[10] The 'big tent' approach eased the smooth running of the ANC – an amalgam of races, classes, religions and politics – as it adjusted from being a revolutionary movement to government. But consensus had its disadvantages. His loyalty to officials even when they were demonstrably inept set a poor example. He fired only one cabinet minister in his term in office, and that was a matter of party politics rather than for poor performance. The tolerance of underachievers encouraged a climate of complacency the country could ill afford.

There were other blemishes. As the years passed, it emerged that Mandela had had to make his share of grubby compromises. His close relationships with business people were from time to time called into question. In August 1996 he faced the type of fund-raising scandal that has beset governments all over the world: it emerged that Sol Kerzner, a prominent gambling tycoon who had had good relations with the Afrikaner Nationalists, had helped to fund the wedding of Mandela's younger daughter, Zindzi, and had also contributed to the ANC's coffers. Bantu Holomisa, a rebellious deputy minister, accused Mandela of agreeing to help to secure the dropping of bribery charges against Kerzner in a pending trial. Kerzner denied the allegations, but then Mandela later sought to draw a line under the matter, saying that he alone had known about the donations. A short while later Holomisa received a dawn phone call from Mandela and was summoned over to his house. There was scant chitchat. Holomisa was fired. Kerzner was never tried.

After Mandela left office, commentators felt emboldened to highlight his failings more critically than before. It was not that his claim to greatness was in dispute. Rather the question was asked whether South Africa – and the world – had not been so beguiled by the idea of 'Mandela's miracle' that the many pressing difficulties the ANC faced as soon as it took power, and also its stop–start progress in confronting them, were overlooked. I was one of many correspondents who were unashamedly dazzled by Mandela when he was in office. Small groups of us would gather at his Johannesburg home for impromptu press conferences, when we would sit at his feet, acolytes before a sage. We *were* more forgiving of his weaknesses than we would have been of a more ordinary politician's. Several of the crises that tarnished Mbeki's presidency, in particular the epidemics of crime and AIDS, had festered under Mandela. And yet, as he marked his ninetieth birthday a decade after leaving office, his record appeared to many South Africans even more magical than it had when he was in the presidency. He and his contemporaries, Oliver Tambo and Walter Sisulu, were from a generation imbued with a mythical status. His successors, in contrast, were rather more human and flawed. As the country stumbled under their direction, the benefits of having a leader who led with vigour and moral conviction were all the clearer.

The failure of leadership is one of the greatest curses to have afflicted sub-Saharan Africa since it won independence. The history of the continent in the second half of the twentieth century is littered with the examples of 'Big Men', independence heroes who came to power vowing to liberate their people from the tyranny of the colonial past and then never left office, invariably garlanding their actions with the rhetoric of liberation to justify their misdeeds. The intensity of their misrule varied, but their governing rationale was identical. It was the philosophy attributed to Louis XIV of France: *'L'état, c'est moi.'* History was clear on this point also: once undermined, the independence of demo cratic institutions is hard to recover.

So Mandela's unflinching support for the independence of the courts, the media and state institutions set a vital precedent. The ANC inherited a stronger judiciary and a more vibrant civil society than anywhere else in sub-Saharan Africa. Mandela respected the courts, even when rulings by white judges from the apartheid era went in favour of old Afrikaner Nationalist leaders. When General Magnus Malan, a former defence minister, was acquitted of murdering thirteen civilians in a 1987 massacre, ANC supporters were outraged. Mandela, however, called on them to respect the judgement. He himself appeared in court when subpoenaed in a dispute over the national rugby squad. He regularly submitted himself to questioning by the press.

His respect for the judiciary was in contrast to the approach of Mbeki and Jacob Zuma, who were both to stand accused of undermining the independence of democratic institutions. Mandela, however, believed in leading by example. He was prepared to break ranks with his fellow African leaders and condemn oppression. He did not indulge the ruinous culture of relativism and solidarity that had led to so many abuses in Africa passing unrebuked. He led. He also knew when to go. Mandela was the last of a long line of African liberation leaders to take charge. He was acutely aware of the need to buck their trend by serving just one term.

His timing seemed perfect. Under him South Africa had gone from being an outcast to being something of an icon. As he prepared to leave office, the consensus abroad and in South Africa was that it was time for a more vigorous leader to build on his successes and address the next phase of the post-apartheid story – and that the right man had been identified for the task.

The elegant balustrades that grace the front of the Union Buildings, the light sandstone headquarters of the South African government, command one of the more imposing views in southern Africa. Designed by Sir Herbert Baker, the British colonial architect, they dominate the capital, Pretoria, overlooking rolling lawns and gardens that stretch to the city centre below. It was in the Union Buildings that the dour leaders of the National Party made so many fateful decisions about their country and region.

On 10 May 1994, tens of thousands gathered there for the most joyous moment in the birth of a free South Africa, the inauguration of the country's first democratically elected president. Under a diamond-bright sky Mandela took the oath of office and swore to 'build a society in which all South Africans both black and white will be able to walk tall, without any fear in their hearts'.[11] An eclectic mix of leaders was at hand. The Duke of Edinburgh all but brushed shoulders with Fidel Castro and Mu'ammar Gaddafi in the inevitable shambles of official cars. In a dramatic climax, military jets flew overhead piloted by the very airmen who had been trained to bomb the ANC. The world celebrated.

Just over two years later I was in the shadow of the Union Buildings once again. I had just spent an hour with Thabo Mbeki, Mandela's deputy president and successor-in-waiting. I had emerged confident that South Africa would be in safe hands once Mandela stepped down.

Mbeki had been wearing a cardigan and puffing on a pipe. Our conversation ranged from international economics to European history and the best literature on the Highland Clearances, the eighteenth-century eviction of Scottish crofters by clan chiefs. In a state of some rapture I was later to describe him as a philosopher-king.

I was not alone in concluding that South Africa needed a less deified head of state. Mbeki's insistence that it was time to move beyond the fuzzy nation-building ethos of the Mandela era perturbed many in South Africa's white minority. But ANC supporters, in particular members of the nascent black middle class, were convinced that a shift in focus was overdue and that reconciliation had to shift to 'transformation'. In the last years of Mandela's presidency the violent crime that had been a grim hallmark of the last years of the apartheid era, far from decreasing, raged unchecked. The economy was in the doldrums. There was clearly the need for a firmer hand at the tiller.

Rather than the reconciler, it seemed Mbeki would be the implementer or fixer and would not shy away from speaking uncomfortable truths. 'He left no doubt his laid-back pipe-smoking image masks a formidable political brain,' I wrote. 'Discussing the challenges ahead he made no pretence that he would be a Mandela clone. He would seek to inject a note of realism into the national debate even at the expense of reconciliation. Starry-eyed rainbowism is not his style.'[12]

Many had been impressed by Mbeki over the years. He had been groomed from his youth as a potential leader of the movement. He came from a middle-class family in the Eastern Cape region, the breeding ground for Mandela's generation of ANC leaders. His father was an ANC intellectual. As the apartheid regime started to clamp down on the ANC, he was sent into exile to keep the anti-apartheid flame burning. When studying at Britain's University of Sussex he charmed both the British establishment and the radical left-wing fringe. After a stint studying in Moscow, he became the aide-de-camp of Oliver Tambo, the ANC's leader-in-exile.

His mellow and reflective manner won over countless visitors to the headquarters of the liberation movement in Lusaka, the capital of Zambia. There he

held court late into the night over bottles of fine whisky, espousing his vision of
a liberated, non-racial South Africa. Afrikaner academics, writers and business
people who travelled to Senegal in 1987 to meet the ANC for the first time
came away deeply reassured. He was, as Margaret Thatcher once said of
Mikhail Gorbachev, a man they could 'do business with'. This after all was a
man who in the mid-eighties had argued for talks with the apartheid regime at
a time when many in the ANC were still dreaming of a military triumph. For
this he was to face a whispering campaign within the movement that he was a
CIA spy. But he understood that Umkhonto we Sizwe (MK), the ANC's
armed wing, for all its romantic reputation in the townships, would never defeat the South African military machine, and that the only way to end apartheid
was across a negotiating table.

Patrick FitzGerald, an ANC member living in exile in the last years of white
rule, recalls a car unexpectedly arriving at his home in Lusaka in late 1984 to
take him to Mbeki's office. FitzGerald, a veteran of the underground movement, was due that afternoon to catch a flight to Angola, where he had been
promised training as a sniper. Mbeki told him to unpack his bags. The military struggle was a sideshow, he told FitzGerald. Liberation would be won by
negotiations.[13] It seems obvious now, but it was heresy in the ANC at the
time.

Mbeki finalised an equally bold decision a decade later, when he served as
Mandela's deputy and de facto prime minister. With the economy failing to fire,
he oversaw a fundamental review of the ANC's policies. The party's old
redistributive approach had to be discarded. Instead, the ANC would stabilise
the nation's tottering finances by bending to the winds of globalisation then
gusting across the world and adopting an orthodox free-market programme. It
would push for balanced budgets, low inflation, free trade, even possibly
privatisation. In short, outraged opponents on the left argued, he advocated the
approach of the ANC's Western ideological foes of the eighties, Ronald Reagan
and Margaret Thatcher.

His pragmatism won him an admiring audience abroad. He was held as a
statesman in the making and a worthy successor to Mandela. The business
people, editors and politicians who trooped to see him as he prepared to take
office emerged from their audience deeply reassured.

There may, however, have been another factor behind Mbeki's favourable reviews. Judge Edwin Cameron, a prominent human rights lawyer in the eighties, who became one of Mbeki's most outspoken critics, believes that the young Mbeki received similar fawning treatment in his time in exile in Britain in the sixties partly because he did not seem threatening, in short because he wore tweed suits, smoked a pipe and quoted classical poets. This had a disastrous effect, Cameron argues. He believes that it blinded people to Mbeki's faults and also that the attention encouraged him to think he was a genuine policy intellectual and superior to his political peers and his people. Cameron says, 'It's an intellectual form of hubris. He was determined to make his own stamp on the country and to do it through his intellect.'[14]

So were Mbeki's many admirers in the West subconsciously applying a racist stereotype to Africa? Was it that the liking for malt whisky; the liberally scattered quotations from Yeats, Shelley and Shakespeare; and the well-fitted grey suit that almost always adorned his dapper frame made him stand out from the wild stereotype of post-colonial leaders, built up in the West over several decades of failed governments across Africa? Were Western and, indeed, some South African commentators so struck by his detailed knowledge of Western literature and his British affectations of dress that they suspended their critical judgement and thought he was more brilliant than he was?

Towards the end of his presidency, several commentators who were traditionally sympathetic to the ANC concluded that they had blinded themselves to his faults. After spending seven years in Britain in the sixties, Mbeki would have been well-attuned to subtle racial slights, and the effusive reception he received from many of the 'great and the good' may have reinforced an innate resentment towards the West that was to become one of the hallmarks of his time in office and was to have a baleful influence on some of his policies.

Mbeki's supporters complained that by putting Mandela on a pedestal the media had made it impossible for his deputy to succeed and had set him up to fail. Mbeki himself was infuriated by the hero-worship of the 'old man'. When he was preparing to take over, there was only one question informing international perceptions of South Africa: What will happen when Mandela steps down? The clear presumption was that Mandela was all that was holding South Africa back from the brink. Time and again Mbeki was asked about taking up the great man's mantle. His frustration at this implicit slight bubbled over in his address to the ANC conference when he succeeded Mandela.

'Madiba,' he said, addressing Mandela by his honorific clan name, 'members of the press have been asking me how it feels to step into your shoes. I've been saying I would never be seen dead in such shoes. You wear such ugly shoes!'[15]

Mandela was stunned by the remark, one of his aides later revealed. The bluntness may have had as much to do with Mbeki's awkwardness on a political platform as his exasperation at being constantly compared unfavourably to the 'old man'. But the comment reflected his clear desire to step out of Mandela's shadow and be his own man. In deliberate contrast, he aspired to be a philosopher-president who would speak truth to his people, however unpopular that might be. 'I say things very foolishly I shouldn't,' he once told me. 'Then a debate begins about what is wrong and what is right. And then your nice deputy president ceases to be a nice deputy president. That's fine. I don't mind. Thabo Mbeki might be terribly bad, might be late for meetings [a regular accusation of his critics]. But it doesn't take away the validity of the issues he raises.'[16]

Many of the policies he championed served South Africa exceedingly well, in particular his drive to reform economic policy, his push for fiscal discipline and the creation of a black middle class. Others, in particular his blinkered stance on AIDS, were disastrous. His questioning of the orthodox science on AIDS hampered the provision of the antiretroviral drugs that could have kept hundreds of thousands of people with AIDS alive. He took a similar contrarian stance towards the country's appalling levels of crime, arguing that the problem was exaggerated by whites who wanted the country to fail. For the outside world, however, it was most of all the crisis across the northern border in Zimbabwe under the increasingly despotic Robert Mugabe that undermined Mbeki's reputation.

Mbeki had taken power espousing a vision for Africa that echoed the ambition of Kwame Nkrumah, Ghana's fiery independence leader, whose African nationalism had inspired a generation of freedom fighters. Mandela had led South Africa back onto the world stage. Mbeki would go a step further and champion the continent. He would be a latter-day Nkrumah, only, unlike the Ghanaian, he had the stature to be heeded by the world and the authority and power to make his aspiration more than a mere dream.

The era of Africa's 'petty gangsters' who stole elections and ruled as tyrants was over, he declared. An African renaissance was at hand. His South Africa would take the lead. 'You cannot have a stand-up success in South Africa and great disaster further north and hope you can insulate yourself from the rest of the continent,' he said. He added, however, in a critical caveat, that South Africa had to be wary of hubris. 'We need to avoid a sense of arrogance that South Africa is a great moral power. You can overreach yourself, and then fail and misspend the moral force that you have. What you find is that you have changed nothing and that no one is listening.'[17]

Mandela's voluble human rights foreign policy would always have to be tempered by a dose of realpolitik. A defining moment for Mbeki had come during Mandela's presidency, when the Nigerian military junta hanged the Nigerian writer Ken Saro-Wiwa, spurning Mandela's pleas for clemency. Outraged, Mandela pushed for sanctions against the junta, only to find that the rest of Africa was not behind him, and he had to back down. At the next meeting of the ANC's national executive committee, Mbeki excoriated Mandela over the debacle. Never again should South Africa break ranks with its fellow African states, he argued. The logic of trying to solve crises via diplomacy and forging alliances rather than by shouting from the rooftops is clear. But Mbeki took that to such an extreme, with his policy of not speaking out about Mugabe's excesses, that he was to be accused of appeasing a tyrant.

When asked a year into his presidency how the crisis in Zimbabwe would be resolved, he responded munificently. He was addressing a briefing at Windsor Castle, where he had spent the previous night at the start of a state visit to the old colonial power. He was the guest of the queen, whose forebear had sent armies to fight his Xhosa ancestors 150 years before. Dressed as was his wont in a charcoal-grey suit, he looked very much at home. African leaders in a new regional initiative he was founding would bring rogue leaders to heel, he said. A peer-review mechanism would ensure that rules of good governance in

Africa were upheld. He moved on to discuss global trade with the editor of the *Economist*.

This was classic Mbeki. He probably had a better understanding of how Africa fitted into the world's economy than any other African leader. His authoritative style of leadership helped to ensure that Africa was on the agenda at summits of world leaders. Yet he had a more cryptic side to his character. He was also known for so cloaking his pronouncements in policy jargon and so gilding them in subclauses that when you reread them it was all but impossible to ascertain his thinking or to pin him down. He made repeated pledges to world leaders that he was on the brink of a breakthrough in Zimbabwe. Initially the West was happy for him to take the lead. It made sense to defer to the region's dominant power and also to try to talk Mugabe out of power. But by the end, after several deeply flawed elections blithely endorsed by South Africa, few believed his repeated claim that a deal was in sight. Western officials and Zimbabwean opposition leaders came to believe that Mbeki had no interest in reaching an agreement and would rather maintain solidarity with a fellow African leader than stand up for the trampled human rights of the ordinary Zimbabweans.

The humouring of an ageing autocrat did not ostensibly accord with Mbeki's renaissance ideals. But standing by Mugabe against the West did fit with his belief in pan-African solidarity. This tattered philosophy had shined brightest in the 1960s and 1970s, in the heady first years of independence. Mandela, with the clarity of one who had spent twenty-seven years in prison, had repudiated it as soon he was a free man. Mbeki sought to revive it, driven as he was by a committed anti-Americanism.

So determined was Mbeki to create a counterweight to the United States that South Africa even sided with China in voting against a UN Security Council resolution condemning the Burmese junta, a move that Tutu blasted as a repudiation of all that the ANC had fought for in the anti-apartheid struggle. A senior Western official who has known Mbeki for decades believes his world view was underpinned by the lessons he learned studying in Moscow in the late sixties. These included an opposition to US hegemony, a fury about the British imperial legacy and a belief in the solidarity of liberation movements. 'His vision has not changed in twenty years,' the official said. 'It is one that believes the benefit of the Cold War was a bipolar world. He believes a national liberation movement cannot be seen to fail, and so he's prepared to turn a blind eye to its failings.'[18] Mbeki found huge comfort for Africa in the certainties of the Cold War, he added.

Nothing seemed to crack Mbeki's position on Zimbabwe. As inflation reached 2 million per cent in 2008 and state repression intensified, he still shrank from toughening his stance. He argued that as the regional mediator he was honour-bound to act as more of a referee than a judge and to hold his tongue. There was no easy option for South Africa. But the stark truth was that many of Mbeki's aides did not seem bothered by the tyranny across their border. Indeed, some openly sympathised with Mugabe as he took on the old colonial master. It is not our problem – it is Britain's problem, Nkosazana Dlamini-Zuma, Mbeki's foreign minister, once told me.[19] When people questioned their inaction, South African officials claimed that the world wanted them to 'send in the tanks', as if there were no middle ground between doing nothing and regime change. In a rare open discussion about the crisis, Sydney Mufamadi, Mbeki's boyish Zimbabwe envoy, employed a script that could have been drafted by the Zimbabwean government. Both sides faced allegations of human rights abuses, he said.[20] I had just returned from Zimbabwe, where I had reported on the brutal campaign of intimidation Mugabe's supporters were meting out on opposition supporters. I had last heard such a specious attempt to apply a false moral equivalence in Bosnia in the early 1990s, when British officials desperately tried to reduce public pressure for military intervention by talking down the atrocities of the Serbs and suggesting that the Bosnian Muslims besieged in Sarajevo were as guilty as their aggressors. Mufamadi's statement was a terrible indictment of Mbeki's policies. It was also a reminder of the moral contortions of a man who had dreamed of surpassing Mandela's greatness on taking power.

So why did the highly regarded heir apparent become the more controversial figure of the later years of his presidency? Tutu cites the insecurity of Mbeki's disjointed upbringing as a child of the 'struggle'. 'When you are insecure, you are unlikely to take kindly to a collaborative approach,' he said. 'So when you are top dog, you tend to make sure that you remain there. You tend to be assertive, to lay down the law, and you find it not easy to admit when you have made a mistake, because it subverts your sense of being macho.'[21]

Mbeki's upbringing had certainly been austere. His father, Govan, had been one of the intellectual titans of the ANC and had sparred with Mandela for many years in Robben Island over ideology. A committed Marxist, he saw the overthrow of apartheid as the precursor to a communist revolution and viewed Mandela's African nationalism with contempt. For him, the movement was all that mattered. Parenthood came a very distant second, as was clear when the two Mbekis met each other in January 1990 in their first encounter in nearly three decades.[22] The senior Mbeki was one of a group of ANC leaders recently released from prison. At his side was Walter Sisulu, another veteran prisoner. Sisulu rushed into the arms of Max, one of his sons. The Mbekis merely shook hands, and then the father turned to the next 'cadre' in line.

Soon after the end of white rule, I paid a visit to 'Oom Gov', as Govan Mbeki was known, to glean some insights into his son. He greeted me in a blue-and-white-striped dressing gown and delivered a half-hour political lecture, talking repeatedly of the need not to lose sight of the working class. Most striking was his use of the third person to refer to the deputy president, his son. He never referred to him by his name.

The shadowy ethos of life in exile clearly also affected Mbeki's presidency. For nearly three decades he had roamed the world, always looking over his shoulder, such was the fearsome reputation of the apartheid security services, and at times despairing of ever returning home. In the 1960s the exiles believed that apartheid would soon collapse under the weight of its contradictions. But as the years passed, it became clear they faced long years in exile. Then finally, when they did return, it was to find a very different country from the one they had left.

Dali Tambo, the son of Oliver Tambo, the late ANC leader who groomed Mbeki as his successor, says it is hard to overestimate how disorienting and alienating life in exile was. When he had returned in 1990, having spent almost his entire life in exile, he found South Africa unfamiliar and even unfriendly.

'I walked into Shell House [the ANC's headquarters], and this ANC leader said, "Dali, you look lost." And I said, "I know, Chief. I'm really lost." On my second week back here I was in Bree Street [a bustling central Johannesburg street], and I was struck because this guy looked so like me. I went up to him, and I couldn't understand what he said. I'd lived in Rome, New York and Paris. For the first time I had encountered someone who had my features, my voice, even my backside, and yet I could not speak to him. To this day I can't speak Xhosa or Zulu. I can't debate in it. I can't give speeches in it. I'm to some extent culturally alienated.'[23]

Mbeki, who left South Africa as a young adult, could at least speak Xhosa fluently, but this was a man who had a foot in both Britain and Africa and who, one old friend said, seemed more at home in the former. While he delivered several powerful eulogies to Africa, his words tended to be more analytical than empathetic. His critics in the ANC referred to him disparagingly as a black Englishman and derided him as having no feel for township life. In the introduction to a book by a sympathiser, Mbeki wrote a withering indictment of South African intellectual life, expressing the hope he would one day find time 'to address the issue of the calamitous retreat from the habit of thinking in our country, the atrophy of meaningful critical intellectual engagement and communication, and the occupation of the realm of ideas largely by dearth of originality, superstition, opinionated prejudice, stereotypes and a herd mentality'.[24]

He felt a deep disdain for the traditions that were integral to the lives of many black compatriots, hardly the ideal qualification for a man who wanted to shape his nation. The tragedy of Mbeki is that a man who was obsessed with rebutting stereotypes of Africa and with emerging from Mandela's shadow seldom appeared at home on his own continent and through his obsessive behaviour fostered the very ridicule he was determined to avert.

Mandela had had misgivings about his successor long before Mbeki took office. He told friends privately that he would have preferred Cyril Ramaphosa, an urbane former union leader. But Mandela was overruled by party stalwarts, including Jacob Zuma. Mandela prided himself as being a loyal party man and t his misgivings to himself. A month before relinquishing the presidency of the ANC to Mbeki, he courteously suggested that it had been far harder at times to be in exile than to be in prison. Mbeki would, he said, raise the ANC to a level it had never been on before. He went on, however, to give an oblique hint of concerns over Mbeki's reputation for surrounding himself with sycophants.

'When a leadership surrounds itself with powerful and independent people who can criticise even the president of a party without fear, then you have democracy,' he said.[25] He was yet more explicit when he handed over the baton of the party leadership at its conference in the old Boer War town of Mafikeng.

'One of the temptations of a leader who has been elected unopposed is that he may use his powerful position to settle scores with his detractors, marginalise them and in certain cases get rid of them, and surround himself with yes-men and -women,' Mandela told the party's delegates. 'A leader must keep the forces together, but you can't do that unless you allow dissent.'[26]

That was not to be Mbeki's way. His years in exile had inculcated a cabalist approach to politics. He made it clear that he expected total loyalty, and perceived rivals in the party were ruthlessly shunted to the side. Ramaphosa, his defeated rival, who left politics for business during Mandela's presidency, was called by a friend one day during Mbeki's first term in office and told to switch on the news. Ramaphosa was one of three senior ANC figures who had been accused by a cabinet minister of plotting to overthrow Mbeki. The accusation was based on a blatantly trumped-up charge. Appalled, Ramaphosa went to Mandela's home, and the two of them watched the coverage of the supposed conspiracy on the state broadcaster.

'I was very shocked,' Ramaphosa recalled. 'And Madiba watched in silence.'[27] Mbeki, he said, had initially won over everyone in the ANC on his return from exile. But he had soon concluded that Mbeki was a complex man and faced a number of challenges as a leader. Mandela was sufficiently confident in his own abilities to want to surround himself with advisers who were cleverer than he was, Ramaphosa said, while Mbeki needed to be the brightest in the room. Ramaphosa wished that Mbeki had been bold enough to work with people 'with diverse experiences and not just people who had the same views. Barack Obama's courage to appoint people who think differently provides a great lesson to leaders.'

'When I was at the ringside, I saw in him great qualities of intellectual analysis,' Ramaphosa said. 'It's the advantage that he got by being in exile, having time to think and to read. It's like someone who had time at university on his subject. You read and read and read. And you cannot but be extremely good at your subject.'

Mbeki's enemies seized on this trait of his to trot out the old cliché that he was a latter-day Nero, fiddling away while South Africa 'burned'. That was a little unfair. While he was a micromanager and was known for whiling away hours late at night polishing his trenchant weekly online address to the party, he was no Nero, a weak and vacillating figure. A more apt classical analogy would be with Tiberius, the second emperor of Rome. Wily, brooding, increasingly paranoid and autocratic in his later years, he is portrayed as having been resentful of the cult status of his predecessor, the godlike founding father of a reborn state. Just as Tiberius knew that he was not Augustus's first choice as successor, so Mbeki knew that Mandela had wanted Ramaphosa to succeed him and that he would never be loved as Mandela was.

Mandela, ever the showman, was not above occasionally upstaging his successor. He arrived at one ANC conference just as Mbeki had finished speaking, and promptly the delegates switched their gaze to the beloved statesman and forgot about applauding their president. But that does not excuse Mbeki's petulant stance towards Mandela. Far from deploying Mandela as his most potent asset, at one stage he would not even take his calls. Three friends of Mandela say that halfway through Mbeki's presidency he confided to them that he could pick up the phone to talk to any president in the world, with the exception of his own president.[28] Sometimes he told confidants he had to wait six months to see Mbeki.

Mbeki's allies thought that the world had seized on Mandela as if he were the 'good African' to counterbalance all the bad leaders the continent had had since independence. Mbeki's spin doctors even went so far as to suggest Mandela was something of an Uncle Tom. At an international concert to mark Mandela's eightieth birthday, Mbeki delivered a distinctly loaded tribute by quoting from Shakespeare's *King Lear* the ageing king's words to Cordelia shortly before their deaths. By citing literature's most famous befuddled old ruler, Mbeki's message seemed clear: leave the governing to me. 'As Lear wished for himself and his offspring,' he said, 'we too urge you to live and pray and sing and tell old tales and laugh at the gilded butterflies which will continue to come to you to tell you all manner of idle gossip.'[29]

Towards the end of Mbeki's presidency a truce was declared. But by then many in the ANC had become exasperated with their eccentric president. Mbeki would have done well to have heeded Mandela's advice on the need to allow dissent and to keep rivals close. It was politics, not his controversial policies, that undermined him in the end, as Saki Macozoma, a close confidant who had become a multimillionaire in Mbeki's era, conceded.

'One thing Madiba was good at was even if he didn't want you to have power he would make sure you were nearby,' Macozoma said. 'Simply spending time together, having lunch, patting backs and giving an audience . . . That is as important in politics as clarity of ideas. That part of politics has been lacking in an Mbeki presidency. When you take into account all those elements, the people expelled, people pushed out, [you understand] the opposition to the man.'[30]

It had always been clear that Mbeki had a political tin ear. In public he cut an unapproachable figure. His disdain for baby hugging and sound bites reflected his shyness and an old-fashioned belief that government was about ideas and policy, not marketing. Watching Mbeki in public was reminiscent of Senator John Kerry, the 2004 US Democratic presidential candidate, or of Gordon Brown, the British prime minister. All three have that debilitating flaw in the modern televised political arena of being unable to connect with large audiences.

Mbeki once confided to Tony Blair wistfully that he regretted never having had the thrill of savouring victory in a competitive election.[31] That may be so, but he never displayed any hankering for retail politics. Rather, he gave the impression that he regarded himself as above the hurly-burly of popular democracy. He believed that he did not need to stoop to sell his policies, still less his personality. He saw himself as a policy intellectual not a mere politician, whereas Mandela, he confided to friends, had a second-rate mind. Mbeki closed an address to an important ANC conference by commending those in his audience who were familiar with European classical music to recall a comment attributed to Beethoven. His audience wanted political red meat, and instead he wanted to flaunt his cultural knowledge by commending a long-dead European composer.

Mbeki had after all been anointed rather than elected as ANC president, and his two general election victories were merely a matter of tallying the scale of the ANC's triumph. He saw himself in the tradition of the early nationalist leaders, whose words were holy writ. It was as if he thought he had a divine right to rule.

In his heyday Mbeki liked to quote from the American poet Langston Hughes. One of Mbeki's favourite lines runs: 'What happens to a dream deferred?' *A Dream Deferred* was the title of an authoritative biography and became something of a catchphrase in the second half of his presidency. Towards the end of his time in office, one of his aides reworked it in a text message, bemoaning what he said was a corrupt and sycophantic culture in the ANC. Too many 'predators, brigands, incompetents and phoneys' had 'jumped on the ANC bandwagon' since 1994, he wrote. They were unworthy of the 'chief' (Mbeki), he concluded. 'It's not the dream deferred but betrayed.'[32]

To this, Ramaphosa, Mbeki's old rival, rolled his eyes. 'It's not a dream betrayed,' he said. 'It's a dream derailed.' Mbeki had had an impossible act to follow. He had also set himself a stiff challenge of moving beyond nation building and implemented crucial stabilising economic reforms. Amid the controversies of his later years over AIDS and Zimbabwe it is easy to lose sight of the pivotal role he played in cementing the new order. His pursuit of an orthodox economic policy was revolutionary and essential. But he was not able to rise above apartheid, as Mandela miraculously had done. Instead, it oppressed him, Mandela's fabled spirit of reconciliation was tossed aside and the scars of the polarised past were laid bare. Future historians will probably judge him more kindly than his political peers. Mbeki, however, was to lead South Africa down several blind alleys from which it would not easily emerge.

Chapter 2

THE OTHER SIDE OF THE RAINBOW

There's a bridge, but no one dares to cross it.

— CHARL VAN DER MERWE,
DEPUTY MAYOR OF THE SMALL TOWN OF KOPPIES,
A YEAR AFTER THE END OF APARTHEID

We have a non-racial society that has not yet come together. Or you can say, we have now truly legitimised apartheid . . . Mandela made us all feel we belong, and that has disappeared.

— PROFESSOR MALEGAPURU MAKGOBA,
VICE CHANCELLOR, UNIVERSITY OF
KWAZULU-NATAL, 2008

Just under a year before the end of apartheid, the small South African town of Koppies (pronounced copees) was in a state of war. The water tower, with its commanding view of Kwakwatsi, the town's satellite black township, had become a makeshift gun emplacement manned by white farmers. A second unit was watching the gravel track that linked town to township. A third patrolled the fields. A fourth guarded a back road. Their instructions were clear: no one should go in or out of Kwakwatsi. The blacks were to be taught a lesson they would not forget. The Berlin Wall had come down three years earlier, but Koppies, like so many small towns in South Africa, was caught in a time capsule.

Koppies is in the heart of the *platteland* (flat land), the six-thousand-foot-high plateau that stretches across most of the old Orange Free State and Transvaal. In the last years of white rule there were about a thousand whites living there in neat homes with trim, well-watered gardens. They sent their children to Sarel Cilliers High School, a handsome red-brick complex named after a nineteenth-century Boer hero that backed onto spacious grounds with rugby pitches and tennis courts. Across the railway track was Kwakwatsi, a sprawling collection of low-cost houses and unsanitary shanty huts that were home to about fifteen thousand blacks. Formally, the old apartheid laws were abolished in the late eighties and early nineties. But in Koppies, as in small towns across South Africa, relations between black and white were as starched as the terrain, and it was always going to take rather more than a stroke of a pen to reconcile the two – if indeed it were possible at all.

On the first day of the siege, *Tannie* (Auntie) Joan, the proprietor of the Hotel Friesland, the town's only hostelry, was wearing a faded sky-blue terylene cardigan and brown-framed rectangular glasses and smelled of stale cigarette smoke. She had a tired, weather-beaten face. Her husband was ill. She was struggling to keep the business going. They had been there for three decades. She would leave overnight if she could. But who would buy a run-down hotel in the middle of the veld at such a time?

The hotel looked as if it had not been decorated since the 1950s. The paint was peeling. The curtains were frayed. The floor in the bar bore the stains of decades of overturned drinks and cigarette stubs. The attitudes were of the same vintage. On a typical night, in June 1993, a policeman with pockmarks over his face was playing darts with a passing truck driver. They were drinking rum and Coke, the staple of conservative Afrikanerdom. A young farm worker in battered jeans sat in the corner. None of them looked up when I entered. After a faltering greeting in Afrikaans, I volunteered a half-hearted introduction about having come to understand what was 'really' happening in South Africa. The driver grunted. 'I don't want my daughter living with blacks,' he said. The policeman said something in Afrikaans. They all laughed.

Four days earlier hundreds of gun-toting right-wingers had tried to derail the transition to democracy by storming the conference centre outside Johannesburg, where delegates from South Africa's political parties were negotiating a post-apartheid settlement. The right-wingers had been escorted away but only after driving an armoured car through the plate-glass front of the conference centre and forcing the ANC delegates to run for safety. The mood in Koppies was equally defiant.

In its broad central street, tanned farmers in *bakkies* (pickups) raced up and down for the three days of the siege, ferrying khaki-clad youths to take up their shifts. Most had shotguns, sidearms or *sjamboks* (rawhide whips), although, like the emblem of one of the nineteenth-century Boer Republics fluttering from a tailboard, these were as much for show as for action. Charl van der Merwe, the deputy mayor, and the other members of the 'Action Committee' masterminded the siege from the local supermarket. They barked instructions into radios, as behind them the town's womenfolk baked scones and brewed coffee for the volunteers.

Van der Merwe was rather reluctantly put forward as the spokesman. A tall, thin man with soft blue eyes and a diffident manner, he picked his words carefully, avoiding talk of 'them' and 'us'. The delicate matter of race was not mentioned. It was in essence a matter of economics and governance, he explained. The blacks had launched a consumer boycott of the whites' shops. Koppies had had enough.

'We are not anti-black or racist or whatever,' he said. 'But every year you reach a frustration point. How can you build up an economy when you are dealing with endless strikes?' For three months a group of blacks had squatted on the corner outside his shop and intimidated other blacks from entering. His revenue had shrunk by 85 per cent. 'This is not the way in the land of reconciliation and cooperation. We want to help them but . . .'[1]

Across the railway line half a mile away, past the checkpoints and an armoured police car, Johannes Tladi, the local ANC leader, was addressing an angry crowd. Kwakwatsi was the usual township sprawl of cramped and higgledy-piggledy streets. Piles of rubble and rubber tyres blocked the entrance. The residents were penned in and furious. The first they had known of the siege was when people heading to work at dawn had come under fire. No one had been hurt. The farmers manning the checkpoints said they had deliberately aimed wide. But it would have surprised neither whites nor blacks if someone had been hit. This was merely the latest instalment in a long-running saga of antagonism, oppression and mutual distrust.

In his T-shirt and jeans the gangly Tladi looked even younger than his twenty-odd years. Van der Merwe, he suggested, had a strange view of 'reconciliation and cooperation'. He related a saga of racial injustices the people of Kwakwatsi had endured over the years. A month earlier an ANC comrade called Solomon Mahlatsi had been shot dead by the police he said, but no one had been arrested, still less charged.

Apartheid was at its most stark in *dorps* (small towns) like Koppies. In the first three years of the 'new' South Africa, Koppies experienced minor triumphs. In December 1994 a beaming Constable Bafana Pule stepped into the township shebeen (illegal bar) for a pre-Christmas drink. As a policeman, he would have been lynched a year earlier if he had set foot in the township after dark. A month or so later van der Merwe and Tladi, the young ANC leader, formed a multiracial transitional local council. 'I don't have a suit,' Tladi said after the first council meeting. 'But it doesn't matter a jot.'[2]

The swimming pool was desegregated. So was the doctor's surgery, after a local Afrikaans paper picked up an article published in Britain highlighting the doctor's practice of maintaining two reception rooms. In October 1995 van der Merwe could be seen exchanging a cheery greeting with two of his old ANC adversaries as he put up a National Party poster ahead of the first democratic local elections. 'Just remember you would do better voting for my party,' he joked.[3]

The two races remained apart, yet there was, however briefly, a shared sense of purpose and hope. One Sunday after the handover of power, the white congregants of the Dutch Reformed Church filed past a memorial to the Anglo-Boer War, heads down, men in suits, women in sombre formal dress, to give thanks for peace and for Nelson Mandela in their morning service. Later that afternoon Kwakwatsi was hosting a local choral competition. In a riot of bright choral outfits the teams had come from townships all over the *platteland*. In those early days of the new order their singing reverberated into the veld a chorale of hope that the old divisions could be broken down.

There were also, however, setbacks. Van der Merwe was the F. W. de Klerk of Koppies. Like South Africa's last white leader he was by birth, upbringing and conviction deeply conservative. He understood – unlike some of the yahoos who had been careering around on the *bakkies* at the time of the siege – that change had to come. But the changes threatened to sweep away far more than he had anticipated. Only belatedly did he appear to appreciate the timeless lesson of revolutions: once the floodgates of reform are opened, change takes on its own momentum and can be impossible to control.

The transitional council collapsed when van der Merwe resigned after he said he was insulted by a black councillor. No sooner was the swimming pool desegregated than it was boycotted by whites. Township dwellers remained unwilling and in many cases unable to pay the 35-rand-a-month flat rate for basic services. Tired of subsidising the township and aware that the number of shacks on the edge of Kwakwatsi was growing by the day, the people of Koppies threatened to stop paying their own dues to bring the council to its knees. Each time I returned, Charles Masibi, a young teacher and ANC activist, was more depressed about the chances of reconciliation.

As for the Friesland, the characters in the bar changed, but the scene was always the same, as was the desolate nature of the conversation. One night, a few months after Mandela's inauguration, Johannes Hattingh, the local Afrikaner greybeard, said that blacks would cross the threshold of the bar over his dead body. He had spent his life on the gold mines. We knew how to keep them in line there, he said. A passing black traffic policeman had recently been assaulted when he walked in and ordered a drink. A white farmer listened in silence.

Presiding over this acrid scene was the owner. She had recognised me immediately on my first return visit. So why had I returned? I told her I was trying to understand the 'new' South Africa.

'It is new? Is it good? You will find changes.'[4] Her husband had died of a suspected heart attack. He had returned from a trip to the town of Kroonstad looking a bit yellow. She told him to lie down. He was dead before the doctor came. She recounted this without a trace of self-pity. But the whiff of hopelessness, of defeatism that had hung over her on my first visit, seemed even more evident than before. She lingered in the doorway after showing me to my room. There was something, she said, she wanted me to understand.

'This is the *platteland*,' she said. 'And the Afrikaners don't like the blacks. We let them drink on the *stoep* [porch], but the boys don't like them in the bar. It's OK [for] the clever ones who dress well, but the farm *kaffirs*,[5] smelly and all that, they'll never be accepted. One or two come in talking about the new South Africa. But the boys soon tell them where to go.'

Her thoughts kept returning to race and the new era and the sense of 'entitlement' that 'they' seemed to feel.

'After pay day they come in by the lorryload. They line up and make straight for the bar [at the back]. They want this. They want that. They have four schools. It is not as if they are lacking . . .'

'So how will Koppies and Kwakwatsi be reconciled?'

'I don't think there is a future here,' she said. By way of illustration she recounted how her chairs kept disappearing from the *stoep* if she was not keeping an eye on them. And reconciliation? I repeated.

'It'll take time. I hope I'll be long gone by then.'

Such was the troubled inheritance of the 'rainbow nation', Tutu's flamboyant coinage for post-apartheid South Africa. When the ANC took power after the first democratic elections in April 1994, race relations were, on the surface, swiftly transformed. Television, radio and advertising reinforced the message that the country was changing with images of blacks and whites happily working together. Soon after the election the South African Broadcasting Corporation (SABC), the state television channel, aired a soap opera that poked fun at the country's racial hang-ups and misunderstandings. *Suburban Bliss* was based on the jarring exchanges between the Molois, a black family who had moved out of Soweto to a former white suburb, and the Dwyers, a middle-class white family trying to do the right thing and yet privately appalled by having black neighbours.

'This is just the medicine the doctor ordered; it's very close to the bone,' the actor who played Ike Moloi, the father of the black family, told me. 'Black people can laugh at themselves, but white people traditionally didn't like that at all. All the years they've been labelled *baas* [boss], and now we're saying, "Hey, man, relax." '[6]

His comment was in keeping with the exuberance of the times. Every now and then someone would say or do something that would jolt the post-election narrative of a new multiracial nation. There was outrage in early 1995, when a tape was published of an inflammatory exchange between white and black police officers. The blacks had gone on strike against racism in the force and blockaded themselves within their Soweto station. The whites from the elite Internal Stability Unit were deployed outside with orders to end the protest.

'When are you *kaffirs* going to stop? Didn't you have enough?' said one of the ISU members over the radio to his black colleagues. 'It appears that you *kaffirs* have forgotten Blood River' – an 1838 battle in which a few hundred Afrikaners annihilated several thousand Zulus.[7]

The publication of the exchange led to angry condemnation of the police. In liberal white circles in Johannesburg and Cape Town some agonised over how such language could still be aired now that apartheid was over. There was a similar response in South Africa's newspapers in 1997 after a coach of the national rugby teams was caught out using the K-word in a tirade against the new rugby authorities over their pressure for affirmative action in the selection of the team. The outrage was a little naive. South Africa was hardly going to wake up the morning after Mandela's inaugural address to Parliament, when he vowed to eradicate the use of the word *kaffir*, awash with sentiments of cross-cultural understanding.

But for a few years, by force of his personality and his example, Mandela encouraged the belief that true reconciliation between the races really was attainable. During his first eighteen years in prison he had not been allowed even to hold hands with his second wife, Winnie, on her few sanctioned visits, and they had had to communicate through a glass screen. Nor was he allowed to attend the funerals of his mother or his eldest son, who was killed in a car accident. And these tribulations were, he maintained, relatively trivial when set against the suffering of so many compatriots in the fight against apartheid. That a man who had suffered so much and for so long was willing to embrace his old oppressors was all the more inspiring against the backdrop of the genocide in Rwanda and the civil war in Yugoslavia, which were raging as he took power.

Sometimes there was a touch of pantomime to his drive for reconciliation, such as when he invited the widows and wives of former Nationalist heads of state and black liberation leaders to tea at his residence. Then there was the lunch he hosted for Percy Yutar, the state prosecutor who had argued for the death sentence when he was on trial for his life under apartheid, and who had expressed disappointment when Mandela was jailed for life.

His critics in the ANC suggested privately he had taken his mission too far when he travelled to one of the most remote spots in South Africa to pay a call on the widow of Dr Hendrik Verwoerd, the most polarising of the apartheid leaders. Verwoerd's speeches and policies had provided the ideological under-pinning of apartheid. As prime minister from 1958 until his assassination by a deranged parliamentary messenger in 1966, he had presided over some of the more notorious events in the history of South Africa: the massacre of sixty-nine unarmed black protestors at Sharpeville in 1960, the banning of the ANC and Mandela's trial. He had also been reputed never to have shaken a black man's hand. His widow, Betsy, lived in Orania, a small whites-only settlement on the fringes of the Kalahari Desert. She was ninety-four and wrinkled like a dried-up fruit when Mandela came to call. She spoke with a quavering voice as she offered him coffee and *koeksusters* (sweet pastries). At an impromptu press conference on her doorstep, a black journalist asked Mandela a pointed question about his visit. The clear insinuation was that he was frittering away his time and should have been focusing on changing the lives of the poor. He replied testily that his reconciliatory drive had cost him only a few moments and yet had helped to bind the nation together.

Mandela knew how difficult the post-apartheid settlement had been to achieve and how important it was to keep the Afrikaner establishment loyal to his government. There was nothing inevitable about a peaceful end to apartheid, however logical it seems in retrospect. Without Mandela the story of South Africa's transition from white rule might have had a far bleaker end-ing. Years after he stepped down from office, one of his advisers said that even after taking power Mandela had still been worried that the security forces might try to sabotage the new democracy. Mandela also knew South Africa could not afford a mass exodus of whites with their skills and their capital. He cited many times as a cautionary tale the histories of the former Portuguese colonies Angola and Mozambique, which lost most of their skilled workers and professionals at independence when the Portuguese colonists fled. So he masked his anger over the decades of brutality and injustice – he always said he had forgiven but not forgotten the past – and strove to make the Afrikaners feel they belonged in the new nation.

The apex of this drive came at the 1995 Rugby World Cup finals, which were being hosted for the first time in South Africa. While it was something of a cliché to say that rugby was a religion for Afrikaners, it was certainly 'their' game. Adopted by Afrikaners after their defeat in the Anglo-Boer War, it was seen as a way of getting back at the hated *rooineks* (red necks), the Afrikaner nickname for English-speaking whites. Under apartheid it became a symbol of all that was robust and defiant about white South Africa – or aggressive and pugilistic, depending on your perspective. Sensing an opening into the Afrikaner soul and so another way of ensuring stability, Mandela embraced the game with a passion.

Wilhelm Verwoerd, the grandson of the assassinated prime minister, attended the opening game. His delicate frame and slight stature marked him out as an improbable Afrikaner. This is a race that has long taken pride in muscular physique forged by outdoor life and a meat-heavy diet. He was indeed something of an apostate. He had joined the ANC in the early nineties and was seen in the family, he said, as a *hensopper* (the word used in the Boer War to describe one who surrendered to the British). He was instinctively sceptical about the idea that Afrikaners were really changing and so was all the more struck by the atmosphere at the first match of the tournament when, after being publicly blessed by Mandela at the opening ceremony, South Africa's team beat one of their great rivals, Australia.

'To sit amongst a white male Afrikaner crowd with everyone cheering for Nelson Mandela was the ultimate postmodern *volksfees* [people's party],' he recalled. 'Not many could sing "Nkosi Sikelel' i-Afrika" [the liberation hymn that had become part of the national anthem], but that didn't matter. It felt wonderful.' The international sporting sanction imposed under apartheid and lifted after the unbanning of the ANC had been far more devastating to whites than economic sanctions, he reckoned. 'It struck people's daily lives. It struck at the core of their being.'[8]

The hype over the tournament was a little synthetic. There was only one non-white in the squad, a dashing athlete of mixed race called Chester

Williams, whose face adorned a thousand billboards advertising the tournament. Soccer was the game of the townships. Black commentators noted drily that rugby was essentially a sport played and watched by white people. But some cynics might have been softened by a magical paean to reconciliation from a young black woman called Thandi on a talk-radio show. 'I have no idea what they are doing or why. I can't see why they spend all that time sitting on each other or making themselves into that tortoise thing,' she said of the rugby scrum. 'All I know is I am glued to the screen, and when I see the team in green hugging each other, I get damp in my eyes: those are my boys; that's my team.'[9]

Mandela surpassed himself at the final, arriving wearing the green-and-gold jersey of the Springboks, the South African team, with the captain's number 6 on the back. It was a masterstroke. As he pumped his fists in the air when South Africa scored the winning points, the world reprised its awestruck wonder at seeing the old pariah state apparently breaking the mould. Even the *Sowetan*, then the country's best-selling daily newspaper and arguably the most authentic voice of black South Africa in the print media, was tickled by the tournament. It ran the headline '*Amabhokobhoko*' (the Boks), a wordplay on *amabhakabhaka*, a Zulu corruption of the English word 'buccaneers', the nickname for the Orlando Pirates, one of the country's top soccer teams. More than a decade later François Pienaar, the golden-haired giant who led the Springboks to victory, told me he was still being greeted by black South African strangers as 'our captain'.[10]

A few nights after the final, around midnight, Gigi Mafifi, a young black student, returned home seething. He had been hit by white policemen a few streets away for no apparent reason.[11] Given his confident, outspoken manner, it was likely that in their minds he 'provoked' the assault. To them he was, in the old apartheid mindset, the ultimate 'cheeky *kaffir*'. His feelings about white South Africans after this were barely more civil. It was a salutary reminder of the world that lay behind the Chester Williams posters and the jolly chanting by white radio hosts of 'Shosholoza', a jaunty old Zulu miners' song that had become the rugby tournament's anthem.

It was always going to take more than an inspirational leader to overcome the legacy of centuries of discrimination.

If Mandela was the demigod of reconciliation, then Tutu was his high priest. For two sapping years from 1996 to 1998 the 'Arch', as his aides called him, toured the country as head of the Truth and Reconciliation Commission, a body set up to try to unearth and then exorcise South Africa's past. His mandate was to expose and, in return for confessions, forgive human rights abuses in South Africa's troubled history. He had to act as an umpire, as the commission faced criticism from all sides. Yet in his heart he, like every other black South African who had grown up under apartheid, knew all too well how racist and unjust the country had been in the old days. He recalls fuming with his classmates over why history books referred to blacks as 'stealing' cattle but whites as 'capturing' them.

'We thought it was a strange choice of language,' he said soon after the commission started work. 'You really lived in two worlds. In white areas there would be the birds tweeting in leafy avenues. And then as you entered Soweto you had to put on headlights to see in the smog.'[12]

As the experiences of Eastern Europe after the fall of communism and South America after the fall of its right-wing dictatorships had shown, delving into the past was always going to be difficult. Former Soviet-bloc countries faced wrenching decisions over what to do with their secret-police files. The experience of Romania, where the files remained under lock and key after the fall of communism, testified to the risks of trying to bury the past as a drip-drip of allegations poisoned the new dispensation. But at least in Eastern Europe, as the years passed after the fall of the Berlin Wall, the more obvious scars of the past faded. South Africa faced a far greater challenge. It had to tackle a past that was divided by race and not just politics, and a past whose consequences were starkly apparent to South Africans every day as they lived their lives in their largely segregated communities.

Tutu embarked on his mission with the same fire and emotion he had devoted to confronting the white government in the 1980s. Yet for all his evangelism on behalf of the commission, he was among the first to admit it had a daunting task. We are trying to 'heal a deeply traumatised, wounded and polarised society,' he said. 'So many South Africans, particularly whites, see me laughing and are unaware that we sat in cells wondering why we were there.'[13]

His credo was an old African saying, *Ubuntu ungumuntu ngabanye abantu*, which loosely translates as 'people are people through other people'. *Ubuntu* is seen by many Africans as a powerful moral corrective to the West's perceived cult of the individual. Inspiring as it was as a guiding principle, this was a judicial process. The commission was the fruit of a vital compromise agreement between the National Party and the ANC and was intended as a middle way between the victor's justice of the Nuremberg trials and collective amnesia. White rule was not overthrown at the barrel of a gun, however much the ANC liked to romanticise the role of Umkhonto we Sizwe, its armed wing. Rather – and somewhat incredibly in hindsight – the Nationalists negotiated themselves from power as they slowly came to the conclusion that while they could probably beat back the insurrection in the townships for many years, ultimately they would have to reach a settlement. The promise of amnesty played a critical part in this capitulation, as it helped to ensure that senior generals in the army and police did not oppose the post-apartheid agreement. National Party and ANC negotiators haggled over it until just a few hours before finalising the interim constitution in November 1993. In the end agreement was reached by crossing out the word 'may' from the clause that had read 'there may be amnesty' and replacing it with the word 'shall'.[14] The technicalities were left unresolved. It was left to the post-apartheid Parliament to spell out the terms. After an intense debate the legislators came to the critical conclusion: perpetrators of human rights abuses would be eligible for amnesty if they confessed their misdeed and if their crimes were deemed political.

Unsurprisingly, the commission had a stormy ride. The white right accused it of conducting a witch-hunt of Afrikaners; the ANC accused it of imposing a false moral equivalence between the apartheid secret police and the anti-apartheid movement; victims argued that the apartheid torturers and secret policemen should not deserve amnesty even for full confessions. Academics suggested that Tutu's emotional and overtly religious approach to his task conflicted uneasily with the commission's judicial status. Some of this was political point-scoring. But as Tutu and his fellow commissioners toured the country to hear the stories of past human rights abuses, you had to be fairly heartless not to sympathise with the victims' complaint: How could you reconcile yourself to a former member of a death squad?

Dirk Coetzee, a one-time leader of the most notorious apartheid hit squad, decided the best way to approach the commission was by grovelling. In 1989 he had fled the country and become a whistle-blower about apartheid dirty tricks after he was on the brink of being exposed by one of his former colleagues, who was on death row for murder. In the countdown to the first hearing of the Truth Commission in 1996, he took me and other correspondents on a televised tour of Vlakplaas, a farm outside Pretoria where, in the last years of white rule, he and later Eugene de Kock, a notorious policeman known as 'Prime Evil', masterminded the murder and torture of dozens of opponents of the regime. It was more hit-squad reality show than confessional.

'I am worried the light will fade and we won't be able to film,' Coetzee said, breaking off his reminiscences as he approached a row of empty graves. He turned to the producer. 'Just in case, do you have lights for your camera?' The producer nodded. Coetzee's sing-song tones continued. 'So where was I? Oh yes. You see these were dug in advance for victims. It sounds terrible. It was terrible, but . . .'[15]

'This was the canteen where the boys drank themselves to pieces,' he said gesturing to a low brick bungalow. 'We had our own little clubhouse. This was the place where Gene [De Kock] congratulated the guys and they had their Chivas Regal . . .' We moved on down to the remains of an old *braai* [barbecue] pit, the traditional heart of any white South African farm.

'It was here that Japie Maponya was tortured. He was tortured to pieces.' Coetzee pointed up at a grove of willow trees. 'This was his last sight of normal surroundings. You look at the picnic spot. They made him dig his own grave . . .'

Maponya was killed in September 1985. He had been kidnapped by policemen who were looking for information about his brother, an ANC member in exile. The final details of his murder emerged in court after the end of white rule, when de Kock went on trial for multiple crimes. The trial was unfolding even as Coetzee took me on his grisly tour. 'He [Maponya] was kicked, he was punched . . . It was a free for all. They were like bees attacking a man,'[16] one of his interrogators told the court. Another recalled that they discussed within

earshot of the battered Maponya about how they were going to kill him. They
eventually took him handcuffed and blindfolded just over the border with
Swaziland. De Kock administered the *coup de grâce* by cleaving his skull with a
spade.

The Vlakplaas tour was part of a long-running public relations campaign by
Coetzee coinciding with his appeal for amnesty from the Truth Commission
for the 1981 murder of a prominent human rights lawyer, Griffiths Mxenge,
one of the more infamous killings of the apartheid era. As the sun started to
sink over the low surrounding hills and the group moved on to Daisy Farm, the
site of a separate security police operation, Coetzee's face was set in a permanent ingratiating pose. He had long since appreciated that his only way to
avoid a prison cell – or even a knife in the back – was to assist the Truth Commission.

So how could he justify his crimes? He gave a nervous giggle before replying.
'It's difficult to explain nowadays, but we believed we were fighting a war,' he
said. 'And the fact that the world was against us just meant they didn't
understand. If you look back now, it seems so absurd, but we boasted we were
the last bastion of Christianity in the continent . . . and joining the police was
like joining an elite club.' As a car drew up with his lawyer, Coetzee switched
back into reality-television mode. 'Don't get out yet,' he shouted at his lawyer.
The television crew, he said with an expansive sweep of his arm, needed a few
more minutes to get ready to film his arrival.

De Kock was convicted of eighty-nine crimes, including six murders. He
was sentenced to two life terms for two specific murders and a further 212
years in prison for other crimes. The camera-savvy whistle-blower, Coetzee,
won his appeal for amnesty.

How is one to set his relative lack of penitence against the account of Nohle
Mohapi, the first to testify to the commission in its opening hearing in a
draughty hall in the town of East London? With her head held high, she moved
slowly to the front, supported by a friend, to tell of her love for her activist husband, Mapetla, the birth of their children, and their life together through endless police harassment. Her voice did not falter as she reached the terrible day
in 1976 when a policeman came to their door and claimed her husband had
hanged himself in a prison cell with his jeans.

'I was never happy in the twenty years since Mapetla died,' she said. When she went to the mortuary to identify the body, a black policeman laughed, she recalled. 'He said: "They call themselves leaders and yet they cannot take pressure, they kill themselves,"' she told the hearing.[17] She herself was subsequently detained in solitary confinement. On one occasion she was fastened to a grille, assaulted and forced to denounce her comrades as terrorists.

Such harrowing testimony, emerging day after day, produced bit by bit a version of truth of South Africa's murky past. Sometimes the precise details of what had been a particularly shocking murder were at last confirmed. Security policemen confessed how Steve Biko, the charismatic leader of the black consciousness movement who had kept the anti-apartheid flame alive in the seventies, died in custody in 1977 of brain damage after a brutal assault by his interrogators. Sometimes the revelations were less newsworthy yet shed light into the shadowy recesses of the apartheid mindset. In one hearing a low-ranking civil servant, Jeffrey Benzien, demonstrated how he administered the 'wet bag' treatment – a form of water-boarding – which involved placing a cloth over a victim's head, taking them to the brink of suffocation, and then bringing them around before starting all over again. Every day he returned home to his wife and family like any other dedicated civil servant. It was, his psychiatrist testified, all in a day's work. Sometimes the hearings reminded their audiences that whites too had been innocent victims in the vortex of political violence that engulfed South Africa in the last years of apartheid.

With the publication of the Truth Commission's report at the end of Mandela's presidency, South Africa moved closer to knowing its history. But the second part of the commission's mandate, reconciliation, was rather more elusive. As many of the victims argued, it was a little too slick to suggest that two years of hearings, however graphic, could bring down a curtain on the past. 'By granting amnesty to the tormentors, society made the hard choice to suspend these victims' civil rights,' wrote Joel Netshitenzhe, Mbeki's chief strategist. 'To crow about "closure" is premature and insensitive. The search for the truth and lasting reconciliation continues. Many hard choices still have to be made, so that as partisans of a better tomorrow, we can all escape the legacy of apartheid.'[18]

Many in the ANC were infuriated that South Africa's whites, whose comfortable existence had been protected by the dirty work of the security police, carried on with their lives without having to apologise for having benefited from apartheid. As the death squad leader, de Kock, argued bitterly: What about F. W. de Klerk and the other leaders of the National Party, who denied any knowledge of the hit squads and dirty tricks and blamed their actions on rogue elements? Why were they allowed to get away with a bland generalised statement to the commission about their past? On this de Kock had a rare meeting of minds with Mbeki.

On the eve of publication of the commission's final report, as president of the ANC, Mbeki tried to censor its condemnation of the ANC's human rights abuses. His gripe was over what he saw as an implicit moral equivalence between the deeds of apartheid security forces and its opponents. Mandela, still the country's president, appreciated that the commission was the product of a political trade-off and forced him to back down. But the die was cast for the less reconciliatory era that was to unfold under Mbeki.

Mbeki had long made clear that he was sceptical of the fuzzy idea of a rainbow nation. 'When we begin to grapple with the real issues, when you pass beyond the "Gloria! Hallelujah! What a lovely thing we've done!" then the problems begin,' he told me while he was still deputy president. 'You cannot have real national reconciliation of a lasting kind if you don't have a fundamental transformation of society. You have to de-racialise. It is a painful process.'[19]

Once in power he moved fast to reinforce that impression. Through his weekly online address to the ANC he promoted a pricklier message. The saccharine banalities of the weekly presidential radio address in the United States were not for him. White critics were demonised as racists steeped in the mindset of centuries of colonists in belittling Africans. Sympathetic columnists followed his lead. Black critics were labelled as Uncle Toms, coconuts (white on the inside), or even *askaris*. In the colonial era in Africa, *askaris* were native soldiers. Under apartheid they were liberation fighters who had been turned by the security police to fight against their old comrades.

It was always clear that after Mandela's era it would make sense politically for the government to devote fewer of its statements to reconciliation. But Mbeki pushed too far in the other direction. Over halfway through his second term, he sparked a furore by wading into a dispute involving　　　　 Africa's banks, in which a black intern resigned while accusing it o... ing that white managers did not train black staff through fear they w... their jobs.[20] Only eleven years earlier Mbeki had said that the 'nice' deputy president would sometimes have to say things that would make him no longer seem like a 'nice' deputy president. Should he not as president, I asked him, be more of a cheerleader?

When pressed on this point, Mbeki recalled a friend who had moved into a white suburb and been shunned by his white neighbours.[21] His irritation with the small-minded white suburban mindset was understandable. Within months of the end of white rule it became something of a cliché to say that it was impossible to find anyone who had voted for apartheid. But Mbeki's blanket indictment of all whites as being as racist as the proprietor of the Hotel Friesland was unfair. It was also counterproductive, as it helped to entrench the very isolationist white mindset that so irked him. When Tony Trahar, the mild-mannered chief executive of Anglo American, the giant mining house, suggested that a few uncertainties remained over South Africa's future prospects, Mbeki responded with a 2,900-word polemic accusing South Africa's most influential businessman of being just another racist reared to believe a black government would fail. When allegations surfaced about corruption in a controversial multibillion-dollar arms deal, he said the criticism was prompted by a 'racist conviction that Africans . . . are naturally prone to corruption, venality and mismanagement'.[22] As Mbeki's presidency unfolded, many whites, including some white members and supporters of the ANC, came to suspect that the reconciliatory ethos of Mandela's term in office had been a brief post-liberation honeymoon before the onset of an African nationalist era in which they would be a politically disenfranchised minority.

Mandela himself had occasionally issued a swinging indictment of reactionary white attitudes, most notably in his speech when handing over the leadership of the ANC to Mbeki. But the impact of these critiques was softened by his reconciliatory refrain. Mbeki, however, dispensed with the latter. Instead, he constantly picked at the country's racist scab. It had always been apparent that Mandela's reconciliatory vision was going to need cultivation, but that was not to be Mbeki's way, and he undid much of the work that

Mandela had done in trying to encourage whites to stay committed to the new nation.

A decade after the end of white rule, race relations had outwardly been transformed. In the last days of white rule, adult black men had still frequently been referred to as 'boys' and treated like children. In the early nineties it had been common even on the streets of the most cosmopolitan city, Johannesburg, for a black passer-by to avoid a white man's gaze. Rather, the standard – that is, safest – response had been one of downcast eyes and a preemptive cringe. The opening lessons in my Zulu textbook in the early nineties reflected such hierarchical thinking. 'Come here, Jo, I say' and 'Jo smokes a lot' were two of the opening phrases I was taught should be used when speaking to staff. More than a decade into majority rule, for most South Africans the days of such defensive deference were over. Black South Africa had collectively regained the dignity denied for so long.

Shortly before the end of white rule an entertaining tale did the rounds about a black American newspaper correspondent. She was supposedly queuing in Thrupps, the Whole Foods of Johannesburg, when an elderly white woman looked over her shoulder at the French cheeses in her basket.

'What good taste your madam has,' the shopper is said to have commented.

'I am the madam,' the correspondent replied.

Such exchanges were impossible to imagine a decade later. Whatever some might feel privately, whites could no longer be dumbfounded at encountering a black compatriot as an equal, rather than an underling. Year by year the black middle class expanded, as did black enrolments at the previously whites-only universities. Tutu ventured with his usual linguistic brio that he was regularly astounded at how South Africa had matured. 'I am frequently amazed at some of the things that our people take in their stride, when you think for instance that we had something called the Immorality Act and the Mixed Marriages Act that said no to any intimate relationship between whites and people of other races, and I mean, you look around and you . . . you see mixed couples walking hand in hand, or more often they are in a clinch, you wouldn't get a razor blade between them.' He had recently seen a group of black male students stride through the campus of Pretoria University, one of them arm in arm with a white girl. 'And so far as we were able to make out, the sky seemed to remain very firmly in place,' he said. 'That is amazing, given where we come from.'[23]

Tutu was right to cite how race relations had improved since apartheid. Also in the early years after liberation, the ANC had for the most part been careful to eschew triumphalism. Just outside the main gates to Parliament in Cape Town stands a squat stone statue of a Boer horseman. It was erected in memory of Louis Botha, the first prime minister of South Africa. *Boer Krugsman staatsman* (farmer warrior statesman) reads the inscription. It was a mark of the ANC's commitment to building a new nation that a statue of the man who had implemented many of the laws that paved the way for apartheid still stood facing the president's office in Cape Town.

And yet, as Tutu agreed, fourteen years after the end of white rule, the two worlds, black and white, were for most people very separate. A casual unacknowledged racism remained embedded in the consciousness of many whites. A reciprocal suspicion was lodged in the mind of many blacks, compounded by a lingering resentment that most whites appeared to regard the past as another country. Racial boundaries were increasingly crossed at the workplace and in schools, but most interracial friendships did not extend into out-of-office hours, and many whites and blacks still tended when in their own racial group to talk of the other as 'they' and 'them'. 'The whites won't let us talk in our African languages at work, as they are afraid we are speaking about them,' a senior black accountant said. 'But we don't listen to them. It makes them mad.'[24] The 'rainbow nation' was very much a work in progress.

The post-apartheid career of Malegapuru Makgoba encapsulates the racial complexities of the new order. In 1994 he returned home to South Africa, having had a successful career as an immunologist in Britain, to be feted as one of his country's most distinguished academics. He was welcomed onto the campus of the University of the Witwatersrand, a sweeping series of grand Victorian stone buildings and quads, reminiscent of an Oxford college, just north of the centre of Johannesburg. For the authorities of what had been traditionally a pillar of white liberalism, he was the answer to their dreams. He was a bona fide, world-class, black South African academic. The university moved fast to groom him as the first black vice chancellor as a way of proving to the ANC and the militant public service unions, which had been disrupting the university with protests and marches, that they were changing.

But an influential group of white academics in the senior common room had other ideas. They were convinced that he was unfit for high office, believing that he had falsified his credentials and also that he was temperamentally ill-suited to the post. He in turn accused them of racism and passed on his trenchant views of his colleagues to the media. Overnight, the sort of petty row that electrifies universities across the world all the time became a cause célèbre. For the new black establishment trying to find its bearings in the post-apartheid era, Makgoba was a hero challenging old patriarchal and racist assumptions. To his detractors his candidacy was a test of the rigour of the new age. Just because he was black and had fine qualifications did not mean he should automatically be promoted to high office, they argued.

The row was one of the few occasions when the racial undercurrent in many South African institutions and offices became a public spectacle. It ended with his suspension after he leaked confidential files about his detractors, the suicide of one of them, and the university in even more disarray. Thirteen years later, he was the vice chancellor of the University of KwaZulu-Natal in the eastern city of Durban. Once again he was grappling with the difficulty of how to change a university, and once again he found himself caught up in a row with a group of white academics who accused him of pushing too hard to Africanise the curriculum. So had race relations improved in South Africa over the intervening years? He gestured towards his campus before replying. His was a non-racial university with about 40 per cent black students, 18 per cent white, and about 30 per cent Indian and of mixed race, but there was little mixing, he said.

'If you walk around the university, you see African students are by and large together, white students are by and large together, Indian students are by and large together. In classrooms you see the same thing. We have a non-racial society that has not yet come together. Or you can say, we have now truly legitimised apartheid. We live in different orbits all the time, sometimes quite comfortably, but at other times we collide. We are still suspicious of each other. We still view the world in our racialised terms. What Mbeki did was to sharpen this. He was saying these are the realities society needs to take on board. But such an approach intimidates. It creates fear. It leaves a sense "I am not listened to. I do not belong." Mandela made us all feel we belong, and that has disappeared.'[25]

The endurance of a rift between white and black long after the end of white rule was hardly surprising. Apartheid governments had not just entrenched the colonial oppression of the black majority by the white minority. They had legislated to create a make-believe all-white country, in defiance of the demographics of black population growth and urbanisation, not to mention justice. Laws barred blacks from living in areas designated for whites except as domestic workers and gardeners. These ensured that long after the end of apartheid most blacks and most whites would still live apart.

The traditional division of wealth broadly along racial lines exacerbated the rift. It was misleading to suggest that all whites were prosperous. The trade union Solidarity, which catered mainly to blue-collar white workers, calculated fourteen years after apartheid that 10 per cent of whites should be designated as poor, in contrast to 50 per cent of blacks.[26] Whites argued that they were atoning for apartheid by paying high taxes to fund the uplift of the townships, and that they were being penalised by a far-reaching affirmative action programme to promote blacks into employment and higher education. Yet nonetheless Mbeki was essentially correct when he spoke of South Africa's two economies: one white and wealthy and the other black and poor.

In the annual Nelson Mandela Lecture, a decade after liberation, Tutu had warned the ANC that it was sitting on a 'powder keg' of unmet expectations, prompting a withering counterblast from Mbeki, who accused him of meddling in affairs he did not understand. The riposte had pained but unsurprisingly not silenced Tutu. South Africans and the government should be doing far more to address the divisions and to reach across the racial divide, he told me. The gulf between the 'leafy avenues' with 'the birds tweeting' and the townships sadly, he concluded, remained all but intact.

'We still have these huge, huge disparities in wealth and poverty, and although people can now live anywhere if you can afford it, what were white suburbs are still largely white suburbs, and the townships are still . . . What has amazed me is the fact that people can live under those conditions. They get up in the morning and go to the white suburbs, affluent, salubrious, and they work

in homes that have all the modern conveniences. And in the evening they go
back to the squalor . . . and deprivation . . . And you wonder how they have
maintained the patience that they have shown. I mean, you would have
thought that by now they would have said, "Oh no, this freedom dividend,
where is it?" '[27]

Economists agreed that the creation of a black middle class, one of Mbeki's
priorities, was the best way to bridge the gap. According to one survey the average income in black households in the central Gauteng province, the engine
room of the economy, rose by 47 per cent to over 90,000 rand a year between
2000 and 2006.[28] But still, the country's extremes broadly split down racial
lines. A trade union report in 2008 found that fourteen years into democracy
whites enjoyed on average incomes 450 per cent higher than blacks, and 400
per cent higher than people of mixed race.[29] The survey's results were not surprising, given the legacy of apartheid education. But they highlighted a trend:
despite the growth of the black middle class and the government's anti-poverty
measures, including an annual social welfare budget of over 70 billion rand, the
inequality gap between rich and poor was increasing.[30] The Gini coefficient,
the international measure of economic inequalities, rose between 1995 and
2005, identifying South Africa as having one of the world's sharpest divides between rich and poor.

As ANC ministers faced increasing criticism over their record in tackling the
inequalities, some found themselves all but parroting the language used by the
old white government. Essop Pahad, one of Mbeki's senior advisers,
argued it was unfair to highlight the rift in South Africa. Racial 'ghettos' occurred
all over the world, he said.[31] He was right. They are often a matter of cultural
choice, as much as the product of an economic division. Such a stark divide in
society is hardly unique to South Africa. The racial divide in Washington DC,
where three of its quadrants are mainly black and poor, seems if anything starker
than in Johannesburg. But South Africa's poisoned racial history makes its
wealth gap more perilous than in most countries.

Cyril Ramaphosa was one of the first to warn that whites had to find ways of
showing more public commitment to understanding the lives of their black
compatriots if only as a matter of security for their future. Enduring bigotry
was all too apparent in the 'well practised and well-finessed way of white

people just hiding their heads in the sand like an ostrich, completely oblivious to what's happening in this country,' he said. Many implied they had not been aware of apartheid abuses, and some of them did not even want to know, he said. 'But . . . it is very, very sad that white people are indifferent and this is something that is going to catch up with us as a nation.'[32]

One of the great wonders of South Africa in the years leading up to and away from the transition was the extraordinary tolerance and patience articulated by so many blacks. In conversation after conversation in Kwakwatsi in the mid-nineties, Tladi, the local ANC leader, and one of his colleagues, Charles Masibi, a young teacher, stressed that they did not seek retribution from the whites. They just wanted at long last a fair chance and an end to such outrageous behaviour as the siege. This magnanimity was amplified across the country in the early years of democracy by Mandela. But as Tutu warned me, such patience cannot be infinite. Yugoslavia or, nearer to hand, Zimbabwe offers a grim example of how historical grievances can lie fallow for decades before being whipped up by unscrupulous leaders.

As the years passed after the end of white rule, from time to time South African newspapers would fasten on a reminder of how the attitudes of the Hotel Friesland were taking a long time to die. For a week in February 2008 front pages were dominated by what became known as the 'hostel of hate'. A video had surfaced showing four white students from an all-white residence at the University of the Free State forcing five black cleaners to take part in humiliating mock initiation rituals. The students had made the video as a protest at plans to make their hostel multiracial. In one clip a student is shown urinating on food before the cleaners are made to eat it, on their knees. Two of them spew it out almost immediately. They are also repeatedly called 'whores' and made to do Afrikaner folk dances and play rugby. 'Once upon a time the Boers lived happily here . . . until the day the less advantaged discovered the word "integration" in the dictionary,' intones a calm voice in Afrikaans over the opening footage.

News of the video was greeted in the outside world as final proof that the 'rainbow nation' was little more than a marketing slogan. Headlines suggested with a hint of *Schadenfreude* that racism was alive and well in South Africa. It was a vile video. It cast a depressing insight into the entrenched attitudes of conservative Afrikanerdom. It also raised an important question as to why for fourteen post-apartheid years the university authorities had condoned segregated university hostels. But the outrage missed the point.

Such incidents were rare – and certainly far rarer than they had been under apartheid. I was tempted to agree with Zuma when he told me he thought the furore was overblown. It was not, he told me, representative of the state of race relations. All in all, given its racial history, he concluded, South Africa was doing pretty well. Addressing a dinner for the *Financial Times*, he argued that it was not as if racism was unique to South Africa. He went on to illustrate his point by jokingly imagining a South Africa without blacks and yet still plagued by racial divisions.

'The following day it would start between the Afrikaners and the English speakers. And if all the English speakers left South Africa, the problem would start between the Afrikaners from the old Free State and the Transvaal. And if you said just the Xhosas stay, you would see problems between the Mfengus and the Xhosas. And if you said Zulus only can stay . . . Phew.'[33]

His remarks were typical of his informal style of politics. They also reflected how South Africa could be on its better days: a country of blacks and whites and Asians and people of mixed race united by their love of *braa*ing (barbecuing) meat in the sunshine, their appreciation of the smell of fresh rain on the dry earth, their veneration for Mandela and their willingness to laugh at each other and the awful absurdity of their past.

Yet the underlying story of race relations in post-apartheid South Africa was more subtle and complex. It was one in which incomprehension and resentment dominated uneasy racial encounters across the country every day.

More than a decade after the end of white rule it was still broadly true that everything that blacks hoped for whites feared they would lose, that many whites could not appreciate that the arrival of a pothole just might be the price to be paid for the building of a road in a township, and that many blacks saw whites as interlopers and did not appreciate that many whites saw themselves as Africans and regarded South Africa as home. Outside the multiracial elite and some very poor communities, South Africa's races were like tectonic plates. Much of the time they glided smoothly past each other, but there was intermittent friction, and every now and then, they crashed against each other, sometimes with spectacular results.

Professor Shadrack Gutto, a government adviser, maintains that 'national reconciliation is sometimes when you smile at each other even if you hate each other like hell'.[34] It is a jaundiced view from a man with strong Africanist convictions but one that it's not unlikely many South Africans privately share or at least fear that many others share. The former certainly seemed true in the small town of Koppies fourteen years after the end of apartheid, even if the certainties of the days of the siege in the last year of white rule had long since been eroded.

Tannie Joan had long since left the Hotel Friesland. Our last conversation had been rather blunt. After hearing from Tladi, the local ANC councillor, that he had been thrown out when asking for a drink at the bar, I wrote an article about the survival of the old prejudices in the local hotel. When a South African read my piece in London, he was so incensed at the besmirchment of his country that he traced the number of the Friesland and telephoned the owner to upbraid her. A few weeks later she stood at the door with arms crossed.

Since her departure the hotel had been renamed the Paradys. In a sign of the changing times a wooden board pinned to the neighbouring gate advertised the services of a Dr Mula, a herbalist and specialist in *muti* (traditional medicine). The new owner, like her predecessor, was a chain-smoker. She had moved down from Pretoria a decade earlier and still affected the Afrikaner chic common to the capital in the heyday of apartheid: beehive hairdo, layers of caked make-up, high heels and a 1950s flowery dress. She had painted the reception hall in apricot pink and torn down one of the internal walls. She was less blunt than her predecessor had been and never used the word *kaffir* in my presence. But she too was convinced that the arrival of a black government was leading inexorably to disaster.

'Everyone is leaving Koppies because of the black happenings,' she told me flatly. 'There is nothing to stay for now.'

There were many more black people on the streets by day than under apartheid. A few had even moved into the town, including Hansie Buka, a tall, thickset man with a hearty laugh, who under white rule had run the only liquor store in Kwakwatsi. Five years after the end of white rule he had moved his family across the tracks to Koppies, where he lived in a bungalow with his wife and had opened a second store.

But Koppies and Kwakwatsi, while as dependent on each other for survival as before, were still two different universes: racially, white and black; politically, the past and the future; socio-economically, developed and developing; emotionally, resentful and angry. His white neighbours ignored him, Buka said. The principal of the main primary school in Kwakwatsi could barely restrain herself from shouting when asked about race relations. Apartheid was alive and well in Koppies, the principal said. There was no mixing of races. The whites just wanted to be alone. She cited a local white farmer who had recently, in a fit of vindictive pique after a row with a black farmhand, forced him to dig up the body of his dead infant son, just three days after he had been interred on farmland, and take him elsewhere.

Christo van Greunen, the town clerk, a veteran white civil servant who had been responsible for providing electricity and water to the township since the 1980s, did not question the continuing polarisation; rather he regarded it as inevitable. The tensions of the time of the siege had at least abated, he said.[35] He could remember a late-night meeting brokered by Buka with angry township activists in 1993, when he had carried a gun fearing for his life.

The antagonism had gone, as had the subservience. Blacks no longer called him 'baas' or 'sir'. He felt unthreatened driving through Kwakwatsi. As for the future, he said it was a matter of destiny: the blacks were poorly educated; they would not govern well; the roads and public services in Koppies would slowly deteriorate; all but the poorest whites would leave.

So is reconciliation possible on the front line of the first and third worlds? Van der Merwe, the deputy mayor at the end of white rule, had remarked a year after the end of apartheid that there was a 'bridge' between Koppies and Kwakwatsi but no one dared to cross it. A decade later Koos du Plooy, the acting principal of the Sarel Cilliers High School, still believed – publicly at least – that the two races were starting to reach out to each other. But he knew it would be a long haul. He, like most white South Africans, had had to accept huge changes to the world in which he had been raised. By 2008 the school had long since opened its doors to children from Kwakwatsi, but as the enrolment of black pupils increased, many of the white families had opted to take their

children to schools in nearby larger towns. They cited the decline
'standards' at Sarel Cilliers, but black parents were convinced it w
they did not want their children to mix with children of other rac
dozen teachers in the schools in Kwakwatsi started teaching at Sarel
Cilliers and then left after a few months, saying that the school staffroom was
still racist and treated black pupils with vindictive disdain.

'In the beginning there was a lot of struggle between the cultures . . .' du
Plooy said, slipping unconsciously into the euphemistic language of apartheid.
'Black culture is a loud nation. They don't talk softly to one another. Also a
black person doesn't have the same sense of time. In our culture it's important
to be on time.'[36] It would take some years, he reckoned, for people to forget the
past, but with commitment a multiracial school could emerge.

One of Buka's sons had been one of his star pupils. Buka himself was optimistic that his children, who were in their teens and early twenties, were breaking free of the country's racial straitjacket. One had recently married a lawyer.
At the wedding in Koppies there were twenty white students, even though
none of his white neighbours attended. His story was a reminder that bit by bit,
as more black South Africans entered the middle class and deployed their talents to business or building a family rather than politics as in the old days, post-
apartheid society gained fresh injections of glue.

That is the principal hope for South Africa: that the poison of apartheid can
be steadily diluted as the years pass and that, after a period of dutiful arm's-
length cooperation, future generations can somehow grow up free of the prejudices that have so long divided the country. But it will take a long time if it
happens. Much depends on the ANC and its ability to resist the temptation to
play the politics of race when it is under threat.

Chapter 3

LIBERATION MOVEMENTS HAVE A HABIT OF NOT AGEING GRACEFULLY

A movement without a vision is a movement without moral foundation.

— NELSON MANDELA, 1994

The ANC is one of the most loved organisations internationally because it always does the right thing.

— JACOB ZUMA,
AT HIS SIXTY-FIFTH-BIRTHDAY DINNER, 2007

João Domingos has a dim view of African liberation movements. He supported the Popular Movement for the Liberation of Angola (MPLA) in the mid-seventies, when it was one of three liberation movements vying to take over the Portuguese colony. He was euphoric in 1975, when its founder leader, Agostinho Neto, became the first president of an independent Angola even as the armies of Neto's two rivals marched on the capital, Luanda, determined to depose him. He celebrated as the MPLA imposed Marxism and then again when South African forces backing a rival movement were forced twice to withdraw. Yet long before decades of fighting finally ended in 2002, Domingos had lost faith in his liberators.

From the late nineties he had been reduced to living with his family on a rubbish heap in the heart of Luanda. Their shack was barely half a mile from a pink-marbled government complex adorned with some of the grandest residences and ministries in sub-Saharan Africa. When I met him in 2007, his foot was wrapped in a dirty red bandage. A trickle of sewage ran down the track past his doorstep. In the tropical haze one could make out the shapes of dozens of container ships from China, the latest 'colonial' partner, waiting to dock in the city's harbour. Further out, much further than the eye could see, were Angola's offshore oilfields, then pumping out about 1.5 million barrels a day. Someone presumably with a very wry sense of humour had named the slum Boa Vista (Good View).

When asked whom he would vote for in forthcoming elections, Domingos threw up his hands in the air. There had been no election since 1992, when a disputed result led to a flare-up of the civil war. He did not expect a vote to change anything. The MPLA would stay in power for eternity, he said, however badly it ruled.

'The country is rich, but they don't allow us to develop,' he said. 'It's like living under a dead dog.'[1]

Across Africa, liberation movements came to power in the 1960s, 1970s and 1980s espousing great dreams for their peoples. But the dreams invariably faded against a backdrop of corruption, authoritarianism and ethnic conflict (if one tribe was too closely identified with the ruling party). Many newly independent states formalised a one-party system, which they justified as in keeping with African traditional village democracy and also as a way of avoiding ethnic parties. Others went through the ritual of a fake election, which required party officials campaigning against a candidate who would never be allowed to win. While the symptoms of liberation movements' malaise varied, the history of their time in office tended to follow the same depressing course.

There were mitigating factors. Many African states were pawns on a global chessboard during the Cold War, when Moscow and Washington were more interested in creating a network of client states to stymie the other's global ambitions than in fostering good governance, even if this meant funding devastating proxy wars. The newly independent states also inherited minimal infrastructure and few skilled personnel. But possibly the greatest factor in the fifty-year-old saga of disappointment across much of sub-Saharan Africa has been a failure of its ruling parties to adapt from revolutionary movements to government.

Aguinaldo Jaime, the silver-haired deputy prime minister, was one of the reformist technocrats in charge of Angola's economy in the first decade of the new millennium. A graduate of the London School of Economics, he tended to be wheeled out to visiting Western officials to assure them the government was reforming its ways. He was the model of a modern technocrat: he spoke perfect English, wore an immaculate grey suit, and was fluent in the argot of the International Monetary Fund and the World Bank.

'The money is never enough to cater for all the needs of the people,' he told me silkily. Some people were not yet benefiting from the peace dividend, he conceded. But the government lacked the skilled workforce to carry out the necessary reforms. 'Can we do more? Yes, probably. But if you compare Angola today to the Angola we had twelve years ago, my assessment is we have made a lot of progress.'²

Angola certainly had made progress in that time. Twelve years earlier it had been embroiled in a terrible civil war. Artillery and aerial bombardment had reduced several of the main provincial towns to rubble. Luanda was home to at least two million refugees. The sight of a brand-new washing machine dispatched from United Nations' headquarters in New York in 1995 to a remote outpost of UN peacekeepers, where there had been no electricity or running water for twenty years, had epitomised for me the haplessness of international efforts to restore peace. But in the early years of the new millennium the country's economy was booming, courtesy of its fabulous oil revenues, worth $29.9 billion in 2006 according to official figures. Just down from Boa Vista, prime office space overlooking the lagoon was worth $6,500 a square metre.

Despite the push by reformists to open up the economy, the MPLA was one of the most corrupt regimes in the world. In 2004 a report by the New York-based agency Human Rights Watch said $4 billion of oil revenue was unaccounted for between 1987 and 2002. It was a staggering figure in a country where, according to the UN, most people lived on less than $2 a day. Many in Luanda lived in slums as bad as any in Africa.

The same sorry saga of mismanagement and autocracy had unfolded across the continent and indeed elsewhere under dominant parties. India's Congress Party, which ruled for forty-eight of the first sixty years after independence in 1947, and Mexico's PRI (Institutional Revolutionary Party), which wielded power for seven decades, provide case studies in how decades in power lead to corruption and stagnation. The challenge the ANC faced as it prepared for office was whether it could take a different path.

From the outset Mandela – inevitably some might say – posed to the party the question that lay at the heart of its necessary metamorphosis from a revolutionary movement to political party: How could it buck the depressing trend of other African liberation movements?

'We must never forget that power corrupts and absolute power corrupts absolutely,' he told an ANC party conference in its first year in government. 'It has happened in many countries that a liberation movement comes to power and the freedom fighters of yesterday become members of government. Sometimes without any idea of mischief they concentrate so much on portfolios that they forget about the people who put them in power and they become a class, a separate entity who are not accountable to their membership.'

The ANC would, he concluded confidently, avoid heading down the path of tyranny and misrule. But the ANC leaders had to work hard to avoid such a fate. 'It is not our good wishes that are going to avoid that disaster.'[3]

His speech was greeted rapturously by his audience. But not all in the ANC were so confident that the party would keep in mind the needs of its constituency. As it prepared to take office, Harry Gwala, one of the ANC's veteran left-wing ideologues, was already grimly convinced that it would not take its officials long to be seduced by the perks of power.

Gwala was a committed Stalinist. In his two stints on Robben Island under apartheid, he had sparred relentlessly with Mandela. The ANC's multiracial African nationalism was bourgeois and ineffectual, he had contended. When the time came, there would have to be a genuine communist revolution. In the mid-seventies, when he began his second term of imprisonment, his fiery rhetoric resonated with his comrades, many of whom thought Mandela had grown soft in prison and lost touch with the struggle. Mandela himself recalls having to argue long and hard to win them over.

On his release after his second term in prison, Gwala became a warlord. From his base in the townships around Pietermaritzburg, in the eastern province of Natal, he led the local fight against supporters of the ANC's main black rival, the Inkatha Freedom Party, a conflict that was to claim twenty-five thousand lives between 1983 and 1996. He was also an idealist. After the unbanning of the ANC he argued in vain against 'sunset' clauses in the post-apartheid settlement, guaranteeing cabinet seats for the Nationalists. He saw himself as a guardian of the ANC's true faith. In the last year of white rule I went to see him; four heavily armed young men drove me in a battered car from the edge of a township outside Pietermaritzburg. Half a dozen more youths in ANC T-shirts were waiting at the entrance to a simple brick bungalow.

Gwala was wearing a string vest and jeans. With his silver hair and formal manners he cut a genial grandfatherly figure. But his thick glasses and stern gaze lent him the appearance of one of those intense European Marxists photographed in the early twentieth century. He was badly paralysed from a rare motor neuron disease. He gestured with his eyes for me to take a seat opposite him before expressing his deep misgivings about the direction of the ANC. The party, he said, had to avoid being beguiled by business into thinking only of deals and forgetting about the poor.

All leaders had to learn that their strength lay not in themselves but in their supporters, he said. Separated from the masses, they became ordinary people, and this applied to all great leaders, even Churchill, Mandela or Roosevelt. If he himself failed to provide the right leadership and to deliver the fruits of liberation, then he too should be cast aside. 'If I can't deliver, I will march against myself.'[4]

After proffering political analogies from dozens of countries, from Scandinavia to New Zealand, he compared the great revolutions of history to the one unfolding in his own country. He even recalled a visit to Charles Dickens's home in Great Britain to amplify his point.

'You should think of *Great Expectations*,' he said. 'People are expecting a lot. More than half of South Africans live in shacks and squalor and deprivation . . .

For every child to go to school there must be drastic change. When Mandela
came out of Robben Island, there were tens of thousands at a rally in Durban.
They thought Mandela was a messiah. But he will have problems in delivering
those dreams. You mark my words.'

He was wrong about perceptions of Mandela, who would remain the messiah to South Africans long after he had stepped down from office. But the old
Marxist was right to have doubts about the ANC's ability to deliver the
dreams.

As the ANC settled into government in April 1994, its leaders bridled when
commentators compared their beloved party to other liberation movements or
even predicted they too might lose their way. They were different, the ANC
said. They had spent decades planning for liberation. They would avoid the
mistakes that had so blighted independence in the rest of the continent.

The ANC could indeed draw inspiration from a longer and more distinguished history than any other African liberation movement. The party dated
back to 8 January 1912, when the white residents of Bloemfontein, one of
South Africa's most conservative cities, had had the unaccustomed and presumably disconcerting experience of seeing large numbers of blacks gathering
in the streets, accompanied by the haunting strain of 'Nkosi Sikelel' i-Afrika',
the liberation hymn 'God Bless Africa'.[5] It was just two years after the Afrikaners and the British had formally ended decades of enmity and forged the Union
of South Africa. Far from extending the relatively liberal provisions in the
British-ruled Cape to the rest of the country, the constitution of the new state
had made no provision for the rights of blacks. Congregating in Bloemfontein,
the ANC's middle-class founders, lawyers, journalists and academics were determined to oppose this. They were, in Mandela's words, 'pioneers who braved
uncharted waters driven by a noble ideal',[6] but they faced a longer battle to gain
their rights than they could ever have predicted.

The first major turning point for the ANC came in 1948, with the landslide
election of the National Party on a platform of uplifting Afrikaners and intensifying segregationist laws. The result was a devastating blow to Mandela and
other young leaders in the ANC who appreciated that their fight for a non-

racial democracy had just become far harder. The following year he and others in the ANC Youth League ousted the party's then leader, Dr Alfred Xuma, a middle-class lawyer who was unwilling to confront the authorities with mass demonstrations. 'I think after so many years I must now confess what we actually did,' Mandela told ANC colleagues nearly half a century later to loud chuckles. In Xuma's place they put a feistier figure, Dr James Moroka, who was not at the time even a member of the party. They wrote out and gave him a party membership card on the spot, Mandela recalled.[7]

For a glorious decade the party dared to dream of one man, one vote. It organised protests. It wrote petitions. It enlisted the support of white liberals. In June 1955 it unveiled the Freedom Charter, a sweeping policy document laying out the principles of a non-racial democratic country and also detailing a series of social reforms, including free education for everyone regardless of race, land for the landless and shorter working hours. But as soon as the ANC and its rival liberation movement, the Pan-Africanist Congress, which had broken away from the ANC in opposition to its non-racialism, posed more than the most token threat, the state reacted ruthlessly. In 1960 police shot dead sixty-nine unarmed protesters, including ten children, many in the back, in the township of Sharpeville, after they marched to protest against the law requiring them to carry a passbook. Later that year the two parties were banned. The clampdown ushered in three grim decades with the party's leaders in prison, in exile, or underground.

The exile years posed huge challenges to the ANC. The party benefited from widespread international support for its opposition to such a noxious racist system. Yet its leadership was scattered across the globe, and many of its most impressive and authoritative figures were in prison on Robben Island. While it eventually learned how to harness public sympathy for its cause in the West, it was hardly the brilliant revolutionary mastermind that its propagandists suggested. It could not even claim credit for the two principal uprisings against the white regime. The exiled leadership was taken by surprise by the Soweto Uprising in 1976, when a protest led by schoolchildren and students and organised by the black consciousness movement spiralled into a rebellion. The ANC also had a relatively minor role in organising the township revolts in the mid-eighties. These were internal rebellions. In exile the ANC was, according to the memoirs of Mac Maharaj, a senior party member, divided and hopelessly indecisive.

Then, after the ANC was unbanned in 1990, just when it wanted to start making detailed plans for running the government, most of its leading figures were caught up in the increasingly bloody drama of the transition from apartheid. Not only did the ANC have to negotiate with the National Party over its departure from office, it also faced secessionist threats from the white right wing and from a nationalist Zulu movement, the Inkatha Freedom Party. Over ten thousand people were killed in political violence in the four years between Mandela's release from prison and his assumption of office. On a sunny March day in 1994, the fighting washed up against the door of the ANC headquarters itself, as thousands of Zulus aligned to Inkatha marched through the centre of Johannesburg brandishing spears, machetes and clubs. At least eight of them were killed when ANC security guards fired on them as they massed outside the party headquarters, apparently planning to attack. An hour later dark pools of blood glistened on the tarmac just beyond the entrance. The pavements, which were usually lined with fruit and vegetable hawkers, were strewn with abandoned spears, shields and leopard-skin headdresses. Incongruous amid the traditional weaponry and dress were three baseball hats and a white trainer.

So in May 1994, when the ANC's MPs took their seats in Parliament, while excited by their mission and delighted by the idea of debating and legislating in a building that had been a symbol of white power, they were also weary and unprepared. Cheryl Carolus, one of the foremost anti-apartheid activists in the eighties, said that they 'hopelessly underestimated' the scale of the challenge of being in government, not least because almost until the day the movement was unbanned they did not think liberation was at hand.[8]

'In the eighties we did not think we would be free in our lifetime,' she said. She slipped out of South Africa illegally in 1986 for a meeting with Oliver Tambo, the ANC's leader-in-exile, in Sweden. He wanted to run past her and a few colleagues the constitutional principles of a democratic South Africa. 'We thought he was out of his tree.' She and other activists had bemoaned in those days how unjust it was that Africa's oldest liberation movement would be the last to win freedom. They had appreciated that they were at least able to learn from the others' mistakes. But they had not realised 'how many talented people we would need to run this country'.

After six months in Parliament, in late 1994, Blade Nzimande, then the head of the parliamentary committee on education and one of the former protégés of the old communist Harry Gwala, conceded with a long sigh that the transfer to government had been far harder than he had anticipated. There was a bulging blue sack of unread papers on his desk. He looked exhausted. On his wall was a double-page cut-out from the newspaper *The Star* with the headline 'Inside Parliament: How It Works'.

Many ANC MPs were still coming to grips with parliamentary responsibilities, he acknowledged. Also many had not appreciated the parlous state of the country's finances on taking power. They had assumed that the country was fabulously wealthy and that it would be just a question of redirecting the flow of money. Rather, it transpired that the ANC inherited a country in financial crisis. In short they hadn't appreciated, he suggested, either the complexity of governing or the scale of their task.

'It's been a lot of work. I don't think any of us anticipated the amount of work.'[9] He and others had had to acknowledge that they had not known the country was 'on the edge' of bankruptcy and collapse. Sometimes he reflected wistfully about how much easier it had been opposing than governing. 'It's funny to realise I am now part of the system.'

Nzimande and other ANC leaders faced two major challenges. The first was national: they had to transfer state resources previously devoted largely to the white minority to improve the lives of the majority of blacks, Indians and people of mixed race without jeopardising the economy and the stability of the state, or rather without prompting a mass flight of whites into exile. The second was internal: the ANC was determined to maintain the unity of the party, an amalgam of different politics, ideologies, races, religions and beliefs, whose only bond had been the opposition to apartheid. Nzimande shrugged off the question of whether the ANC would stay together with its partners in the 'tripartite alliance', the unions and the Communist Party. A 'robust' internal debate over policy had been the hallmark of its brief time in power, he said. They had a very 'lively' caucus. If there was a problem, it was that they had too many competing voices, but the ANC would not split. 'There is too much at stake that binds the ANC together.'

It was a balmy early evening in mid-November 1994. The parliamentary benches were empty, as the session had ended a few days earlier, following a magisterial closing address by Mbeki, then the deputy president. But Johnny de Lange, another ANC MP and the head of the ANC's parliamentary study group on justice, was still hard at work at his papers, planning a new judicial system for South Africa. A burly Afrikaner, he talked of how his fellow MPs had reformed the budget process, given parliamentary committees more say in decision-making and checked executive power. He saluted the way former 'torturers' and the 'tortured' had been sitting opposite each other and debating.

Parliament was at the heart of the transformation of the country, he said. The ANC's tradition of participative democracy would ensure that government would not get strangled in bureaucracy. 'In the past government was top down. We've totally opened it up. The National Party missed the boat. Their idea was that the executive could do everything. For them the cabinet was everything, dictating the pace. Our job is to keep the executive accountable. Suddenly people have to answer. People can't talk nonsense any more.'[10]

His enthusiasm was infectious. Under apartheid the massed ranks of the National Party MPs had in most debates behaved like automatons. Now MPs in the new ruling party were talking of holding their ministers to account. It was, however, something of a false dawn.

The ANC, like so many revolutionary movements, was determined that once in power it would at all costs maintain its unity. The obsession was rooted in its long years underground, when it was convinced that its enemies were constantly trying to undermine it by peeling off potential defectors. To keep it united after the end of apartheid was always going to be a challenge. While it had been founded by a group of like-minded black middle-class professionals, in the second half of the twentieth century it had become an eclectic grouping of liberals, communists, African nationalists, activists, clerics and even warlords. There was also a strong argument that a split was just what South Africa's fledgling democracy needed, given the ANC's electoral dominance and the tendency of ruling parties to become lazy and autocratic. But the party's strategists unsurprisingly took a different view. It became a mantra for party officials to treat speculation of differences of opinion as tantamount to treason. That was counter-revolutionary thinking, they stoutly maintained.

When it was unbanned, the ANC managed publicly at least to coalesce under the messianic leadership of Mandela, disappointing the hopes of National

Party leaders, who had dreamed that, once legalised and back in South Africa, the ANC would split under the weight of its internal contradictions. But behind the scenes two major rifts imperilled the party's unity: between the left and the centre and between those who opposed apartheid from inside South Africa and those who fought it from exile. When the exiles returned in 1990, they came back expecting to be treated as conquering heroes, only to meet a slightly cool reception from many of the anti-apartheid leaders and activists. There was a strong sense among the 'inziles', as members of the internal wing were known, that they had been on the front line, while the exiles had been the equivalent of staff officers in the First World War, issuing instructions from the comfort of cushy offices abroad. The exiles thought many of the inziles were amateurs who had been merely preparing the ground for the accession to power of the revolutionary titans. However much the ANC sought to present an impression of unity, behind the scenes the rivalry festered. It was not just about personalities: it was also about a style of politics. The exiles were known for their close-knit conspiratorial ways, the secretive habits of exiled revolutionaries across the ages. The inziles had a tradition of participative democracy in which everyone should have his or her say.

Carolus, the activist who had met Tambo in Sweden, was one of the best-known inziles. Raised in a working-class family in one of Cape Town's townships for people of mixed race, she had been one of the founders of the United Democratic Front, the umbrella group of unions, churches and civil society that was formed in 1983 as a surrogate for the then-banned ANC. She was one of the more outspoken members of the movement and one of the few in the ANC to address in public the distinction between the two strands. She was quick to salute the exiles and to suggest that her years dodging the police in South Africa had been far easier than the shadowy existence of life abroad. But she did say that the exiles' autocratic leadership tradition was alien to what she had known as an inzile.

There was a big difference between the exiles' culture of 'taking orders' and the inziles' culture of 'sitting around and debating. You operate differently. You relate to comrades in a different way. Your styles are different.'[11]

The split burst rancorously into the open in 1991, at the ANC's first conference in South Africa after its unbanning, when Cyril Ramaphosa, a former union leader and prominent inzile, startled the exiles – in particular Mbeki – by

winning the race to be the party's secretary general. With that victory he became the unofficial champion of the inziles and an anti-Mbeki wing of exiles,
paving the way for a behind-the-scenes title fight between the two that would
only be resolved in 1994, when Mandela picked Mbeki as his deputy president.
Two years later Ramaphosa elected to move into business. He had not been
pushed, but he had appreciated that he would not prosper politically in the
years ahead, as Mbeki moved to consolidate his control of the party.

Mandela, who as a Robben Islander was in neither camp, rose above the rift.
He did his best to smooth over the differences. He once mused that he had had
a far easier time in prison 'with three meals a day' than Mbeki had had in his
peripatetic life in exile.[12] Mandela picked his ministers and senior officials from
all the ANC's different traditions. Under him many inziles flourished. Among
them was Manne Dipico.

At the end of white rule, Dipico, then just thirty-six, was appointed premier
of the Northern Cape, the largest and least populated of the nine new
provinces. In the old days, as a trade union organiser, he had traded off his boyish features and quick wit countless times to trick the police when he was carrying prohibited texts across the country.

'The police loved me because I spoke Afrikaans and I said "*baas*" when driving up to their roadblocks,' he said. 'They didn't know I was always hiding
something. One time at a roadblock I hid a book up a woman's skirt. After we
got off OK, we gave a quick prayer to God!'[13]

He dedicated the same irrepressible energy and mischievous spirit to government. He saw himself as something of a mini-Mandela. He liked to hurtle at
180 kilometres per hour across the arid expanse of the southern Kalahari
Desert that encompassed his vast 'empire', delivering lessons in reconciliation
and leadership. Once, when visiting a hospital in a very conservative town, he
strode up to the Afrikaner matron, thanked her in fluent Afrikaans for caring
for an ANC comrade, and then much to her astonishment gave her a quick
hug. She had probably, he later explained with a laugh, never been addressed
before as an equal by a black man, let alone embraced by one.

His unassuming style was typical of ANC leaders in the early years of majority rule. As a premier, Dipico was entitled to police outriders and flashing
lights. Yet he drove unescorted. For lunch he tended to stop off at a cheap

steak house for a takeaway. In one typically whirlwind forty-eight-hour period, he brokered a deal between groups of land reclaimants, assessed a township housing project, addressed a dinner honouring Tutu, hosted a visiting British minister, teased her about Britain's foreign policy, and escorted Mandela on the campaign trail for the local elections. At the end of it all he repaired to his simple township home. Yet under Mbeki his star waned. After a stint as a presidential adviser, he left politics for business.

Carolus was another inzile to fall from prominence under Mbeki. She was a favourite of Mandela's. He appointed her to be high commissioner to the United Kingdom, South Africa's most prestigious diplomatic post. There, with her love of late-night dancing, she was one of London's most unconventional envoys and a brilliant marketer of South Africa. After returning from London she assumed a lesser post as head of the country's tourism board. Like Dipico she later moved into business. She always insisted she had left politics of her own accord.

Some inziles flourished under Mbeki, notably Trevor Manuel, his acclaimed finance minister, and the Reverend Frank Chikane, his director general. But most in Mbeki's inner circle were friends and allies from his days in exile. The sidelining of a perceived rival faction is not unique to former liberation movements. But in South Africa it reflected a shift towards a centralised and more autocratic ethos in the party. It not only represented a squandering of political talent but also led to the dominance of members of a close-knit grouping who had cut their teeth in the conspiratorial and at times paranoid world of exile politics. Loyalty was to be prized above all else.

Tutu, who had fought apartheid alongside many of the inziles (but as a churchman), was never a member of a party, and had long opposed the ANC's armed struggle, felt no compunction about speaking out.

The domination of the exiles was a betrayal of the ideals of the struggle, he said. Exiles understandably had been a bit paranoid and had needed a very short line of command to minimise the risk of betrayal. But that style was not suited to government. Someone like Ramaphosa might have made a better leader than Mbeki. He laughed wistfully as he recalled the chaotic decision-making processes of the inziles in the eighties. 'At any meeting you had to justify your position. And it made no difference whoever you were. We had this wonderful saying: "Where did you get your mandate from?" '[14]

Such a tradition of popular democracy was not best suited to the quick decision-making required of government. It was always going to need tempering with hard-headed realism. But the inziles' love of open democratic debate was to be missed in the Mbeki years.

A second cancer that was to eat away at the unity of the ANC once in power and distract it from its mission of addressing the legacy of apartheid was one familiar to ruling parties across the world: its relationship with business.

As the party approached the centenary of its foundation, it was clear that students of political history were not advised to go to its headquarters in central Johannesburg if they were seeking inspiration from the party's past. The building is named after Chief Albert Luthuli, the first of the anti-apartheid movement's three Nobel peace laureates. At briefings there was no shortage of vacuous revolutionary rhetoric, but there was also a striking lack of ideology. With its terracotta walls, blue-flecked carpets and new Ikea-style desks, Luthuli House was not unlike a B-grade corporate head office. It was about as far removed from the endearing chaos of Shell House, the scruffy tower block that housed the ANC in the countdown to the 1994 election, as could be imagined.

The order and efficiency reflected how the ANC had transformed itself into a party of government. As ANC officials from the early nineties were the first to concede, Shell House was a shambles. But the changed decor and tempo also symbolised what the left saw as a fundamental and disturbing shift in the party. They had watched in dismay from the mid-nineties as the traditionally left-of-centre party promoted business-friendly macroeconomic policies in a bid to stimulate much-needed economic growth. By embracing the markets, they raged, Mbeki had overseen nothing less than the selling of the party's soul.

Their denunciation of policy was a little simplistic. Mbeki's orthodox free-market policies had been vital for the health of South Africa's economy. But there was no shortage of evidence to support the idea that many of the party's officials were more interested in making money than governing. By one reckoning, 40 per cent of ANC MPs in early 2007 were directors of companies, with many 'owning them outright'.[15] Most officials in the party headquarters professed not to see a conflict of interest between their positions in the governing party and their involvement in state contracts – which were awarded by the ANC in government. For instance, Ronnie Mamoepa, the spokesman of the ministry of foreign affairs, led a consortium that aspired to buy the country's most influential media house. In possibly the most infamous example, Smuts Ngonyama, the senior spokesman for the ANC, and Andile Ngcaba, the former director general of the telecommunications department, led a consortium that bought a 15.1 per cent stake, worth 7 billion rand, in Telkom, the national telephone provider. Andrew Feinstein, a former ANC MP who resigned after the party leadership quashed his attempts to investigate government corruption, spoke for many inside and outside the party when he queried the foundations of the deal. 'How does a man earning a fairly average salary in a full-time job manage to be party to a shareholding of that magnitude?' he asked.[16]

Ngonyama said with a sigh that it was a daunting task to move from being a liberation movement to a modern political party. It had been difficult to adjust from being 'total activists', he said. In the old days they had assumed 'a culture of struggle', and they had sought to retain those traditions in government. He concluded with a resounding critique of the party's materialism. To become 'true cadres' ANC members had to remember to be 'servants of the people', he said. The party was, he added trenchantly, suffering from 'affluenza'.[17]

The hypocrisy was blatant. If the party was indeed riddled with 'affluenza', then he was clearly one of the more afflicted. This, after all, was a man who once said, 'I did not struggle [only] to remain poor.'[18]

The sight of former communists rapidly finding their way to a place in the boardroom suite is not new. In the old Eastern bloc, former members of the nomenklatura were the first to prosper from the influx of capital, as they had the best connections to take advantage of the new order. An obvious and important difference in South Africa was that it was the formerly oppressed – or at least a subset of the formerly oppressed – who were cashing in on the change of regime. But that was no excuse for the blurring of the divide between politics and business and for the ANC's use of state tenders to raise money for the party. In 2004 the ANC was exposed as having established a front company known as Chancellor House, to which the government awarded stakes in private corporations through contracts aimed at uplifting blacks, in order to raise money for the party.

In its exile days the ANC had warned of this danger. In 1969 the ANC's Strategy and Tactics document had cautioned against the temptations of money: 'Our nationalism must not be confused with a classical drive by an elitist group among the oppressed people to gain the ascendancy.'[19] Halfway through his second term in office Mbeki delivered an impassioned outburst bemoaning the new acquisitive culture. 'Thus every day and during every hour of our time beyond sleep, the demons embedded in our society, that stalk us at every minute, seem always to beckon each one of us towards a realisable dream and nightmare. With every passing second, they advise, with rhythmic and hypnotic regularity – Get rich! Get rich! Get rich! And thus has it come about that many of us accept that our common natural instinct to escape from poverty is but the other side of the same coin on whose reverse side are written the words: At all costs, get rich!'[20]

And yet anyone outside the ANC who talked about the corruption of the party faced accusations of disloyalty – if black, Indian or of mixed race – or, if white, racism. When it emerged that two senior cabinet ministers, the parliamentary speaker and a deputy minister, had stakes in a consortium with a share of the tender to build the Gautrain, a high-speed rail link connecting Johannesburg, Pretoria and the international airport, commentators, the unions and the opposition accused them of a conflict of interest. Mbeki was apoplectic. Such criticism, he argued, merely contributed to the centuries-old racist slur that blacks were 'inherently amoral and corrupt'.

One of Mbeki's closest advisers, Essop Pahad, his best man, was to deliver an extraordinary eulogy at the funeral of Brett Kebble, a disgraced mining magnate who was involved in a network of shady business deals. Kebble had poured millions of rand into the ANC's coffers, had close links with several senior ANC leaders, and was ensnared in multiple corruption scandals before he was shot dead on a motorway off-ramp in Johannesburg in a hit the national prosecutors later said he had orchestrated. A distinguished ANC delegation graced the funeral, including the speaker of Parliament and the ANC's chief whip. Pahad used his address to attack the media for its exposés of Kebble's shadowy past.

The existence of a revolving door between business and politics is long established in Western democracies. Ex-politicians in Britain and the United

States have for decades headed to business on leaving power, trading their contact books for seats on boards. Over a third of former members of the US Congress, by some accounts, end up working as lobbyists. Individual ANC politicians argued that just because they had fought against apartheid they did not have a moral obligation to stay on a public service salary.

Still, the scale and speed of the stampede from the ANC into business was startling. In 2008, when the ANC was riven by internal disputes, a local newspaper published a list of senior party figures who in the view of the paper had failed the country by not speaking out about the turmoil in the party.[21] More than two-thirds of the figures on the list, who included clerics, ex-Marxists and trade unionists, had made fortunes in business and largely by virtue of their political connections rather than their business sense.

When Eskom, the state electricity provider, was being excoriated for its inept handling of South Africa's power supplies, which had led in 2008 to rolling blackouts across the country and a sharp drop in business confidence, there were calls for the chairman to resign. He was none other than Valli Moosa, a veteran ANC leader. He was a dynamic young ANC negotiator in the democracy talks that brokered a deal with the National Party. His qualifications for overseeing a state electricity company were rather less obvious. *City Press,* a Sunday newspaper targeting black readers, once focused on deals involving several leading politicians turned businessmen, including Moosa and Manne Dipico, the former Northern Cape premier, and asked rhetorically if the ANC was 'mortgaged to private capital'.[22]

ANC members across the country were continuing to devote themselves to improving the lives of the poor, as were some officials in government. But for all too many senior officials, the purpose of a career in the party had clearly shifted from opposing one of the most notorious regimes in history to making a fortune – and as quickly as possible.

For the rank-and-file members of the union movement and the South African Communist Party, the two junior partners of the governing tripartite alliance, the profusion of post-apartheid business deals involving senior members of the

ANC was the symptom of a fundamental flaw, the party's repudiation of the left. It was a shift that they argued threatened the very foundations of the party's tripartite alliance.

Under apartheid, opponents of the ANC liked to demonise the party as the puppet of the communist powers. In the seventies, when socialism was a global force, many senior party members, including Mbeki, were also members of the SACP. In the eighties and after its unbanning in 1990, the SACP provided much of the liberation movement's intellectual heft. Yet the SACP's influence had always waxed and waned, and the alliance had always had its strains. Mandela had fought with the communists for control over policy back in the 1950s and then again on Robben Island, when Mbeki's father, Govan, and the Marxist firebrand Gwala regarded him as too moderate. Mbeki allowed his membership to lapse in the late eighties.

For as long as the white government was still in power, the alliance's integrity was all but guaranteed. The ANC relied on the unions' muscle and organisation to ensure that vast demonstrations could take to the streets at critical moments. The unions needed the ANC to be sure of gaining seats in Parliament in the April 1994 elections. The allocation of seats was arranged according to a party list rather than by constituencies. Standing on their own, communists or unionists would never have made much headway against candidates campaigning under the banner of the ANC.

After the April 1994 election, as the ANC shifted its economic policies to the centre, the left became increasingly disgruntled. It was also increasingly marginalised. Mandela from time to time delivered sharp putdowns to the communists. For almost a decade the SACP was able to do little but carp from the sidelines. Thousands of its members trooped into Johannesburg City Hall in August 1996 to attend its seventy-fifth-birthday celebrations, flanked by members of European Communist Parties wearing caps adorned with the hammer-and-sickle slogan and singing 'The Internationale'. But despite the bombast their fortunes were at low ebb. It was not just that communism had crumbled in Europe, but also that the ANC was vigorously pursuing policies aligned to the so-called Washington consensus: fiscal discipline, deficit cutting and inflation targeting.

Jeremy Cronin, the deputy general secretary, valiantly tried to rebut the idea that the party was heading for oblivion. They were changing, but they were also biding their time. If they had stood still since they were founded in 1921 to defend the rights of white workers against black competition, or if at any other time they had lost sight of their goal, they would have become a 'museum piece', he said.

'Every last brick in the Berlin Wall has been rubbed in our noses, and that has hurt. We supported the Soviet Union. Were we right? You can't just chug along and pretend nothing has changed.' But they were not going to follow the route of Boris Yeltsin, the first post-Soviet president of Russia, and push for unbridled capitalism. And if the ANC were to 'trample on its mission', then there would be problems.[23]

Mbeki was yet more dismissive than Mandela had been. He publicly disdained the SACP and the unions as fringe radicals who had lost touch with the real world. More than halfway through his presidency he said there was no chance the unions would break away. 'It would be suicide,' he said. 'It will not happen for a long long time.'[24]

Confident the left was a spent force, he made no secret of his preference for hobnobbing with business people and economists from the World Bank or the IMF. One of his favourite gatherings was the World Economic Forum in Africa, which was invariably held in Cape Town. In 2007 he shared a podium with Cynthia Carroll, the newly appointed head of the mining giant Anglo American, and President Abdoulaye Wade of Senegal and posed a series of searching questions to the floor. But even as he was speaking, a revolt on the left was gathering momentum.

On the streets outside, public service unions were on strike in the most serious display of union muscle since the end of white rule. In a hall adjacent to the World Economic Forum, POPCRU, the Police and Prisons Civil Rights Union, was holding its Sixth National Congress. The members' uniform was a red baseball cap, red overalls and a T-shirt with the slogan 'Consolidating the Workers' Power'. There were angry murmurs when it was drawn to their attention that Mbeki was addressing business leaders nearby. Abbey Witbooi, the secretary general, picked his words carefully, but he did not hide his disdain for his president. 'It's clear he has not used the goodwill for the benefit of everybody but only for a few,' he said. 'We did not expect this kind of attitude from our comrades. We thought they would understand better. It's regrettable. Our members have been helping to give the ANC leaders a majority [in

Parliament] and so expect to see some improvement in their lives. Members
are bound to be unhappy.'[25]

The growing divide between Mbeki and the left prompted talk of a battle for
the soul of the party between centrists and socialists. Professor Kader Asmal,
one of the party's most respected thinkers, scoffed at the idea. The ANC had
traditionally been petit bourgeois, he argued, not socialist. It was wrong of the
unions to claim the party was betraying its roots.

'People who talk about the soul of the ANC don't like the idea of a social
democratic party. They think the ANC is socialist, but it never was,' he said.
'They are trying, as James Joyce would say, to transmogrify the ANC. You can't
say the economic policies of the ANC have compromised its soul. Pragmatism
is at the heart of the relationship with power.'

Asmal had joined the party as a young man in the 1950s, when Chief
Luthuli was its leader. He was something of an intellectual firecracker. He had
been one of the party's better known figures in exile as a law lecturer at the University of Dublin. He served in Mandela's and Mbeki's cabinets, and such was
his loyalty to the movement that for many years he kept his misgivings over
Mbeki's missteps and Zuma's failings to himself. But towards the end of
Mbeki's presidency he started to speak out. The talk of an ideological rift was
cover for a crude takeover of the party, he told me.

'This is not a struggle for the soul. It's a struggle to take over the ANC, and
it's a frantic one that has not been thought out.'[26]

The professor was unquestionably right. The unionists who tramped the
streets to put pressure on Mbeki's government, just as in the old days they had
put pressure on the National Party, thought they were marching to push the
government to the left. But they were as much the foot soldiers in a party
putsch as the standard-bearers of a revolution. Zuma had relied on the support
of the left for his comeback after he was fired from his position as deputy president early in Mbeki's second term. But he was not fighting an ideological battle; rather, it was a battle for control.

For Zuma and those of his supporters who had been sidelined by Mbeki,
this was an opportunity for revenge. For some of his allies, the idea of reversing
Mbeki's economic policies was paramount. But for others it presented an opportunity for lucrative deals. Many of the leaders of the ANC Youth League,

the most outspoken supporters of Zuma, had extensive business interests. In the words of one commentator, many Zumaites were interested as much in *dipolotiki tsa ma* (the politics of filling one's belly) as in the idea of wielding a new broom.[27]

And yet an old guard in the ANC, including close friends of Mandela, had a more principled reason to see Mbeki thwarted in his bid to extend his leadership of the party. They had been dismayed by the showdown, which they believed pitted two flawed candidates against each other and which also wrecked the party's consensual tradition. They had also, however, been increasingly concerned about an autocratic bent to Mbeki's leadership. That had been the hallmark of too many other liberation movements after a period in power.

Soon after the end of white rule, Carolus, the prominent inzile, had talked candidly about the risks posed to South Africa's young democracy by the ANC's overwhelming electoral dominance.[28] There were all sorts of potential pitfalls ahead for the party, she said.

'We are becoming a vaguely normal democracy . . . [But] there isn't a real opposition in South Africa. We have to be our own watchdog.'[29]

From his perch in the Union Buildings, Mbeki saw himself as the man to play that watchdog role. He was convinced that the only way to head a party with so many divergent strains was with strong centralised leadership. With this in mind he made the regional premierships presidential appointments. With the enemy, apartheid, vanquished, the party did need clear direction from the top. But the longer Mbeki was in power, the more it appeared that under his leadership the ANC risked becoming subservient to one man – and also of seeing itself as synonymous with the state.

The ANC had long stressed the importance of loyalty to the party line and also the need for members to be 'deployed' into all spheres of public life. Under Mbeki these two trends intensified. In the words of Andrew Feinstein, a disillusioned former ANC MP, the ANC ceased to be a 'broad church'. Instead it became 'a more disciplined, choreographed, and constrained party, a party fearful of its leader, conscious of its power to make or break careers, conscious of his [Mbeki's] demand for loyalty, for conformity of thinking'.[30] All the while the ANC sought to extend its influence over the state. Joel Netshitenzhe, one of Mbeki's closest aides and a leading party theorist, outlined in a policy paper the party's goal as 'extending control over all levers of power: the army, the police, the bureaucracy, intelligence structures, the judiciary, *parastatals* [state-owned companies] and agencies such as regulatory bodies, the public broadcaster, the central bank and so on'.[31] On first taking office, ANC cabinet ministers were justifiably uneasy that the state bureaucracy was in the hands of civil servants from the old regime.[32] But by the time of the next election in 1999, the party was completely in control. Its continuing ambition to extend its influence smacked, its critics said, more of a desire to rein in checks on executive power than a legitimate concern over the reach of its authority.

The most obvious encroachment was on the South African Broadcasting Corporation. Under apartheid the SABC had shamelessly punted the government line. After a few years of independent journalism post-1994, the SABC reverted to its old sycophantic ways. The head of news blacklisted a number of analysts and commentators who had been critical of the government. In a sign of his contempt for due process, Mbeki drew up a list for members of the new SABC board and forwarded it to the party's MPs for their signature.

Parliament itself became little more than a rubber stamp for the executive, as Andrew Feinstein found at the start of Mbeki's presidency, when he sought to expose wrongdoing by senior party members and arms companies in a controversial multibillion-dollar arms deal. The same de Lange who, at the start of the ANC's first term in government, had extolled the brilliance of the ANC in holding the executive to account was one of the many senior ANC MPs who failed to support Feinstein's investigation into the arms deal and backed the leadership's drive to bar South Africa's most prominent anti-corruption judge from presiding over an inquiry.[33] Feinstein was subjected to vicious denunciations by Mbeki's senior aides. In despair he resigned from Parliament.

Tony Leon, a white Jewish liberal who led the parliamentary opposition from 1994 to 2007, regards the first two years of South African democracy as a Prague Spring in Parliament. He recalls how in 1994 Joe Slovo, the Communist Party leader who was to die of cancer the following year, challenged fellow ministers about the wisdom of the arms deal in Parliament.

'We had very vigorous interrogation of ministers in Parliament. Committees bared their teeth despite the ANC's majority,' Leon told me. 'A lot of that has disappeared. A lot of Parliament itself has been reduced to a branch office of the ANC's headquarters and hasn't displayed any kind of institutional fortitude or independence. Zimbabwe, AIDS, all these great issues that have crowded in on the national agenda have barely been properly debated in Parliament.'[34]

All politicians gain inflated ideas of their brilliance – and tire – after long periods in office. Margaret Thatcher, and then later Tony Blair, the two most successful British prime ministers in recent decades, had by their third term in office and a decade in power run out of ideas, alienated too many allies and become dangerously convinced of their infallibility. Second presidential terms in office in the United States regularly prove disappointing: the best ideas are spent; sharper members of staff are wearied; skeletons from the first term are waiting to be revealed. The ANC was showing similar signs of fatigue after a decade in office. But with its overwhelming majority it faced scant chance of being booted out of office. So it was all the more important that the ANC resist the temptations of abusing its power.

An old friend of Mbeki's once revealed that as a student at Sussex University Mbeki's contemporaries teased him that he had an autocratic streak. They imagined being lost in Africa and having to decide whether they would rather be judged by a village chief or Mbeki – and, so the joke went, they would opt for the chief.[35] With his time in the presidency limited by the constitution to two terms, Mbeki moved to entrench his domination into the future by floating the idea of a third term as ANC president. He could then emulate Vladimir Putin of Russia and be the *éminence grise* behind a handpicked successor, safeguarding his legacy, policies and allies long into the future. For a while it seemed the ANC might accept this passively. He had not counted on the party proving for the first time in many years why it deserved its reputation as superior to other liberation movements.

The rejection of an African liberation movement by its own people is a seismic event that tends to happen only after several decades in power. In Zambia it took nearly thirty years for Kenneth Kaunda, the independence leader, to be turned out of office. Much to his surprise, he was beaten at the polls in 1992, after he had ceded to pressure from Western donors and agreed to hold an election. In neighbouring Malawi, the eccentric despot Hastings Banda, who had demanded obedience to the crankiest whims, including a ban on miniskirts, lasted thirty years before he was voted out. Robert Mugabe of Zimbabwe suffered his first defeat at the polls in a referendum in 2000, after twenty years in power, and eight years later he was still in office. The ANC, however, moved rather more rapidly.

Mbeki was re-elected to a second five-year term as South Africa's president in 2004 with an increased share of the popular vote. And yet just a year after his re-election, there came the first portent of a rebellion when a council of senior party members orchestrated a comeback for Zuma following his dismissal earlier that year as deputy president over allegations of corruption. Mbekiites had hoped to finish him off politically once and for all by formalising his suspension as deputy head of the party. They failed. Instead, Zumaites took charge of the meeting and insisted that their man was fully reinstated.

The disillusionment with Mbeki's style of government stretched beyond a clique in the party elite. After long years of dutiful obedience, members of party branches were finally voicing exasperation at the instructions coming down from the head office, in particular the insistence that Mbeki knew best on policy. In April 2007 several thousand Sowetans gathered to question their president in a sweltering marquee in the heart of the township. Mbeki was holding an *imbizo*, a Zulu word for a chief's community gathering. Before the meeting he remarked on how much he enjoyed such chances to hear the people's opinions. After the *imbizo* the SABC radio news dutifully led its afternoon news bulletin with a report on the rapturous reception he had supposedly received. But the report did not reflect the view of a group of half a dozen angry men looking in at the *imbizo* from the side of the road. They were unmoved by the sight of the bright green-and-gold ANC banners draped over the official limousines and buses and the piercing ululations of the women chanting Mbeki's name.

Martin Baloyi, a thickset twenty-something with a keen grasp of political history, was their unofficial spokesman. He had grown up in Soweto in the eighties amid the turmoil that accompanied the end of apartheid. He was scratching out a living as a security guard earning 4,000 rand ($550) a month. 'Mbeki is doing nothing for us,' he said. 'He thinks a lot for himself but not for other people.'

Mbeki and his aides remained blithely confident that the party would not betray him. There had not been a fight over the party leadership since 1949, when Mandela and other young firebrands had ousted the party's moderate president. But Mbeki was too complacent after long years in office. 'It was a classic hostile takeover of the company,' one senior government official said. 'They [Mbeki's aides] were asleep, playing golf and making money. They never saw it coming.'[36] In December 2007 a powerful force in the party struck back. Mbeki and his senior allies faced the humiliation of being heckled on the podium at the party's quinquennial leadership conference by a noisy crowd of delegates chanting the name of his rival, Zuma. When on the eve of the vote a friend told Mbeki that he faced defeat, he ridiculed the idea, saying no liberation movement would reject its leader, still less the president of the country. The following night he was voted out as ANC leader. To compound Mbeki's embarrassment, eight government ministers closely linked to him were voted off the party's national executive committee.

On the night that the results were announced in the shabby university campus hosting the conference, a euphoric party veteran came up to me, glass of wine in hand, dancing a little jig for joy. Mbeki's bid for a third term as ANC leader had risked turning South Africa into Zimbabwe with Mbeki playing the malign role of Mugabe, he said. 'We were saying we could not be Zimbabwe. No, no, not here – in South Africa, we are better than that. Thabo should have listened to us. But he did not. He thought he knew best. Now the ANC has taken back control of the party.'[37]

Such disdain for a head of government and party would not be surprising in mature democracies. But in South Africa, coming just thirteen years after liberation, it was astounding. A colossus had been toppled. Pallo Jordan, one of the party's most respected thinkers, argued that such irreverence was very much in the party's tradition. It had always been a broad church and could be relied on to maintain a rebellious spirit, he said.

'From the day I walked in the doors of the ANC in the late fifties, we were arguing, and we are still arguing today over everything under the sun. People in the ANC are – well, it's not that they are fractious, but they don't put up with a lot of crap. They had to be stand-up people all those years to be in the ANC.'[38]

Jordan was no mere party spin doctor. He had a history of speaking his mind and challenging the party consensus. He was detained in 1985 by the ANC's security police, locked up for six weeks in a corrugated-iron hut in Lusaka and, according to one ANC informant, nearly died of dehydration.[39] Since the end of white rule he had served in Mandela's and Mbeki's cabinets, but his abrasive manner and intellectual self-confidence had led to a number of clashes with Mbeki. He did not speak out about the controversies over AIDS and Zimbabwe, in a reminder that in Mbeki's heyday the ANC was not quite so argumentative and democratic as Jordan liked to contend. But in the countdown to the 2007 leadership election he did break ranks and dared to argue in public that Mbeki and Zuma should step aside in favour of someone younger, an elegant solution that the two men in their fight to the death had inevitably ignored.

The ANC might ossify, he conceded, as had India's Congress Party in its long initial stint in power. If ANC politicians grew like the average 'machine politician' of a Congress Party MP, then he would despair. But that scenario, he concluded, was unlikely. The brilliance of the ANC was its tradition that people could speak out whatever the point of view. That was far preferable to 'a sullen silence or subservience to some führer principal, where you just bow and scrape before leaders'.

The vote *was* a sign of a healthy and long-buried democratic pulse still beating in the party, and it offered a badly needed opportunity for the ANC to renew itself. But that was only one step towards its shedding the outdated mantle of a liberation movement and becoming a modern and accountable political party. The result reflected as much the canniness of Zuma's political machine in managing to manoeuvre a majority of the party's four thousand delegates to vote for him as any innate integrity at the heart of the ANC. More than a quarter of the members of the new seventy-strong NEC either had criminal convictions or were being investigated or had had to resign from office over ethical lapses.[40]

For Kader Asmal, who had long seen himself as a guardian of human rights, the ascendancy of Zuma's faction was deeply depressing. The turmoil signified, he thought, that the ANC had become 'another grubby political party'. He winced as he realised what he had said.

'We deserve better.' He turned to his wife. 'Did I say that? Did I say we've become another grubby political party? No, we haven't. I can't believe that.'[41]

He and other ANC elders had long tolerated – if not blinded themselves to – the party's flaws out of a belief that it always ended up making the right decision. Zuma liked to rekindle this old conviction. At his sixty-fifth-birthday party dinner he told his guests, 'The ANC is one of the most loved organisations internationally because it always does the right thing.'[42]

His guests accorded him rapturous applause. The time for such exceptionalist talk was over, however. The ANC had fought bravely against a terrible and repressive system. It had also initially moved into government with an impressive vigour as it set about addressing its daunting task. But after fifteen years in power, it had become subsumed by a torpor that ill served South Africa. It had become conformist, smug, defensive, and prone to responding to criticism with a blast of repetitive Marxist–Leninist rhetoric.

For the mass of the electorate, revolutionary slogans had long since lost their potency. Talk of being the 'vanguard movement' or of the threat of 'counter-revolutionary' forces still drew dutiful cheers at rallies. But for most South Africans the test of the ANC was its record in delivering on its promises. In its first fifteen years in power this was very mixed.

Chapter 4

THE DIFFICULTIES OF DELIVERY

It is the question of delivery that frightens me. How to deliver – people have been dispossessed, their birthright has gone.

— TOKYO SEXWALE,
1993

We were told that after liberation we would be free and there would be jobs for all. They did not say jobs for a few.

— 'COMRADE SAM' MAKGOKA,
TOWNSHIP ACTIVIST, 2007

If you don't want flies, don't put rotten meat on the table.

— MOSIUOA 'TERROR' LEKOTA,
DEFENCE MINISTER, 2007

In an informal settlement just outside Johannesburg's city centre, a mob chased a young Mozambican down a back alley. They cornered him in a patch of urban wasteland against a wall and pelted him with rocks and stones. Then, when he could resist no more, they wrapped him in his duvet cover, piled wood on top of him, and set him alight. A few stood watching his smoking and crackling body. Some shouted and danced. One woman laughed.

The image of the man's hunched frame under a smouldering blanket was all too familiar. On seeing the shocking photograph on the front pages of the South African newspapers in May 2008, I was taken back nearly fifteen years, to August 1993 and another charred body lying in another unmemorable patch of ground in the township of Tembisa, one of the many largely un-recorded battlefields in the uprising against white rule. The body wore what looked like jeans and a T-shirt, the uniform of the townships. Attempts to set him alight had been only partly successful. Another blackened body was laid alongside his like a vegetable in a market stall. The deaths were barely noted statistics in the next day's papers.

In the eighties and early nineties, hundreds of suspected township inform-ers, opponents, rivals and unfortunates who spoke with the wrong accent or wore the wrong T-shirt in the wrong place were summarily executed in this hideous way. The phenomenon, which became known as 'necklacing', entailed throwing a rubber tyre filled with petrol around someone's chest and arms, and then setting it alight. Its emergence had marked the time when South Africa's good versus evil narrative lost its stark simplicity. Images of mobs dancing around their blazing victims sent a chill through more sober leaders of the ANC as they realised the extent to which apartheid and the battle against it had bru-talised the country's youth. The return of the necklace to the country's news bulletins in 2008 marked another turning point for South Africa.

The young Mozambican was one of dozens of immigrants from elsewhere in Africa killed in a week of ethnic cleansing that led to thirty thousand people having to flee their homes. The outpouring of anger was a cry of anguish from the dispossessed over the competition for scant services and jobs. It was a re-minder of the passions that lay just below the surface of society. It also marked the moment that the ANC could no longer convincingly argue that it had done enough to alleviate poverty. The necklace reflected not just the failure of South Africa to escape the brutality of the past but also more broadly its failure to overcome the inequalities of the apartheid era.

The media and the authorities blamed the violence on 'xenophobia'. The implication seemed to be that this was somehow an alien syndrome that had poisoned South Africa. Winnie Madikizela-Mandela was the first politician to challenge this self-righteous theory. For her to seize on a necklacing to reprise her anti-apartheid role as the conscience of the nation was rich with irony. In the seventies she had been the indomitable heroine of the struggle. Her refusal to be cowed or even silenced when banished to a remote township had inspired the anti-apartheid movement. In thirty-three years of marriage she spent barely five weeks in broken stretches with her husband, Nelson Mandela. But in 1985 her halo slipped when she appeared to exhort the township comrades to more necklacing. 'With our boxes of matches and our necklaces we shall liberate this country,' she told a rally.

Since then her reputation had fallen precipitously. Her thuggish entourage in the late eighties, known as the Mandela United Football Club, terrorised her section of Soweto, kidnapping and assaulting youths suspected of being informers. One, a fourteen-year-old called Stompie Moeketsi, was murdered by the 'coach' of the club. In 1991 Madikizela-Mandela was convicted of kidnapping him and being an accessory to assault, but her six-year prison sentence was commuted to a fine and a two-year suspended sentence on appeal. Mandela, whose relationship with her didn't survive his long incarceration, fired her as a deputy minister early in his term in office over a corruption scandal. In the subsequent decade she incurred convictions for fraud and theft. But the Winnie legend retained some of its lustre. She swept back to prominence in December 2007, when she won first place in the ANC's national executive committee.

She was something of a Gucci populist, sweeping into shanty towns in a limousine flanked by bodyguards. And yet she more than most in the ANC kept her fingers on the township pulse. She was one of the first senior ANC leaders to visit the township of Alexandra, where the anti-immigrant riots first erupted. Essop Pahad, one of Mbeki's senior aides, preposterously blamed the violence on shadowy elements trying to undermine the government. It was, he suggested, the work of a 'Third Force', the term used in the last years of white rule for the apartheid hit squads. Winnie had in the past been happy to indulge conspiracy theories to explain away inconvenient facts, but not this time. At fault, she said bluntly, was the government's failure to 'deliver' the fruits of freedom.

'It is most tragic that xenophobia should be used as an explanation for the crisis,' she said. 'It is an explosion caused by lack of delivery. People say the conditions under which they live are conducive to this kind of violence; it's not xenophobic.'[1]

The violence came as no surprise to Gigi Mafifi and his family. They lived in Diepsloot, an expanse of low-cost housing and shacks that sprang up on the veld north-west of Johannesburg at the end of white rule. There they had an existence that mirrored the lives of many millions across Africa and the developing world. Mafifi had left school with good grades and had half completed a mathematics programme at a technical college. His girlfriend worked for an advertising agency. And yet still they were struggling to make ends meet to support an extended family. He was unemployed. They lived in a Diepsloot shack from which his girlfriend emerged every day to compete in a high-powered office. For more than a year the pressure on amenities had been intolerable as more immigrants arrived. The lines at the clinic were filled with foreigners, resentment was mounting, and still more Zimbabweans were coming from their troubled homeland looking for shelter, willing to undercut South Africans in their desperation for work. The global rise in food and fuel prices in the first half of 2008 and a steep rise in South Africa's inflation had been, it appeared, the final straw.

Diepsloot was one of the first townships where the tensions exploded. After two days of violence a fragile calm was restored. For Isaac Maela, an ANC councillor, they had been the most stressful forty-eight hours of his short political career. He had presided over a rally of four thousand people in a campaign to say 'to hell with *tsotsis*'. He had patrolled the streets with a force of community volunteers. A slick young man with a crisp turn of phrase and an apparent liking for command, he stood outside the local clinic handing out leaflets to residents as a sharp wind lightly dusted his pressed khaki trousers in debris and sent rubbish skimming over his well-polished shoes. The situation was in order, he said. The criminals responsible had been caught. Life could return to normal.

Then Mafifi walked up to him and started remonstrating with him over the ANC's record. Diepsloot was an overcrowded slum, he said. The party had not done enough, since coming to power, to help the poor. It was time for a change. The councillor was apoplectic with rage.

'You are dangerous because you don't have the right information,' he said, jabbing his finger in Mafifi's face. 'I have the information. You are telling lies about this community.'

'No, you are lying,' said Mafifi. 'You are not telling the truth about Diepsloot.'

'You can't say I'm lying!' shouted Maela. 'I am a leader of this community.'

'But we elected you.'

'You are totally devious,' Maela said. 'Who are you? Where are you from?'[2]

The accusation that lazy or entrenched critics of the ANC like to level against the government that nothing has changed for the poor in South Africa since the end of white rule is unfair. Maela rightly pointed to the new tarmac road and to the shopping mall in the middle distance. He outlined the programme to extend electric street lighting across the township, an initiative aimed at reducing the high levels of crime.

'We don't have any doubts [about the ANC's record],' he said. 'When you talk about fourteen years, it's just a few years. We have achieved a lot, a lot, a lot.'[3]

His outburst, however, also reflected a creeping arrogance in the party after its long years in office. Maela's conviction that the ANC was right and knew best was echoed higher up in the party. It was when Maela said that the violence was the fault of 'criminals' and had nothing to do with poverty that Mafifi could not restrain himself. He had matriculated from high school when white rule was coming to an end. He had had high hopes of the new era, and they had been disappointed. It was easy enough to talk of the changes unless, as he was, you were still living in a shack.

As the councillor still fumed at the clinic's gates, scores of people were lining up for treatment. Three days earlier, the chief nurse said, a man had burst in and ordered all 'Vendas' to go outside. Vendas are a minority South African tribe from the far north of the country. They are regularly mocked by the country's larger tribes as country bumpkins. But there can be more dangerous currents in such sentiment. The implication behind the eviction of Vendas was clear: they were aliens, and had to go.

'No one moved at first,' the nurse said. 'Then one by one everyone left . . . The foreigners are many. We treat more of them than South Africans. But we've never seen anything like that [the forced eviction of the Vendas]. The pressure is growing.'[4]

In early May 1994, on the evening that F. W. de Klerk conceded power, Mandela hosted a spontaneous victory party at the Carlton Hotel in central Johannesburg. Hundreds of people were dancing and singing and skipping in the streets. A white chef in the apron and tall cap of his trade appeared on one of the hotel balconies and bellowed '*Amandla*' (power), the liberation cry. A jubilant crowd of party hierarchs and hotel staff watched Mandela appear on a stage and dance a victory jig. He saluted his comrades who had not lived to see that day, before concluding with a typically peremptory piece of advice. 'Tomorrow the leadership of the African National Congress will be at our desks. We are rolling up our sleeves to begin tackling the problems of our country. Let's get South Africa working.'[5] Then he abandoned the floor, as old men do at parties, as he prepared for the task ahead.

It was always clear that the capture of political power was only the first hurdle for the ANC. Kwame Nkrumah, the first president of Ghana, the first sub-Saharan country to attain independence, inspired his continent with the slogan 'Seek ye first the political kingdom, and all things shall be added unto you'. But the focus of many newly independent countries, including Ghana, on building up the state – and usually a bloated civil service – rather than tending their economies led to their ruin. Surveying post-colonial Africa's tale of economic mismanagement in the nearly forty years after Ghana's independence, the newly elected ANC's leaders appreciated that the capture of the political kingdom was just a first step. If their victory was to mean anything, they had to address the economic legacy of apartheid. They had, in short, to give meaning to the election slogan of building a 'better life for all', and to do that they had to steer sub-Saharan Africa's largest economy.

The ANC's policies had moved a long way from the socialism of the Freedom Charter, which had called for the nationalisation of the mines, banks and 'monopoly interests' and which Mandela endorsed on the day of his release from prison. Shortly thereafter, Western officials and business people had persuaded him to rethink his approach. When he paid his first visit to Davos, the annual summit where 'the great and the good' gather in an Alpine resort to talk about the global economy, he was still ambivalent about which course to pursue. After conversations, however, with sympathetic left-wing delegates from China, Vietnam and the Netherlands, he tore up his prepared speech and effectively renounced nationalisation.[6] It was seen as something of an epiphany. But a more decisive break with the past was still to come.

The ANC came to power trumpeting an ambitious Reconstruction and Development Programme (RDP). It promised to build a million new homes, redistribute 'a substantial amount of land', and provide clean water and sanitation for everyone in five years. But how the party was going to fund this munificent list was from the outset unclear. Trevor Manuel, the then head of the party's economic policy unit, talked of streamlining government spending and cutting the defence budget, which had ballooned during the last years of white rule. But there was no clear rubric for macroeconomic policy. Many in the ANC still believed that South Africa's treasury was in rude health and that a flow of funds just needed to be redirected to the underdeveloped townships. As it was, they had a shock on entering office and finding that after years of sanctions and overspending on defence, and in the wake of a series of last-minute splurges by the Nationalists in particular on the civil service, the economy was in a desperate state. It was hobbled by debt. In the decade before 1994 it had grown at an average of just half a per cent a year. It needed to grow at 6 per cent if the government was to make inroads into unemployment, estimated at the handover at over 30 per cent of economically active adults.

The sound of trade union slogans and pounding feet along the streets of Johannesburg just a few months after the 1994 election left little doubt of the pressures on the government to deliver on its promises. At the shabby headquarters of Cosatu, the main union federation, its secretary general, Mbhazima 'Sam' Shilowa, a huge man with a bald head the size of a small basketball, held court, warning that the unions expected to reap a reward for its alliance with the ANC.

'Our workers are saying no one declared a honeymoon with the government,' he said. 'It must come to an end.' They had 'sacrificed' many of their leaders to serve as ANC members of Parliament, and it was time for the debt to be repaid. If they were to tell their members to accept the wage offers, people would tell them they had taken the route of other African unions 'who went soft when their partners came to power'.[7]

These were defiant words, but even as Shilowa's unionists were tramping the streets, Mandela and his then de facto prime minister, Mbeki, were seeking the advice of very different interlocutors – big business and economists from Washington – to abandon the RDP. In early 1996, towards the second anniversary of Mandela's presidency, the rand plunged by 20 per cent in two weeks amid mounting concern in the markets over South Africa's economic policy and in particular the influence of the left, which was pushing for a vast government stimulus package. Perturbed by the negative signals from potential investors, Mbeki took control of the debate over policy and promulgated what for the ANC was a revolutionary new approach to economics.

The Growth, Employment and Redistribution programme (GEAR) encapsulated the core ideas of an orthodox free-market macroeconomic policy, envisaging a tight deficit target of 3 per cent, low inflation, a savaging of public debt by huge cuts in state expenditure and privatisation of non-essential state assets. This was at the time seen in Washington as fairly standard fare for a developing economy. But for the ANC it was a radical break from the past. Mbeki introduced it in effect by fiat, bypassing both the cabinet and Parliament. He taunted the left at its launch, saying, 'Call me a Thatcherite.' It was a far more significant moment in the evolution of the party's thinking than Mandela's 'road to Davos' conversion.

Julian Ogilvie Thompson, the chief executive of Anglo American, a towering patrician figure who used to dominate his staff by the pertinence of his questions and the ever-present cigar stub in his mouth, was one of the unofficial kitchen cabinet of business people advising Mandela on the economy. He recalls going to Mbeki in Cape Town with a delegation of business leaders to air their concerns and put their case for growth. They anticipated a cool reception. Instead they found that Mbeki had independently come round to this idea.

'We thought he would say, "Uh-oh." But instead he said, "Why don't we publish our proposals?"'[8]

This was the moment when South Africa was saying to the outside world that it wanted to compete for investment in the new globalised economy and that it would not go down the path of so many other newly independent African states, which ended up emptying their treasuries. It was a brave and important decision.

Mbeki's advisers briefed that, within three years, growth would triple to 4.2 per cent and more than a million new jobs would be created. They anticipated that foreign capital would pour in to drive the economy.

A few years later, in one of his regular meetings with Mbeki, Ogilvie Thompson saluted GEAR. 'I told him we like it,' he said. 'I said, "Our concern is that you are only in second gear. You need to be in top gear, and you may slip into reverse gear." He had the grace to laugh.'⁹

Unfortunately, the aside about the need to move into 'top gear' was to prove all too prescient.

Trevor Manuel, the architect of South Africa's post-apartheid economic recovery, recalls wryly how sceptical the financial world was in 1996, when he was appointed South Africa's first non-white finance minister. A former activist who had grown up in one of the Cape's townships designated by apartheid for people of mixed race, he had no background in economics before he took over the party's newly formed economics policy unit in 1990. Mandela kept on the Nationalists' last finance minister in his first cabinet in May 1994, to reassure the world that it was business as usual. Manuel's appointment two years later sent jitters through the financial markets. There was a racist edge to the reaction. The markets had an engrained scepticism of Africa's finance ministers stemming from the decades of independence in which the continent's economies had been systematically looted and mishandled. But Manuel did also have much to prove.

To reassure investors, Treasury officials and business leaders took him on a world tour. Among his destinations was the *Financial Times*, where he 'became a meal for everybody' and where some commentators were, he sensed, not impressed. 'They were saying, "This monkey is going to screw up that South African economy; he doesn't know what he is doing."'¹⁰

A decade after his appointment he was one of the world's most respected finance ministers and seen as the talisman of South Africa's economic stability. His budget speeches had a punch that was all the more striking in a parliament that within a few years of liberation had lost most of its talented ANC members to business or to retirement. In 2002 he was elected first in the vote for the party's national executive committee. If he had been black, an unofficial pre-requisite for the leadership of the ANC, rather than of mixed race, he might have been a possible successor to Mbeki. Under his stewardship the economy enjoyed the longest uninterrupted period of economic expansion since the Second World War. As the growth rate reached 5 per cent in 2004, officials argued that South Africa could yet reach its official target of halving poverty and unemployment by 2014. All seemed rosy.

There are few better ways of sampling the success of Manuel's plan than by surveying the skyline of the township of Soweto. In the last years of white rule there was only one reason for correspondents to go there: the struggle. Soweto was the crucible of the fight against white rule. Yet in 2007 a rather more mundane saga, one familiar to villages and small towns across the developed world, was unfolding there: the battle of small shopkeepers to survive against the powerful supermarket chains. Under apartheid, informal *spaza* shops, named after township slang for camouflage, were the principal source of groceries in townships. In one of the many petty injustices of apartheid, supermarkets were effectively kept in the control of whites and were built away from townships. Operating out of one-room shacks, *spaza* shops were profitable twenty-four-hour convenience stores. One of the most striking symptoms of Mbeki's and Manuel's boom was the fact that in Soweto they were struggling to keep going against the competition of the supermarkets springing up all over the township.

The Jabulani Mall was one of five shopping malls that opened in Soweto between 2006 and 2008. It gleamed with the allure of its counterparts in Johannesburg's traditionally white northern suburbs. The logos of the best-known fashion chain stores and cafes vied for attention on the sandstone walls. Rebecca Sebolecwe was one of the thousands flocking to Jabulani Mall every day after its opening, savouring the simple delight of not having to trek forty minutes by bus into Johannesburg to shop. She was one of the stalwart Soweto grannies who in the old days did much to keep the fabric of society together as younger generations fought on the streets. Some days, she said, she went just to window-shop.

'Before, I was a lady of the *spaza* shop,' she said. 'Now I am a supermarket lady!'[11]

Aiding Manuel's cause was a surge in government revenue, courtesy of another of the more successful public servants of the new era, the country's 'activist' tax collector. A former communist who once hectored the country's disparate parties into consensus at the multiparty talks, Pravin Gordhan had turned his formidable abilities at organising underground party structures to winkling tax out of the corporate sector. So successful was the tenure of this headmasterly figure at the South African Revenue Service that tax revenue increased by an annual average of 10 per cent between his appointment in 1999 and 2007. As part of what he called the 'normalisation' of society, he had also started to overturn the ethos of the anti-apartheid era, when the ANC had urged people not to pay their rates and taxes. In the decade beginning in March 1996, the tax base more than doubled, from 1.9 million individuals to about 5 million. In a striking sign of the economic turnaround and of the surge in tax revenues, but also of the inefficiencies of local government – which proved unable to spend its budget on worthwhile projects – in 2007 and 2008 Manuel ran a budget surplus.

And yet there was another side to the sparkling statistics. In the shadow of the new malls and the grand infrastructure projects in the main cities, there were many who were not experiencing the benefits of the boom. A decade after the introduction of GEAR the divide between rich and poor had increased. Unemployment hovered somewhere between 30 and 40 per cent. After taking five years to fire after the launch of GEAR, the economy did grow at a healthy average of 5 per cent between 2004 and 2007. But at a time when China and other developing economies were achieving double-digit rates of growth, and as the global appetite for South Africa's commodities, the traditional backbone of its economy, soared, the growth rate should have been higher. It fell stubbornly short of the magical 6 per cent figure that was supposedly required for unemployment to start plummeting. The government trumpeted that 1.6 million jobs were created in the five years up to 2007, but unemployment remained precipitously high.

One of the unofficial spokesmen for the disillusioned ranks of the underclass was 'Comrade Sam' Makgoka, a reflective and unflappable man in his late-middle age. A fortnight before the ANC's leadership election in December 2007, Makgoka was dressed in raggedy blue overalls and surrounded by fifteen-foot-high mounds of soiled plastic and dirty bottles. He was fed up. His was an attitude encountered not infrequently in informal settlements in countries across sub-Saharan Africa once the euphoria of independence had dissipated.

Makgoka was hard at work at a recycling project in Orange Farm, a hybrid shanty town and township south-west of Johannesburg. For sorting and cleaning bottles he and his six helpers earned around 2,000 rand, then about $290, a month. He had last been in formal employment a decade earlier, when he was made redundant after sixteen years as a security guard. When he was asked about the ANC's record, a look of deep irritation flitted across his face.

'We've been patient. They promised a better life for all,' he said, quoting Mandela's 1994 election manifesto. 'But we don't see changes.' The ANC's policy did not help poor people but only the wealthy. 'We were told that after liberation we would be free and there would be jobs for all. They did not say jobs for a few.'[12]

The mastermind of his recycling project was 'Bra' (township slang for brother) Bricks Mokolo, a legendary anti-apartheid activist with the build of a prizefighter. In 1985 he had been arrested, tortured by the police, kept in a mortuary fridge overnight and left for dead on a desolate patch of veld. In 2007 he was an enthusiastic supporter of the protests that erupted in several Johannesburg townships targeting the authorities' poor 'delivery' of basic services. Like many black South Africans in Johannesburg's townships, he was extraordinarily politically literate and had a view on everything from globalisation to international trade policy. He had founded the Itsoseng (Stand Up on Your Own) recycling project in 1997 on the site of a farmhouse abandoned by its white owner shortly after the 1994 election. Some three hundred people earned about $100 a month by bringing in glass and plastic. His opinion of his old comrades in government was tart.

The shopping malls were, he said, a chimera. The capitalists who installed them were interested only in building businesses, not helping the poor. Only those in government and the officials who got the tenders prospered. The poor, he said, were struggling, condemned to live in small and inadequate houses. So who was to blame? Mandela, he replied. He was the first to sell out to business, and then Mbeki and Manuel followed his lead.[13]

For Manuel, the most diligent minister in Mbeki's government, such barbs were familiar. They were also inaccurate. Far from implementing a textbook neoliberal doctrine, the government retained a high degree of confidence in the role of the state in steering the economy. The idea of privatising non-core state assets was off the agenda. The post-1994 labour laws enshrined sweeping rights for workers that were far better suited to a developed economy than to South Africa and led to a rise in unemployment. As for the charge that the plight of the poor had been forgotten, that too was unfair. Between 1994 and 2007 the ANC built 2.6 million houses. The number of homes with electricity doubled to 8.8 million. By 2007, over 87 per cent of people had access to clean running water. As of March 2008, 14.1 million people in South Africa were benefiting from the largest social welfare programme in sub-Saharan Africa.

Yet there was more to the criticism of Manuel and Mbeki than a frustration on the left that old comrades had not kept the faith. In their determination to disprove the international sceptics about the ANC's grasp of fundamental market economics, Manuel and Mbeki had arguably been excessively doctrinaire. Mbeki's younger brother, Moeletsi, a political scientist and noted critic of the government's policies, was a little harsh when he maintained that when power changed hands, all that happened was that a new political order was imposed on the old economic order, focused on big business and excluding the informal sector.[14] But the government's policies were tailored more to the skilled than the unskilled half of the economy. When in 2007 the government revealed that it would have a budget surplus, the criticism that it was pursuing policies better suited to a developed country with low levels of unemployment than to one struggling with huge social inequalities intensified.

In response to Comrade Sam's predicament, Manuel argued bravely that South Africans had to have realistic expectations. With Comrade Sam's 'spirit of enterprise and his determination not to let life get him down', all things considered his life was not too bad, Manuel said. His salary would not buy him a German car. Nor would it enable him to live a fancy life in Johannesburg's swisher suburbs. But his life was sustainable. He would be able to afford heating at home and to put food on the table. South Africans should not get into the frame of mind where making US $300 a month was inadequate and so the state needed to intervene.

'When I say these things, I am just a callous so-and-so,' Manuel said. His critics, he joked, saw him as 'to the right of Attila the Hun'. But when one was tackling poverty it was important not to lose sight of what was a legitimate expectation.

His closing remark went to the heart of one of South Africa's most acute dilemmas. As the joy of liberation dissipated, the country had had to come to terms with the realisation that it was just another middle-income country with a host of pressing problems and that it could expect no special favours from the outside world. Under apartheid about 80 per cent of the budget was directed to about 15 per cent of the population. That ensured that many in that minority had a lifestyle to compare with the most affluent countries in the world. But as Manuel appreciated, wealthy as South Africa was in comparison with other sub-Saharan African countries, whatever the government did, the inequalities could not be evened out. Rather, South Africans had to tailor their expectations of the state to the realities of a developing country.

Compounding his difficulties – and frustration – there had been no post-apartheid dividend. Foreign investment had not poured in to South Africa after the unveiling of GEAR. Rather, it had come in a trickle. There were other, more attractive destinations in Asia and Eastern Europe, where societies were not still embroiled in debates over how to deal with the past. A decade into the post-apartheid era, like many other developing countries, South Africa found itself battling against the unforeseen phenomenon of jobless growth. But the greatest frustration for the millions of impoverished people like Comrade Sam was not the policy, nor the failure of foreign investors to show confidence in the new country, but rather the ANC's mixed record in delivering basic services.

Five minutes drive from Bra Bricks and Comrade Sam's recycling project, past municipal walls covered with biting socialist-realism graffiti satirising fat-cat business people, was a new housing project on the edge of Orange Farm. The concept was splendid, Bra Bricks said. The only trouble was that the ones being built by the ANC were smaller and of poorer quality than the houses built by the apartheid government. Under apartheid they had fought against the building of five-hundred-square-foot houses. 'They were an insult. Now the government is building us even smaller ones.'[15]

Overlooking the project was a row of government-prefabricated blocks housing the local civil servants. Surprisingly, Ernest Rambau, a government housing officer, did not make the slightest attempt to defend official policy. Once he started speaking, his frustrations bubbled forth in a torrent. The government was incompetent, uncommunicative and overwhelmed, he said. They would not meet their target of building five thousand houses in Orange Farm in 2007. That figure anyway was not nearly enough for demand. Third, the houses they were building were substandard. He dismissed out of hand the government's goal of building a house for everyone in South Africa by 2014. 'We'll never make it.'

So what was the underlying problem? He had a number of gripes, including the top-down style of the national government. But the biggest problem was the low quality of officials at the provincial and local government. 'There is poor management of everything,' he said. 'I cannot run away from the truth.'[16]

His complaint could be heard across the country. When asked about the quality of the local government and its employees, South Africans always gave the same response: dire. The issue exasperated Trevor Manuel and his Treasury officials. One of the reasons behind the budget surplus of 2007 was that many provincial government departments were so incompetent, overwhelmed and, in some cases, corrupt, that they were unable to draw up viable plans to spend their budgets. So money provisionally allocated to provincial governments was often not disbursed or was returned unspent to the Treasury. It might be controversial to have a surplus, Manuel argued. But he was not going to endorse ill-considered plans just so the budget was spent. Between 2003 and 2008 municipal governments massively underspent on infrastructure, according to a government report, potentially undermining prospects for growth and the reduction of poverty.

There were several factors behind the failings of local government. One was a shortage of skilled personnel. 'Eeeergh,' exhaled Dudo Mazibuko, the mayor of the town of Ladysmith, in response to the word 'skills'. At the turn of the twentieth century the small market town made international headlines as besieging Boer forces lobbed shells at the hapless British garrison. In 2007 the town was, the mayor suggested, all but besieged again.

'It's quite a nightmare.' They had one engineer for the municipality of three hundred thousand people. They had one urban planner. They had grants to build and mend the roads, but, with just one structural engineer, it was impossible to carry out the work. 'What happens when there is a flood? There were several last year. You can imagine our frustration.'[17]

Second, there was the difficulty of retaining people with good qualifications in the provinces at a time when there were far more lucrative contracts in the cities. In a town such as Lichtenburg, an old white right-wing stronghold three hours' dusty drive from Johannesburg, the problem was particularly acute. The Reverend Moses Moshelane, the municipal manager, said it was impossible for the town to keep engineers. A government programme had deployed trainee engineers to small towns such as Lichtenburg. But as soon as they were qualified, he said, they left for better jobs in the cities.[18]

Third, as Manuel had told me, there was the delicate matter of expectations. In the last year of white rule many whites feverishly predicted that on the day of liberation blacks would start moving into the suburbs and measuring up whites' homes for themselves. It was clear, however, to anyone who spent any time in the townships that that was nonsense. The apparent willingness of so many blacks to be patient for the fruits of liberation was as remarkable as was the modesty of their aspirations. Time and again, ahead of the April 1994 elections and then in the years afterwards, people across the country said that all they were looking for was the opportunity to live a life in dignity, have access to running water and electricity, and to have a roof over their heads. Yet after a decade or more of patience, residents in some townships started to become more restive. The huge fortunes that small numbers of black business people were making in Johannesburg fuelled frustrations, encouraging the sense that there was money to be made somehow, somewhere in the new order, if only they were not held in check and the government gave them their due.

A few miles up the road from the Reverend Moshelane's office, in Lichtenburg's satellite township of Boikhutso, scorch marks on the roads and piles of rocks and paving stones on street corners testified to two days of rioting. The residents had been protesting over a shortage of clean water, jobs, decent houses and a lack of street lighting. Since the end of white rule time had not stood still. There was an asphalt road through the centre of the township, a welcome change from the potholed track of the apartheid era. A giant furrow signalled the start of a storm-drainage scheme. A web of cables over the rows of cheap houses testified to a new electrification project. But life was hardly the material of post-apartheid dreams, and it was even grittier in the adjacent shanty town, a sprawl of ramshackle corrugated-iron huts that were ferociously hot in summer and freezing in winter.

One state employee who would not give her name gave the local government 'three marks out of ten'. There was only one clinic for five thousand people. It was always full. They still had to use the bucket toilet system at home rather than a flushing lavatory. 'The community has been observing in silence, but no longer,' she said.[19]

Moshelane was outraged by the accusation that not enough had changed. 'People don't differentiate between basic needs and wants.'[20] He conceded, however, that all was not going to plan. Projects were proceeding at glacial speed. Poor coordination between the different tiers of government had ensnared housing projects in red tape. A bureaucratic logjam had imperilled his chances of meeting the government's deadline of ending 'bucket' lavatories by 2008. (He was right. The deadline passed unmet.)

The fourth factor behind the dismal record of provincial and local government was the most politically delicate: affirmative action. Reports into South Africa's 'skills crisis' tended to shy away from addressing this because of the sensitivities of race. But the unvarnished reality of government was that in the understandable post-liberation drive to promote blacks rapidly to positions of authority, many experienced white civil servants, surveyors, engineers and other professionals were encouraged to take early retirement, and their replacements were not always as well qualified for their jobs.

Under apartheid the civil service was dominated by Afrikaners. Mandela moved cautiously to change this. The post-apartheid settlement had included a sunset clause for civil servants. Mandela was wary of alienating the Afrikaner establishment at a time when he was still trying to cement the foundations of the new country. But on taking office Mbeki stepped up the pace. He drew on the precedent of the National Party, which had introduced a sweeping affirmative action programme for Afrikaners on taking office in 1948. Previously, the civil service had been dominated by English-speaking whites. Within a decade it was a preserve of Afrikaners. Half a century later history repeated itself. Under Mbeki the civil service underwent a rapid transformation.

The need for a comprehensive and rapid affirmative action programme was undeniable. While many of the Afrikaner civil servants had done their jobs very efficiently, these were the people who had implemented the apartheid policies. So it was not just for appearances that the ANC needed to promote blacks to senior positions. Many in the old guard were never going to be enthusiastic about crafting new policies to tackle apartheid's legacies. Also, employing blacks in the civil service was a relatively straightforward first step for a government mandated to reverse the inequities of the past.

But a decade later it was becoming clear that in some cases the transformation had been overzealous. It was done in an orderly and fair manner. The departing officials received handsome pay-offs and pensions. But across the country there were examples of new officials who had been overpromoted and who were unable to do their jobs even as their predecessors were kicking their heels in retirement. South Africa was always going to have to pay a price for the rapid sidelining of public servants. In many cases the new officials learned quickly how to tackle their responsibilities. But that was not always the case.

In the small town of Koppies, in the Orange Free State, the town clerk told a story that encapsulated the triumphs and failings of the change of guard. Christo Van Greunen had been the town clerk responsible for services in the satellite township Kwakwatsi through the eighties, the most turbulent years of the anti-apartheid struggle, including the time of the siege. Life had improved markedly for Kwakwatsi since the end of white rule. Each household had a flushing lavatory and electricity, and refuse was removed twice a week. Yet he estimated that only about 20 per cent of the town's development goals were being met.

He conceded that the new authorities of the joint community faced huge challenges. When he had started his duties in 1983, there had been 327 households in Kwakwatsi. Fifteen years later, as people poured in from rural areas looking for work, there were five thousand households. Yet, he argued, the difficulties were accentuated by the shortcomings of the new civil servants, many of whom had not been trained to do their jobs. The chief financial officer was not trained to read financial statements, he claimed. 'You can never buy knowledge.'

He himself had been retained at the level of town clerk but was allotted only minor responsibilities, including maintaining the library and refuse removal. Another experienced white public servant at his level was being paid to do nothing. 'They don't want to utilise him or to get rid of him.'[21]

It was easy to see how the new councillors would have been wary of retaining Van Greunen. He had been a policeman before becoming a town clerk. In the eighties he was public enemy number one in Kwakwatsi because of the government's poor record in maintaining the township. In those days the money raised in Koppies was spent on Koppies, and the money raised in Kwakwatsi was spent on the township. But his critique of the new authorities was echoed by many in the township. Clearing out too many of the old public servants had left a deficit of talent. This was compounded by the tendency of the ANC to appoint some officials on the basis of struggle credentials rather than merit, an approach that affected the highest levels of government.

Cheryl Carolus, the veteran anti-apartheid activist whom Mandela appointed as high commissioner to London, suggested that the time had come to rethink affirmative action. The ANC needed to stop relying on an old boys' network. It would do much better at 'service delivery' if it assessed people according to their talents, she said. 'We need to think of what people are best at doing.'[22]

The best way to change this was education. Unfortunately, the notoriety of education under apartheid continued after liberation. 'South Africa's Worst School', ran one headline about a local school in a rural township. 'One Pass, 659 Fail.'

The crisis in South Africa's education was rooted in the bigoted mindset of the National Party officials. The Bantu Education Act of 1953 was drawn up on the understanding that blacks were to be educated to do menial jobs. They should, in short, be reared to 'hew wood or draw water' but not much more. At the height of apartheid, the government spent barely a fifth as much on educating a black child as a white child. Blacks did not need to be educated to a high level in maths and science, the officials decreed. Jobs requiring such qualifications could be better done by whites. This unjust and short-sighted approach, premised on the idea that apartheid relied on cheap black labour, was to cast a long shadow over South Africa's future.

Thamsanqa Kambule was the headmaster of Orlando High School in the 1970s. He was nicknamed 'the Rock' for his clear principles and adamantine authority. His pupils included the Reverend Chikane, Mbeki's chief presidential adviser, and several other leading figures in the anti-apartheid fight. In a conversation not long after the end of white rule, his eyes flashed to recall the awfulness of the old education he had been meant to teach. 'It was just to make you a good servant,' he recalled. 'Maths and science were taboo for blacks.'[23]

By the seventies, as the economy boomed, it was becoming clear to business people that the country needed a larger educated workforce. Then, just when some officials were starting to appreciate the need to improve education for black children, schools became swept up in the fight against apartheid. The explosion came on the sunny morning of 16 June 1976, when anger over the authorities' decision to impose Afrikaans, the language of the oppressor, as the medium of instruction for secondary schools erupted in violent protests in Soweto. Kambule's pupils were among the children who took to the streets in defiance of police firing live ammunition. It was the start of what would become known as the Soweto Uprising, a turning point in the fight against white rule.

Kambule had been one of the few to predict there would be an explosion. The students had told him that they would not accept being taught in Afrikaans and that they thought their parents were too timid. On that first morning he told his pupils to disperse and not to challenge the police. But he also gave them 'the nod' because the situation was so intolerable. 'I saw them take on bullets with stones,' he recalled. 'And they did not mind.'

One of the first children to be killed was twelve-year-old Hector Pieterson. The poignant photograph of another schoolchild running through the streets carrying his bleeding body next to his distraught sister was on front pages all over the world the following morning. That terrible day sparked six months of protests across the country. One morning Kambule and his pupils were under siege from the police for three hours. The police had guns and were ordering the pupils to come out. The children shouted, 'Mr Principal, give us a break – we can take those guns from them.' The Rock's authority, however, remained undimmed. He told them to go out one by one. The boys left with the girls, and the police were unable to identify the ringleaders, whom they had wanted to arrest. The government closed the school in 1978. 'They wanted to fumigate it, but how can you fumigate an idea? They strung up Jesus Christ, and he has two billion followers. That day I knew the history of South Africa had changed.'

The Rock was right: South Africa's history had changed. After six months of upheaval across the country, in which more than five hundred people were killed, most shot by the security forces, the police had just about regained control of Soweto and other townships. But the flames of revolution, which had been dormant for a decade following the imprisonment and exile of the leadership of the ANC, had been rekindled. Scores of young activists were sent to Robben Island. Thousands of youths headed into exile. Soweto had become synonymous with racist repression. The clock was ticking for the end of apartheid.

The revolt, however, came at a price for black South Africans and not just in their blood. When the protests were reignited in the eighties, the phrase 'no education before liberation' became a rallying cry. In 1987 it was estimated that more than one million black children between the ages of seven and sixteen did not attend school.[24] Combined with the legacy of 'Bantu education', as the schooling for blacks was known under apartheid, this bequeathed the ANC a generation of poorly educated adults and a tradition of lawlessness. The education system had been bankrupted, Kambule told me in 1996, twenty years after the uprising. Half a million pupils had left school the previous year and were sitting at home with 'useless certificates'.

On the very morning of the twentieth anniversary of the Soweto uprising, I visited Morris Isaacson High School, where the first protest had begun. Fidgeting and giggling in their black-and-white uniforms, the pupils trooped into a large tent to hear of the heroism of old boys and girls, including Tsietsi Mashinini, who had roused his fellow classmates to take to the streets by quoting Tennyson's epic, 'The Charge of the Light Brigade'. But if the pupils expected platitudes, they were to be disappointed. Clarence Mlokoti, who had been a teacher in 1976, lectured them about how they were desecrating the memories of the '76 generation.

Pupils were using the slightest grievance to vandalise classrooms and entire schools, he said. Their behaviour was no different from that of 'the children of Israel, who, after crossing the Red Sea, started misbehaving and mismanaging things'.[25] They had to start studying.

Over the following decade the pass rate for the school-leaving exams steadily declined, from 73 per cent in 2003 to 66 per cent in 2006. The Institute of Race Relations, a think tank that had charted policies for decades, concluded grimly in 2008 that it was debatable whether state education was any better than it had been under apartheid. Two of South Africa's most prominent black women, Wendy Luhabe, a leading businesswoman, and Mamphela Ramphele, the legendary anti-apartheid activist who served as a managing director of the World Bank, endorsed this devastating conclusion.

The quality of education had deteriorated, there was absolutely no doubt, Luhabe said. 'I'm a product of Bantu education, and when I look back, it really seems much better than what education appears to be today.'[26]

The dire results in mathematics and science were of particular concern. In 2007 just 1 per cent of black schoolchildren in South Africa gained a decent pass in mathematics in their school-leaving exams. For businesses this was a major disincentive to invest in South Africa. A survey of chief executives and managers in 2007 concluded that companies were 'creaking under the strain' of the 'skills shortage'.[27]

In a savage irony, a decade into ANC rule, thousands of middle-class Zimbabweans fleeing the implosion of their own economy landed well-paid jobs in Johannesburg by virtue of their qualifications and their excellent English.

Funding was not the issue. The ANC spent 18.5 per cent of the budget on education, a higher percentage than many other developing countries.[28] Teachers were, in Trevor Manuel's words, 'not poorly remunerated'. Rather, the problem was management. To the frustration of Treasury officials, more than 800 million rand of the education budget in the Eastern Cape was unspent in 2007, a reflection of the notorious incompetence of its provincial government. It was better that the money was saved rather than frittered away on ill-considered and poorly managed projects. But what was required was a root-and-branch overhaul of education. There were too many poorly run schools with appalling levels of absenteeism among staff that were not being held to account.

The ANC had rightly moved fast, on taking office, to open up education in the last traditionally white schools resisting integration. The most famous case was in February 1996, in the northern town of Potgietersrus. The most dogged of the Afrikaner Voortrekkers escaping from British rule in the Cape by heading into the interior had made their way there in the nineteenth century. The same intransigent spirit infused their descendants as they tried to prevent the enrolment of black children in the town's primary school, arguing that taking black children would dilute the Afrikaner culture of the school and would infringe their minority rights. The case eventually went up to the Supreme Court, which ruled in favour of the regional government. Early one morning twenty-one black pupils were escorted into the school for the first time since it had been founded a century earlier. The armoured cars stationed outside the school gate evoked memories of the bussing in of black pupils to schools in the southern states of America. It was an important milestone, as was the rewriting of the curriculum, in particular the history syllabus, which was no longer to present a one-sided version of the founding myths of white rule.

But overcoming a last bastion of white conservatism was primarily a symbolic victory. The legacy of apartheid went far beyond the recalcitrant mindset of a few dozen Potgietersrus parents. The schools in the former tribal homelands, the regions that had been set aside by apartheid governments nominally as semi-independent states but in reality as impoverished dumping grounds for blacks, had long been underfunded and were in an atrocious state. The power of the teachers' unions needed to be shattered. Such was their grip on the profession that government officials said it was all but impossible to fire negligent, incompetent or corrupt teachers. But the ANC did not have the stomach to take on the unions. Year in, year out, new government initiatives for education were unveiled and yet went unenforced, and the pass rate dropped lower and lower.

The more thoughtful ANC ministers conceded their progress had not been as smooth as it should have been. Mosiuoa 'Terror' Lekota, the defence minister in Mbeki's second term (whose nickname stemmed from his reputation as a soccer player), once cited a Congolese saying: 'If you don't want flies, don't put rotten meat on the table.' His message to the ANC's critics was that he accepted that sometimes the ANC moved 'at an extremely slow pace' and sometimes 'we slide backwards'.[29] But the party's noble intentions, he said, remained undimmed, and he urged investors not to lose faith.

That faith was tested to the limit in early 2008, when Eskom, the state electricity provider, ran out of power. For several weeks the country suffered sustained power cuts, often imposed without any advance warning. The mines had to close for a week. Hospitals had to rely on generators. When the situation eased, it was made clear that there would be more power cuts for at least another six years. Eskom's financial director went so far as to advise investors not to plan big new projects until 2013, when new power stations were due to come online.

For South Africa this was a stunning reversal of fortune. At the end of white rule, Eskom had boasted an excess of cheap power, which it hoped to export to neighbouring countries. But in early 2008 the reserve margin was down to 4 per cent, barely a quarter of the international norm. Solidarity, a trade union for mainly white blue-collar workers, blamed affirmative action policies at Eskom. While the early retirement of many experienced technicians was clearly a factor, there was a more fundamental problem: the government's failure to plan. Nine years earlier Eskom had warned officials the country would run out of power within a decade if it did not plan a new generation of power stations. For several years after that warning the government dithered over how to proceed. By the time it finally made up its mind and started to plan for new power stations, it was too late. As predicted, in 2008, the power ran out.

The crisis reflected a particular weakness in the ANC's style of government: it was rather better at discussing policy than implementing it. AIDS activists became wearily accustomed to reading well-worded policy papers on health whose policies were never implemented.

Renier Schoeman, a former National Party minister, spent two years witnessing the ANC's inner workings when he served in Mandela's government of national unity after the 1994 election. He concluded that the quality of the discussion was far superior to the debates in National Party cabinet meetings, but that the National Party had been better at reaching a conclusion. Often in ANC meetings there would be long debates that ended without a decision, he said. The danger, he concluded, was that 'you end up with the process being king, and you lose sight of the goal'.[30]

That was the unofficial maxim of many in the ANC government.

Trevor Manuel is the first to accept that Mbeki's government could have done better. In May 2008, in the wake of the worst six months for South Africa's reputation in a decade, a period that had seen the electricity crisis and the violence in the townships, he gave a nuanced defence of his record. He looked tired, having just taken the dawn flight from Cape Town to his office in Pretoria. It was tempting, however, to see his fatigue as having deeper roots. Domestically, his stock had fallen as abruptly as South Africa's international reputation. Having gained the most votes in the 2002 election for the ANC's national executive committee, the party's inner council, five years later he only just secured re-election. Ever since then, the trade union leaders had been openly mocking him, insisting his economic policy would have to be refashioned.

The budget surplus that was lambasted by the left as an extravagance was not about getting 'a gold star from the fiscal police', he said. It was an essential insurance policy, given the global economic uncertainty and also the country's high current-account deficit. The policy of inflation targeting, another bugbear of the left, could be revisited, he suggested. But it had been an 'anchor' of monetary policy. If every time there was a storm you 'cut loose the anchor, you don't have many choices'.

So after twelve years in charge, what would he do differently if he could do it again? In his pomp, this titanic figure of the post-apartheid era had gained a reputation for swatting aside impertinent questioners. But he sounded a reflective note. Maybe the government had been too fixated on the grand architecture of economic policy, he said. It was important to have a debate about fiscal and monetary policy. But one should not 'get stuck there'. Ricardo Haussman, a prominent Harvard economist, had told him to think of his job as conducting an orchestra.

'What the macro does is to provide the beat. It is just there as the percussion. To listen to just the percussion is not very pleasant. You need symphony.

You take the percussion out of the symphony, you can't maintain the necessary rhythm . . . You need two hands.'

This 'symphony' is what Zuma promised to provide as he swept into control of the ANC, propelled by the support of the unions and the Communist Party. In his campaign for the ANC presidency he brilliantly exploited Mbeki's failure to explain his policies. The new order would be 'pro-poor'. They would 'deliver'. Yet he insisted he would also maintain the broad thrust of Manuel's market-friendly policies. But it was hard to see how he would achieve this in practice.

Cheryl Carolus, the veteran activist turned businesswoman, says the ANC cannot afford to fail. Blacks had 'put their anger to one side as a trade-off for a better future', but their patience could not be expected to last forever.[31] She did not elaborate on what might happen if the better future never came, but the return of the necklace was clearly a portent.

There is a culture of violence at the heart of South African society. It manifested itself in the brutal attacks against immigrants in 2008. It is also daily apparent in the violent crime that eats away at the nation's confidence. If the ANC does not improve on its record, there will be more explosions of violence, and as one of the country's senior law enforcement officials warned me, the next time it might not only be innocent Mozambicans being murdered by township mobs. Wealthy South Africans could be in line.

Chapter 5

A CITY UNDER SIEGE

*You must kill the bastards if they threaten you or
the community. You must not worry about the
regulations – that is my responsibility.*

— SUSAN SHABANGU,
DEPUTY MINISTER OF SAFETY AND SECURITY,
SPEAKING TO POLICE OFFICERS, APRIL 2008

*Today the law is dead in this country. You can kill,
you can steal, and you can get away with it; crime
does pay in South Africa today.*

— MAMPHELA RAMPHELE,
VETERAN ANTI-APARTHEID ACTIVIST

On the night of the reception in honour of John Major, the first British prime
minister to visit post-apartheid South Africa, at the British High Commission
in Pretoria, a man was beaten to death just outside my office window, and it
became inevitable that my long and happy association with the Royal St
Mary's Building was to end. For eighteen months the shabby office block in
downtown Johannesburg had been a second home. The paint was flaking, the
lights were dim, and the lifts rattled and creaked. But it was a fine base for

journalism – ten minutes' walk from the ANC headquarters and just a little further from the headquarters of the main union federation. In the countdown to the 1994 election, at least once a week demonstrators filed noisily past with their cries of 'viva ANC viva' and more cumbersome, but no less articulate, 'forward to a non-racist, non-sexist South Africa, forward'.

It was there that a dozen international newspapers and agencies had their offices. In the tiny shopping centre on the ground floor, Costa, a lugubrious Greek cafe owner, and his sparky Sowetan waitresses kept us fuelled with weak coffee and toasted sandwiches. I would stop off most mornings at the newsagent's opposite for the day's papers and a chat with Anil, the Indian owner, to hear the latest of his beloved Manchester United football team. A telex machine at the end of our corridor on the fourth floor churned out the most recent anodyne reports from the South African Press Agency. I had just left the office when I received an 'urgent' message on my pager. It was from Mark Suzman, a correspondent for the *Financial Times*.

'Don't wait for me. Go on to Pretoria,' it said. 'Man being shovelled to death outside.' I messaged him back instantly, assuming the receptionist at the pager service had misheard him. Back came another message with more details. 'Man on ground, police on way.'

He later filled me in on the gruesome saga. A crowd waiting for a minibus taxi caught a suspected pickpocket just outside the Royal St Mary's Building. They surrounded him just below the office window and started battering him with a shovel and any other implements to hand. By the time the police arrived, he was dead, and the perpetrators had scattered into the night.

Neither Suzman nor I nor indeed as far as I am aware any other correspondent in the building thought to write about the incident. It was just another murder in a city that had become known as the murder capital of the world. A year after the shovel attack, I came out of the lift on the ground floor of Royal St Mary's to see a man shot through the stomach, groaning on the ground in front of me. There was a trail of blood leading to one of the exits. An exultant man in jeans was brandishing two kitchen knives and claiming to have foiled a robbery. Two bullet holes had pierced Anil's front window. Another round had embedded itself in the display of the neighbouring boutique. Dr Robert Müller, the Austrian doctor whose practice was next to Anil's, had seen it all. A bank courier was collecting the takings from a boutique when seven or eight men pounced.

Müller had thrown himself to the floor with a patient as the gang chased the man into the arcade. 'They tried to get his gun, and then he shot.' Two of the gang were hit. A bullet pinged past his window. Then another of the gang, a young man, ran into his reception demanding sanctuary. 'Then there were more bullets. It was like the Wild West, the Wild West.'[1]

A month later the Royal St Mary's foreign correspondent caucus drew to a close, leaving only the team from the Voice of America. We moved to the leafy suburbs to the north, vowing we would come back to the centre of town once a fortnight – well, at least once a month – for a coffee so we did not lose touch with the 'real' Johannesburg. Few, if any of us, kept our pledge. We had fled north, just as tens of thousands of South Africans of all races, but mainly white, emigrate each year primarily to escape from the epidemic of violent crime.

South Africa's crime statistics are extraordinary. A decade after apartheid an average of fifty people were murdered *a day*. In a population of about fifty million people that meant about forty-one people were murdered a year for every hundred thousand residents, eight times higher than in the United States and twenty times higher than in Western Europe. The government correctly highlighted that the rate was higher in parts of Latin America. They also argued that South Africa only had its unenviable reputation as the world's capital of crime because other countries with worse levels of violence did not have the means or will to record them. But that was small consolation to South Africans. Few believed that the official statistics, extreme as they were, took into account all the crimes that were being committed. Their country remained, as one analyst of the crime wave put it, 'a country at war with itself'.[2]

Roelf Meyer contends that South Africa's crime wave is not 'exceptional' for a country in transition to democracy.[3] In the early nineties he was one of the pivotal figures behind the settlement that steered South Africa to majority rule. As the chief constitutional negotiator for the National Party, he formed a fabled partnership with his opposite number from the ANC, Cyril Ramaphosa.

At one of the stickiest patches in the talks the two went on a fly-fishing week-end to talk over the difficulties. When the boyish Afrikaner hooked his hand with his fly, it fell to the black former union leader to pull it out. A bond had been formed that was to help to keep the talks going behind the scenes in 1992, even when formally they had broken down amid terrible bloodletting. They paired up again sixteen years later to form an anti-crime initiative seeking to bring private sector funds and leadership to help the government address some of the social factors behind crime, including drugs and alcohol.

Meyer argues that many countries emerging from tyranny suffer a sharp increase in crime. In parts of Eastern Europe, liberation *was* mistaken for licence after the fall of communism, and the police, the old enforcers of a hated system, found their authority spurned. But as the years of democracy passed, they gained credibility. In South Africa, however, more than a decade after liberation, crime was rampant, and the police's reputation abysmal.

What was particularly shocking was the brutality that was the hallmark of South Africa's criminals. In 2007 there were over nineteen thousand murders and more than fifty thousand reported rapes, and more than eighteen thousand people were the victims of violent robberies, including the hijacking of cars. Johannesburg, in particular, was a city under siege. At night its suburbs were dead zones. The streets were deserted. The silence was broken only by the warble of alarms. Most residents of all races seemed inured to living with appalling levels of crime and regularly swapped stories of brutality that individ-ually would have provoked a political outcry in many countries. In January 2007, an old friend was shot dead in an apparent botched robbery. Two months later, a near neighbour, a newspaper columnist who worked two floors below the *Financial Times*'s office, was shot in the stomach one Sunday evening when he challenged two assailants who had broken into his suburban house. Soon afterwards the mother of one of our elder son's friends was held up at gunpoint at her front gate, half a mile from the school. So many friends had had a similar experience that the incident appeared to cause barely a rip-ple. Later that year, the office manager of the *Financial Times* bureau in Johan-nesburg was shot in the arm on her doorstep in a township formerly for people of mixed race while defending her grandchildren from two men who wanted to steal her car. Our elder son's French teacher was held up at gunpoint in daylight and decided to move with her family back to Beirut. These cases were culled from a small circle of people. The murder rate was far higher in the formerly black townships and in rural areas. While the murders that had the most international impact were of prominent business people or expatriates, the overwhelming majority of the victims were black. The two provinces with the worst crime rate, KwaZulu-Natal and the Eastern Cape, had the largest black rural populations.

Then there were all the other attacks that were part of the background noise of life in Johannesburg: in the first six months of 2008, nearly three hundred bank cash dispensers were blown up, a 3,000 per cent increase over three years, attributed to the thriving trade in explosives from the gold mines;[4] one in ten of the three thousand members of the Restaurant Association of South Africa were robbed in the 2007–2008 financial year;[5] official statistics for 2007–2008 showed house robberies, carjackings and business robberies – the three categories, excluding murder and rape, that spread the most fear – had all increased. Such was the climate that it seemed perfectly natural for many householders from affluent suburbs to rehearse with their children what they would do in the event of a man approaching them with a gun in his hand. It did not seem remotely surprising to the parents of children at our boys' school that the role of Snow White in the school play had been adapted so she carried a panic button, a standard accessory for householders in wealthier suburbs.

Thabo Mbeki liked to challenge the popular belief that crime was raging unchecked. In the last session of the first democratic parliament, in November 1994, he was asked whether he thought that having three police vehicles for eight hundred thousand people in the township of Mitchells Plain constituted an emergency. He countered that people agitating about crime had lost perspective. The figures were high, he said, because crime was better reported than before. When an opposition MP warned of anarchy, Mbeki demurred. Anarchy means 'rampaging through the streets', he said, and that was far from the case. His measured tones were well received. He was speaking at a time when people dared to hope that with the dawn of a new order, crime would finally decrease. Over the next decade he regularly reiterated his claim that the scale of the problem was exaggerated, and implied that whites were racist when they complained about crime. But in time this approach came to be seen as blinkered denialism. When he argued in January 2007 that it was just a perception that crime was out of control, he prompted outrage. The country had had enough of his semantics.

Fears of crime undoubtedly fed into an old white prejudice about life under a black government and even a fear of Africa. The history curriculum in white schools under apartheid had dwelled at length on the hardship of the Great Trek, when Afrikaners headed north from the Cape to claim land and freedom from British rule. At the heart of the narrative was the encounter between Piet Retief, one of the Voortrekker leaders, and Dingaan, the Zulu king who ordered his warriors to slaughter the Afrikaner pioneer and his companions. In the 1960s, 1970s and 1980s, waves of white immigrants moved south from the independent Congo and then from the former Portuguese colonies of Angola and Mozambique and finally from Zimbabwe, bringing with them lurid tales of life under majority rule. Frequently when talking to conservative whites, I sensed a note of 'I told you so' in their comments when the conversation turned to crime, as if to say, 'What more could you expect?' For some, crime gave them a pretext to vent their regrets over the passing of the old order without appearing wistful about apartheid.

Mbeki was infuriated by this. Whites were, he told me, subsumed by a racist fear that any black man in their neighbourhood was a potential criminal, a supposition that he thought was linked to an old paranoia of 'black hordes that are coming at us'.[6] This was the mindset that had underpinned apartheid. He talked to me at length about the case of a black family moving into a traditionally white-dominated suburb. One of the white residents supposedly approached the only other black family on the street and asked them privately about the credentials of the newcomers. 'Do you know these new arrivals, these other black people? You know my family is feeling a sense of unease at these new arrivals. How do we know they are kosher? How do we know they are not criminals?'

Mbeki was right that many of the whites lambasting the government over crime had blissfully feigned ignorance about the violence that plagued the lives of so many of their black compatriots under apartheid. Until the apartheid population controls crumbled in the late eighties, the residential areas reserved for whites had crime levels to compare with the most gentrified and tranquil areas in the West, even as many of the townships were racked by crime. Following his president's lead, Charles Nqakula, Mbeki's minister of safety and security, dismissed whites who complained about crime as 'whingers'.[7] Another cabinet minister lambasted as racist and unpatriotic an eighty-year-old white grandmother who had moved to Australia, where she was born, after a close relative was brutally attacked at home.[8] Such rhetoric, however, was not only deeply insensitive but also failed to take into account that despair about crime was one of the few issues that united the races. Criminals did not discriminate on grounds of age, sex or race.

So why was the crime so terrible? There were three explanations most often cited to explain the crisis: the yawning inequality gap, poverty and the brutal culture of apartheid. The first two were clearly important. But they did not explain the chilling violence that accompanied so much of the crime.

The vast disparity between haves and have-nots in Johannesburg, where swanky suburbs and shopping malls were within half a mile of the township of Alexandra, made the city an obvious and easy target for criminals. Mandela recalled the daily hardship of life in Alexandra when he lived there in the 1940s. Sixty years later, most of its houses had electricity and running water, but it was still an overpopulated slum, with tens of thousands of shacks where people scrabbled for survival. In the early nineties it witnessed running street battles between the ANC and inhabitants of migrant worker hostels, strongholds of its rival, the Inkatha Freedom Party. It experienced the first of the anti-foreigner pogroms of May 2008, when mobs went on the rampage, driving immigrants from their homes. Isaac Moyo, a young Zimbabwean decorator, was camped out in the shadow of Alexandra's police station. Six years after he fled to South Africa from his troubled homeland, his dreams of a new life had come to an abrupt end when a mob of machete-wielding South Africans yelling xenophobic slogans smashed down the door of his shack and forced him and his three brothers to run for their lives. Clutching a small mirror and a bucket of old clothes, all he could grab, he had fled for sanctuary to the very building that under apartheid had been a symbol of oppression.

Alexandra was just a few streets from Sandton, a few acres of office blocks and corporate headquarters surrounded by thousands of the most coveted homes in the country. It was no coincidence that Sandton also had one of the highest rates of carjackings in the country. The wife of Tokyo Sexwale, the ANC politician turned tycoon, was held up in broad daylight just outside Sandton while dropping off her children at one of the country's more prestigious private schools.

Yet in many other cities in the world, notably Angola's capital, Luanda, slums are more inextricably interwoven with wealthy areas than in Johannesburg, and yet the rate of crime is lower. Luanda's statistics may be less reliable than South Africa's. Angola's terrible prisons and notoriously thuggish police force are powerful deterrents to would-be criminals. But still it was noticeable that a country awash with weapons, after enduring off and on for thirty years one of the worst civil wars in Africa, was safer than South Africa. There are even Angolans in Luanda who had fled to Johannesburg during their country's long civil war but are now delighted to have returned home and escaped from South Africa's crime.

As for poverty, the second factor regularly cited, this clearly provided a steady supply of new potential criminals. Investigations of carjackings in South Africa revealed these were largely coordinated by syndicates, which relied on desperate young men to steal cars to order and drive them to safe houses. There they were paid the rand equivalent of about $300 and the cars were then stripped overnight before being smuggled across the border, often with the connivance of corrupt policemen.[9] South Africa's misfortune was to come of age at a time when the international crime networks were expanding their reach. For drug-smuggling syndicates South Africa was an ideal haven in the nineties: a wealthy country with good air and sea connections to the rest of the world and a dysfunctional police force. Yet plenty of impoverished countries in Africa and other continents are far less violent than South Africa, including even Zimbabwe at the height of its economic and political crisis, when food was short and inflation at 2 million per cent. Zimbabweans faced the risk of appalling violence from their own government if they dared to support the opposition. But however impoverished the country became, it faced only a tiny fraction of the criminal violence that South Africa endured.

That leaves apartheid. It is hard to avoid concluding that centuries of race-based repression, applied for the last half of the twentieth century with scientific and brutal rigour, embedded a culture of violence. Apartheid was predicated on force – the evictions and relocations of whole communities, the separating of families, the bulldozing of homes, the dawn raids by policemen searching for infringers of the pass laws, the shooting at crowds of unarmed protesters and the torture of prisoners. Too many families have been dispossessed, uprooted and torn apart over the years. Too many relations have been killed or imprisoned. There are too many grieving and aggrieved.

Then there was also the legacy of the resistance to apartheid. The struggle was fought in townships across the country. It was a brutal fight that led to the collapse of many of the traditional codes of behaviour. In the eighties in the townships that encircled Johannesburg, young men abandoned their classes and joined 'self-defence units' to defend their streets against the security forces. Later, in the early nineties, when the fighting between the ANC and the Inkatha Freedom Party spread from the eastern province of Natal, Johannesburg's townships experienced a small-scale guerrilla war between supporters of the two parties.

Mandela repeatedly lectured the youths in the self-defence units and urged them to put down their weapons and to resist the temptation to become embroiled in crime. But it was always going to be hard to put the genie back into the bottle. Dr Gomolemo Mokae, a scholarly medical doctor who had been a leading member of the black consciousness movement, the inspiration behind the 1976 Soweto Uprising, concluded after the end of white rule that South Africa was 'reaping the whirlwind' not just of apartheid but also of the ANC's decision to make the townships ungovernable. In the eighties, supporters of the black consciousness movement had been brutally targeted by the ANC. Mokae was not going to spare the ANC from blame. In the eighties the leaders of the liberation struggle had sanctioned youths to kill their opponents, he said. 'Correctly we didn't have confidence in white courts and settled for an even more monstrous force, kangaroo courts.' A few years earlier, township youths had caught a notorious criminal called Korumbi, whom the police were ignoring. Schoolchildren beheaded him, put his head on a stick and paraded it around the township. 'It is a *Lord of the Flies* syndrome,' he said.[10]

The lawlessness was the most terrible legacy of apartheid. For the ANC it posed an acute dilemma on taking office, as it exposed the tension between its liberal ideals and the hunger of many South Africans for a crackdown. In 1995 the Constitutional Court outlawed the death penalty, to the acclaim of the ANC. Mandela was among the ANC members who had been on trial for his life. In the eighties, more than a thousand people had been executed. Archbishop Tutu said the ruling had made South Africa a 'civilised' country. But within months, at rallies and meetings in townships and meetings in former white suburbs, people angrily called for its reinstatement. In the decade after the abolition a steady groundswell spread in favour of restoring it. Jacob Zuma gave voice to this when he refused to rule out a referendum, much to the horror of ANC intellectuals, but to the approval of many South Africans. He also backed Susan Shabangu, the deputy minister of safety and security, when she denounced the laws as too soft and all but authorised police officers to shoot to kill.

'If criminals dare to threaten the police or the livelihood or lives of innocent men, women and children, they must be killed. End of story,' she told police officers at an anti-crime rally. Post-apartheid laws[11] were too soft, she argued. 'You must kill the bastards if they threaten you or the community. You must not worry about the regulations – that is my responsibility. Your responsibility is to serve and protect.' Lest anyone had missed her point, she continued: 'The constitution says criminals must be kept safe, but I say: No!'[12] Speaking a few days later, Zuma made clear he supported her views. 'If you have a deputy minister saying the kind of things that the deputy minister was saying, this is what we need to happen,' he told a dinner audience. 'What the deputy minister was saying is, what we are to be doing is dealing with the criminals rather than talking about it.'[13]

Judge Edwin Cameron was outraged by such talk. In 1986, as a young human rights lawyer, he had been one of the most outspoken critics of the apartheid judiciary over the death sentences handed down to six residents of Sharpeville for the mob killing of a councillor. In defiance of the chief justice and the minister of justice, who publicly condemned his stance, he championed a campaign for the 'Sharpeville Six'. After an international outcry their sentences were commuted. 'I saw that the executions would only add to the injustice and resistant rage that apartheid had spawned,' Judge Cameron later wrote.[14]

And yet twenty years later, there was a drive to undermine some of the rights so many had fought so hard to win. Judge Cameron did not doubt that apartheid had brutalised society. But he had no doubt where the main problem lay: it was not the constitution but the police, who were 'hopelessly corrupt and hopelessly managed', he said. No one he knew believed the police's crime figures. The only crime that was not under-reported was murder, and that was because 'in each case there is a body'.[15]

Just over a year after the 1994 election, the South African Police Museum in Pretoria unveiled a new exhibition dedicated to the anti-apartheid struggle. Some of the history was a little brief, not to say one-sided. 'On 21st March 1960 about ten thousand people armed with knobkerries, knives, sharp irons and rocks crowded around the Sharpeville station,' read the note under an exhibit devoted to the Sharpeville massacre, when police shot dead sixty-nine demonstrators protesting about having to carry a pass. There was no mention of the grievance. Nor was it made clear that most were shot in the back while fleeing. The exhibit on Steve Biko, who died in police custody, took a similar approach. 'He was never found guilty of any of the accusations against him, except the breaking of his banning order,' ran the note beside the sculpture. 'After his death he was falsely accused of participating in sabotage.' More germane was the point that no policeman had been found guilty of his murder.

In 1977 Jimmy Kruger, the police minister, said of Biko's death that it left him 'cold'.[16] Now the museum had a model of Biko lying unconscious, naked and handcuffed. A display case had some of the shotgun rounds used to quell the 1976 Soweto student uprising. There was even a placard admitting that between 1963 and 1989 there had been eighty deaths in detention. 'Because of the new policy of transparency of the SAP, the SAP opened the new exhibition,' a poster informed visitors.

This was, however stilted and faltering, a genuine attempt at public relations. Under apartheid the police had been the enemy in the townships. They patrolled in armoured vehicles as if an occupying force – which, in a sense, they were. But by the late eighties, they deployed in townships in an array of fearsome military vehicles: *casspirs* (large armoured cars), *nyalas* (smaller, square, armoured vans), and *buffels* (baby *casspirs*). Designed for combat in the bush in the 'frontline states' to the north, they rumbled through the townships like giant crustaceans, occasioning anger, fear and despair – the very emotions many of the police felt on the other side of the lines. In early 1994, when I travelled with one unit in a township battle, it appeared that the armoured shell of the *casspir* was ample protection against the stones and petrol bombs of the township's 'self-defence unit'. But there was no triumphalism in the patrol. 'I don't understand this,' the young Afrikaner police officer in charge of the unit kept telling me. 'I don't understand.'[17]

Major Leonie Wagner, the curator of the museum, was in a side office. With a purple lace bow in her hair, wearing a wool cardigan and floral-patterned skirt, she looked like a small-town librarian. She had been in the police since 1980 and at the police museum since 1982. She was deeply proud of the new exhibition. She had sculpted the Biko statue. She was preparing work on a Robben Island exhibit, although she said they were still awaiting permission from 'Mr Mandela'.

'In the past we had only the police viewpoint because that was all we knew,' she said. 'So we decided to update our exhibits.'[18] Many in the police had been worried about the idea, she said. They had not known what to expect. She had tried to make the exhibits 'as balanced as possible by going through the different newspapers for different viewpoints. It's one of our aims to build a bridge to regain trust.' She chatted away happily about her time in the police. The police had been used 'politically in the past'. That was 'unfair'. She had seen a documentary film about Biko. In the heyday of apartheid she had been 'very innocent'. She 'didn't know what was going on . . . The ordinary policemen were very confident we were going to win this war, but I told them, "Look what happened in other countries like Rhodesia." '

The Wit Wolf (White Wolf), the nickname for Barend Strydom, a notorious racist murderer who had shot dead eight black people and wounded sixteen in cold blood in Pretoria in 1988,[19] had come in, she added, and insisted that they display his case in a particular way. 'Of course we refused . . .

And when he came and looked at it, he said it was balanced and that he was pleased with the whole thing . . . Everyone was suffering on all side.' The more she talked, the more it was evident that changing the police from agents of repression to officers of law enforcement was going to be one of the harder adjustments of the new era.

Under apartheid the police had two principal functions: to suppress threats to white rule and to protect white lives. Some dutiful policemen diligently investigated crimes in black areas. Several newspapers had separate 'black' sections that addressed crime in the townships. They would carry reports of murders with *pangas* (machetes) and stabbings in shebeens. But these crimes were not a concern for the police generals. They saw themselves as the upholders of white 'civilisation'.

The bloodline and curriculum vitae of Colonel Johan Nothnagel, the commander of Pretoria Central police station in the first year after liberation, suggested that he was steeped in the old authoritarian ways. Policing was in his blood. His father had been a police general and had retired in 1982. As an Afrikaner, Nothnagel was part of the ethnic inner circle that under apartheid dominated the police command. He had the gargantuan build, Aryan colouring and pale blue eyes of a Viking warrior. He asserted, however, that he had been viewed as a 'liberal' by his peers. Such a rating was, of course, relative. But still, his recent appointment to command one of the more notoriously racist police stations in the country had been intended to transmit a signal of change. He had lived in Venda, one of the former nominally independent 'homelands'. He knew the 'diversity of Africa's cultures' and appreciated that some differences had to be 'respected'.[20]

So what of his colleagues? We were all brainwashed in the old days about the threat of communism, he said. Some still believed it was on its way. A year after the end of white rule, the police force, he implied, was close to psychological and institutional collapse.

Nothnagel was the sixth commander in three years. His predecessor had 'thrown in the towel' after three months. He had apparently belonged to the 'old guard' and had been 'mentally unfit' to adapt to the changes. Soon after retiring, he shot himself and his wife. Nothnagel's subordinates were dealing with their stress in different ways. His wife was a music teacher. He tended to go home at night and sing as she played the piano. He would then have a couple of drinks before taking the children to the park. He avoided taking tranquillisers. A move to community policing, a radical change of focus, fitted him 'like a glove'. But some of his colleagues were 'physically and mentally broken' by the changes and the pressure. There were countless attempts at suicide. Police figures recorded 172 suicides in the force in 1994. As the years passed from the end of white rule, the figure dropped, but it was still high. Between 2000 and 2006 about one hundred policemen committed suicide a year.

'It's often when youngsters are involved, when they are shot at. And the next day they do a stupid thing and use a firearm where they shouldn't have . . . They fear for their future,' said Nothnagel. 'Some also are from the old guard. They know they can't change.'

Morale among black policemen, the cannon fodder of the old force, was if anything lower than among the old Afrikaner officers. They had traditionally suffered a double stigma. They had been treated with racist disdain by many of their white colleagues and hatred by their black compatriots. Between 1991 and the election in 1994, 950 policemen were killed, according to official statistics. Most of these were black constables ambushed in the townships. In late 1995 Major Mlondi Nhlangulela was in charge of the police station in the township of Atteridgeville, outside Pretoria. Under white rule, his home in another township, Soshanguwe, had been burned down.

'They used to call us dogs,' he said. 'They were killing us policemen because we were defending the wrong system. We were not recognised by our black community, and in the [white] town people did not want us because we were black.' As he started talking, the major lost his initial reserve.

'There is no black man at the top of the police. Rather there are those who want us to fall down. They [white officers] will do things behind your back and say you are incapable of running a station. There are those who still believe they are superior because of the colour of their skin.'[21]

One of his subordinates, Warrant Officer Lazarus Mosesi, had joined the police in 1981 out of desperation to have a job. Liberation had done nothing for the police, he said. The ANC wanted them to learn 'community policing'. Yet every time they tried to make an arrest, they risked being shot. Many policemen were so demoralised and underpaid that they considered resorting to crime on the side. His monthly salary after taxes, he told me, was about 1,400 rand, then about $300. One constable he knew, who had been a 'good policeman', had become so desperate to make ends meet that he had joined a criminal syndicate. He had been caught attempting to carry out a robbery in an official vehicle.[22]

Over the years the authorities invested heavily in the police. More than a decade after the end of white rule, analysts estimated that South Africa allocated three times as much per capita on criminal justice as the international average. And yet, as was the case with so many other government departments, the force was unable to devise adequate policies to justify its budget. In 2007 the South African Police Service returned 2.5 billion rand ($350 million) to the Treasury.

Yet more damaging to its reputation than its evident incompetence was the taint of corruption. The national police commissioner, Jackie Selebi, an ANC veteran, blithely conceded he had a close friendship with Glenn Agliotti, a notorious racketeer who was on trial for drug running and murder. Mbeki stood by Selebi. He even suspended the head of the national prosecutions authority in 2007 when it emerged Selebi was about to be charged. But much to Mbeki's embarrassment, national prosecutors in 2008 pressed ahead and charged Selebi with bribery over his 'generally corrupt relationship' with Agliotti. The charge sheet accused him of taking 1.2 million rand ($170,000) in bribes from Agliotti. Selebi was also accused of passing on to Agliotti details of British intelligence reports into his drug trafficking, and of tipping him off that he was being investigated over the murder of a corrupt mining magnate, Brett Kebble. Selebi denied the charges. As for his relationship with Agliotti, he said he was just a 'close friend, finish and *klaar* [end of story]'.[23]

For more than a decade, business leaders heeded the government's request for cooperation. But towards the end of Mbeki's presidency, business lost patience with his continuing equivocations over crime. For major companies, so dire was the country's reputation for crime that it was becoming increasingly difficult to recruit people from outside South Africa to top managerial posts. Employees in Anglo American's office in central Johannesburg told me that most middle managers were angling for jobs in the company's London headquarters. In 2008 Mark Lamberti, the head of Business against Crime, a private

sector initiative, finally abandoned the group's traditionally diplomatic deal-
ings with the government and accused it of being 'out to lunch' on crime.

'Those who deal with government know it's exceptionally difficult to get
things done,' he told a gathering of international business people and politicians. Most of the policies were fine, but 'when it comes to making things happen, it doesn't happen'.[24] For once Mbeki's government did not respond to a
critique with a withering counterblast. The deputy justice minister, Johnny de
Lange, who had enthused to me in the early days of the ANC government
about the new culture of accountability, conceded what most South Africans
had long since known: the system was 'dysfunctional'. The statistics, he added,
did not reflect the scale of the crisis.

Alluding to the estimated eighteen thousand murder cases of five years earlier, de Lange said it was impossible to say what had happened to the investigations.[25] More than 50 per cent of crime scenes were not being combed for
forensic clues. Just over two thousand forensic investigators had to confront
over six hundred thousand 'very serious contact crimes' a year. It was going to
take a 'huge effort' to take the criminal justice system out of the technological
Stone Age to the twentieth century, let alone the twenty-first century, he said.

Jonny Steinberg, an award-winning South African writer who spent more
than three hundred hours on patrol with policemen between 2004 and 2007,
formed a damning assessment of their culture. He closed his book *Thin Blue:
The Unwritten Rules of Policing South Africa* with a striking anecdote about a
policeman whose beat included a Johannesburg suburb where, in 2007, residents had effectively seceded from the police's authority by setting up their
own force.

'About a year ago an entire suburb in this man's jurisdiction turned from the
police and erected a substitute agency,' the author concluded. 'To all intents
and purposes several thousand people here have severed their relationship
with the South African Police Service. He appears not to have noticed.'[26]

With the police clearly unable to cope, South Africans of all races resorted to
self-defence. In the wealthier suburbs privatisation was seen as the solution.

The private security business was one of the boom industries of the post-apartheid era. When Millicent Chuene founded her security firm Amantombazana [the Girls] Security Services five years after the end of white rule, she had two guards. Eight years later she had more than ninety. She had been a policewoman at Alexandra police station in the early nineties. Night after night she had sat up with her husband, Moffat, who was also in the police in Soweto, pondering the appalling levels of crime and the shortcomings of the police, and plotting when to leave the force. In 1999 she took her chance, invested about a month's salary in training herself to be a security guard, and set up her own private security business in a neat whitewashed block in the down-at-heel industrial area that separates Alexandra from Sandton.[27]

She dressed as snappily as a soldier on a parade ground, with a beret perched to the left, a tie, a crisp sleeveless sweater and creased trousers. The logo on her epaulettes depicted a Zulu club, spear and shield, with the martial tone offset by the image of three African women bearing a cooking pot. She put her staff through pre-breakfast drills before dawn. Every day her guards put their lives on the line.

Her business was a post-apartheid success story. She was a black woman operating a successful business in an industry traditionally dominated by white male veterans of apartheid's defence force. According to the Private Security Industry Regulator, by 2007 there were about three hundred thousand private security guards in South Africa. That figure had been increasing by more than 10 per cent a year in the previous decade. Between 1990 and 2002 the industry's revenues rose ten times to nearly $2 billion.

Yet the burgeoning revenues also testified to the increasing scale of the problem. From Chuene's perch on the front line she could see – literally sometimes – the ebb and flow of criminals heading from Alexandra to Sandton and back. One of her guards was shot in the hand after he chased a 'thug', who turned and shot him.

In the mid-nineties private security firms concentrated on 'armed response'. Houses would be equipped with alarms that, when activated, would prompt armed security guards to rush to the scene. As, however, it emerged that the proliferation of such firms was doing little to deter would-be criminals, wealthier people resorted to ever more expensive and bellicose measures. In 2007 residents in several of Johannesburg's more exclusive suburbs banded together to fund their own private militias. One such firm provided armed units that patrolled in four-by-fours, escorted cars home and monitored 'suspect' vehicles and pedestrians. After an initial collective investment of several million rand to buy the vehicles, householders were expected to pay 2,000 rand a month for the patrols, on top of the monthly fees they were paying for the services of armed-response security firms.

Crime plunged in the suburbs with these new private militias – and promptly rose in adjacent, less well-protected areas. Johannesburg's suburbs were, after dark, a no-man's-land patrolled by rival units of armed men, each in their own distinctive uniforms and vehicles. Meanwhile, residents lived behind ever higher perimeter walls. One of the most striking physical changes in Johannesburg over the first fourteen years of majority rule was the growth of the suburban fortress: the average height of walls rose by several feet; gated suburbs and office parks sprouted on the fringes of the city like medieval walled towns; more and more roads were fenced off with booms and sentries. Yet analyses of crime statistics suggested that higher walls had no impact on the number of break-ins. Rather, there was a spurt of cases of people being hijacked as they entered or left their homes. Gates and drives had been identified as the weak point in defences, just as drawbridges had once been for forts. Armed robberies increased by nearly two-thirds from 77,000 per annum to 126,000 in the decade from 1996.[28] In the same period the ratio of robberies at gunpoint to burglaries of empty premises had risen from 1:4.1 to 1:2.4.

In abandoning faith in the authorities, the former white suburbs were merely following the lead of the townships, where residents had long since given up on relying on the police to maintain law and order. After the end of white rule, the numbers of *casspirs* in the townships declined precipitously. But still, few residents trusted the police. Rather, many continued to rely on the community to enforce justice, just as they had when the townships were in flames.

Late one evening in Soweto's Zola section, two years after the end of white rule, a gang of shadowy men was circling around 1061a Ndlovu (Elephant) Street, preparing for a raid. There was a low whistle. Three men scaled the front fence. Two went round the back. Then the leader barged through the front door shining his torch.

'Rise and shine,' he shouted. 'Tell us where your gun is.'

The householders nervously rubbed sleep from their eyes as their home was ransacked. Cupboards, fridge, nothing was left untouched. After two minutes the intruders left, dragging the son of the house with them. He was, they claimed, handling stolen goods.

The scene was reminiscent of the police raids in the apartheid era, when police stormed into township houses before dawn to enforce the pass laws. But these 'raiders' were former African National Congress paramilitaries. Led by Jerry Marobyane, an ebullient twenty-three-year-old who had had his hand blown off fighting the police in the eighties, they had founded Intokozo (Joy), one of several semi-formalised groups of vigilantes that emerged in Soweto after the end of white rule. They liaised with the commander at the local police station, they said, before making a citizen's arrest. The arrangement was simple: the youths provided the intelligence and sometimes the muscle; the police provided the facade of the law.

The police chief had been '100 per cent our enemy', Marobyane chuckled. 'I never thought I would go to him for advice.' Marobyane's headquarters was lined with files with portentous labels, including 'constitution', 'conduct', 'membership', and 'cases'. But then again, the apartheid police had liked to dress up their behaviour in the cloak of laws and had shown scant respect for human rights. Shortly after the Ndlovu Street raid, a large middle-aged woman strode down the street in a flowery nightgown, shouting and wagging a finger at Marobyane. Jeanne Moshodi was a teacher. It was her house that had just been ransacked by Marobyane's men. She was incensed.

'Who are these guys?' she screamed. 'You just burst in asking for my son? I was asleep in bed. Who is in charge of you? Who is in control?'

Marobyane was unabashed. 'It's bad to hit people, but how would you feel if someone shot your mother and you saw him, but he insisted he had done nothing wrong? It's not in our code of conduct, but obviously you have to knock him about. The police are soft. It's not like that with us. Five minutes will be enough for anyone to confess.'[29]

Moshodi's outburst and Marobyane's insouciance underlined the moral and legal complications of the resort to street justice. There was also a more chilling aspect to the phenomenon: lynch-mob killings. In the first five years of democracy I reported on several kangaroo courts, including the murder of a young Sowetan by a gang of schoolchildren after he hit one of their classmates, and the stoning to death of an ANC councillor. While the circumstances varied, the context was invariably the same. The traditional codes of behaviour had broken down under apartheid, and the police had either long since forfeited – or never had – authority.

One afternoon in April 1996, in the village of Sekororo in the far north of South Africa, hundreds of people gathered on the top of a small hill to decide the fate of the family of an eighty-one-year-old suspected witch. Johannes Baleaga had had the misfortune of hobbling through the village the day after an itinerant witch doctor decreed that the 'witch' responsible for a lightning strike on a tree in the school playground would be revealed by a limp. Baleaga had fled his home just ahead of a mob intent on burning him to death. Since then, the villagers had turned their attentions to his family. They were squatting in a corner of the family homestead – two low clay houses, three rounded huts and a cattle *kraal* (enclosure) linked by a perimeter wall. It was not that Baleaga was a witch, they told me. It was just that he was a successful farmer and his principal accuser coveted his crops.

'We were never given a chance to respond,' Harris, the old man's youngest son said. 'We wanted to put our side of the story at the first village meeting. We were shocked, but when the others saw we were pinpointed as the relatives of a witch, we were told to sit down.'[30]

As the sun set over the northern Drakensberg Mountains, the villagers bowed their heads. The trial could begin. It was over in barely twenty minutes. The old man's family had to leave the village. It was a gross injustice, but they were at least alive. David Sekgobela, the chairman of the proceedings, was a young urban sophisticate in a flashy suit who had recently returned home from Johannesburg. He dismissed the idea that he should have steered the assembly into letting the Baleagas stay. If he had, he said, someone would have gone to their house and burned it down. Scores of suspected witches had been burned in that province in the previous two years. The practice, local officials told me, had been propagated by youths returning home from urban townships, where they had seen their peers taking the law into their own hands and necklacing suspected informers. The traditional structures of leadership had faltered in the face of these challenges to their authority. Headmen felt powerless to intervene.

In a previous era a wise chief would have been expected to stay the eviction of the Baleaga family. But the authority of Chief Joshua Mongadi had been swept away in the turmoil and amid the clamour for change of the last years of apartheid, when chiefs and headmen often faced the wrath of politicised youths. He was sitting in a battered old deckchair as the assembly prepared to meet. He was not planning to attend, he said. He had other pressing matters at hand. The old order had decayed, but there was a vacuum in its place.

The following year, in the township of Swanieville on the western fringe of the city, Eric Ndeleni, an ANC councillor, had been stoned to death by a mob of schoolchildren in front of his wife. He had addressed countless rallies during the struggle, but his liberation credentials gave him no protection. His brother-in-law was suspected of killing a youth at the local school in a brawl in a bar. When his classmates heard the news at school assembly, they went to Ndeleni's house, showered stones on his roof and demanded he hand over the suspect. When he remonstrated with them they pelted him with stones before cornering him in a nearby ditch when he tried to escape.

'The children felt the police never did anything when they reported a murder,' Mbulelo Musi, a spokesman for the regional government told me. 'So they just charged outside, jumped into the buses that had taken them to school, and drove to Swanieville.'[31] The *coup de grâce* came, he said, when a boulder the size of a basketball landed on Ndeleni's head. Even ANC councillors had to watch their step.

There is nothing uniquely African about such barbarism, as witnesses to the terrifying force of mob violence anywhere in the world can attest. In June 1990 thousands of miners rampaged through Bucharest, the Romanian capital, attacking supporters of opposition parties, students and 'intellectuals' with clubs, hammers and pit props. One young woman in a red shirt was beaten in front of several journalists until her back was a bloody pulp. The behaviour of the Sowetan and Swanieville mobs was no different. It was an irrational outpouring of rage and violence. There were clear parallels between the political situations in South Africa in 1994 and Romania in 1990. Both societies were emerging from an authoritarian past with a police force that was distrusted, discredited and dysfunctional. But unlike in Romania, where the explosion was a one-off and society swiftly stabilised, in South Africa the rage remained, erupting unexpectedly, drawing on the lawlessness that was arguably the most terrible legacy of apartheid, feeding on grievances over the past and present, and thriving in a world over which the police had long since ceded control.

Why else did Masilo Mathebula have to die? His 'crime' was to have intervened one Saturday afternoon in a run-of-the-mill family squabble between his mother and a younger brother, Thomas. When Thomas returned for a second argument, this time accompanied by a school friend called Jerry, the row became heated and ended with Masilo hitting Jerry on the head with a bottle. Three days later, Jerry returned with a group of classmates from his school armed with *pangas*, knives and stones.

Mathebula would have understood what the gang's arrival portended. He had grown up in Soweto in the eighties, when mobs murdered suspected informers. 'Masilo said it was a family affair,' his mother told me. 'They said he should shut up. He ran away, but they hunted him, the whole class . . . They caught him, stripped him and frog-marched him naked through the streets. They then hacked him to death outside their school.'[32]

A week later a handful of pupils congregated outside the school gates. It had just reopened. No one from the school had visited the family. Jerry had not been seen since.

'He was very angry,' one pupil said. 'He was trying to show his friends he could kill someone.'[33]

One of the most successful anti-crime initiatives drew on the township tradition of a collective response. Hout Bay, a valley that stretches down to the Atlantic from Table Mountain, just south of Cape Town, was a sleepy fishing community under apartheid. A decade after liberation it had become a microcosm of the country's racial and economic divides. In the centre of the valley was a wealthy, mainly white community of some fifteen thousand people. Sol Kerzner, the gambling magnate, was one of the super-rich part-time residents who had houses there. Clinging to a hillside overlooking the white village was a rapidly expanding squatter camp, Imizamo Yethu. Most of its fifteen thousand residents, who included many from other African countries, lived in shacks with the most basic sanitation. Sandwiched between them – economically but not geographically – was Hangberg, a former 'coloured' township, home to some ten thousand people, tucked away at the far corner of the valley, all but out of sight of the old 'white' area.

Under apartheid, when the village was restricted to whites and heavily policed, it had minimal crime. But a decade later, as Imizamo Yethu expanded, crime soared. Then a tourist was murdered in a bed and breakfast, and a neighbourhood watch scheme was launched, linking all three racial communities. It was to become a model for the country.

'Hout Bay got together and said, "Thank you, that is enough," ' said Captain Gerhard van den Bergh, the deputy police chief in the two-storey pillbox of a police station that faces the main entrance to Imizamo Yethu. 'I thought there was no way a neighbourhood watch scheme would work. But when people stood up and said, "We're tired of crime," they meant it. If we all change attitudes, stop blaming each other and get involved, we can beat crime.'³⁴

It was a hugely successful initiative. Residents of Imizamo Yethu patrolled the shanty town every night. In the village Rod Panagos, a businessman, and other coordinators of the neighbourhood watch scheme ran a mobile response service and took turns to be on duty to respond to calls. One night he had been on duty barely five minutes when the radio in the control room crackled into life. A woman called Josephine was on the line in a panic. A man was in her garden trying to break into her home.

'Josephine, can you see him?' said the radio operator. 'Lock the door. Don't put the phone down. I am still here.' Moments later a message was being sent to hundreds of people tuned into the neighbourhood watch frequency: 'We have an intruder at 35 Penzance.' Panagos was on his way, with his night-vision goggles, two-way radio and pepper gun at his side. As he waited just down from 35 Penzance Road, his radio crackled into life: 'Suspect wearing red cap, with dark top and stripes on sleeves.'

'We have changed people's thinking,' he said later, when the tension had subsided. 'This has had a very positive impact.' But, he went on, 'we don't want to live like this'.³⁵

Neighbourhood watch schemes and community policing programmes are alleviating the problem in some towns and townships but only as a stop-gap measure. For South Africa to have a chance of combating the crime and stemming the flood of middle-class professional emigrants seeking a safer life for their families abroad, not only do the criminal justice system and the police need a profound overhaul but they also need clear moral and credible leadership. There was one law enforcement unit that shone in the early years of the twenty-first century amid the incompetence, inefficiency and corruption of the police, but unfortunately it then came up against the obstacle that has stymied so many anti-corruption forces in developing states over the years: politics.

The Scorpions were founded at the start of Mbeki's presidency as an elite anti-corruption force. At the peak of their powers they were 550 strong, including 100 prosecutors, 200 investigators and 100 analysts. Their first batch of investigators was trained at the FBI academy in Quantico, Virginia, earning them the tag 'the FBI of South Africa'. They took on and won a string of criminal cases, from drug smuggling to white-collar fraud. They also investigated a number of high-ranking public officials, including Jacob Zuma.

Their death knell was sounded at the ANC's conference in December 2007, when Zuma was elected party president and several other prominent victims of Scorpions' investigations were voted on to the party's national executive committee. The party resolved to dismantle the Scorpions, bolstering their case with an array of arguments, including claims that the unit had too much autonomy, that it selectively leaked material to the media to bolster a 'Hollywood' image, that it used old apartheid agents, that it gave too many plea bargains to secure evidence against its targets, and that it had been abused by Mbeki to pursue his opponents.

Of these the most serious charge was the last. The history of the Mbeki era suggests that there was an occasional pattern of selective prosecutions. In September 2008, the judge presiding over a long-running corruption case against Zuma delighted his supporters by suggesting that there may have been 'political meddling' in the case. While four months later the Supreme Court of Appeal overturned the ruling saying the judge had 'taken his eye off the ball', in April 2009 taped conversations released in court suggested politics had influenced the timing of the Scorpions' moves against Mr Zuma. Yet by defying Mbeki and taking on his close ally, the police chief Jackie Selebi, the Scorpions had made clear that they were not merely the president's puppets. The problem for the Scorpions was that many of its former targets had taken control of the ANC and were hell-bent on exacting revenge by destroying them and in particular their charismatic head, Leonard McCarthy.

McCarthy is a bear of a man, big of body and personality. Yet like a number of men of his bulk, he moves with a feline grace. There was something of the panther about him. His deftness helped him for several years to outmanoeuvre powerful enemies. He inspired fierce loyalty among his staff, and he was seen as one of the most successful public servants. But in the middle of 2008, as the row over the Scorpions intensified, he announced that he was leaving South Africa to become head of the anti-corruption unit at the World Bank. His announcement came soon after the publication of a powerful exposé of how international criminal syndicates saw South Africa as the ideal conduit from Africa to the West.[36] Shortly before McCarthy left the country, he bumped into one of the ten biggest drug dealers in South Africa. The man was driving a Humvee. He opened his side window and said, 'Mr McCarthy, let me say something. We, the members of the Firm, are celebrating. The Scorpions are closing down.'[37]

McCarthy rolled his eyes in response to the accusation of Zuma's supporters that his unit had been selective in its prosecutions. It was 'complete bullshit', he said, to claim that he was the 'extension of Mbeki'. He had met the president only a few times. Out of five thousand cases they had investigated, fewer than a hundred had a political connection. The most prominent, after Zuma's, was of the police chief, Selebi, the very man whom Mbeki had tried to protect.

Two months into his new post, McCarthy flew from his new home in Washington DC to an anti-corruption summit in Norway. En route, he made his first public comments about the drive to end the Scorpions. It was, he told me, 'unfortunate'.

'If you have something that was great and has worked well and has become part of the psyche of the country, but it has problems, then my inclination is to fix the problems,' he said. As for the accusation that the unit had been politicised, he gave another one-word answer: 'Nonsense.' Maybe he had been guilty of bad judgement once or twice, he said, but to accuse him of bad faith was a calumny.

McCarthy had earlier that morning met the head of a European anti-corruption body who reckoned that the removal of the Scorpions could set back the fight against crime in South Africa by several years. 'I'm not an absolutist; I don't believe that if the Scorpions are not there, then South Africa's going to turn into a criminal haven.' McCarthy paused and then added wryly, 'Some people are saying it is, in any event, the case.'

He had three thoughts on how to improve law enforcement. In 1999 the newly formed Scorpions had asked: Who are the top twenty criminals? The law enforcement authorities needed to ask who were the top two hundred criminals and then work with the Revenue Service and intelligence agencies to target them. Second, there needed to be more police on the beat. Third, police needed to appear more authoritative.

'Do people sit up when they see you in the street or in your car? Or do they say, "Ah, look at the police! That policeman is slouching in his van sitting there. Look at how loose his clothes fit!"?'

McCarthy had a touch of flu. He apologised for being off-colour. It probably was just the flu, but it was hard not to see his malaise as more profound. Six months later his reputation in South Africa suffered a blow when the National Prosecuting Authority suggested he had timed charging Mr Zuma to have an adverse impact on his career. But the abolition of the Scorpions by a vote in parliament in late 2008 was a loss that South Africa could ill afford.

Chapter 6

THE WHITE AFRICANS

*My generation of Afrikaners does not want to say
sorry any more. This is a democratic South Africa,
and we have moved on.*

— BOK VAN BLERK,
TWENTY-NINE-YEAR-OLD
AFRIKAANS ROCK SINGER, 2007

*Whites have never had it so good. Wealth has been
pouring out of their ears. It has been business as
usual.*

— RENIER SCHOEMAN,
FORMER APARTHEID GOVERNMENT
MINISTER TURNED MEMBER OF THE ANC, 2008

When Marthinus van Schalkwyk, a plump, baby-faced National Party appa-
ratchik known as Kortbroek (Shortpants), took over the party leadership in
1997, he was following some of the more uncompromising leaders of the twentieth century. While his predecessor, F. W. de Klerk, had taken the momentous
decision to lift the ban on the African National Congress and release Nelson
Mandela from prison, before him there stretched a roll call of dour leaders who

for four decades had dominated South Africa with their ethnic nationalist vision and warped racial programme. From 1948 until 1989, when de Klerk took over, the National Party was led by D. F. Malan, Hans Strijdom, Hendrik Verwoerd, John Vorster and P. W. Botha, hard, dogmatic men who had built up a military powerhouse designed to entrench white supremacy while enforcing a race-based repression that went so far as to ban sex across the colour line and impose separate benches for different races.

Van Schalkwyk was schooled in their thinking. In the eighties he had been a founder of Jeugkrag (Youth Power), an organisation supposedly set up to oppose the Nationalists but in reality a front of military intelligence. His leadership failed to staunch a haemorrhaging of support, as the party lost its *raison d'être* after the end of white rule. But he did make one memorable decision. Just over a decade after the National Party lost power, he voted to dissolve the party, and he joined the ANC. 'What we do today is part of our contribution to finally ending the division of the South African soul,' he said. 'What we do today is liberating. It empowers us to throw off the yoke of history.'[1] With that, the National Party effectively ceased to exist. It was a capitulation. Yet it also reflected how the Afrikaner establishment had reached an accommodation with the new order. They had chosen to acquiesce rather than criticise. They had, in short, decided to accept that they had lost power and to curry favour with the new rulers.

In its heyday the National Party was all-powerful. It took office in 1948 on a programme of uplifting Afrikaners, the white tribe whose forefathers had come to the Cape from Holland and France in the seventeenth and eighteenth centuries to escape discrimination. They were determined to guarantee white supremacy by a sweeping extension of segregationist laws. They were also determined to ensure that Afrikaners no longer felt like second-class citizens. Their old foes, the English-speaking whites, many of whose forefathers had fought theirs in the Anglo-Boer War at the turn of the twentieth century, had dominated government, the civil service and business since the formation of the Union of South Africa out of the British colonies of Natal and the Cape and the Boer republics of the Orange Free State and the Transvaal in 1910. They achieved both goals in swift order, the former by a blizzard of draconian new laws codifying apartheid and the latter by affirmative action.

Once in office, the National Party rapidly cemented its power on a platform of white privilege. The Nationalists' victory had come at the expense of the United Party of Field Marshal Jan Smuts, a former Boer War commander, and friend and close adviser of Winston Churchill in the Second World War. The United Party withered in opposition. While many English-speaking white South Africans liked to bemoan the Afrikaner Nationalists as crude and uneducated, in fact apartheid suited most whites well. From 1961 to 1974 the Nationalists faced just one opponent of apartheid in the whites-only Parliament, the feisty Helen Suzman, who infuriated the Nationalists with her probing questions. Her party steadily gained supporters and parliamentary seats in the eighties, when the townships were in flames and it was hard to see a peaceful solution to apartheid, but still the National Party easily retained the support of the majority of whites.

Then came the astonishing moment on 2 February 1990, when F. W. de Klerk, the country's last white president, stood up in Parliament and announced the unbanning of the liberation movements and the release of Mandela. It is tempting with hindsight to see this as inevitable. The climate was favourable for change. The collapse of global communism had removed the Nationalists' old fear of a communist takeover. But Afrikaner leaders had baulked at taking major reforms several times before and contented themselves with tinkering at the edges of apartheid. The military generals were rightly confident that they were in no imminent danger of defeat. De Klerk's history and genes suggested he too would shrink from reform: he was a blue-blooded Afrikaner Nationalist and a member of the strictest branch of the Dutch Reformed Church; his grandfather had been a friend of Paul Kruger, the Boer leader in the Anglo-Boer War; his father had been an apartheid cabinet minister. But in one bold gesture he paved the way for a new era.

While his colleagues did not appreciate it at the time, they were on a path towards negotiating themselves from power, as the long years of Nationalist domination drew to a close far more smoothly than most had dared to hope. De Klerk was often compared to Mikhail Gorbachev, the reformist Soviet leader. The analogy was unfair on the Afrikaner. While Gorbachev proved unable to adapt his vision and was overtaken by the process he had unleashed, de Klerk kept modifying his plans as he went along, as his initial vision of a permanent coalition entrenching whites' interest proved unsustainable. In a continent where, for most of the previous three decades, leaders had tended to leave office only in a coffin or by a coup, his abdication was remarkable. Years later he recalled the heartache his decision had caused: 'The decision to surrender the right to national sovereignty is certainly one of the most painful that any leader can ever be asked to take.'[2]

For a while it was feared that the reformist drive might fuel a surge of support for the far right. In those days foreign correspondents loved to rootle out fire-breathing would-be secessionist Afrikaners. They did not require much hunting, and they seldom disobliged. Eugene Terre'Blanche, the leader of the Afrikaner Weerstandsbeweging (AWB), or Afrikaner Resistance Movement, could be counted on to deliver blood-curdling rhetoric. He had exploded into South Africans' consciousness in 1979, when he burst into a Pretoria hall and tarred and feathered an Afrikaner history professor who had dared to question one of Afrikanerdom's founding myths, the claim that God had been on their side at their defeat of a Zulu army at Blood River in 1838. In December 1993, just five months before the election, the black-uniformed paramilitaries of Terre'Blanche's Ystergarde (Iron Guard) put on a display of their prowess at the Voortrekker Monument. Under apartheid this was a shrine to Afrikaner Nationalism, a squat totalitarian monument commemorating the covenant the Boers believed they made with God at Blood River. On the eve of the battle's anniversary, Terre'Blanche's supporters did their best to instil the idea that whites were again facing a potential annihilation – by marching into the amphitheatre beside the monument with military precision before giving a display of high kicks and karate chops.

'Mandela does not want peace,' Terre'Blanche bellowed. 'He wants war. If he wants war, he'll get it. No government can govern without the Boers. No government can govern without God. The Afrikaners have been asked: Who would you rather have, Jesus Christ from Blood River or Barabbas from Robben Island?'[3]

The scene made great television. But it was little more than a pantomime. Three months later his ranting was exposed as bluster in the violent last days of President Lucas Mangope, the tinpot leader of the homeland of Bophuthatswana. In its chaotic denouement Bophuthatswana ended once and for all speculation over the threat posed by the white right wing and also shattered the far older myth of whites' invincibility. After three days of protests by people pushing for the end of the homeland government, several thousand white right-wingers, including AWB supporters, mobilised to support Mangope. In the words of the Afrikaans press, the AWB diehards thought they were embarking on a *kaffirskietpiekniek* (a nigger-shooting picnic) as they drove through Mafikeng taking potshots at blacks. For the Bophuthatswana security forces, until then loyal to Mangope, that was too much. They turned on their nominal allies and opened fire on the last car in a convoy, a light blue Mercedes. The driver was killed outright. One of the two passengers, a caricature of a Boer with a tree-trunk frame and a flowing brown beard, lay on the ground for fifteen minutes pleading for help. A third man lay silent, bleeding from the hip. Then a young black policeman strode through the throng of journalists and locals and shot dead the two Afrikaners pleading for their lives. He then lifted his rifle in the air and kicked the bodies.

The image of the three khaki-clad Afrikaners slumped in the dust became a symbol of the change of the guard. No longer was the white man *die baas*. This time it was the black man that had held the gun, and it was whites cowering on the ground. It was clear that the militant Afrikaners would not take up arms again. Appalled by what had occurred, the more moderate right-wing leaders pushed for a settlement with the ANC.

In the final months before the April 1994 election, white extremists let off a series of bombs, killing nineteen people. Terre'Blanche, the AWB leader, continued his fire and brimstone racist ranting. Eighteen months into the new era, I attended a rally at an old cattle showground outside a small town in the expanse of the veld, where he was addressing about three hundred mainly khaki-clad supporters. 'We are heading for total destruction,' he told me. 'Out of the chaos of smoke and disaster we will take a part of this land and keep it as a Third Boer Republic.'[4] But even his diehard supporters knew his time was past. In 1997 he was sentenced to six years in prison for assaulting a petrol-station attendant and the attempted murder of a security guard. The only flicker of life on the far right was a clumsy attempt by a group called the Boeremag (Boers' force) in 2003 to set off bombs in Soweto. One person was killed; the conspirators were swiftly arrested and put on trial for treason.

In the countdown to the 1994 election, the vast majority of Afrikaners had already decided that the man from Robben Island and his negotiating partner, F. W. de Klerk, had a more tempting vision than the man evoking Blood River. The majority of Afrikaners were too affluent and had too much to lose to flirt with irredentism. The quasi-intellectual foundations of the apartheid edifice had been crumbling for many years. The absurdity of trying to fence in blacks in so-called tribal homelands had long since been manifest, even if many whites still turned a blind eye to the injustice. The economy clearly needed to tap into the African market if it was to grow. In 1992 nearly 70 per cent of whites voted yes in a referendum on whether they supported de Klerk's drive for a negotiated settlement. While de Klerk's hopes of hiving off some black supporters from the ANC in the April 1994 election were disappointed, the Nationalists came a clear second with 20 per cent of the vote, leaving its old liberal bugbear, the Democratic Party, trailing with just 1.7 per cent and the main right-wing party, the Freedom Front, with 2.1 per cent. Then the monolith imploded. Deprived of the rationale of apartheid, the party collapsed with vertiginous speed.

Tim du Plessis, a leading Afrikaner journalist, said a few years after the end of white rule that there was a spirit of subservience running through the Afrikaner psyche that would help them to adapt more easily to the new order than white English speakers. 'Once we Afrikaners can overcome racism and bigotry, we will slip easily into the African way of thinking,' he said. 'The Afrikaners are used to defending corruption and bigotry in the old government. They will easily adapt to the inefficiencies of the new.'[5] The career path of van Schalkwyk, de Klerk's successor, appeared to bolster this contention.

The party had nine cabinet seats in Mandela's first government, in line with the agreement that parties with more than 10 per cent of the vote were entitled to join a government of national unity. But in 1996, after two uneasy years, de Klerk took the party into opposition. Some Nationalists still entertained dreams of coming back to power. At a caucus of the party's MPs soon after they had walked out of the government, the chief whip argued confidently that within a decade he would be back in government. 'You wait, once the Mandela glue goes, we will get 30 or 40 per cent of the vote.'[6] Within seven years, the party had ceased to exist.

It is never easy for once dominant parties to regain power after the rationale behind their original authority has disintegrated. The communist parties of Eastern Europe struggled for a while for relevance after the collapse of the Soviet bloc, but most then regrouped as parties of the left, exploiting disillusionment with free-market reforms. Some even regained power. The pernicious role that race had played in South Africa's history ensured that such a recovery was not an option for the National Party. In a last gasp, it attempted to relaunch itself as the New National Party in 1997, when de Klerk handed over the reins to van Schalkwyk. The difficulties the party would always face over its past were underlined when the new leader was almost immediately exposed as having been an informer for the security police. In the second post-apartheid election, in 1999, the party's share of the vote plummeted from 20 per cent to less than 7 per cent. It allied itself briefly with the Democratic Party, its old opponent from the whites-only Parliament, to become the Democratic Alliance. Finally, after polling just 1.7 per cent of the votes in the 2004 election, it merged into the ANC.

On pledging in 2004 to dissolve the party, van Schalkwyk became an ANC MP. As a reward he was appointed minister of environmental affairs and tourism in Mbeki's cabinet. Addressing Parliament, he lavished praise on Mbeki and denounced the Democratic Alliance as representing 'old apartheid privileges'.[7] For Mbeki this was a political windfall, giving him a riposte to the opposition's persistent accusation that he was reracialising politics.

By subsuming the Nationalists, the ANC was following the lead of other post-independence governments in Africa that had sought to envelop potential opponents in a consensual government. The most recent example had been in Zimbabwe, where Mugabe co-opted his old rival liberation movement leader, Joshua Nkomo, into a 1987 unity accord; the deal removed the last trace of any meaningful opposition in the country until the rise of the Movement for Democratic Change more than a decade later. Mandela used this arrangement as an analogy when he tried to entice Tony Leon, the leader of the Democratic Party, into his government in 1996. 'We must go out and face the world with one voice, just as Mugabe and Nkomo do,' Mandela said. It was, Leon commented, an 'unfortunate and revealing analogy'.[8]

But the collapse of the National Party in the first decade of white rule also reflected a remarkable subnarrative of the post-apartheid story: the ease with which some of the old oppressors appeared to adapt to the new order. Renier Schoeman, a veteran apartheid functionary, proudly liked to claim he had served in three very different governments, de Klerk's, Mandela's and Mbeki's. His political career started in 1972, when he was an assistant private secretary serving the government of John Vorster and the National Party was at the peak of its powers. He was one of the ministers whom de Klerk took into Mandela's government, which he served as deputy minister of education. Then, after a stint in opposition, he served as Mbeki's deputy minister of health after the dissolution of the National Party.

The end of white rule was a terrible shock, he said. Overnight Nationalist MPs went from forty posts in government to just nine. 'We were walking around like shipwrecked survivors,' he said. '"The ship has sunk," we thought. "We have nothing to do. We have outlived our purpose." It was a very unacceptable truth for white people.' And yet he said he soon realised that an Afrikaner could be relevant if he was humble or, as he put it, 'provided he did not magnify himself'. Some Afrikaners might see him as a *hensopper* (a Boer War insult for someone who surrendered to the British) or even a *kaffirboetie* (the apartheid-era term of abuse for an Afrikaner who evinced sympathy for blacks), he conceded, but such critics were prejudiced and wrong. 'Whites have never had it so good. Wealth has been pouring out of their ears. It has been business as usual for most whites.'[9]

Schoeman was something of an opportunist and was decried by his foes as utterly lacking in political principles. In 2007, as a member of the ANC, he found himself serving a new master, Jacob Zuma, as national coordinator of the ANC's Progressive Business Forum, responsible for selling businesses time with government officials. The Progressive Business Forum was a controversial operation whose existence underlined how some in the ANC had lost sight of the distinction between the party and the state. It was designed to raise money for the ANC by selling appointments with government ministers. But Schoeman's story *was* an illustration of how, far from being financially ruinous, democracy was liberating for and even to the advantage of many Afrikaners.

Koos Botha, a thickset former far-right MP, was among the more striking converts. In 1989 he was elected to Parliament for the Conservative Party, the ultra-right party that opposed moves to end apartheid. Two years later he was dubbed 'Koos the Bomber' after he and a friend blew up an empty school in

Pretoria that had been set aside for the children of ANC members returning from exile.

'I said, "Let's make some music,"' he recalled three years later. 'It was a big bang, one of the best. But we were two stupid bastards. I gave twenty years of my life to the *volkstaat* [an Afrikaner homeland], and it was a bloody dream. We were wasting our time.'[10] He strode around a black squatter camp outside Pretoria, which in the old days had been in his constituency and he would never have dreamed of visiting. Now it was a business opportunity. He had set up a company liaising between the squatters and construction firms to build new housing. His partner was an ANC veteran. There had been no blinding flash of light, he said, but rather self-interest, and he claimed somewhat unconvincingly that guilt had fuelled a reappraisal.

Such evolutionary stories in the early years after white rule ran against the trend of history for whites in sub-Saharan Africa, where independence had usually prompted a mass exodus of the former colonial masters. Most Afrikaners, however, whose very name means 'Africans', had nowhere to go, having long since cut ties to Europe. Their forefathers had come to Africa before the US Declaration of Independence, and they had liked to cast their nineteenth-century trek north from the Cape to escape from British rule in the same light as westward expansion in the United States. They had long seen themselves as part of the continent, even if their romanticised view of Africa had tended to exclude a role for black Africans except as their servants. With the stigma of apartheid removed, many of their cultural and intellectual leaders liked to argue that Afrikaners would find it easier to adapt to black rule than the English speakers, many of whom still thought of themselves as Europeans.

A few years after the end of white rule, Professor J. C. van der Walt, the head of Johannesburg's Rand Afrikaans University (RAU), a traditional bastion of Afrikaner Nationalism, travelled to Soweto and forged a link with the township's main football club. He was then able to trumpet that connection to persuade a delegation from Howard University, the traditionally black university in Washington DC, to sign a twinning agreement.

'You see the image of the granite Verwoerdian is not correct,' he said. 'We Afrikaners are very adaptable. The coming of the new dispensation has been for many of us a relief.'[11]

As the years passed, many of the old Afrikaner corporations, which were founded by the Nationalists to take on the English speakers, prospered in the new order. With sanctions removed, they were at last able to exploit the market in Africa and elsewhere. Naspers, a media company that originally published conservative Afrikaans newspapers, became something of a corporate pin-up of the new order. It expanded its pay-television service into the rest of Africa and was one of the first South African companies to invest in China. Afrikaner chief executives tended to demur when asked if they regarded themselves as trailblazers for a new breed of post-apartheid Afrikaner businessman. They saw themselves as South Africans, they said, not Afrikaners.[12]

Then in early 2007 there was talk of a new restiveness in Afrikanerdom. The focus was an elegy to a legendary Boer War commander, but it reflected more an uncertainty over the future than a hankering for the past.

The song rolled through the night air with the timbre of a high-veld storm. It is the sort of Old Testament voice that at the end of the nineteenth century might have enthused young Afrikaners to join a commando for a tilt at the 'khakis', as the British forces were known by the Boers in the Anglo-Boer War – or that is at least what many in the crowd of Afrikaners listening to it one balmy night in 2007 clearly yearned to dream as they rejoiced in hearing their beloved Afrikaans delivered with such power. It was hard to see against the flare of candles and torches, but there must have been at least six hundred people gathered under the stars in a grassy school arena. They had come to hear the latest idol of Afrikanerdom, a young rock musician named Bok van Blerk, perform his ode to Koos de la Rey, a legendary Boer War general.

One by one they got to their feet as the concert reached its climax. Matrons in floral-print dresses, students, barefoot children, bureaucrats – they all started swaying to the music. A few had tears in their eyes. Some were in the uniform of the South African farmer: khaki shirt and shorts, long socks. A couple of jokers had dressed up in Boer War regalia. Most were of middle-class urban Afrikaner stock, the sort who had time and again voted the National Party back into power.

A tubby Afrikaner policeman directing *bakkies* (pickups) disgorging latecomers waved me past a melee of families busily barbecuing their supper. It was as if I had slipped back in time to the last year of white rule. Then I had come to know all too well the death rites of Nationalist rule. I had gone to small towns across the *platteland* to hear conservative politicians address the *volk* and supposedly to take the pulse of Afrikanerdom. The scene seldom varied: families, the sizzling of *boerewors* (spicy Afrikaner sausage) on *braais*; ample servings of Castle beer and brandies mixed with Coke; plates of *koeksusters*; and the blending of culture and history by politicians.

In early 2007 Bok van Blerk's elegy to de la Rey had shot to the top of the Afrikaans music charts. De la Rey was one of the *bittereinders* whose guerrilla campaign frustrated the British for years. It was his wiliness that led the British eventually to take the harsh step of interning Afrikaner women and children in concentration camps. The English translation of the chorus was banal: 'De la Rey, de la Rey, will you come and lead the Boers? General, general, we will fall around you as one.' But its military beat sent many Afrikaners' pulses racing – not least because it allowed them to celebrate something from their past after years of having to feel ashamed of apartheid. For six months the young singer Bok van Blerk criss-crossed the nation, performing night after night to packed audiences in theatres, school playing fields and stadiums. Many Afrikaners had seized on the song as a reminder of a happier and simpler time when they had leaders sticking up for their beliefs and they did not have to feel guilty about their past. It also clearly tapped into a feeling of alienation that was creeping over whites in the second decade of majority rule. Liberal Afrikaner commentators agonised over whether it was a sign of a new confidence or a paean to white rule.

To assess the ballad's appeal I had driven one night to the Protea Park elementary school on the edge of the town of Krugersdorp, where Johannesburg's sprawl gives way to the veld. It was just beyond a road junction where a sign read, 'Hijacking hotspot. Beware.'

Bok van Blerk, whose real name is Louis Pepler, was still at school when white rule ended. His father worked for the National Productivity Institute, part of the sprawling state bureaucracy that set aside jobs for Afrikaners in a scheme similar to the one the ANC introduced to promote blacks, which cost Bok's father his job in 1995. Bok's singing career, however, in many ways exemplified how Afrikaner culture had been able to flower under ANC rule. While Afrikaans lost its predominance in 1994, when it became just one of eleven official languages, in the early years of the twenty-first century, Afrikaner literary and music festivals thrived. Afrikaans websites testified to the emergence of a zappy new urban Afrikaner set.

I vaguely expected Bok to be a khaki-clad throwback to the past, the Afrikaner equivalent of the bearded young folk-rock stars who whipped up Serbian nationalism in the early nineties. Instead, he was a clean-cut young man who could have been a Scandinavian entrant in a 1970s Eurovision Song Contest. He was wearing bracelets, a crisp white T-shirt and ripped designer jeans, and was clearly bemused by the attention.

'Maybe it was a trigger for something bound to happen. My generation of Afrikaners wants to be proud of who we are, and where we come from, and our language. We grew up with the guilt of apartheid. We don't want to say sorry any more. We have moved on.' His contemporaries were fed up with being told that because they were white they were not eligible for a job. 'You walk into an interview and are told "Sorry". The younger generation says "Enough".'[13]

His focus on affirmative action and crime underlined the two trends that most clouded whites' perceptions of the new order and undermined their commitment to South Africa. It also highlighted how some whites were increasingly assailed by a siege mentality. In 2008 Eugene Terre'Blanche, who had been released from prison a few years earlier, was once again addressing rallies. His apocalyptic talk did not represent a threat to the state nor was the ageing racist appreciated by more than a fringe of whites. But his return to podiums before cheering crowds did reflect the same concerns that had fuelled the sales of the de la Rey song.

The ANC contends with some exasperation that it has acted with sensitivity towards Afrikaners and their symbols. Sometimes in Mbeki's second term in office there was an overhasty drive to change the name of a town or landmark. But in most cases there was an intense and public debate over the changing of names. The reaction to the de la Rey song was clearly about more than specifics. It reflected a broader sense of uncertainty and disquiet. Pallo Jordan, the minister of culture and arts, who was responsible for matters of 'national identity', laughed off the furore over the de la Rey song. 'Look, let the guy sing,' he told me. 'Who knows? It might become an international hit, although I don't think the tune is that great.' He broke off to muse about the parallels between Afrikaner and Appalachian music and gave a tuneful rendition of the old Scots-Irish folk ballad 'On Top of Old Smoky'. His measured approach to de la Rey was prudent politics, but Jordan was far from starry-eyed about the state of race relations. 'What did Oscar Wilde say? The truth is seldom simple and very rarely plain. The new South Africa is a work in progress. It hasn't come together. It hasn't gelled.' In particular he was worried about Afrikaners' insularity. The defensiveness over the future of the Afrikaans language reflected a resurgence of isolationism linked to a desire to be on a 'little island, on their own' rather than a genuine concern for the future of the language.[14]

The de la Rey phenomenon perplexed and troubled Carl Niehaus, one of the ANC's more prominent Afrikaners. He had been Mandela's spokesman in the early nineties, and his cropped blond hair and square-rimmed glasses can be seen just behind the ANC leader in much of the famous footage of that era. He fretted that Afrikaners were slipping back into the *laager* of ethnic identity, if they had ever left it.

'Bok has obviously touched a chord,' he said. 'How articulate those feelings are and how well thought through, I don't know. Part of this relates to a lack of understanding from young Afrikaners of where we come from. They somehow feel they are the victims of the sins of their fathers. They don't want to cope with or carry the baggage of the past.'[15]

After growing up in a small conservative town under apartheid, Niehaus had broken with his tribe to join the ANC and was still seen as something of an apostate by conservatives in his family. He was expelled from the Rand Afrikaans University as a student for his political activities. When his sister enrolled at the university a few years later, she was taunted as the sister of 'that communist'. Convicted of high treason in 1983, he was sentenced to fifteen years in prison. On the eve of his sentencing, an Afrikaner warder took him from his single cell to a communal cell, where he was assaulted by about twenty prisoners, a torment he only felt able to acknowledge in public more than a decade after his release.[16] Fourteen years after the end of white rule, his parents had still not come to terms with his politics.

Niehaus saw the song 'as a hankering for an idealised past where the Afrikaner was heroic and strong and didn't have to be apologetic for being an Afrikaner'. It was indicative of a dilemma, he said. How were Afrikaners to define themselves? Should they see themselves first as South Africans and then Afrikaners, or first as Afrikaners and then as South Africans? The de la Rey fans were right: there was no strong Afrikaner leader. But should there be? Niehaus believed that they were 'extraordinarily fortunate to be in a society that has worked through the ravages of apartheid and hasn't turned on the white community'.

It *was* remarkable that blacks had not turned on whites over the years. But, then again, the transition was a negotiated settlement that was designed to allay Afrikaners' concerns for the future and to ensure that whites had a home in the new country. A decade after the end of white rule, the guardians of Afrikaner culture feared this agreement was under threat. In particular they were unsettled over the steady diminution of Afrikaans. Nearly half of the 1,396 schools that taught solely in Afrikaans in 1993, the last full year of white rule, had by 2007 ceased to be Afrikaans-speaking. The University of Stellenbosch, the intellectual cradle of Afrikaner Nationalism, was one of several traditionally Afrikaans universities embroiled in a bitter fight over what should be the language of instruction. In 2002, in a bid to encourage more black students to apply for places, university authorities agreed English could be used for teaching in the first year of undergraduate courses.

Hermann Giliomee, a well-known conservative Afrikaner historian, was in the front line fighting against moves to dilute Afrikaans culture and Afrikaner history in founding South Africa. Sitting on his *stoep* in a quiet Stellenbosch suburb, as two teams of Afrikaner youths played rugby on the pristine grounds of a nearby school, in a scene unchanged for generations, he volunteered that a good 50 per cent of Afrikaners had done 'fairly well' in the post-apartheid era. But the bottom 25 per cent were 'really suffering', a reference to the 'poor whites', some of whom could be seen begging at traffic lights in cities.[17] The furore over the de la Rey song reflected, he contended, an inevitable clash between Afrikaners' need to assert their identity and a growing intolerance in the ANC. His concern for the survival of Afrikaans had recently intensified, when the police chief in the Western Cape said police statements should be in English. The province is home to the greatest concentration of Afrikaans speakers in the country, as it is dominated by people of mixed race. For many of them, Afrikaans is their mother tongue.

Giliomee took a conservative stance on Afrikaans at the university. Stellenbosch, perhaps more than any other university, had to show it had left behind a past in which it had been a tradition to ask the head of the National Party to be the chancellor. His position would in effect require a Nobel Laureate coming from abroad to learn to speak Afrikaans in two or three years so he could teach in it. The ANC said it showed he was unwilling to see Afrikaners interacting with people from other cultural and racial backgrounds. But Giliomee argued that shoring up Afrikaans at Stellenbosch was a vital part of sustaining Afrikaans and Afrikaners' history. He liked to quote the contention of Eli Wiesel, the Holocaust survivor, that 'to live without a past is worse than to live without a future'.

'The froth of the miracle has disappeared. Those Afrikaners who have decided to stay have said, "I need to know my roots, or I will get swept aside." They must know their history because the ANC's version is one of guilt and shame. It believes it must somehow restrain public discourse; it can't allow something surging up.' The de la Rey song had come just in time to encapsulate these concerns. 'It was a unique stroke of luck. It hit just the right note.'

As Bok's concert neared its climax, Kyle Esterhuyse and Shawn Luppa, both in their last year at high school, were in the queue for drinks at the makeshift bar at the Protea Park concert. They nearly belonged to what was known as the 'born free' generation. They had been five when white rule ended. Liberated from the stigma of apartheid, they could travel abroad at will without facing the hostile grilling their parents used to face. They exuded the good health of eighteen years growing up in relative affluence under bright sunny skies, but they were deeply disillusioned with the new South Africa.

'The blacks at our school act as if it's apartheid in reverse,' said Kyle. 'My girlfriend's aunt used to be a chartered accountant, and they gave her job away because she was white.'[18]

Shawn had been held up recently on his way home from the local shop. Kyle had the last word. Two days previously one of his neighbours had returned home to be confronted by men with guns who tied him up. Kyle was in his family's garden checking on their pet rabbits when he heard noises from next door. On investigating he found his neighbour bound and gagged. 'The police said they were planning on shooting him, but they must have heard me coming.'

Behind them Bok was singing one of his favourites, a riff mimicking Nelson Mandela supposedly welcoming his 'favourite singer of all time: Bok van Blerk'. Watching from the fringes were Kobus Koekemoer, a former civil servant who had been made redundant, and Conrad, his twenty-three-year-old son, a recent graduate from Potchefstroom University, one of the traditional centres of Afrikaner Nationalist thinking. Conrad had a defiant racial slogan scrawled on his baseball cap.

'Where is the Boer leader?' he asked. 'We need a leader. We just want someone to stand up for us.'

So how should whites respond to the new order? Should they speak out about their concerns? Or would it not be better – even safer – to keep a low profile, given their history as overlords? The dilemma over whether to atone for the past by staying out of politics has long vexed whites in post-colonial states. A handful decide to do their bit by putting their skills to use in education, the economy and social programmes. A few choose to engage in politics when they think that the government is stepping out of line. Most, however, decide to focus on making money and opt out of their country's daily life. The last is a tempting routine but not necessarily the wisest, although, as the years since independence have passed, many whites have concluded that whichever route they take, they will ultimately be penalised for their forefathers' role in the past.

The de la Rey song provided a catalyst for this debate for Afrikaners, who comprise two-thirds of South Africa's whites. It was a debate that had been played out acrimoniously across Africa since the end of colonial rule. Its course was vital for the future of South Africa.

There are no accurate figures for white emigration, still less for the Afrikaners. But the population of white South Africans has a striking characteristic: there are fewer in their twenties, thirties and forties than in their teens or in their fifties or older, the opposite trend to most First World population groups, which tend to be at their most numerous in those three middle decades. Demographers concluded that the twist reflected a steep rise in emigration among people in their twenties, thirties and forties. At the end of white rule there were an estimated 5.2 million whites in South Africa, including 3 million Afrikaners. A report extrapolated from official household surveys estimated that over three-quarters of a million whites emigrated in the decade after 1995. The report concluded that the white population had sunk from 5.1 million to 4.3 million between 1995 and 2005.[19] Given the history of whites in South Africa, some in the ANC openly said, 'Good riddance.' Such disdain was not just callous but also misguided. The emigrants tended to be the professionals the country badly needed to retain. It was estimated in 2008 that nearly one qualified engineer left South Africa every day,[20] at a time when municipalities and businesses were bemoaning the lack of engineers.

In Kenya and in Zimbabwe at independence, whites opted to abide by an informal compact with the government to keep clear of politics and abstain from criticising the government. As the Kenyan government became increasingly corrupt, Richard Leakey, the celebrated conservationist, was one of a few whites to break the 'compact' and get involved in opposition politics. He had worked with Daniel arap Moi, the country's second post-independence president, when he was head of Kenya's Wildlife Service between 1989 and 1994. Then they had a cordial relationship, but it changed dramatically when Leakey helped to form the opposition Safina Party. He was dubbed a racist and colonialist. His rallies were attacked. He was whipped and beaten by police officials.

A similar saga unfolded in Zimbabwe. After independence, most whites elected to stay out of politics. Many turned out in the first post-independence election to vote for the party of Ian Smith, the last leader of what had been known as Rhodesia. But once the constitutional clause guaranteeing whites a share of parliamentary seats lapsed, very few whites saw any point in voting, given the dominance of the ruling party. Then twenty years after independence, dismayed at the growing corruption and misgovernance, many joined, funded and campaigned for a new black-led opposition party, the Movement for Democratic Change. Heidi Holland, an acclaimed biographer of Mugabe, believes the old autocrat felt betrayed and thought that they had spurned the offer of reconciliation he had made on taking office.[21] His response was brutal. The majority of the country's 4,500 white farmers were driven off their land. The compact had been broken.

Whites were always likely to be more prominent in public life in South Africa than other African countries after independence. In 1994 South Africa had a far larger white minority, about 12 per cent of the population, than any other African state. But the vitriol that Tony Leon faced as the leader of the main opposition in South Africa for the first thirteen years of ANC government underlined the challenges that white politicians faced in the post-apartheid era. He took over the leadership of the Democratic Party shortly after the 1994 election, after it was all but eliminated at the polls, winning just seven seats and less than 2 per cent of the vote. The DP was the successor to Helen Suzman's original party and the inheritor of her outspoken liberal tradition. In her thirty-six years in Parliament, from 1953 to 1989, she infuriated the Nationalists with her probing questions. On average she asked two hundred questions a year. When accused by a minister of asking questions in Parliament that embarrassed South Africa, she famously replied, 'It is not my questions that embarrass South Africa; it is your answers.'[22]

After his release from prison Mandela frequently lauded her record. They had always had their disagreements, as both readily conceded. As a liberal she was opposed to the armed struggle and argued with Mandela about it when she visited him on Robben Island. But that did not affect their mutual admiration. Around the time of her ninetieth birthday, he called her out of the blue to ask if she had any of her oxtail stew on the simmer and promptly popped round to her flat for lunch.[23]

But under Mbeki, Suzman and her political tradition faced a more hostile hearing. His supporters sought to rewrite history by ignoring her contribution to the fight against apartheid and demonising her as a hypocrite steeped in a colonial mindset. In a book about Mbeki's philosophy of government, Ronald Suresh Roberts, a Trinidadian and sometime government adviser, referred to Suzman repeatedly as 'illiberal'.[24] The book provided one of the more convincing insider accounts of Mbeki's thinking. Mbeki's white critics were depicted as imbued with nineteenth-century stereotypes of blacks as 'inscrutable natives'. His black critics were seen as pandering to their old colonial overlords and failing to throw off the yoke of subservience. As for Suzman's political successors, they were 'illiberal' opportunists.

While the criticism of the white liberals was unfair, the idea of a contrast between bluff Afrikaners, who were true Africans and who were at least racist to your face, and English speakers, who had one foot in Europe, was not a mere political contrivance. Under white rule there were many hypocritical liberals. My first Johannesburg landlady appeared to personify the breed. She was an academic who abhorred apartheid and its enforcers. As she showed me round her house in 1993, I became aware that we were not alone. From time to time a short black woman in a matching yellow tunic and skirt slipped into my peripheral vision. Once we almost bumped into her, but she slipped away before anyone spoke. Near the end of the tour I was ushered into a walk-in cupboard. The same shadowy woman was head down picking up some cleaning equipment. My landlady-to-be barged past her, pointed out the contents of the cupboard, turned and shut the door. She was striding away to show me the garden when she realised her mistake and returned to open the door.

Briefly the woman met my gaze. She moved out of the cupboard at an ever so slightly sluggish pace. Her face was blank – not sullen but several shades short of a smile. It was, I came to appreciate, the form of unimpeachable protest that many black South Africans chose to adopt against their employers. On the day of the handover of her home, the landlady let her guard slip. Sometimes, she explained, when she was feeling a little sleepy, she used a dog whistle to summon an early-morning cup of tea.

My landlady was better than many employers. She had rescued her maid from a nightmarish former 'madam' and had allowed her husband to share her room at the back of the house at a time when it was against the apartheid laws. And yet for the first four years of employment, her maid was expected to work from 7 a.m. to 8 p.m. Monday to Friday, from 7 to 10 on Saturday mornings, and from 8 to 9 on Sunday mornings. This meant it was impossible for her to spend more than an afternoon a week, on Saturday, with her children, who lived two hours away in a homeland township. She worked for eleven years without a pension.

Such stories chimed with the view of many in the ANC that at least Afrikaners tended to be open about their views. Mbeki in particular liked to make much of the idea, most strikingly when he delivered a bizarre eulogy to P. W. Botha, the hard-line Nationalist leader of the eighties. Botha and Oliver Tambo had been 'partners in the peace of the brave that is our blessing', he wrote.[25] Botha had started to reform apartheid, relaxing the Group Areas Act and lifting a ban on interracial marriage, but his response to protests was ruthless. During his presidency thousands were detained without trial and many tortured. Mbeki's paean to him can be seen only in the context of the change in the political climate. The Afrikaner Nationalists had accepted defeat and disbanded. The white liberals, however, continued to champion open and accountable government, highlighting scandals, wrongdoing and poor policies. Mbeki's riposte was to accuse them of racism. He once wrote that white liberals 'remain the colonial boots of the colonial "mother" who has to stamp her foot down hard to frighten the native "child" into cowering obedience'.[26] The criticism of one man in particular infuriated him: the opposition leader, Tony Leon.

From early in the first post-apartheid session of Parliament, Leon made it clear that he would not pull his punches. A hyper-confident former lawyer, he had, his friends conceded, an extraordinary ability to irritate politicians, and not just in other parties. He had a spectacular row with Suzman after he ran for and won the party primary for her constituency, defeating one of her oldest friends. On taking over the Democratic Party after the 1994 election, he upset many of its traditional members by the vehemence of his criticism of the ANC. By coming down hard on the ANC from its first days in office, he sounded, at times, insensitive to the racial overtones of a white man hectoring a black-led government. His natural style was pugnacious, he later conceded. But he had set his sights on refashioning the party and overtaking the National Party as the main opposition. He also believed that his best service to South Africa was to keep the ruling party on its toes, and by exposing scandals and humbug over AIDS, Zimbabwe and black economic empowerment, he performed an invaluable service to South Africa's democracy.

Five years after the 1994 election, the Democratic Party became the largest opposition party, with 9.6 per cent of the vote. In 2004 it increased its share of the vote again to just over 12 per cent. The success came at a price. To entice Nationalist supporters from their old political home, he ran an aggressive anti-ANC campaign in 1999 under the slogan 'Fight Back', for which he was accused of pandering to nostalgia for white rule. Old liberals lamented his repositioning of the party to the right. Leon was unapologetic. 'I took over a bankrupt shell, and I set out to grow the party,' he said on the eve of his retirement as leader in 2007. 'Maybe it wasn't appreciated, but, frankly, to have a good relationship between the opposition and government is nice, but I don't think it's an essential precondition. The party had to grow, and in order to grow it had to change.'²⁷

The difficulty Leon faced was how to avoid sounding like the representative of a privileged white minority seeking to retain past advantages. If South Africa was to have a truly non-racial democracy, there had to be a place in politics for a member of the former ruling race. But after years of enforced racial division, it was always going to take time to break down the polarisation of the electorate, which in the first three non-racial elections broadly split down racial lines, with the overwhelming majority of ANC votes coming from blacks and the majority of votes for the Democratic Party and its successor coming from the white, Asian and mixed-race minorities. Pallo Jordan, the veteran ANC intellectual, argues that in the first fifteen years after the end of white rule the Democratic Alliance painted itself into being a party of 'white irreconcilables'.

The party's natural area for growth among the black community should be the property-owning classes and the business elite, he said. 'But every time they [the DA] open their mouths about the black businessmen, it's just to put them down and curse them and say they are scoundrels and thieves and disreputable. It might well be that some are, but if there are scoundrels, you pick them out; you don't say the whole appear like that. Which black business person would feel comfortable voting DA? They will say, "Fuck you. We won't vote for you."' The other obvious group would be the educated elite, yet the DA opposed affirmative action. 'So why should the educated elite vote for them? They've placed a glass ceiling on their growth and that's why it is unfortunate, because at the end of the day, even people who don't necessarily like the ANC end up voting for it.'²⁸

For him to dub as 'irreconcilables' the white liberals, who had opposed apartheid, rather than the Afrikaner Nationalists, who had imposed it, was extraordinary and unfair. Yet having ousted the National Party as the main opposition, the DA did face a harder challenge of having to break out of its racial electoral straitjacket by attracting significant numbers of black voters. It had to have a black leader if it were to be a contender for power rather than a mere pressure group, as it was under apartheid. But while there were many weaknesses in the ANC's record that the DA's MPs could exploit in parliamentary debates, it was far harder to convert those victories into a sizeable black support base. The few prominent black members the DA enticed over the years to its ranks faced relentless accusations of racial treachery from the ANC and inducements to defect.

'The pressures that black people come under when they join the DA are quite unbelievable,' Leon said. 'They get vicious anonymous notes from ANC MPs. They are put into Coventry in the parliamentary villages. They are treated as sort of enemies of the people.'[29]

An even greater test for South Africa's democracy, however, was the ANC's attitude towards white opposition politicians. Mandela set a good precedent. He was sometimes infuriated by Leon's jibes. He once referred to the opposition parties as 'Mickey Mouse organisations', prompting a tart retort from Leon that Mandela ran a 'Goofy' government. But Mandela never suggested that by virtue of the colour of his skin Leon was not entitled to be heard. He consulted him on policy as an opposition party leader. Famously, when Leon was in hospital for heart surgery, Mandela paid him an unnannounced visit, alerting him to his presence by saying in a loud voice outside the door to his ward, 'Hello Mickey Mouse, this is Goofy. Can I come in?'[30]

Under Mbeki, however, there was an influential Africanist wing in the ANC that shared Mugabe's view that whites should not be involved in politics and indeed were not truly Africans. Vibrant opposition politics was clearly essential for keeping the flame of multiparty democracy alive. By the end of his tenure, Leon believed that the ANC had grudgingly come to accept that the Democratic Alliance was part of the political landscape. But it had been 'quite a hard swim in waters that are ethnic and racially nationalist'.[31] In December 2000, as the DA appeared to be gaining momentum, Joel Netshitenzhe, one of Mbeki's closest advisers, gave an intriguing insight into official thinking when he described the DA as 'undermining the state'.[32]

It was not just opposition MPs who sensed this hostility to whites in politics. Under Mbeki's leadership many whites in the ANC felt cast aside. There were exceptions. Two of Mbeki's most loyal ministers – Ronnie Kasrils, an old friend from exile, and Alec Erwin, a former trade unionist – were white. But many other prominent whites in the ANC, including Carl Niehaus, were sidelined by Mbeki. Niehaus was an ANC MP in the first non-racial Parliament.

Yet just five years after the advent of democracy, he found he was an outcast from the leadership of the ANC.

'Some of the positions taken by people around Thabo led to a lot of white people feeling there wasn't an environment that made them feel comfortable in the ANC,' Niehaus said. He could understand Mbeki's frustration with white attitudes and believed that many whites had not 'made the jump into accepting a multiracial country'. But there was a sudden, almost indefinable shift in approach to whites in the ANC when Mbeki succeeded Mandela. 'It was like a change of temperature. People felt alienated, and it pushed them away.' It later emerged that Niehaus had committed fraud when working for the government of Gauteng, the Johannesburg and Pretoria metropolitan area, and had had to resign from a job in the presidency under a cloud. But his account of a strong Africanist impulse in Mbeki's presidency was not disputed.

After the ANC forced Mbeki to resign from the presidency in August 2008, Niehaus resumed a career in the party and served as the party's chief spokesman. His rehabilitation, before having to resign in 2009 because of the corruption revelations, reflected the more easy-going non-racialism espoused by Zuma. But Leon's successor as DA leader, Helen Zille, a redoubtable former journalist who had as a young reporter helped to expose the official cover-up related to the death of Steve Biko, was subjected to the same rancid name-calling that her predecessor had faced under Mbeki. In 2008 she was accused of being a 'counter-revolutionary' and a backer of apartheid for opposing the ANC's attempts to close down the Scorpions elite anti-corruption unit.

She was undaunted. She would not 'go soft' on the ANC, she said.[33] Her exchanges with the ANC highlighted how South Africa had been more successful than other African countries in accepting white involvement in adversarial politics. But if a healthy democracy was to take root, three things needed to happen: the Democratic Alliance to become blacker, the ANC to become more tolerant to opposition criticism, and whites to become more involved in the lives of their black compatriots, whether through local government, community policing or schools. The post-independence history of Zimbabwe contained an implicit warning for white South Africans. White Zimbabwean farmers thought the country could not do without them because of the scale of their contribution to the economy; they thought they were fireproof from criticism. But that argument did not endure when the country hit difficult times and they became the regime's scapegoats.

Chapter 7

THE NEW RANDLORDS

I don't think I will ever be a common businessman.
In my heart of hearts I am a freedom fighter.

— TOKYO SEXWALE,
POLITICAL PRISONER
TURNED BILLIONAIRE, JUNE 2007

There is nothing wrong with being 'filthy rich'.

— PHUMZILE MLAMBO-NGCUKA,
DEPUTY MINISTER OF TRADE AND INDUSTRY

When the Queen Mother of the Royal Bafokeng Nation strode through the foyer of the single-storey office block that serves as the *legato* (royal palace), members of staff jumped to their feet and muttered 'Mmemogolo' (Queen Mother) just as the Bafokeng have to the mother of their nation for hundreds of years. While she was dressed simply in African-print cloth, she had a regal air, and no wonder. After her marriage as a young woman to the last king but two, for more than thirty years she was queen of the Bafokeng's traditional rural community of some three hundred thousand people in South Africa's north-western bush. Following the death of her husband in 1995, and then in quick succession a few years later the deaths of her two eldest sons, one of suspected

AIDS and the other in a car accident, her third son, age forty, ascended the throne. She was, in traditional African circles, roughly the equivalent of a dowager duchess. Then again, in early 2008, the kingdom had recently acquired a multibillion-dollar fortune in platinum-mining stock, and 'industrial grandee' or 'heiress' might be a more appropriate tag.

The Bafokeng's homeland, a tract of about 1,200 square kilometres northwest of Johannesburg, looks no different from the scrubby bush that blankets much of southern Africa. For hundreds of years the Bafokeng eked out an existence there, tending their livestock and fending off most invaders through a mixture of diplomacy and guile. Only the hardiest Afrikaners trekking north from the Cape in the nineteenth century chose to settle there. Yet the Bafokeng kingdom also happens to sit on a section of a two-billion-year-old rock formation that contains nearly three-quarters of the world's known platinum reserves. Mining companies started full-scale production there in the 1960s, but it was only at the end of the twentieth century that the Bafokeng won their share of the area's fabulous wealth. After decades of legal battles, in 1999, the tribe won from Impala Platinum, the world's second largest platinum miner, the rights to an equitable share of the royalties from the platinum mined on their land. Seven years later, the Bafokeng went a stage further and negotiated a deal to convert the royalty payments into shares. Its 13.2 per cent stake was the crown jewel in a community-based investment fund, which at the end of May 2008 was valued at $4.9 billion.

The Bafokeng had become one of the wealthier tribes on the continent. Decades of injustice dating back through apartheid to the colonial era had been overturned. It was one of the most dramatic events in the financial revolution that was essential in South Africa if the handover of political power was to have real meaning.

The Queen Mother was the first to concede that gaining the rights to the wealth was only a first step towards rectifying the inequalities of the past. Fortunately for the Bafokeng, she did not appear to have a taste for the profligacy that has seduced so many rulers who have come unexpectedly into extraordinary wealth. With its orange-foam chairs and stack of magazines, her reception area had the no-nonsense feel of a dentist's surgery. Outlining health and education initiatives, she came across as more of a management consultant than a matriarch. It is an analogy that fitted the vision of her son the *kgosi* (king), who was endeavouring to impose a corporate structure on the nation's finances. He was in charge of an extraordinary hybrid: the Bafokeng were, in the words of one of his advisers, part tribe, part development agency and part global commodity corporation.

The Queen Mother chuckled to recall the opening of the mines in the sixties, a repressive era when apartheid was at its height. 'I was a young woman, just married. As for the administration of the tribe, there was just my late husband and an elderly man who was general secretary. I was secretary number two and typist at all times. In those days the mines didn't mean much. All you could hear was that the mines had occupied our arable lands, our ploughing lands . . . And there were no women whatsoever at the mines then, just men, living in hostels. So when they saw a skirt, they would just shout. One particular day they came out shouting when I passed. And someone stopped them and said, "Don't do that. Don't you know she is the chief's wife?" And they said: "Ah. She is also a woman." They had no shower blocks in those days. They would just come out with towels round their waists and stare.

'So you can see how far we have come. Women are now allowed on the mines and in the accommodation. The men are working peacefully. They no longer shout.' She paused for effect. 'Now they have to stop when I pass!'¹

Phokeng bore striking architectural testimony to the tribe's changed circumstances: in a few years it had become the capital of Africa's equivalent of a Gulf oil principality. Before 1999 the town was little more than a few streets of tin-roofed box houses and a handful of municipal buildings fringed by informal settlements that petered out in the bush. Nine years later, the skyline was dominated by cranes and, in pride of place, the stylish modern profile of the civic centre, the new administrative headquarters. It was the work of a Singaporean firm of consultants, who worked with the *kgosi*, a qualified architect. In a gesture to Bafokeng traditions, it was adorned with the nation's ancestral symbol, a crocodile with a closed mouth and a lowered tail, which according to local folklore signals a desire for peace. The top floor of the civic centre looked out onto the platinum smelters and mine-heads that testified to the nation's wealth.

South Africa had its diamond rush in what is now Kimberley in the 1860s, and then its gold rush in what is now Johannesburg in the 1880s. In the early years of the twenty-first century, as those industries in South Africa waned, with the remaining known deposits ever deeper and more dangerous to mine, Phokeng was enjoying a platinum rush on the back of soaring global demand for the metal for catalytic converters.

The Queen Mother was not, she insisted, resting on her laurels and was all too aware of the 'mineral curse'. Rather than leading to prosperity, great mineral wealth has frequently led to the enrichment of a few and also to conflict. War is out of the question in the land of the Bafokeng, in its remote corner of South Africa. Ensuring, however, that the benefits of this transfer of wealth from the traditionally white-run and white-owned mining companies trickle down to the people is a challenge. South Africa's mixed experience of Black Economic Empowerment (BEE), the policy designed to redress the financial inequities of apartheid, offered salutary lessons. While the justice and strategic wisdom of a transfer of stakes in white companies to black entities are indisputable, a decade after the end of white rule the initiative was tarnished by perceptions that the principal beneficiaries were an elite with good connections to the ANC.

'There have been a lot of mistakes on the way,' the Queen Mother said of the Bafokeng's handling of its wealth. 'As I keep telling the women of the nation: If we spend all the money, what will happen tomorrow? We must always think about that. The platinum is not our wealth. Our wealth is through leadership. That's why I am saying that we have to be on our knees all the time to say, "Please, Lord, do whatever You do, but make sure that we remain focused. If we get a leader who is not focused, we could go backwards to where we came from."'

It is a humility that some in the ANC would have done well to bear in mind.

Few people talk more forcefully and colourfully about the need to spread South Africa's wealth to the 'formerly disadvantaged' than Tokyo Sexwale. Then again, few if any have benefited more from what the former freedom fighter and political prisoner would call the second stage of the struggle. Fifteen years into majority rule his business empire straddled mining, liquid fuels, property and the media; encompassed interests in Africa; and, his aides suggested, was worth between $3 and $4 billion. His ascent to such fabulous riches, occurring in just a decade after he left formal politics in 1998, encapsulates the triumph and yet also the compromises of the Black Economic Empowerment programme.

In 1993, Sexwale was voted South Africa's sexiest politician on Radio 702, Johannesburg's main talk-radio station whose prime audience was white housewives, for whom for long years the name Sexwale meant 'terrorist'. He combined charm with charisma, and his capacity for empathy was never more apparent than when he was one of the first on the scene of the assassination of his friend and commander, Chris Hani, the hugely popular leader of the Communist Party. Sexwale wept openly over Hani's body in the suburban street, where he had been shot dead by a white extremist.

Even then, as the country teetered on the brink of anarchy in 1993, he was looking ahead to the challenges of government. The most difficult issue facing the ANC, he argued, was not writing a constitution or a bill of rights but bringing black South Africans into the economy. 'We're not represented in primary sectors of economy, such as mining and banking,' he said. 'There's not one single black man in this country in mining.' If that did not change there would be an uprising. 'I have the feeling that the horses' hooves are behind us. Right now they are soft feet, but the sounds are frightening.'[2]

After 1994 he assumed one of the most powerful positions in the country as the premier of the central Gauteng province, the engine room of southern Africa's economy. Unlike some of his more ideological comrades, Sexwale was at ease with business people. He even garlanded his political speeches with corporate metaphors. On the first anniversary of the April 1994 election, he introduced Mandela to a crowd as 'our director of the company that is the new South Africa'. For a year or so after the election he even aspired to succeed Mandela. But he was outmanoeuvred by Mbeki, and in the wake of a smear campaign in 1998, he stepped back from the fray and resigned to go into business. He had been 'deployed' to the corporate sector. He was going 'humbly to join those black people at this rock-face of change'.[3]

His business partners stoutly maintain that he was always a businessman at heart. They recall his role in a prototype black empowerment company that was set up by ANC officials in 1992. When he left politics, he set up a board in a games room at his home and drew on it an 'organogram' of how he saw his business unfolding. He was then relying on the income from his wife's fast-food franchise. His domestic finances were so straitened, one former colleague says, that he could barely pay his staff. Unlike most other aspirational entrepreneurs across the world, however, Sexwale had a trump: BEE.

Sexwale's knowledge of business was minimal. When in the early seventies contemporaries in the West who aspired to become captains of industry were learning the ropes at a corporation, he was studying guerrilla tactics in Moscow; on his return to South Africa in 1976 he was captured by the South African police. He spent the following thirteen years on Robben Island.

Even if he had opted for a quiet life and stayed out of the struggle, he would have found it all but impossible to apply his talents to a career in business. Apartheid did not just deny political and social rights. It also aimed to exclude black South Africans from business by impeding the development of a black middle class. The figures for state investment for helping putative black businesses in the tribal homelands were dwarfed by the financial support the state gave to white businesses on the borders of the homelands. Against the odds a few black entrepreneurs built businesses in the townships. But when white minority rule ended in 1994, the boardrooms, where South Africa's economic power was wielded, remained much as they had in the century since the foundation of the Johannesburg Stock Exchange: white-led, white-owned and primarily with whites' interests at heart. It was this as much as the domination of the bureaucracy by Afrikaners that led many in the ANC to mutter a few years into majority rule that they were in power but did not wield power and drove their determination to implement a black empowerment policy.

The premise of Black Economic Empowerment in its first incarnation was simple: white businesses would be encouraged to transfer stakes to new black entities. The pressure was part moral and part financial. BEE deals would be a way for companies to make amends for the depredations of the past. It would also be a way of proving their commitment to the new era. As business people were all too aware, compliance offered a chance of safeguarding their interests and securing future contracts. At its simplest it was a question of businesses handing over a stake to a fledgling black entity at a favourable price in return for being left alone. As mining houses and banks cast around urgently for credible partners to give them political cover, it was the perfect time for ANC grandees to be leaving politics and going into business even if they did not have a clue about balance sheets. 'I was a novice in terms of real hard business transactions,' Sexwale said years later. 'You have to learn on your toes.'[4]

Sexwale's staff from his days as premier have no doubt that politics, not business, was his obsession. But he did have Mandela's backing, and indeed more significantly, given how little Mandela knew about business, he had solicited the advice of Harry Oppenheimer, the industrial magnate and for many years the richest businessman in Africa. Buoyed by these encounters Sexwale was even then confiding to associates that he aspired to be the first black Oppenheimer.

Oppenheimer was one of the legendary dynasts of the twentieth century. His father, Sir Ernest, was one of the early mining grandees who founded the Anglo American Corporation in 1917. Harry was to build it into a conglomerate that not just dominated gold and diamond mining but had a major stake in just about every sector of the South African economy. His success reflected his canniness as well as South Africa's needs under apartheid, as the economy adjusted to the pressures of sanctions and international isolation. He ran Anglo American much as Sir Alfred Milner, who, as British high commissioner, had run the Cape colony at the turn of the twentieth century with an elite inner circle of Oxbridge graduates. In its heyday it was responsible for about a quarter of South Africa's economic output. 'You couldn't get up in the morning in suburban Johannesburg without coming in contact with Anglo,' one senior employee recalled of the eighties. 'The newspaper on your breakfast table, the cardboard on the cereal packet, the sugar in your teacup – all were products of an Anglo subsidiary.'[5]

In the last years of white rule, to be the chief executive of Anglo American conferred on you the authority of a cabinet minister or the Reserve Bank governor. Every drama in the frenetic final decade of apartheid led to a statement from Anglo's imposing headquarters in central Johannesburg seeking to steer the country back from the brink. The company infuriated the National Party in 1985, when its chief executive led a delegation of businessmen to Zambia to meet the ANC's exiled leaders. It was Anglo that provided a plane for the Kenyan mediator who at the last minute persuaded Chief Mangosuthu Buthelezi, the leader of the Inkatha Freedom Party, to drop secessionist threats and take part in the April 1994 election. Mandela had regular conversations with Harry O, as he was known, at the Oppenheimers' Johannesburg home, Brenthurst. A palatial residence with one of the most rarefied gardens in sub-Saharan Africa, it was reminiscent of the grand East Coast estates of the nine-teenth-century US industrial barons.

But how was Sexwale to achieve his dream of attaining a similar status? Less than a decade after leaving formal politics, he was holding forth in a handsome villa overlooking Houghton, one of the grander Johannesburg suburbs, where many of the early randlords, including the Oppenheimers, had had their homes and where he had the headquarters of his Mvelaphanda Group, a min-ing and resources holding company. In the nine years since its launch he had become one of the richest men in South Africa. He had also become some-thing of a social grandee and was a popular member on the corporate dinner-party circuit. He had long been confident he could hold his own in social chit-chat on literature and the arts. In Johannesburg circles he teased his hosts that he knew more about Shakespeare than they did, having read the entire canon when he was on Robben Island. He and his white wife, Judy, whom he met and fell in love with when she was a legal clerk and he was on death row, were the toast of the exclusive corporate set.

He had acquired for himself a Croesan fortune and at vertiginous speed, but not without controversy.

Indigenisation programmes had been enacted across Africa in the decades of decolonisation, and usually with disastrous results. Aware of these poor precedents, the ANC was determined, as it prepared to take power, to move more judiciously. There were two prototypes that particularly interested the ANC in the early nineties, as it started to consider what form BEE should take. In 1994, the year of liberation, Thomas Nkobi, the veteran ANC treasurer, who was legendary in the struggle years for travelling around the world with an empty suitcase beseeching sympathetic rulers for funds, embarked on a series of visits to Kuala Lumpur. His attention had been caught by a long-standing programme in Malaysia aimed at bridging its wealth and ethnic divide.[6] In the wake of race riots in 1969 the government had implemented a programme known as *bumiputra* or 'sons of the soil', which was aimed at narrowing the wealth gap between the 37 per cent Chinese minority, who dominated local business, and the remainder of the population, including the 52 per cent Malay majority and indigenous people. Businesses were to have a *bumiputra* partner with a 30 per cent equity stake. Affirmative action programmes were to give them preferential access to university places and state jobs.

The policy became increasingly controversial over the years. Economists suggested it was hampering the country's growth prospects and needed to be brought to an end. Chinese complained they were suffering from a form of apartheid and emigrated by the thousands. Even many of the intended beneficiaries started to weary of the policy, as it emerged in time that the main beneficiaries were not the poor but an oligarchy and their hangers-on, who won the bulk of government contracts and share allocations in the private sector. But the Malaysian policy did succeed in its primary objective of reducing poverty among Malays and creating a class of ethnic Malaysian business people. In 1994 it was still seen as a success and regarded by the ANC as a viable model for what South Africa needed to do, as the country embarked on one of the most ambitious transfers of wealth in modern history.

The other model for the ANC was closer to home and came from none other than the old enemy, the Afrikaner Nationalists. When the National Party swept to power in 1948, it capitalised on a grievance among poor Afrikaners that they were on the margins of the economy and were second-class citizens compared to the English-speaking whites. It swiftly implemented a far-reaching affirmative action programme for the civil service and state bodies, such as the post office and railways. It also set up Afrikaner-dominated insurance companies and banks. These were aimed at the economic upliftment of the *volk* but also more fundamentally the vanquishing of the images of poor Afrikaners scrabbling to eke out an existence that had so often in the past illustrated international magazines' articles about South Africa. Afrikaners were to hold their heads high in boardrooms and no longer be mocked as uncultured halfwits, as they had been traditionally by the English-speaking business elite.

Thabo Mbeki's father, Govan, cited the success of the Afrikaners in setting up businesses as a possible prototype for South Africa.[7] He reached this conclusion a year after the unbanning of the ANC, as party ideologues were still arguing over the merits of nationalisation. Thabo's younger brother, Moeletsi, argued, however, that that the Afrikaner model for BEE was adopted far too enthusiastically and that it was rather more successful on paper than in practice.

The younger Mbeki looks and sounds very like his more famous brother, the president. Yet on several of the signature policies of the Mbeki government the two had very different views. Moeletsi was especially outspoken over the initial phase of BEE, which he dismissed as little more than a cosy compact between white business and the political elite. The former benefited, he suggested, because they retained control of their companies, as BEE deals required the transfer of only minority stakes. By cooperating with the government, businesses also hoped to pre-empt more radical measures, such as nationalisation. The political elite benefited by becoming stupendously wealthy. But South Africa was the loser, as it amounted to nothing more than a crude asset transfer and, rather than fostering a new black entrepreneurial class, encouraged an expectation of handouts.

Moeletsi was first involved in planning BEE in 1991, when he was working for Cosatu, the trade union federation, in Johannesburg. There were then regular meetings with business leaders to plot the way forward. At one of these the then director of the department of trade and industry outlined a simple plan for black economic empowerment, calling for white businesses to transfer a shareholding to a black business entity. This was, it transpired, the blueprint for the first wave of BEE.

'There were no bells and whistles in the [initial] policy, no requirements for training black staff or anything,' Moeletsi Mbeki recalls. 'It was to be purely asset transfer. I said, "This is not what we want. We want to put pressure on blacks to become entrepreneurs." I argued this asset transfer was a disincentive.'[8]

He concluded the ANC had been seduced by white business into joining their 'club' without really analysing how best to create a black business class. He later learned that one of the initiators of that approach was a manager of Sanlam, one of the giant Afrikaner financial houses founded in the National Party's economic empowerment drive. The manager happened to be the brother of the National Party's finance minister, Barend du Plessis. 'There was no black input into BEE,' Moeletsi Mbeki argued. 'It was handed to the ANC by Afrikaners who wanted to co-opt them into their world.'

His judgement is bracing. BEE, after all, had to start somehow and quickly. But he is right to be jaundiced: the early history of BEE was dismal. The larger

white businesses swiftly learned after 1994 how to navigate and take charge of
the new world of black economic empowerment. In the mid- to late nineties
several initiated BEE deals, clearly aware it was prudent to try to pre-empt
potentially more radical measures. Cyril Ramaphosa, the former ANC secretary
general, was the most prominent beneficiary of this impulse. He was at the centre
of the country's first important empowerment deal, leading the successful bid by
a black investment consortium[9] to take over Johnnic, an industrial holding
company in Anglo American's stable.

The deal was to be a BEE prototype. Anglo sold its stake off at a generous
discount of 6 per cent of its market value. Ramaphosa became chairman. The
banks lent the new shareholders money to buy their stakes. The shares in turn
were the collateral for the debt. The assumption was that the share price would
keep rising, ensuring the debt payments were easily met. It was hailed as one of
the great South African deals and all but presented as yet another chapter in
the fairy tale of the rainbow nation. The lustre of the deal was dulled by only a
few sceptics, who suggested the deal said more about Anglo American's need
to ingratiate itself with the new regime than about a genuine bid to create a
black business class.

Sexwale was one of half a dozen would-be magnates starting a business career
at this time. Soon after leaving politics in 1998, he embarked on a series of deals
with mining companies, the first of which was orchestrated by Brett Kebble, the
mining magnate who, it was later to emerge, was embroiled in corruption
scandals and had distributed largesse to prominent ANC figures.

The Johnnic deal swiftly proved something of a false dawn. One of the few
who prospered substantially from the deal was Dr Nthato Motlana, a veteran
member of Soweto's business establishment who was Mandela's doctor and a
co-founder of the consortium that took over Johnnic. Motlana made a fortune
from this and other deals. Mandela once quipped that if he wanted to contact
his doctor, he had to call the Johannesburg Stock Exchange.[10] But Motlana appreciated that black economic empowerment might prove rather more complex
and controversial than was broadly understood on the sunny morning when
Ramaphosa announced he was going into business.

'We black businessmen have been attacked because it is said black empowerment means empowerment of the few,' Motlana said two months after the deal.
'And then when you don't succeed, people look at you and say, "Oh look at that

so-and-so. He couldn't make it." If blacks are recipients of largesse, then nothing will come of empowerment. If we sit back and wait for manna, we won't be a successful nation.'[11]

His comments were slightly disingenuous, given the riches he had made from BEE, but they were prescient. Within a few years Johnnic was a shadow of its former self. Many of the new shareholders were unable to meet their debt payments after a crash on the Johannesburg Stock Exchange (JSE); the Asian financial crisis in the late nineties eviscerated share prices and the per centage of black ownership on the JSE. The sorry saga was repeated several times in that period, as other newly 'empowered' companies went bust or struggled to stay afloat. It was a reminder that it is rather difficult to create value out of nothing, which is effectively what the original deal-makers had sought to do.

The caustic commentary to be heard in some conservative white business circles that the new consortium had not been up to the task was a little unfair. They had also been victims of the plunging market. But the new owners of Johnnic had made a series of poor strategic decisions for the company. When it was taken over in 2005, it had nothing left of its original portfolio of assets but a casino and hotels' group, and Johnnic was seen as a BEE cautionary tale. Few of the new black investors had made any money. As for the original black investment consortium, it had become a byword for having done little beyond enriching a few.

Moeletsi Mbeki and other critics of BEE are unsympathetic. Mbeki compared early BEE deals to the strategy of the British colonists on their arrival in the Eastern Cape region in the 1830s: divide and rule. After backing the Boers in the battles against the local Xhosa tribes, the British decided the war was unwinnable. So instead they went for a policy of co-option and split the Xhosas.

As he explained it, 'British missionaries persuaded one side to defect and to take their rivals' cattle, and then they could not go back, as they were seen as thieves. They had become totally compromised. This is what has happened to someone like Cyril Ramaphosa. He is a former trade unionist. I don't know what trade unions think of him, but I can guess. They [the moguls] can't be role models when they have just been given something. They are not role models. In fact the great majority suspects them of selling out.'

BEE, he continued, far from fuelling the creation of an entrepreneurial black middle class, was encouraging a culture of dependency and expectation. 'This new black middle class, what does it do? Where do they get their money from? I know they are not industrialists. There are very few accountants, very few engineers. The consequence of BEE is that blacks are perennial victims.'

That is the flaw that lay at the heart of BEE, both the initial model that relied entirely on asset transfers, and a subsequent more equitable version that compelled businesses to go beyond doling out shares to a prominent member of the ANC. BEE encouraged people to parlay political influence but not to build a career.

Cyril Ramaphosa raises an eyebrow at such a critique, which is as close as he comes to expressing strong disagreement. By dint of his political record he is the unofficial leader of the BEE tycoons. In a crowded field he is also the most urbane of the ANC leaders. His is not the old-fashioned Henry James-era charm of Mbeki, nor the back-slapping George W. Bush style of Sexwale. It is subtler and so more seductive. He deployed this to great effect in negotiations over setting up unions in the eighties and in the constitutional talks in the early nineties. Yet there is steel behind the congenial exterior, as mine owners and National Party negotiators had learned to their cost. While Ramaphosa had a patchy record as a businessman, leading some to query whether his heart was really in the clinching of deals, few doubted his desire to reform BEE. He chaired a commission on BEE in 2000, at a time when the policy faced mounting criticism, and pushed for legislation to reform the policy. In the nineties he visited Zimbabwe several times to learn from its experience of black economic empowerment. He returned appalled at the crony capitalism, he says. The Zimbabwean government had not formalised a policy but rather had allowed corruption to flourish. South Africa had to go down a different route.[12]

The commission, backed by Mbeki, led to a renewed impetus behind black economic empowerment. Amid concern in the ANC that BEE was not achieving the desired results, the government moved to formalise what had previously been a voluntary process. In 2003, a charter for the mining industry decreed that 15 per cent of the equity of mining houses had to be in black control by 2008 and 26 per cent by 2013. Those that did not comply would not have their old mining licences renewed.[13] The financial sector came up with its own guidelines. But notwithstanding this new drive to codify the process, in the early years of the twenty-first century, as the policy unfolded, BEE remained intensely controversial.

While there was still a pressing moral and strategic reason to transfer business stakes from white to black ownership, it soon became clear that most of the beneficiaries were former politicians with close ties to the party who brought little to their businesses beyond their name. The best-known half-dozen were dubbed the 'usual suspects' for their regular involvement in empowerment deals. One of them was Patrice Motsepe, who founded African Rainbow Minerals, South Africa's first black-owned mining company, and was named the country's first black billionaire by *Forbes* magazine in 2008, with a net worth of $2.4 billion. Motsepe was regularly cited as a genuine deal-making businessman. He had started his career as a lawyer and not in politics. He liked to recall how he learned business beside his father, who ran a successful grocery chain. But the successful arc of even his business cannot be seen outside the prism of politics. His family was closely connected to the ANC. One of his sisters was married to an ANC cabinet minister, ran her own empowerment company and was one of South Africa's richest black businesswomen.

Sexwale liked to laugh off talk of the 'usual suspects' and insisted that he remained at heart a campaigner for social justice. The size of his chequebook and the contents of his pockets, he said, did not determine the size of his social conscience. He liked to remind unionists that Engels had been a capitalist, not a worker, and his businesses had provided Karl Marx with access to printing presses for *Das Kapital*. 'We must be very careful not to say a business person cannot play an important role in society,' Sexwale said. 'My history speaks for myself. It is the history of a freedom fighter. My people understand where I come from.'[14] He had always been known for his soaring rhetoric. But such claims by the tycoons to have remained in touch with the people sounded increasingly unconvincing amid mounting criticism of the BEE magnates from the left and the right. In 2007 Sexwale determined to run for the presidency of the ANC, but his campaign was too flashy for the traditionalists of the ANC,

who liked to pretend that no one campaigned for high office. He was also accused by his opponents' supporters of having sold his soul to big business. He
dropped out of the race and threw his weight behind Zuma, pinning his hopes
on another bid for the leadership in the future.

Some of the criticism of BEE was misdirected, including comparisons between the new tycoons and the Russian 'oligarchs' who dominate the Russian
economy. The Russian oligarchs made fortunes from the buying of state assets
at rock-bottom prices on the fall of the Soviet Union. The BEE bigwigs, by
contrast, had minority stakes in businesses, and their investments were in private companies, not the big state companies. So while they became fabulously
wealthy, unlike the Russian oligarchs they did not acquire control of whole sectors of the economy, still less of the state.

But there was another, less flattering difference cited by bankers, who concluded that most Russian oligarchs were genuine business people who then
traded off political connections to become super-rich, whereas most South
African big deal-makers were more adept at parlaying influence than building
businesses. The critical factor behind the success of the new black-owned business empires in Mbeki's second term in office, between 2004 and 2008, was
not the acumen of the business leaders but the buoyancy of the global economy and in particular China's soaring demand for minerals, a mainstay of both
the South African economy and of most BEE businesses, including Motsepe's
African Rainbow Minerals.

Whatever they said to the contrary, most of the multimillionaires in the first
generation of Black Economic Empowerment remained politicians at heart.
Saki Macozoma, a confidant of Mbeki, was a director of Standard Bank, the
country's largest bank, and was one of the half-dozen wealthiest BEE business
people. But insiders in the bank had no doubt he was there for his political
nous and connections rather than his financial acumen. Nor did he trouble to
hide that politics and ideological debate, rather than business and the fluctua-
tions of the market, coursed through his bloodstream.

When First National Bank launched a campaign to get thousands of signa-
tures for a petition urging Mbeki to do more to combat crime, Macozoma responded as if Mbeki was facing a coup. If he had still been the head of the
ANC's press and publicity, as he had been in the early nineties, he would have

called people onto the streets to close the bank down, he told associates.[15] It was a remarkable assertion for one who was on the board of Standard Bank and whose life now ostensibly revolved around boardroom meetings.

Ramaphosa argues that these are early days and that black South Africans need successful black business people as role models.[16] The emergence of a class of black millionaires would encourage the young in the townships to go into business, unlike when he was growing up and the only obvious avenue for the talented was politics. It was good for the collective morale of black South Africans to have super-rich black role models. When a picture of Patrice Motsepe adorned the front page of *Forbes* in its issue on the world's richest men, it was a source of pride to many in South Africa. Ramaphosa was also right to stress that many black business people would need a helping hand. The early experiences of BEE had made clear that the policy could not just rely on voluntary participation by business. But the BEE billionaires were not in the tradition of the self-made plutocrats of the American Dream, who worked their way up from the bottom of a business. They had had their wealth thrust upon them. The most obvious lesson from BEE was that the quickest and easiest way to make money was to trade political contacts for shareholdings. One veteran ANC member involved in several deals once asked me openly to put in a good word for him with Zuma when I next interviewed the ANC leader.

White business people, for the most part, kept out of the public debate. After decades of reaching an accommodation with the apartheid regime, they rapidly found a way of working with the new order. Many established businesses adopted a deeply cynical approach to the policy, appointing token black South Africans to their boards. Trevor Manuel, the finance minister, told me how an acquaintance who was a 'beneficiary' of several BEE deals was often asked to put his name to a deal as a token sign of black involvement.

'All his offers to help with the company beyond just attending the four board meetings a year or whatever are spurned. They are saying, "We want you there. You are a good man. But actually we don't need you close to what we do. We will run the business, but we have bought a licence and an insurance policy through you."'[17]

But it was not just cynicism that bred silence. To criticise BEE risked accusations of insensitivity to the past and potentially losing access to state contracts, which by 2008 were estimated at generating more than 30 per cent of government spending. The Black Management Forum, a lobbying group for black business, was quick to accuse of racism anyone who suggested that affirmative action policies were compounding a shortage of skilled workers. When in 2003 the giant energy company Sasol, which had been set up by the apartheid governments, applied for a secondary listing on the New York Stock Exchange, it noted that the government required that black shareholders should control 25 per cent of it by 2010, and that it could not guarantee that the deal would be at a fair market price and would not affect business and cash flow. Mbeki gave a blistering response in one of his weekly online letters, accusing Sasol's bosses of being unable to free themselves from the 'chains of bigotry'. So when Kevin Wakeford, the head of the South African Chamber of Business, who had done more than most in corporate South Africa to promote the deracialisation of business, lambasted the approach of both business and the ANC towards the policy, it was all the more striking. The results of BEE were, he said, 'characterised in the main by crony capitalism, fronting [the practice of employing a black manager as a token], enrichment and debt burdened deals'.[18]

His comments reflected what many in business and some in the ANC believed privately, but few were prepared to say publicly.

The debate over BEE was made all the more sensitive by controversies over how members of the new black elite should be expected to behave. Phumzile Mlambo-Ngcuka, one of Mbeki's closest cabinet allies, was rather tactless when she said that her black compatriots should not be ashamed to be 'filthy rich'.[19] She was, after all, an official in a party supposedly dedicated to shrinking the gap between the rich and poor. But her comments reflected an irritation among the black elite that, on the one hand, white business was urging the ANC to create a black bourgeoisie and then, when members of the nouveau riche behaved with the flamboyance that the nouveau riche sometimes do, they were ridiculed in the media.

The antics of members of the new elite did sometimes merit all the inches in gossip columns they received. Mandla Mthembu, an activist turned multimillionaire, and his starlet wife lived their lives on the pages of the tabloids in the manner of soccer stars in Great Britain. When their relationship was in trouble, he bought them both matching lemon-yellow Lamborghinis, which could be seen cruising side by side through central Johannesburg. They were hailed in the media as symbols of BEE excess. Such stereotyping infuriated the more august members of the new plutocracy, such as Ramaphosa. He liked to keep a low profile. He was one of the tycoons who invested money and time in schools and other charities. When in 2004 a Daimler Chrysler spokesman claimed that Ramaphosa was one of several moguls to have bought the new luxury Maybach 62, which retailed at about $500,000, he promised to sue and secured an undisclosed settlement for charity. 'For me it's too much of a conspicuous display of wealth in a sea of enormous poverty,' he said later.

He added, however, that the focus on the lifestyle of the new elite had a patronising, if not racist, tinge. 'It's almost like, "Here they are, the Johnny-come-latelies. Look at the type of cars they drive; look at the clothes they wear." I find it despicable. Because quite often black people who are succeeding in business are not recognized for what they are achieving, but for how different they have now become.'[20]

Happy Ntshingila knows all about the social complications and pressures of being a successful black businessman. He is in many ways a poster child for the new South Africa. At the age of fourteen he was shot on 17 June 1976, in the Soweto Uprising and had to spend seven months in the hospital. He attended the University of Fort Hare, the intellectual cradle of many of the great ANC leaders and thinkers, for four years. But unlike many of his contemporaries, he turned his talents to business, not politics. In 1992 he moved out of Soweto and became one of the first black advertising executives. After a stint working for the international agency Ogilvie and Mather, he took the revolutionary step of founding Herdbuoys, South Africa's first black advertising agency. This was not a black empowerment deal. This was a genuine business venture.

'Traditionally if you are black, you run a taxi firm or a fish and chip shop,' he recalled. 'The first challenge we faced was from the industry. People said we wouldn't last a year.'[21]

The night before I met him in April 1996, he had been at a party of black professionals and business people in Hurlingham, one of Johannesburg's more exclusive suburbs. All night they had discussed the difficulties of being an early black success story.

'You don't know how tiring it is being at the top. If anything, there isn't envy [in the townships], but rather you are a role model. We were having an argument all night about what it's like to be at the top. There were affirmative action products, guys who are worth their salt, and also guys like me, the so-called entrepreneurs. I am driven by the fear of failure. I would not be just failing myself but also black South Africa.'

He was then just thirty-five and the chief executive of Herdbuoys. His experience of life in suburbia was an early taste of what other black professionals and business people would find in the years ahead. He did not regret moving to a suburb with neat lawns and swimming pools, reliable electricity and easy access to supermarkets.

'It was the obvious thing to do. There was no soul searching. It's like graduating from a lousy car to a better one. Given the opportunity, everyone would go.' And yet there was a sterility and coolness to his new life that had him pining for Soweto. He had barely exchanged a word with his white neighbour in two years. 'Soweto is not the most beautiful, but shit, it's neighbourly. The neighbours will help you to move house. That's why there's less chance of being burgled there than here. There's a trumpet that calls us back.'

Sometimes the niceties of suburbia became too much. Later that day he was going back to Soweto. 'When white people have fun, they turn off the music. When we have fun, we turn it up. When black people have a ritual slaughter, the white community shudders. I haven't had one yet. It's just, I'm not into rituals, but if I had to, I wouldn't notify anyone. And the priorities here . . . I walk into Pick n Pay [a major supermarket chain] and find people with a trolley full of dog food, but they don't give food to their domestic workers.'

As I rose to leave Ntshingila, I glanced around his home with its blue pillars at the front door, its luxuriant plants and its peach-coloured exterior. My eye alighted briefly on the BMW in the garage. Ntshingila must have seen the direction of my gaze. 'Why is it that when a black person runs a company, the first thing people write about is how many BMWs they have, and yet no one ever writes that about Julian Ogilvie Thompson [the then chief executive of Anglo American]?' he asked.

It was a fair question. Ntshingila was flourishing as any successful entrepreneur might hope to in any capitalist environment. His was a model business

founded on his hard work and not BEE. The story of a savvy black businessman taking advantage of new opportunities to build his own enterprise was a
model for South Africa as it sought to build up a black middle class. But it was
also a rarity.

A decade into majority rule, the ANC came under increasing pressure from inside and outside the party to reform BEE and in particular to ensure that its
proceeds were spread beyond the 'usual suspects'. The ministry of trade and
industry drew up a series of regulations to take BEE beyond the transfer of
equity stakes. This was codified in legislation that came into effect in 2007,
when BEE was renamed Broad-Based Black Economic Empowerment
(BBBEE). Businesses had to comply with a BEE scorecard, for which they
earned points not just for the transfer of equity but also for training black staff,
appointing black managers and board members, and procuring services from
other companies that had earned their BEE spurs.

Patience Bogatsu was an early and deserving beneficiary of this drive. She
was the country's first black female bush game guide. She was one of more than
twenty local employees at the Thakadu River Camp, which was one of two
lodges founded in the northern game reserve of Madikwe with an enlightened
philosophy of trying to benefit the local villages. Outwardly, it resembled any
other African safari lodge, but it was owned and largely staffed by people who
had been dispossessed under apartheid.

The Industrial Development Corporation, the national development finance body, approved a loan to Molatedi, the local village, on the condition
that an operating company managed the lodge for several years and oversaw
training for the villagers before they took over responsibility. If Bogatsu had
been born fifteen years earlier, she could at best have aspired to be a domestic
worker. Instead she aspired to be a future manager of the camp. She had, in
short, become a member of South Africa's burgeoning black middle class, the
most dynamic force in the economy. According to one survey, it had grown by
30 per cent in the previous fifteen months to comprise about 2.6 million
people.[22] Its members could be seen every morning in the dense rush-hour
traffic in Johannesburg, driving along motorways that fifteen years earlier

would have had few black drivers in their own cars. The scene was a vibrant testimony to the emergence of a black bourgeoisie, although the dependence of the black middle class on credit left its future worryingly insecure.

The controversies over the BEE tycoons primed a lazy conflation in the minds of some white South Africans between members of the fledgling black middle class and the more undeserving cases of BEE. Bogatsu was a standard-bearer for the former. In her crisp khaki uniform she led safaris with the same expertise, enthusiasm and calm as any of the tanned white Africans who for decades had dominated South Africa's safari industry. 'Uh-oh,' she whispered one night towards the end of a game drive. In the gathering dusk the outline of an angry bull elephant could be seen closing fast on her jeep. She reached for the radio and gave a crackly warning to other vehicles in the area. Then she spun the wheel and pulled away from the oncoming elephant, only to find several more elephants blocking the track. Again, she abruptly changed tack, and the jeep surged off the track, crushing bushes and bouncing off rocks as the elephant thundered past.

All Bogatsu had needed was the opportunity that had been denied her parents and earlier generations. She was determined to work ferociously hard to give opportunities to her many dependants. Her salary supported her four siblings, her mother, her children, and her nieces and nephews. On the night of the elephant showdown she was planning to study for the next set of ranger exams. 'If you need something, you can't rely on someone else to provide it,' she said. 'That is my slogan.'[23]

If the tale of Bogatsu were the prototype for BEE, then South Africa's long-term economic and political prospects would be extremely rosy. No one would dispute the need for sweeping initiatives to foster the spread of South Africa's wealth more widely. A buoyant black middle class taking an ever larger share of the market is critical to the country's future stability. This is what on paper the BEE legislation was intended to achieve.

By 2008 companies were moving to ensure their empowerment deals benefited more than just the 'usual suspects'. Some schemes were reminiscent of Margaret Thatcher's privatisation drive in the eighties, which created a new class of share owners. Ramaphosa argues forcefully that in the long run the economic benefits of creating a new tier of black business will outweigh BEE's disadvantages. Sexwale likes to say that BEE is an 'artificial constraint created temporarily to adjust for an artificial gap'.[24] He also argues that given the history of racial discrimination, the policies have been minimalist, and that it is remarkable that the ANC did not come into power demanding far greater slices of businesses.

'Traditionally white capital used to own more than 99.95 per cent of this economy,' he told me. 'We could have come in and demanded 70 per cent of businesses in line with demographics. We didn't do that. It is 25 per cent for mining, about 10 per cent in banking . . . What does that mean? In mining 75 per cent is still in white hands.'[25] Taken in isolation such arguments had a resonance. But to judge the success of BEE by the ownership statistics on the Johannesburg Stock Exchange was misleading. The history of other countries trying to effect transfers of wealth suggests that ownership has a short-term symbolic value. What matters is the formation of a new business culture.

In Malaysia in 2004, after years of increasing controversy over its empowerment programme, the prime minister, Abdullah Badawi, signalled the beginning of the end of affirmative action. Further dependence on it would, he argued, affect economic prospects and 'enfeeble' Malays.[26] A critical question for South Africa is whether a national leader will have the courage to take the same step.

One of the most obvious disadvantages of the policy was that it stifled entrepreneurial spirit and encouraged instead a culture of entitlement, an expectation that the state and white business would deliver. Its complex regulations also affected productivity and dissuaded businesses from investing in South Africa. Bankers excited about the prospects in Nigeria and elsewhere in Africa said that the BEE legislation was a major disincentive for investors at a time when there were many attractive emerging markets. In 2008, a Harvard-led group of economists who advised the government on policy called for reforms to BEE, including a sunset clause. Trevor Manuel, the finance minister, was also pushing for reform. But powerful vested interests had no desire to end the policy. One estimate calculated that the ANC's national executive committee, elected in 2007, included twenty-eight people with interests in sixty-nine companies worth billions of rand.[27] Several more had spouses with vast empowerment empires. In Durban, the commercial heart of KwaZulu-Natal, Zuma's home province, business people said openly that they regarded the rise of Zuma as their turn to have a share of the deals.

The worry for investors and ultimately for South Africa is that the policy will become so engrained that businesses will face demands in the future for endless more empowerment deals, and that the ANC will keep going back to boardrooms for further equity stakes. A further fear is that global recession will lead to the collapse of many of the new deals through defaulted debts, a failure that in turn could then lead to calls for a more populist policy. A crash on the Johannesburg Stock Exchange in 2008, when the index of its top forty stocks dropped almost 30 per cent, fuelled such fears amid predictions that many of the larger empowerment companies would go bankrupt in a repeat of the crash of the late nineties.

Moeletsi Mbeki remains a pessimist. He believes that would-be black tycoons will go on stressing their disadvantaged past long into the future, hobbling the economy as they expect handouts from the state. He is also dismissive of the revamped BEE initiatives. 'Training and the rest is camouflage to the real McCoy, which is money. The key part is asset transfer . . . How long can you end up being previously disadvantaged?' The question, he said, reminded him of the old paradox posed by clerics in the Middle Ages: 'How many angels can dance on the head of a pin?'

Kgosi Leruo, the ruler of the Bafokeng, is wrestling with a more specific problem: how many people can prosper from a community empowerment fund, and how quickly? He is a retiring man. He coughed and was clearly embarrassed when I suggested his cautious stewardship could be a model for other mineral-rich communities and also for South Africa. Prudence is in the genes, he conceded. His great-great-great-grandfather set a pragmatic course for the nation in the nineteenth century. When Afrikaner settlers displaced the Bafokeng, Kgosi Mokgatle, who ruled from 1834 to 1891, dispatched the tribe's brightest young men to the Kimberley diamond mines to earn money so they could buy back the land. Lutheran missionaries helped the Bafokeng by holding the land in trust for them, and then advising them to hand over the trust to the government. Decades later, Leruo's parents pursued long negotiations with the apartheid authorities and the mining companies for their birthright.

By 2008 his people faced a new challenge. Public pressure was mounting for a swifter and more obvious disbursement of the Bafokeng's wealth. Phokeng was booming, but parts of the homeland remained very poor, even as the expectation grew – fuelled by the get-rich-quick ethos that had taken hold in Johannesburg – that ordinary Bafokeng too would soon enjoy a more lavish lifestyle. The road from Johannesburg to the gambling resort Sun City, which runs over Bafokeng land, was lined by shacks whose residents hawked fruit and curios at crossroads to make ends meet.

'People are saying, "Our forefathers have worked hard and bought the land, so we expect some benefits from this revenue, from the exploitation of the land," ' Eugene Tsitsi, the *kgosi*'s former chief of staff told me. His principal duty was to appease the nation's seventy headmen, who provided the next tier of government after the *kgosi*. 'The expectations are getting bigger and bigger. That's what the headmen are concerned about. People are saying, "You've established some investment companies. Isn't it time that some of the benefits begin to trickle down?" It's a challenging situation. If we were to distribute this to every household, the benefit wouldn't be as good as if it was kept and grown. People are getting more anxious. We're living in times of economic empowerment and this and that. People refer to Impala as our mine, as our company. But we don't own it.'[28]

The *kgosi* likes to deliver moral lectures to his people on the need for restraint. 'I like to really just focus on getting things done,' he says. 'When I speak, there's got to be something to show. Right now I don't think there is much to show. It's quite easy to conceptualise ideas but quite another to get things done.'[29] But, as his advisers conceded, this is a hard sell to a people with high expectations. All the while migrant workers were pouring into the region to find work.

The *kgosi* predicted that by 2040 the Bafokeng's population would double to about six hundred thousand – an influx that would require careful planning. He refused to be drawn into self-congratulation.

'We can build all these towers and monuments, but unless we have the people who are of the same mind and who are competent and professional . . . we will fail.'[30] He might have been speaking of BEE. The tycoons are the towers and monuments, but they are just expensive adornments. The policy will stand or fall on its ability to create a black middle class.

Chapter 8

THE GRAVES OF THE ANCESTORS

*Mandela was very smart. He said, 'Land reform,
uh-oh, not my baby.' That's why the world called
him an icon. Had he embarked on land reform, the
iconisation would have gone.*

— THABANI KHUMALO,
ANC MEMBER, 2008

*Zimbabwe is way too close to us for us to be com-
fortable with the threat [of the landless losing pa-
tience]. The fact is, there has been no delivery on
land reform. I can understand why the landless
movement is frustrated.*

— THEO DE JAGER,
DEPUTY PRESIDENT OF AGRI-SA,
MAJOR FARMERS' LOBBYING GROUP, 2008

Every morning when he went to school in the 1970s, Bheki Kubheka looked up
the valley at the homestead of the local white farmer. A sprawling whitewashed house, surrounded by a garden and fringed by orchards, it dominated
the area, as did the farmer, Mr Badenhorst, who had a particularly harsh reputation even by the authoritarian standards of Afrikaner farmers of the time. If

children tried to pinch oranges or pears from his trees, they risked verbal abuse and a beating. In those days his farm covered 1,600 hectares of prime agricultural and grazing land. They stretched to the slopes of Majuba Hill, the towering local landmark whose slopes had witnessed a humiliating defeat for the British by the Boers in 1881. They also looked out over Charlestown, a bustling African freehold community on the other side of the valley. Or at least they did until 1978, when the state bulldozers came for the last time and Charlestown ceased to exist.

Charlestown was in apartheid-speak a 'black spot', dating back to the infamous Land Act of 1913, which banned blacks from buying land outside designated 'reserves'. In a stroke of the pen, about 75 per cent of South Africa's population was relegated to about 13 per cent of its territory. The emergence of an increasing number of black farmers successfully competing with white farmers was one of the causes of the act. In a bid to pre-empt the law, leaders of the South African Native Congress, the forerunner of the ANC, frantically tried to buy up plots of land between the tabling of the bill and its passing into law. Such plots, as well as other areas on which black farmers had been flourishing, became known as 'black spots', isolated areas of black freehold land that the National Party sought to expunge from the map when they came to power in 1948.

The most famous was Sophiatown, the vibrant central Johannesburg slum that was a haven for black writers and musicians, including Miriam Makeba and Hugh Masekela in the 1940s and early 1950s. Mandela recalls it fondly as having a 'special character' and being 'bohemian, conventional, lively and sedate'.[1] White developers had originally not wanted to build there because of its proximity to a municipal refuse dump, but its presence was deemed an affront to the whites living in surrounding areas. Technically, it also infringed the Group Areas Act, which had barred different races from living in the same places. In 1954, Sophiatown was flattened by the authorities; its sixty thousand black residents were transported thirteen miles out of town to what was to be known as Soweto; Sophiatown was rebuilt in rows of Identikit houses intended for Afrikaners, and renamed Triomf.

The 'black spot' at Charlestown, a railway hub just inside the border of the old British colony of Natal, dated back to the 1910 Act of Union between the Boer Republics of the Transvaal and the Free State and the British colonies of Natal and the Cape. The union threatened the locals with ruin, since Charlestown's main source of employment, a railway siding, was closed down because it was duplicated in the town of Volksrust just five miles away across the old border with the Transvaal. As its inhabitants drifted away, the white local butcher, a Mr Higgins, took what by the standards of whites of the time was presumably deemed a very desperate measure to prop up his business: he persuaded blacks to buy land.

About a hundred black families took up the offer. Their cattle roamed on communal grazing land. Soon there was a flourishing community, but its existence infuriated apartheid's ideologues. Kubheka awoke one chilly winter's morning in 1977, when he was sixteen, to see a formation of 'ggs', or government garage trucks, as police vehicles were known, bumping towards Charlestown. Within hours his family had been packed off to a township forty-five miles away, in the industrial town of Newcastle. The houses were bull-dozed. The only building left intact was the Catholic Church. No formal reason was ever given for the obliteration of the 'black spot', although the Kubhekas and other dispossessed families harboured suspicions that the neighbouring white farmers had egged the authorities on to act. They later learned that white farmers had taken their pastures for grazing and auctioned off any stray cattle left behind in the chaos of the enforced departure.

So it was with some satisfaction that, in late 2007, Kubheka was striding with a proprietorial air across the very *stoep* on which of an early evening in the old days Farmer Badenhorst could be seen looking down over Charlestown. His spread is now owned by many of the families whose forebears for so long chose to give it a wide berth, and it is run as a collective berry farm. In a gratifying twist, the farmhouse is the collective's headquarters.

Kubheka is a tall, lean man with a high-pitched accent reminiscent of Mandela's. One of hundreds of former residents who had reclaimed their old plots, he was one of the founders of the fruit farm. Yet even as he gave me a guided tour of Badenhorst's steading, it was clearly a wrench for him to recall his carefree childhood years and his family's dispersal from their rural valley. He had grown up with a view from his window that stretched east for dozens of miles across the undulating landscape of northern KwaZulu-Natal. Then abruptly he had been consigned to a tin-roofed shack in a cramped township rife with unemployment and all the stresses of a slum. He pointed across the road, beyond the bungalows and shacks of the new Charlestown. A small grove was just visible in the mist that had swept down off Majuba.

'You see that patch of trees? That was where my school was, Charlestown Secondary School. It won the prize for the best-kept school in Natal . . . and that included white schools too.'[2]

I had first visited Charlestown in early 1994, a couple of months before the end of white rule. Then clumps of weeds, darkened patches of ground, and the odd low wall and heap of rubble on a hillside were, apart from the church, all that testified to the old settlement. I stumbled through these pitiful remains with Peter Nkomo, a friend and fellow journalist who had also been to Charlestown Secondary School, looking for the site of his old home.

Nkomo had a jaunty black cap and a love of braces, which he stretched over his magnificent drum of a belly in the style of the legendary singers of Sophiatown. For once his deep melodious laugh was suppressed. He was visibly upset.

'These used to be the school peach trees,' he said pointing at a clump of couch grass. 'And this,' he added strolling across an old cement floor, 'was the home-craft class for ladies learning to cook.'[3]

A couple of old men were sheltering from the wind in a one-room shack made of corrugated iron and firewood. My friend Nkomo recognised one of them instantly.

'*Baba!*' he exclaimed. The man he addressed as 'father' was Jotham Dube. In the early sixties the young Nkomo and his classmates would run over to the school gate at break time to Dube's wife for one of her 'fat cakes' (sweet dough drenched and cooked in lard). While she had died in exile, after nearly twenty years away Dube had returned in November 1993. His clothes were caked in mud from tending a vegetable patch, but his labour had not dimmed his euphoria over his return.

'Home sweet home,' he said. 'I pity those who died in Newcastle. At least if I die, I will be buried with my ancestors.'[4] His wish was granted when he died later that year and was buried in the old Charlestown graveyard.

His companion, Halban Sangweni, was less starry-eyed. He had had twenty cows in the old days and had been milking one of them in the *kraal* when the police arrived.

'I have just three now,' he said. 'When I was moved out, the livestock was left here. If you wanted to move it, you had to provide transport, and there was no space in the township. All the rest were lost or stolen. It's heartbreaking.'[5] He predicted a tough time ahead for his fellow returnees, and he was right.

Nearly fourteen years later the barren land where the two old men had taken shelter in a shack had several hundred new brick houses. Funding from one of Mandela's foundations had paid for a new school on the site of the old one. The headmaster, Stephen Ngwenya, stiffened with pride as he revealed that he too was an old boy. His family had been evicted in the final assault on Charlestown in 1978. His account of the years since the handover was a tale of short-lived joy replaced by years of grind. It epitomised the hardship facing those seeking to return to their old land.

Many had lost their title deeds in exile or in the chaos of their expulsion and so faced a bureaucratic battle to prove their right to return. The few remaining whites were indifferent if not hostile. There was no obvious source of income: the old cloth factory where Kubheka's father had worked had long since closed down and was a derelict shell. Many had to resort to digging up bricks from the earth to build a home.

At least 40 per cent of the original residents had returned by 2007, Ngwenya estimated, but most were unemployed, and there was mounting frustration about the response of the government. Barely a quarter of the several thousand residents had electricity. All the while more people were flocking to a shanty settlement on the fringes. Many of these had been evicted from farms in recent months, an unintended consequence of the ANC's mandated minimum wage. As for the school, it was not a patch on the old one. Ngwenya had just nineteen teachers and twelve classrooms for 598 pupils. The school still did not have the old silver trophies, which had been taken to a school in the town of Volksrust when Charlestown was flattened. The principal there was refusing to return them.

'*Hai*, it's been tough,' Ngwenya said. 'When I started the school [in 1997], there were no desks and very few books. I had to go back to Newcastle scouting around schools for furniture and books. The government keeps making promises. They say they will install electricity all over, but it's been five years and no sign of it. We are attending meetings and meetings . . . but there is no delivery. That is making people sad.'

So what of Kubheka's berry enterprise? His eyes gleamed. 'Ah. *That* is giving us hope. My people will have jobs and money. It is a dream come true.'[6]

Amajuba Berries was one of the success stories of post-apartheid South Africa. In the late nineties, long after Badenhorst had moved on and sold his hectares and steading to another Afrikaner, Kubheka had lodged a successful land claim to the farm on behalf of the community. The government bought out the new owner at a market price. Then Kubheka set up a trust for the Charlestown returnees and in its name founded a raspberry farm. He became the chief executive of the enterprise and aspired to provide work for hundreds of locals.

Charlestown was a model project of land reform that underlined how South Africa had embedded its policies in a legal framework, in marked contrast to Zimbabwe, where thousands of farmers were driven off their land in a belated crude and disastrous attempt to redistribute land. Not only did it reverse a past injustice, it was also an economic success. Amajuba Berries was backed by a loan from a state development agency. After a difficult homecoming, the Charlestown returnees had a viable and possibly even prosperous future.

Unfortunately for South Africa it was an exception. For every Amajuba Berries there were many more cases of land reform projects that had failed. In early 2008 the director general in the department of land affairs conceded that at least half of post-apartheid land reform projects had failed to make beneficiaries permanently better off, and government advisers were warning that, unless there was a rapid change of policy, South Africa faced a crisis over the land.

Land is arguably the most sensitive and complex issue for post-colonial African governments. This is particularly true in countries such as Kenya and Zimbabwe, where before independence large white settler populations controlled the prime agricultural land. In Zimbabwe the failure of President Robert Mugabe's government to address the issue in the early years of independence, compounded by the failure by some white commercial farmers to take the initiative and effect meaningful reform themselves, sowed the seeds for a catastrophe. In South Africa, the most urbanised and industrialised country in sub-Saharan Africa, land is less important to the economy and to the national psyche than it is in Zimbabwe. Before Mugabe authorised the expropriation of most of the 4,500 commercial farms in 2000, leading to the destruction of commercial agriculture, farming accounted for 40 per cent of exports, 18 per cent of the country's gross domestic product and a quarter of formal employment. In contrast, in 2008 agriculture accounted for less than 3 per cent of South Africa's gross domestic product.[7] Outside a strip down the eastern coast, South Africa's land is not particularly well suited for agriculture. Most white farmers under apartheid relied on subsidies from the apartheid government. Most blacks have long since cut their ties to the land. But the history of land ownership is just as poisoned as Zimbabwe's was at independence in 1980 and the forced removals are more recent. Disentangling the history has the potential for widespread social and political upheaval.

Sol Plaatje, one of the founders of the ANC, travelled across the country in the second decade of the twentieth century to chart the calamitous impact of the 1913 Natives' Land Act. His account rings down the decades as an indictment of white rule and is a telling reminder for English-speaking whites and Britain that the foundations of the apartheid policies pre-dated the election of the National Party in 1948. With the stroke of a pen the authorities formalised the shepherding of blacks into some of the most impoverished and arid corners of the country, a process that had been happening on a more ad hoc basis ever since whites started moving inland from the coast in significant numbers in the early nineteenth century. Between then and the last years of white rule, an estimated six million blacks were uprooted from their homes and then shunted to townships or reserves.

Plaatje was one of the more remarkable South Africans of the twentieth century. Fluent in seven languages, he translated Shakespeare's plays into se-Tswana. He worked as a court interpreter in the small town of Mafikeng when it was besieged by the Boers in the second Anglo-Boer War. In one of the many haunting passages in his book, he described the ordeal of a family he encountered trekking across the country. Two days after their eviction, their baby fell ill and then died. 'The death of the child added a fresh perplexity to the stricken parents,' Plaatje wrote. 'They had no right or title to the farm through which they trekked: they must keep to the public roads – the only places open to the outcasts if they are possessed of a traveling permit. The deceased child had to be buried, but where, when and how?'[8]

The same story could have been written in the subsequent seven decades of the twentieth century, as successive laws refined the restrictions on black land ownership, forcing generations into a twilight existence. In 1951 the apartheid government underpinned the concept of the reserves with ideology by introducing the idea of Bantustans, or ethnic homelands. Black South Africans would have to live in their old tribal territory. Only those with work permits could live in 'white' areas. The borders were drawn up to ensure that more than two-thirds of the richest arable land was reserved for whites. The policy, an integral part of apartheid's architecture, took no account of the increasing numbers of blacks who were urbanised and had started to shed their tribal connections.

The cynicism of the policy was encapsulated by the homeland of Bophuthatswana. To the casual eye, the boundaries of its seven parts appeared to have been drawn up by a cartographer shaking an ink pen over a map, but in reality they had been carefully designed to ensure that most of the prime land stayed in South Africa. Bophuthatswana (also known as 'Bop') was one of the four so-called self-governing homelands whose puppet leaders had accepted a sham independence from Pretoria as part of what was known as 'grand apartheid', the creation of putative states supposedly within old tribal boundaries. The homelands had their own civil servants and security forces, and 'borders'. Bop even had a diplomatic residence in London, where representatives sought to convince credulous and right-wing MPs from the Conservative Party of the viability of apartheid.

Pretoria pumped large sums into the homelands to maintain the illusion of their independence, but the funding was never enough to make them viable entities, and over the years the government faced a series of scandals over the misuse of funds intended for the 'Bantustans', as the homelands were known. For whites the homelands provided a convenient escape from the puritanical ethos of the Afrikaner Nationalists. Gambling was banned by the bureaucrats in Pretoria, but it was legal an hour down the road in Sun City, a resort just across the 'border' with Bophuthatswana, and every weekend thousands of Afrikaner civil servants suspended their Calvinist carapace and drove there to gamble. But for blacks the homelands were a monstrosity. For four decades the homeland policy cruelly divided millions of families, by allowing only those with work permits to stay in 'South Africa'.

On the night of the first all-race elections, the homelands were formally dissolved and incorporated back into South Africa. Their unravelling, however, was the simple part of land reform. Under white rule three-quarters of the land was in the hands of the white minority. In 1994 some 25 per cent of South African land came into the possession of the black majority government. The post-apartheid constitution of 1996 pledged restitution or redress for all dispossessed of their property since the 1913 Land Act. It also enshrined property rights and promised farmers a fair market rate if their land was to be expropriated either for land claimants or for redistribution. Both were laudable principles. But adhering to both was to prove difficult. The two were not unrealisable, but the state bureaucracy lacked sufficient capable civil servants to administer the reforms. The problem was not a lack of land to hand over but rather the competence and efficiency of the officials. As the years passed since 1994, and land reform became ensnared in controversy, the clamour for quicker results grew. So did the impression that the ANC had been rather better at drafting the policy than implementing it.

Amid mounting evidence that the government was slipping far behind its targets for land redistribution, it became increasingly clear that the government faced a fundamental difficulty: how to assuage the land hunger of the rural poor, a shadowy population of indeterminate size, and demands for wholesale redistribution without undermining property rights and endangering the country's food production – and, indeed, the rule of law. To understand this dilemma I went to see a man called Tozi Gwanya.

Gwanya's headquarters were down a long corridor in the department of land affairs, one of the featureless office blocks in central Pretoria. He was not at his desk when I arrived. When he finally wandered in, his face had the harassed expression of overworked civil servants the world over.

The sign on the door said 'Chief Land Claims Commissioner', but it was, by an hour or so, out of date. The director general of the Land Affairs department had been fired that day. Gwanya had just been asked to take over. He was an obvious choice. As chief land claims commissioner from April 2003, he had been responsible for adjudicating tens of thousands of claims for people to be restored to their ancestral lands. Now he was to take on responsibility for the two other major planks of South African land reform: meeting the ANC's target of redistributing 30 per cent of agricultural land to black farmers by 2014 and giving land tenants greater security of tenure after more than a century in which they had been chaff in the wind.

Gwanya drummed out an impressive array of figures that testified to how the government had initially moved steadily and cautiously to rectify past injustices.[9] About six million people had been driven off their land by the series of racist land laws in the twentieth century. The commission had received 79,696 claims for restitution by 1998, the cut-off date for applications. Out of all the claims, 80 per cent were urban. By September 2007, 74,500 had been settled – about 93 per cent of the claims. They had disbursed 4.6 billion rand (about $700 million at the time of the interview) in compensation in lieu of the land. As for the second objective, land reform, they had spent 6.5 billion rand to buy properties from white farmers and 2.3 billion rand to help new black farmers.

Gwanya was also fluent in outlining the many obstacles in his way. His eight hundred staff at the Land Claims Commission had spent nine years assessing claims. Sometimes communities had put in competing claims for a piece of land. With land prices rising, compensation was far more expensive than anticipated. Their budget for 2007 was 3.3 billion rand and would need to increase for 2008. Claimants often had no documentation, let alone title deeds, to support their claim. His staff had to walk over disputed land, asking people, 'Where was your land? Where were your forefathers' graves? Where were your dwellings?' Sometimes there was no evidence left. That's why some people did not understand why they took so long.

Then there was the hoary issue of race. Some white farmers had disputed claims, Gwanya said, by insisting the claimants' forebears had never been more than tenants. Others slowed the process, arguing that it threatened South Africa's food security, a code he said for an old canard that blacks cannot farm.

Many white farmers were hostile to the idea of transferring land from white commercial farmers to less skilled black smallholders, he said. They told him the ANC's land reform policies were 'apartheid in reverse'. He replied that blacks had been shifted without any compensation and that the ANC government was paying a market rate. 'But now the white farmers know the state is buying, they push the price up.' There had been cases of white appraisers colluding with farmers in their valuation report to inflate the price, he said. 'Land owners leave angrily. They bang their doors! They want to be like Americans owning big tracts. We need to change that to people having reasonable pieces of land.'[10]

Gwanya's argument went to the heart of a sensitive philosophical split over the meaning and purpose of land. One of the more heated debates in the talks of the early 1990s that led to the end of white rule was over property. Some in the ANC argued that property rights and large commercial farms were alien concepts introduced to Africa by Europeans and that they conflicted with the traditional African system of communal land tenure. This reflected yet another division that cleaved the country along racial lines. For most commercial farm-ers, land, while cherished, is also broadly a commodity, but for many black African communities it has a spiritual and emotional importance that overrides its economic potential. By 2008, many of the international donors who used to sing the praises of small-scale agriculture for Africa were starting to argue that the continent needed to have large-scale commercial businesses. This favoured the South African model of farming. But in the ANC there were still some who saw such farming as a white or Western approach to be distrusted.

Gwanya was under fire from both the landless and the farmers. Yet his thesis on the farmers was one-sided. Some white farmers under apartheid had been as draconian as Badenhorst and treated their labourers as little more than serfs while making huge profits. But not all were tyrants, and even with the hefty subsidies provided to white farmers by apartheid governments, many were able only to eke out an existence. Farmers' lobbying groups angrily denied Gwanya's claim that farmers were raising their prices in the hope of selling and making large profits.[11] 'The notion that farmers are reluctant to sell is non-sense,' said Theo de Jager, the deputy president of Agri-SA, the main commer-cial farmers' lobbying group.[12] He said he knew of just one case in the whole country of a farmer being unwilling to sell. Rather, there was 'a large number of willing sellers' both because of a sharp rise in attacks on farmers and because it was increasingly hard to make a living from agriculture. He was infuriated that the government was not turning to the open market, which saw up to 5 per cent of agricultural properties exchanging hands each year.

Research by a leading think tank found that many farmers were willing to implement reform and assist restitution but had found the process ensnared in bureaucracy. Some businesses had had their offers to assist land reform spurned partly, the report's authors assumed, because of the ANC's instinctive suspicion of the private sector. In a reflection of the difficulties, swathes of commercial farming land, including as much as 50 per cent of the country's sugar-producing land, faced unresolved restitution claims. This meant the land was effectively frozen, as few wanted to invest in, still less buy, a property with an outstanding claim for its title deed. In short, the report found that the primary issue stymieing reform was not the lack of land on the market or the price, but rather the government's apparent inability to implement its policy.

Between 2004 and 2007 the amount of land redistributed by the state had increased by less than half a per cent, from 4.3 per cent of commercial land to 4.7 per cent. It was estimated that when land transferred on the open market was included in the figure, the true extent of land transferred from white to black ownership was closer to 6.8 per cent of commercial land. But this was still far short of the 30 per cent target the government had set for 2014. Also, many of the farms handed over by the state to fledgling black farmers had collapsed because the department of land affairs had focused its attention on restitution and failed to support the new proprietors. Unless there was a rapid change of approach, there were only two scenarios for South Africa, the report concluded: nobody wins, or everybody loses. The latter nightmare scenario envisaged South Africa embarking on a Zimbabwe-style land-grab. 'If this happens land issues will develop such powerful and harmful momentum that they could spin out of everybody's control with extremely negative consequences.'[13]

More than two hundred miles south of Pretoria, a grove of blue gum trees cast a dappled silvery light over the von Maltitz family graveyard. The trees were not indigenous, nor in the eyes of activists for the 'landless' was the landowner, Friedl von Maltitz, but his family's veneration for the graves of his ancestors matched that of old Jotham Dube, the smallholder whose wife had once served fat cakes at the local school and who had returned to Charlestown in time to die.

The von Maltitzes had run Saxon Park Farm since a young Friedrich Wilhelm, Friedl's great-grandfather, staked out the farm in 1876. He was one of thousands of trekkers fanning out from the Cape and claiming for themselves vast plots of land that had traditionally been hunted over and used as collective grazing by local tribes. The view from his front window was little changed since his great-grandfather completed the first farmhouse. A coat of arms with two lions and a rampant horse sat atop the front gate. A battered signboard proclaimed: 'We plough the fields and scatter the good seed in the land. But it is fed and watered by God's almighty hand.' The inscriptions and heraldry lent a touch of Central Europe to one of the more remote spots on the high veld. Beyond was a horizon of rocky outcrops stretching fifteen miles along dirt tracks to the nearest small town, Ficksburg, a traders' post leading to the mountain kingdom of Lesotho.

'It was not easy in the early days,' Friedl said as we walked past the small fenced-in cemetery at the back of the farm. 'And it is not easy now.'[14] An ornate headstone marked the last resting place of Friedrich Wilhelm (5 June 1860 to 22 July 1921). Alongside was the grave of his wife, Susannah Maria.

By chance I had encountered the most notorious member of the von Maltitz family shortly before the end of white rule, under very different circumstances. Eddie von Maltitz, a distant cousin of the Saxon Park branch, had been marching up an escalator in a giant conference centre outside Johannesburg at the head of a group of khaki-clad, gun-wielding paramilitaries. One of the country's more outspoken right-wingers, he was one of hundreds who had stormed the venue of the multiparty talks, where the post-apartheid settlement was being negotiated. He was regularly on talk radio in those days, warning of a bloodbath if the National Party ceded power. Friedl was cut from very different cloth. A bookish former lawyer, he had taken on the responsibilities of the farm with his wife, Lindi, with some reluctance. He rolled his eyes when I mentioned Eddie.

The von Maltitzes lived much as their pioneering forebears did: in a heavy-beamed farmhouse brimming with old wooden furniture. In pride of place was an antique engraved piano. The farm still operated on semi-feudal lines. To one side was a satellite village of black farm labourers. The children went to a farm school. Four of the women worked in the house. A dozen more helped to sort asparagus, the principal crop, in a giant barn. Half a dozen dogs, led by an ancient Great Dane with white bloodshot eyes, patrolled the grounds. Jackals and *rooikat* (Afrikaans for a caracal, a wild cat) still sometimes broke down the wooden *kraal* walls to prey on their sheep, as they had for a century. But the twenty-first century was starting to encroach. Three of their domestic workers were AIDS widows. There had been a dozen AIDS deaths on the farm. Security was an ever more pressing concern. In the decade after the end of white rule, more than a thousand white farmers and members of their families were murdered, according to farmers' lobby groups. Farmers feared this was an organised campaign to drive them off the land. The police played down such talk. But the attacks were marked by a viciousness that fuelled farmers' fears that they were as much about the past and the future as about crime.

The von Maltitzes had done more than most to ward off potential hostility over the past, appreciating that a dozen acres given freely were worth more than a hundred handed over under duress. In 1999, Friedl's mother, Liela, formed a cooperative with the farmworkers, giving them a 49 per cent share. A year or so later, to comply with requirements that beneficiaries of land redistribution should not be dependent on white farmers, a trust was created for the farmworkers. They then received a twenty-year loan from the Land Bank at a preferential rate. A dream of several generations to be working their own land had been fulfilled.

Von Maltitz drove me through the plot his family had transferred to the trust. At first glance I concluded the farm was being run as had been envisaged. A dozen farmworkers were hard at work in the fields. But the picture was misleading. The project had collapsed. Von Maltitz was now renting back the land to plant asparagus. The workers were casual labourers he had hired to pick the crop. The first season after the trust was founded, the workers planted their crops and paid back the instalment. The second season there was a drought, and they had a poor crop, like everyone else. By the time they had paid for the hire of a combine harvester, they could not pay their dues to the Land Bank. Then the loan was frozen, and they did not have the capital to plant again. They had paid back 190,000 rand, but they still owed 400,000 rand. Since then the debt had been accruing for the last four years. 'I also had a horrible crop, but I could go to a bank as I had more security,' von Maltitz said. 'Since then they have just stood still with no operating capital.'

Since their default on the loan, the trust members had been using the land only for their cattle to graze. An official from the department of land affairs had come to assess the problem, but apparently had reached no conclusion. Von Maltitz and the trust members had written a series of letters to the local department of agriculture, which was based in the former tribal homeland of QwaQwa. But the civil servants were notoriously inefficient, and they had never received a reply. 'We've had four different heads of agriculture in this region in as many years,' said von Maltitz. 'We wrote to all of them, and nothing happens. It is always the same with these projects. The government will help you buy the land, and then there is no follow-up help at all.'

In their frustration the trustees had started fighting with each other, and the trust had become so split that it was unlikely it would ever be able to function again as a business. Half the members of the trust had left the farm and moved to the local small town, Ficksburg. They remained, however, putative beneficiaries. If the farm started to make money, they would probably return. But to plant and pick asparagus they needed money for the labourers, and they did not have any. So instead people were bringing their cattle to take advantage of free grazing. There were three farmhouses on the trust land, and no one was living in them. 'The government ignores that,' von Maltitz said. 'For them it's a numbers game. If they can say they've handed over X million hectares, that's all that matters.'

Von Maltitz fell silent. He was neither angry nor smug. Rather, he seemed resigned to more heartache ahead, not just for the trust but also for Saxon Park. The mood of the white farmers was very bleak, he said. A nagging fear was that the government would renege on its vow not to allow more land claims after the original 1998 cut-off date for the lodgings of claims. The government insisted that the date was sacrosanct. But all across South Africa, von Maltitz said, farmers were reporting fresh claims to their land being lodged informally.

As for the Land Bank, von Maltitz suggested it would be better for our blood pressure to bar it from the conversation. The bank had been embroiled in controversy for several years amid allegations of high-level corruption. A few months after my trip to Saxon Park Farm, a leaked audit into the Land Bank found that one of its former chief executives had 'personally approved' controversial loans worth up to 1.1 billion rand for projects including golf-estate developments and industrial parks.[15] The executive denied any wrongdoing. In July 2008, in belated official recognition of the shambles, control of the Land Bank was transferred to the Treasury. All this was occurring at a time when Ephraim Semahla, the strapping foreman at Saxon Park, was watching a long-held dream of running his own farm collapsing because the Land Bank was heedless of his pleas for help.

'I can remember the day very well when Mrs Liela told us [about the trust],' he said. 'We were on the way to the asparagus fields in the *bakkie*, and she said, "You've worked for me for a long time. I want to give you some land." And everyone understood and was very happy. "You're my children," she said. "I want the government to work with you." '[16]

Semahla's family had been on the farm for several generations. His father had worked with the oxen and raised him with his own father's stories of the Boer War. All they had had was a little pumpkin plot. He had worked his way up to become the foreman and was one of the four directors of the fifty-two-strong trust.

'The government said they could help us. They promised and promised, but in the end they didn't give anything to us. For two years we were so happy. Now we are thinking of selling a few of our cattle to get food and also seeing if we can let some of the land and sell off a farmhouse.' The most painful part of a sad story, he said, was that the trust members were at each other's throats.

Twenty arid miles from Saxon Park, there was a yet bleaker insight into the reality of land reform. '*Welkom* Catarina' said the signboard. The gate was modelled around two wrought-iron wagon wheels. It was still in good repair, but it was the only thing that was. Catarina Farm had once boasted several orchards of peach trees, but it had become a graveyard for cannibalised tractors. The electricity had long since been cut off, and the farmworkers who had taken over seven years earlier when the farmer sold his land to the land affairs department were relying on chickens, sheep and a few cattle to survive. Koos Mosae, a wizened old man with yellowing eyes and a scratchy voice, was sitting in the sun in the old farm courtyard. He had worked on a neighbouring farm for twenty years and in 1999, five years after the end of white rule, had joined a collective of farmworkers taking over Catarina. It had all started well. There had been more than 120 people taking part. But when they ran into difficulties and needed advice, they found they were on their own. Most of the original beneficiaries had moved to Ficksburg. Only seven families remained.

'Mandela said everyone must have a farm, and the government gave us this one,' he said. 'We went to Bloemfontein [the provincial capital] last year for help, and a state lawyer kept promising to come, but until now he hasn't. We don't have any seed, fertiliser or lime. We had four tractors when we started, but we had no money for parts. We have to eat the peaches. We can't sell them.'[17]

Soon there would be no peaches left. In the field stretching from the farmhouse to the road, the farmworkers had been harvesting the orchards. They had clearly worked with a metronomic precision. They had started at the farmhouse end and were making their way towards the road. It was a routine that the orchards had seen over several decades. Only these harvesters were using axes, not their fingers. The stumps were at a uniform height of six inches high. One by one the trees were being chopped down for firewood.

A decade after the end of white rule, the ANC faced an increasing crisis over land, with the costs of market-driven distribution mounting even as impatience among the landless grew. The cost was well within South Africa's reach, in marked contrast to the situation in Zimbabwe at independence in 1980. In Zimbabwe the state needed the financial support of international donors to fund land reform, although the international support was suspended when it became clear that many of the farms that were being handed over were going to members of the ruling elite close to President Robert Mugabe, rather than to the landless poor. In South Africa, with all its relative advantages over its neighbour in wealth and resources, the course of land reform should and still can be far smoother. But the government's record has been so sluggish that the shadow of Zimbabwe's disastrous land reform, which ended with the forced removal of most of its 4,500 commercial farmers and the collapse of its once thriving agriculture sector, hangs over South African white farmers as a harbinger of what could happen in the future if a populist leader takes charge. 'Zimbabwe is way too close to us for us to be comfortable with the threat [of the landless losing patience],' said de Jager, the deputy president of Agri-SA. 'The fact is, there has been no delivery on land reform. I can understand why the landless movement is frustrated. The land is there. There is no excuse for the government other than that the officials do not have the fingers to catch the ball.'[18]

As the years since the end of white rule passed, the pressure for swifter redistribution was fuelled by a wave of evictions of tenants by farmers in the wake of the ANC's introduction of a minimum wage, which farmers said had made it impossible for them to maintain their traditional levels of staff. According to Nkuzi, a land rights non-governmental organisation, an estimated one million people had been forced off white-owned farms between 1994 and 2007. While the figures were disputed, Nkuzi argued that this meant more people had lost land than gained it since the end of white rule.

For Zuma this posed a major problem. He made clear he did not favour a more populist approach. When in June 2008 a prominent newspaper editor suggested to him the only solution was to push to hand over swathes of white-owned land without delay, Zuma laughed good-naturedly, as is his way, and said that that would be a disaster and would lead to chaos.[19] But he will have to juggle the competing claims of the landless and the left urging more interventionist steps, and business and farmers pleading for him to rely more heavily on the private sector. In December 2007 the party passed a resolution calling for an end to market-driven reform and a review of the 'willing buyer, willing seller' principle. This followed calls from the left for more radical measures.

Professor Shadrack Gutto, who wrote a controversial government report advising a moratorium on the sale of land to foreigners, warned that unless redistribution was dramatically accelerated, South Africa would in the future face Zimbabwe-style land expropriations. The Zimbabwe parallel infuriates most ANC officials. They see it as a knee-jerk and racist white attitude and emphasise that, unlike in Zimbabwe, their land policies have been rooted in the constitution. Gutto, however, believes that it is naive to dismiss the idea of land invasions.

Implementation of land reform had been hampered by the inadequacies of local government and a lack of money, he said. Land reform had moved slower than it ought to have done and needed to be speeded up. Otherwise a demagogue could come to power by whipping up public opinion and using the land to gain popularity.

'There are always in society people who can do that. We see it in Zimbabwe. No one says it is an exception. South Africans are not superhumans.' It was not enough just to transfer the land; it needed to transform the lives of the new black farmers, he said. He had attended public hearings where 'very strong sentiments' had made clear that there was a growing frustration with the government's record. 'The landless feel there has not been any intervention [by the state to reverse apartheid land policies and] that apartheid still exists.'[20]

Gutto was something of a hothead but his views did have a resonance. Mangaliso Kubheka was a founder of the Landless People's Movement, a pressure group for the rural poor. His ancestral village was just outside Newcastle, the town that had taken in the displaced people of Charlestown. (He was no relation of the Charlestown Kubhekas, however.) He and his family were tenants on a small plot where he, his father and grandfather had been born. Their forefathers had been there 'long before the demarcation of the land by whites', he said.[21] And yet still he had no rights over the land.

To his fury, more than a decade after the end of white rule, the local farmer was ordering him to move his cattle from the farm's pastures, even though Kubheka's ancestral graves were all over the land. In a reflection of the complexity of the interlocking procedures for land reform, he had lodged a claim as a land tenant only to see it become ensnared in bureaucracy because a separate claim for restitution had been lodged on the same plot.

'We voted for this government and thought they would do the right thing, but they are doing the opposite of land reform,' he said.

He was particularly exercised by the thousands of foreigners who had come to South Africa and bought up properties in some of the country's most beautiful areas, in particular the Cape. This, he argued, had pushed up prices beyond the reach of most South Africans, in particular those whose chances of owning property or indeed accruing capital had been stunted by colonialism and apartheid.

'Land reform is going nowhere,' he said. 'People are being patient, but they are being fooled. Market-led reform has failed in many countries. We must get rid of the property clause [in the constitution]. Land invasions are the only way.'

The ANC's progress, while spasmodic and intermittently accompanied by populist rhetoric, testified to the party's intent to avoid such radical measures. South Africa's private sector had also been far more proactive in initiating land reform than in Zimbabwe. Many large companies pioneered land reform before it was official policy. In 2004 the private sector financed more than double the number of land transactions as the state. The berry farm in Charlestown exemplifies how the old and the new orders, white and black, the private sector and state projects can unite in forming a successful project.

When Bheki Kubheka drove me to the site of the planned berry greenhouses, we came across a silver-haired Afrikaner in his late-middle age at work in the fields in an inversion of the old routine of white farmer and black foreman. Frans Fourie had a 10 per cent stake in the business. In return he was the de facto farm manager. He had started farming in a remote part of the Free State in the mid-1960s, but in the nineties his farm was running into difficulties because of a drought, and he had welcomed the chance of working for the Charlestown community as an adviser.

'If you play the piano, you can use any notes, but you have to use the right notes at the right time,' he said. Too many new black farmers were expected to start out without expertise and capital, and their projects ended in failure. The ANC had to swallow its pride and turn to white farmers for help. 'Every time a man with expertise retires, it's as good as a library burned down.'[22]

Amajuba Berries could at full capacity become South Africa's largest raspberry farm, with 70 per cent of its crop for export. Kubheka hoped to have ninety permanent employees and seven hundred seasonal pickers. For those who returned to Charlestown, many of whom had struggled to make ends meet in an area with high unemployment, this was a remarkable prospect. Among his employees was the son of Halban Sangweni, whom I had first met back in early 1994 deeply depressed about the prospects for the new Charlestown. The government just had to learn, Kubheka said, to provide support and to look to the private sector for advice.

'We need mentors. It's not worth getting back land without support. Just getting land back is not enough. We can get the land back left, right and centre, but if we don't have the expertise, it is meaningless.'[23]

Two men, black and white, working together to build a future for an impoverished black town, Kubheka and Fourie made a picture-postcard image of the 'new' South Africa. But land reform in South Africa is at a crossroads. The ANC needs to move fast with the private sector to stave off a crisis. Good intentions alone will not prevent the country taking the wrong path, with devastating results.

Chapter 9

THE AIDS BETRAYAL

*[South Africa's policies on AIDS are] more worthy
of a lunatic fringe than of a concerned and compassionate state.*

– STEPHEN LEWIS,
UN AIDS ENVOY, 2006

*Mbeki is an intellectual president ... He's not a
classic politician. He paid a price on AIDS because
he approached the issue as an academic.*

– THE REVEREND FRANK CHIKANE,
ONE OF MBEKI'S CLOSEST AIDES, 2008

The wake-up siren sounded as if it had come from the very belly of the earth. It
was 4.30 a.m. at the Great Noligwa gold mine in the heart of the old Orange
Free State. Sunrise was still an hour away. In the gloom one could just make
out the profiles of the mine hoist and the dumps of discarded ore, the pyramid
shapes that enshrined South Africa's troubled past. An icy wind was racing in
from the veld. Draped in blankets, the nightwatchmen were still bent double
for warmth. It was time to do battle underground. Wraithlike, the first miners
appeared on the scene. Scores, then hundreds, and soon three thousand or
more were pouring through the compound, whistling, singing – some still half

dressed, fumbling with their blue-and-white socks and overalls as they came. There was just time for a snatched bowl of porridge and bread at the canteen. Then they were streaming towards the shaft. Soon the first shift was bolted into the 'cage', hurtling nearly two kilometres into the sweltering bowels of the earth at a stomach-defying eighteen metres a second, singing songs and stamping their rubber boots up and down to keep up their spirits.

It was a timeless scene. For all the changes in technology, the pre-dawn rituals had changed little since gold was first found in South Africa towards the end of the nineteenth century. But on the second floor of the main residential hostel, a wiry thirty-six-year-old winch operator with a winning smile had one last thing to do before joining his shift. With its sixteen utilitarian bunk beds, chipped crockery in the basin and peeling posters on the walls, Room 149 was a typical miners' lodging, basic, even spartan, yet luxurious compared to the quarters of twenty years earlier, before the nascent unions started to claw concessions from the mining houses and, with them, chip away at apartheid. Glancing around to check his last two remaining room-mates were not looking, Eric Morake, the winch operator, rummaged in the back of his locker. Hidden on the top shelf were two small packets of pills. He slipped two pills in his pocket: one yellow and one white. Then he stashed the boxes back in his locker and headed out for his shift.

Morake had a confident swagger, and he whistled to himself as he joined his team. It would be hard to guess that a year earlier he had been so weak he could barely get out of bed and that, like so many South African gold miners before him, he was dying of AIDS. He had been reduced, as he put it, to 'walking with a stick like an old grandfather with three feet'.[1] Yet when I saw him in 2003, he had been on antiretroviral drugs (ARVs) for nine months and was a man transformed. He was one of the first to benefit from a revolutionary decision by his employer AngloGold, then the world's largest gold-mining company, to take the costly step of distributing ARVs to its forty-eight-thousand-strong workforce. The ARVs slow down the production of HIV and give the body a chance to build up its CD4 white blood cells, crucial to fighting AIDS. Morake was secretly taking his every morning and night. In nine months his CD4 count had risen from 330 to 530, still low but not lethally so. To his utter joy he had recently returned to work.

'When I heard the catch of the cage on my first day back, I shook and gripped the man in front,' Morake recalled. He was speaking in the privacy of the mine's Wellness Clinic, a spotless whitewashed bungalow that was an oasis of calm amid the relentless hubbub of the mine. In the conservative world of the hostels, such was the stigma of AIDS that you did not discuss it, let alone admit to infection with HIV.

'I had not done a shift for so long. The men [in the cage] said, "Eric, we thought you'd been dismissed. How did you come back?" Even the white men [the overseers] were saying, "Eric, we were not expecting you back."'

The simple story of Morake's recovery would have been unexceptional in the West and in much of the developing world, where ARVs were holding AIDS at bay. But in South Africa, because of the government's refusal to accept the standard science over how to confront AIDS, such a turnaround was shockingly rare. On taking office, the ANC had assumed its major challenge would be countering the legacy of apartheid, but instead it faced a medical emergency that threatened the very South Africans who had been neglected most under white rule: poor, undereducated blacks. It was a terrible saga, but it was not just a humanitarian disaster, as elsewhere in sub-Saharan Africa. It was also a political scandal. First Mandela failed to make it a priority. Then, far, far worse, Mbeki impeded the delivery of the life-saving ARVs, a stance that was to see him accused of complicity with genocide.

According to the UN, in 2003, the year after Eric Morake started taking ARVs, every day in South Africa two hundred babies were born HIV-positive, and six hundred people died of AIDS. Five years later, in 2008, the estimated death rate had increased to about a thousand a day. The statistics are not definitive, but the UN's figures are deemed the most reliable on AIDS. South Africa, with a population of about 50 million, has more people living with HIV and AIDS than any other country in the world. The UN estimated that, of an estimated 33 million people living with HIV worldwide in 2008, 5.7 million were in South Africa. Nearly 1 in 3 pregnant women between the ages of twenty and twenty-four were HIV-positive.[2]

The remote rural villages that had for years provided the workforce for the mines were particularly badly hit. In the mid- to late eighties, when AIDS arrived in South Africa, and through the nineties, the response of mining companies was prejudiced, unjust and obtuse. In 1986 the Chamber of Mines publicised the findings of a study of the blood samples of 300,000 male mine workers. These showed that about eight hundred, mainly from Central Africa, were HIV-positive.[3] At the end of the following year their contracts were not renewed, and they were sent home to meet almost certain death in countries where health facilities were minimal. But at the turn of the twenty-first century, AngloGold was one of several mining houses that made a momentous decision. It had assessed the spiralling costs of having a sick and dying workforce and calculated that in the long run it was cheaper to implement their own ARV programme, both to keep their workers alive and their mines productive. And so in a bitter twist, the mining houses whose reliance on migrant workers had been an integral part of the policy of apartheid and had contributed to the spread of AIDS had upstaged the very government that had come to power vowing to improve the lot of Africans after centuries of subjugation.

Mbeki's quibbling with the accepted science – in particular the denial of ARVs to patients – and his reluctance to provide drugs to prevent pregnant women passing on the virus to their babies caused the premature deaths of 365,000 people, according to a study by the Harvard School of Public Health.[4] AIDS activists argued that Mbeki was responsible for more unnecessary deaths than resulted from apartheid. At the heart of their indictment lay a simple devastating question: How could the leader of sub-Saharan Africa's richest and most developed nation have presided over such a catastrophe?

As early as March 1995, just before the first anniversary of the end of white rule, the head of the Joint United Nations Programme on HIV and AIDS, Dr Peter Piot, had given a sombre assessment of the challenge facing the ANC to combat the crisis. The party had a host of pressing problems competing for attention, he conceded, but the fight against AIDS had to be a top priority. Quacks and crooks were profiteering by hawking fake cures. The cost of treatment was staggering. Overcoming the stigma would be very difficult. But, he concluded, it was not too late for South Africa to avoid the fate of other sub-Saharan African countries, in particular Zambia, Uganda, Botswana, Malawi and Zimbabwe, where the HIV prevalence rate among adults had stabilised at a terrible level of about 30 per cent. Astonishingly in retrospect, the hero of his presentation was none other than Thabo Mbeki, then Mandela's deputy president. Mbeki appeared determined to give the firm leadership that the crisis required, Piot concluded.

The virus had arrived much later in South Africa than in other countries in sub-Saharan Africa, so there was a 'window of opportunity', Piot said. He had been 'very worried about South Africa until quite recently', he added. He had thought all the conditions were in place for a rapid spread. But on hearing Mbeki speak about combating AIDS, he had been deeply reassured. Mbeki's vision was compatible with the UN AIDS programme. 'The right concepts are there. It makes me think there is a commitment, and a will to take it on.'[5] Thirteen years later, Piot's endorsement of Mbeki made Zackie Achmat shake his head.

Zackie – like Winnie Mandela, he is known across South Africa by his first name only – is irrepressible, irreverent, idealistic and impassioned, not to say obstinate. A puckish gay former anti-apartheid activist who became engaged in politics in 1976, when he set fire to his school in sympathy with the Soweto Uprising, and went on to be detained several times, he has (after Mandela) played the most important political role in South Africa since the end of white rule. He tested positive for HIV in 1990, the year Mandela was released from prison. Eight years later he founded a pressure group, the Treatment Action Campaign (TAC), to fight the Western drug companies in the courts for the right to cheap non-generic AIDS drugs and to challenge the government for the right to access to ARVs. He was far more than a litigator, however. He mobilised a community campaign across South Africa to goad the government into action, encouraging tens of thousands of HIV-positive people to defy the stigma attached to the virus and to wear T-shirts emblazoned with the slogan 'HIV POSITIVE'. He brought HIV and AIDS out of the shadows of South African society. It was easily the largest and most successful grass-roots movement in the country since the apartheid era.

Zackie's voice rose when he recalled the spirit of the TAC campaign. The songs had been based on old struggle songs. The use of posters and mass mobilisation had been learned in the anti-apartheid days. So how was it that less than a decade after the end of white rule, he had had to deploy these tactics *against* an ANC government?

'I am still officially an ANC member,' he said. 'But this is a tragedy. Many, many have died. It's very difficult to think of forgiveness.'[6] When he founded the TAC, he had thought its biggest and most expensive fight would have been against the Western drug companies protecting their costly patents. Yet it transpired his biggest battle was against the very man who for much of the nineties was one of the few in authority who appreciated the scale of the crisis.

In the early nineties, when the last white minority government was still in power, Mbeki had been very supportive of the 1992 joint AIDS plan of the government and the ANC, Zackie recalled. 'It was a good plan, superb. Very little of it has not stood the test of time, and Mbeki understood it.' Once in government under Mandela, after the 1994 election, Mbeki continued to burnish his AIDS credentials. He wore an AIDS awareness badge prominently on his jacket lapel and chided cabinet ministers if they did not follow suit. His stance was all the more striking because it came at a time when Mandela was virtually ignoring the issue. Statistics from antenatal clinics in townships showed that the number of pregnant mothers testing positive for HIV was rising steadily. But few people were paying attention. Journalists were too engrossed with covering Mandela's reconciliatory drive and his bid to create a new nation to pay attention to a predicted future catastrophe. In many news organisations in the West, AIDS in Africa was an 'old' story. Most politicians too were turning a blind eye.

Edwin Cameron, an openly gay judge who tested positive for HIV in 1986 and was to be one of the very few public officials to reveal his status, headed a convention of AIDS groups in the mid-nineties. He had been sorely disappointed when, on requesting a meeting with Mandela, he was told the 'old man' had delegated the meeting to subordinates. Yet just ten minutes into the meeting, he was delighted when Mbeki strode in unexpectedly and insisted on taking part. Mbeki opened a 1996 international conference on HIV and impressed AIDS activists. When Mbeki was elected ANC leader the following year, the party resolved that he, as the new party president, and his deputy must both take the lead on AIDS. 'Mbeki was behind that. It was because he was fed up with Mandela's response to AIDS,' said Zackie.

Then came the denial. As awareness of AIDS first spread around the world in the eighties and nineties, many governments responded initially by denying the scale of the crisis. The UN AIDS head, Dr Piot, regarded Thailand as an analogy for South Africa. Like South Africa, it had entered the nineties with a relatively low rate of infection. Then after a period when the authorities, fearful of the risk to the lucrative tourist industry, dithered and denied there was a crisis, the government made AIDS a priority. 'In a period of one year the trend was reversed,' Piot said. The AIDS programme was put in the office of the prime minister, and every minister was forced to have a budget line on AIDS. Under Mbeki, however, the South African government moved in the opposite direction.

In 1999, a contact in the presidency called Zackie with alarming news. He had been told, he said, to remove HIV as a category for unfair discrimination in a new bill about to go through Parliament. Why? asked Zackie. Back came the perturbing answer: 'Because he doesn't believe HIV causes AIDS.'

Zackie called Edwin Cameron to pass on what he had heard. Cameron told Zackie that he was taking leave of his senses and that Thabo Mbeki was 'the best person in the government on AIDS'. Two months later Cameron called Zackie back. He was almost in tears. Zackie, he said, 'you were right'.[7]

Early the following year, Malegapuru Makgoba, the prominent immunologist who was embroiled in the race row at the University of the Witwatersrand a few months after the end of white rule, received a telephone call late one night from the president. A few days later the presidency sent him a thousand pages written by prominent AIDS dissidents who denied the link between HIV and AIDS. Makgoba was stunned. He was also in an awkward position. He was a member of an informal kitchen cabinet of business people, academics and writers sympathetic to Mbeki. But he stood firm on the science. He replied to Mbeki that the dissidents were a discredited fringe. His relationship with the president came to an acrimonious end. Five months later, he was to write that Mbeki's questioning over AIDS could result in his being judged as having collaborated in 'the greatest genocide of our time'.[8]

Mbeki was not dissuaded. At around this time Zackie was called by a friend at the US embassy in Pretoria. President Clinton had received a letter purportedly from Mbeki about AIDS. The friend wanted confirmation that the signature was forged. Zackie could not confirm the signature either way. But the letter was soon proved to be authentic. 'They sent me a copy,' he recalled. 'It was a lunatic rave.'

The letter, a copy of which was sent to Tony Blair, then British prime minister, and other world leaders, was to do terrible harm to Mbeki's and South Africa's reputations. In it, Mbeki expressed clear sympathy for the views of the AIDS dissidents, who argue that HIV does not cause AIDS, and called for a uniquely African approach to confronting the disease. 'Not long ago, in our country, people were killed, tortured and imprisoned because the authorities believed that their views were dangerous,' he wrote. 'We are now being asked to do the same thing that the racist apartheid tyranny did, because there is a scientific view against which dissent is prohibited.'[9]

Mandela has repeatedly and publicly berated himself for failing to do enough about AIDS when he was president. In March 1999, just before stepping down from office, he addressed a meeting on AIDS and formally apologised for not talking about it. He made the fight against AIDS the priority of his post-retirement life, successfully badgering former President Clinton to raise funds for AIDS treatment. In 2005 he took his boldest step yet to confront the taboo when he announced that his son, Makgatho, had died of AIDS. But while Mandela's government neglected the fight against HIV/AIDS, Mbeki's guilt would be of a different order. First he questioned the very nature of the pandemic, and then he impeded the most effective way of treating it.

When the epidemic swept through Uganda in the eighties, President Yoweri Museveni ordered his cabinet ministers to mention AIDS in every speech they delivered, whatever the subject. In South Africa the president, far from addressing it at every opportunity, projected a muddled and misleading message. Not once did he urge people to have an HIV test, the standard first step towards prevention. He once said he would not take a test for HIV because it would confirm a 'particular paradigm'.[10] Not once did he urge people to use condoms. So inadequate was his approach that if he so much as mentioned AIDS in his annual state-of-the-nation address to Parliament, in a throwaway line, his aides cited it as proof that he was taking the matter very seriously. In the wake of an international storm over his interventions, he withdrew from the debate, and some health officials pushed to implement an internationally approved AIDS policy. But its progress was desperately slow, not least because his notorious health minister, Manto Tshabalala-Msimang, and several of the provincial health ministers appeared to share Mbeki's denial. They delayed implementation of the new policies through obfuscation and petty interventions in official reports. All the while, thousands more South Africans were being infected with HIV and progressing to AIDS.

In the mid-nineties Pete Mafifi was a bright young teenager with a gentle manner and wickedly charming smile. As the years of democracy passed, he seemed to embody the hopes of the new South Africa. He had a steady job with a computer company, a mortgage on a house and a car. One chilly winter's morning in June 2007 he suffered from a bad headache. He had just been on a trip for his company in Swaziland. At first it seemed that he had malaria. Mafifi talked to friends about wanting to be driven to his rural village to die. He succumbed to pressure to go to the hospital instead. Within two weeks he was dead.

The cause of death was tuberculosis on the brain. A few days after Pete died, it emerged that, like so many thousands of South Africans, he had died of it only because his body was weakened by AIDS. His mother found out only when she beseeched the nurses at the hospital to tell her the truth. Such is the stigma of AIDS, even a decade into the pandemic, that Pete had not told her. 'I am his mother,' she told the nurses. 'I must know.'

'How am I to know that all of my sons are not going to die of this?' she said later. 'I told him so many times to be careful. And now I, a grandmother, will have to care for his children.'[11]

Then there was Johannes Tladi, the dynamic young ANC councillor who led the party in the small rural township of Kwakwatsi through the great siege and later became the first black mayor of the white town of Koppies. He died in 2006 of AIDS. He was not, his friends thought, taking ARVs. These were two of the many who might have still been alive if the government had given a clear, consistent and correct message.

In 2003 Mbeki told the *Washington Post* that he did not know anyone who had died of AIDS.[12] Zackie snorts at the idea. 'Mbeki and co[mpany] saw people dying in exile. They knew exactly what had happened.' Nowhere was the impact of Mbeki's obfuscation and denial starker than on the mines and in the remote villages that provided their workforce.

In the summer of 1986 Eric Morake had packed up a small bag in his home village near the Botswana border and headed off in the footsteps of millions of Africans before him in search of a job on the great Witwatersrand Reef. The discovery of the 'ridge of white waters' exactly a century earlier in 1886, under what was to become Johannesburg, was one of the defining moments in South Africa's history. It sparked a gold rush; caught the attention of the British colonial authorities in the Cape, whose desire to dominate and exploit the industry was intertwined with their imperial ambitions; and led to two wars between the British Empire and the Afrikaners, then a fissiparous grouping of fiercely independent farmers. The thousands of tons of gold that were hacked out of the Witwatersrand reef over the next 120 years were the foundation of sub-Saharan Africa's only industrialised economy.

Within months of the first shaft being dug, Egoli, the City of Gold, became a magnet for young men from across southern Africa in search of work. They came often with only a kaross and endured long hours of danger underground for the chance to remit a miniscule stipend home. In time the conditions would be formalised, and they would be housed in single-sex hostels. Morake's barracks-like compound housed over four thousand people in nineteen blocks. He lived a few hours from his village and went home most months. Most of his colleagues, however, had come hundreds of miles and would return home only once a year, in the latest chapter of the country's migrant history, which had led to generations of broken families. The arrival of AIDS in South Africa in the late 1980s gave the saga a new and yet more heart-rending hue. Just as AIDS had come south through Africa on the truckers' routes, via sexual encounters between truck drivers and prostitutes, so the multiple relationships miners had with women near the mines helped to drive the epidemic across South Africa.

For Morake, the first sight of his new life was his dormitory compound on the banks of the Vaal River, rearing up on the veld like a giant alien pod. It is an unprepossessing sight, but it is the network of shafts snaking through the rock below, in a Dantean world of extreme temperatures and deafening booms, that counts. Gt Noligwa was on the western arc of the richest vein of gold-bearing ore in the world, a seam that was woven into the political and social fabric of the colonial and apartheid eras. By 2003 South Africa's gold-mining industry was past its prime, but Gt Noligwa was still one of the most productive mines in the world, as Nigel Trevarthen, the ruddy-cheeked mine manager, said proudly.

Trevarthen, a young Englishman, had arrived on the mines shortly before the first onset of AIDS. It was also just as a decades-old culture in the mines was coming under greater scrutiny. Since being legalised in the early eighties, trade unions had pushed to improve the mines' dire safety record. For years the risks had been steadily increasing, as the miners had to burrow ever deeper into the rock, following the exhaustion of the most accessible seams. The unions argued that the mining houses had traditionally been rather more cavalier with black lives than they would have been if the workforce were white. At the heart of the mines' militaristic culture were the traditionally single-sex hostels. There the old values, respect for elders and belief in the power of faith healers and herbalists, rubbed alongside modern urbanised ways, and AIDS thrived.

With the end of white rule, mining houses came under pressure to reform the hostels. AngloGold had by 2003 set up family quarters for miners outside the compound, aimed at reducing casual sex with prostitutes. Yet there were few takers, Trevarthen said. Many miners were from Mozambique, Lesotho and rural Zululand, and so were hundreds of miles from their families. They did not have to pay for their accommodation. They did not have to bother about transport. Food was provided. If there was a hole in the roof, it was fixed. 'They are here to earn money, and they want to earn as much as is possible and then go home and enjoy spending it.'[13] It was into this disciplined and macho world that Eric Morake, a young man in search of an adventure, arrived – at just the wrong time.

He worked hard and lived for the weekend a month he would try to return home to his wife, Janey, and their growing family. By 2003 they had three young girls. He would splurge on some bananas and cold drinks as a treat for them on the way home. And yet the local prostitutes were sometimes just too tempting after a hard day underground.

'Here you'll find lots of beautiful girls,' he said. 'All of us want beautiful girls. In their face you can see beautiful teeth, a beautiful tongue and a beautiful mouth.' He was speaking after having his latest check-up at the clinic. As he talked, he became increasingly animated. The beautiful girls might have HIV behind their back, he said, and you would not know.

The clinic's staff told me later that even if Morake had known the prostitutes were HIV-positive, such was the macho culture of the mines that they suspected he would not have dreamed of using a condom, the first line of defence against the spread of the virus. They were still battling to persuade miners not to consult traditional healers about AIDS. Two were squatting just outside the main gate that very evening, draped in animal skins and with beads and strings of bones around their necks, hawking their own 'natural' cures for the virus.

One of the many interwoven tragedies of the saga is that there was no shortage of warning signs. Traditionally the mine had organised funeral arrangements for workers who died in service. It was in the late eighties that Anton van Hoek, the manager of Morake's residence, noticed he had to arrange more and more funerals. Once they were too weak to work, victims were packed off home with a small medical pension. Even as they wasted away and died in their villages, many more young men were eagerly lining up to take their places underground. Everyone, employers and employees, seems to have been turning a blind eye to the implications of the epidemic.

'Black people thought AIDS was a joke from white culture to bring the number of blacks down,' van Hoek recalled. 'Even now, many don't take it seriously or are ashamed to talk about it. They won't go openly to their boss. They will say, "So-and-so is looking very weak. He is staying in his room."'[14] In the early years of the pandemic, he said, many of the victims were recorded to have died of TB. When, in the 1990s, mine managers started to promote condoms, they were treated with suspicion and ignored. All the while the prostitutes and traditional healers continued to ply their trade outside the hostels, and the miners continued their dance with death, blithely airbrushing the dying miners from their minds.

'Before I was sick I didn't know anyone with HIV,' Morake maintained. 'I just heard about it on the radio or TV. We would be used to seeing a person and then one week not seeing him any longer. We just didn't know what was happening to him. I would ask, "Where is Sipho?" and people would say, "He is not alive any more." ' Sometimes there were clues. Peoples' hair went 'fluffy like a cat'. He would ask what the problem was. 'You did start asking yourself what was happening to all the people.'

By the mid-nineties it was clear to Trevarthen that they faced a serious problem. The doctors were telling him that, unless he moved fast, he would have a sick and unproductive staff. He was struck when a security manager lost 'a hell of a lot of weight' in two weeks. 'One day when he came into my office, I thought, "Jesus, this is not the guy I remember." It took him ninety seconds to get to my desk, and I said, "You don't look good."' Five days later he was in the hospital, and he soon died.

Trevarthen was adamant that AngloGold had been motivated by humanitarian rather than material concerns. Yet he readily volunteered that as the years passed and the toll rose, they appreciated the epidemic was affecting productivity and profits. The timing was particularly poor from the bosses' perspective. In the nineties the costs of mining were already rising steeply in South Africa, as companies had to drill ever deeper and also had to implement new workers' benefits introduced by the ANC. And then they faced the impact of AIDS. But, he concluded gamely, it had not caught them 'off guard', and they had worked hard to educate their workers.

'In the nineties, when you spoke about AIDS, a lot of people were hysterical about the problems, scared to shake hands and share toilets. If I went to one of the shift bosses ten to fifteen years ago and said, "Between 25 per cent and 30 per cent of your shift are HIV-positive," he would have refused to work with them. We have not had any instance of anyone refusing now. Pretty much everyone knows that HIV is different from AIDS. The training has been pretty good.'

The training may have been good, but it was not enough: the stigma remained. In their nightmarish underground world, miners stumbled past like phantoms. Christo Viljoen, Morake's shift supervisor, a short wiry Afrikaner with a wispy beard, gave him a clipped but friendly welcome.

'He is often sick,' he said of his winch driver, in a break from the labour. 'Six months ago he came to me and said he had TB. I knew it was one of those things. He said the doctor was looking after him and that he would work Sunday and overtime to catch up. He was looking a little thin. Two years ago he was much bigger. But we know about this TB stuff. Just yesterday I asked where he was, and someone said he was sick again.'[15]

He did not mention HIV or AIDS. He must have known. But there was clearly a compact underground. 'No one knows,' Morake had whispered to me earlier. 'We don't talk about these things.'

Morake had lived happily in this world of denial until it was his turn to fall ill, to start missing shifts, to get weaker and weaker, and ultimately to be written off. 'The people in my room didn't know what disease hit me, but when they looked at me, they hated me. There were whispers: "You see this guy. He'll die now." They didn't ask me about it. But I heard them. Nothing was working for me. One day I came across some nurses going round the hostel. They said, "It's free. You can find out about HIV." I did not know. I stayed thinking about these things. I just did not want to go to them. I thought maybe they could tell me I am not HIV-positive.'

In September 2002, when he was close to death, he was tested and told he was infected.

'I had a very painful heart. I knew it takes your life. I knew my life was gone. I knew I would leave my kids without a father and my family without arrangements for them.' He did not tell his wife, even though he was still going home and sleeping with her. He saw two other doctors, and they confirmed that he had AIDS. His children knew he was ill but did not know why. 'My wife asked me to go to another doctor, and I said, "You know, sweetie, we are wasting our time and money."'

He was lucky. Two months later AngloGold began its pilot programme distributing ARVs.

Bobby Godsell, the then chief executive of AngloGold, had gained a reputation as a maverick in the traditionalist business empire of the parent company, Anglo American. He was a part-time lecturer in moral philosophy. When I spoke to him about the AIDS programme in the company headquarters in central Johannesburg, he was wearing a green sweatshirt over a rumpled checked shirt and looked as if he had not brushed his hair in days. He had just returned from a trip to New York, where he had released lion cubs on the floor of the New York Stock Exchange to mark the fifth anniversary of the company's listing there. It was a typically unconventional move. Still fired up by the experience, he launched into an impassioned spiel about the antiretroviral programme.

'To present it as something we had to do is not true. It's something we wanted to do ... and were able to do.'[16] He conceded it had taken a long time to take that step. But that, he argued, was to do with the moral and medical complexities of the issue, not the finances. It was like being in the first decade of penicillin. They had wanted to be sure the drugs had been tested. As confidence in administering ARVs had increased, so providing them had become the logical next step.

'When people are sick, over time it's more cost-effective to treat them than not to treat them.' But the final factor had not been cost but 'a moral imperative', he said.

Junior managers and doctors involved in the company's programme were rather franker about the financial imperative. As the miners milled around in their compound after an afternoon shift, one manager gazed down from the top of a staircase leading to a dormitory block. 'AngloGold doesn't have a choice,' he said. 'The industry is labour-intensive, and if this goes on, there won't be anyone left. It's a very costly business to train people to work underground. The mines can't afford to do that.' In 2007 Anglo American was to estimate that, taking into account absenteeism, early retirement, treating AIDS-related conditions, death benefits and recruiting replacements, the overall cost of failing to provide an AIDS-infected employee with ARVs was about $32,000 per person. In the same year it was calculated that the overall cost of treating a gold miner with AIDS was 1,200 rand (then about $175) a month.

For Morake, the initiative came just in time. His doctor told him that drugs were available that could help him. Only then did he tell his wife that he was HIV-positive. 'She was a little frightened. I told her I would get those medicines being talked about on the radio.' After a stint of counselling about the possible side effects and the need to be consistent in taking the pills, Morake was one of the first 250 employees to take treatment. Of those, 90 per cent responded positively and made a rapid recovery.

'Now I don't say I have a HIV,' he said. 'I am a strong man; I am strong.' He took off his beloved Stetson with its fake leopard-skin band and made as if to toss it into the air. 'One thing I know. You take your tablet, and you throw HIV away, and you stay as perfect as can be.'

His response was simplistic. ARVs can have painful and disfiguring side effects. For them to work one has to follow a rigorous routine. ARVs merely keep AIDS in check rather than offer a cure. On about one in ten people with AIDS they have no effect. But the essence of his story was clear: he had been on his deathbed; now he was back at work. This was because of a daily cocktail of three pills, and yet this was a chance that was denied to most South Africans with AIDS, as the government prevaricated over the role of ARVs.

Godsell may have been a little disingenuous when he suggested that moral and medical issues rather than costs had delayed the company's final decision. But his appraisal of the government's position was unimpeachable. 'When we announced our rollout, we were in a dialogue of the deaf,' he said. 'Our country was engaged in the wrong debate at the wrong time in the wrong way.'

In the twilight of Mbeki's presidency it was to emerge that as a young man he had told friends that his favourite Shakespeare play was *Coriolanus*.[17] They protested, arguing that its hero was a tyrant. He countered that Coriolanus was a revolutionary hero because he was prepared to take on his own people when they went astray. This contrarian streak goes to the heart of Mbeki. He had, according to the Reverend Frank Chikane, one of his closest aides, an obsession with challenging the consensus. To understand Mbeki's stance on AIDS, you had to appreciate that he was an 'intellectual president who raises questions,' he said. 'His sin was to raise the question. Because he's not a classic politician he did not back off. At the end of the day, all he was saying is there are lots of unknowns and that poverty worsens the situation. Because he's too intellectual he asks those questions. He read a lot. He paid a price on AIDS because he approached the issue as an academic.'[18]

Zuma, his successor as ANC leader, comments privately that the problems started when Mbeki 'found' the science of AIDS on the Internet.[19] Mbeki certainly believed in doing his own research. He once cited to me a new textbook written by a professor from KwaZulu-Natal on immune deficiencies to back up his argument about AIDS.[20] It showed a keen attention to detail, but it was more the mark of an academic than a politician trying to make his case. When the debate over his policies was at its height, he expressed exasperation with the advice of a former health minister who had become his minister of foreign affairs. She was a doctor, he implied, and that gave her a particular perspective but not necessarily the full picture.

His disastrous liaison with the dissident scientists who dispute the link between HIV and AIDS had begun shortly after taking over the presidency in 1999. He was first alerted to their work when one of them wrote to him. He then read about their views on the Internet. To their delight – and to the horror of AIDS activists – nearly half the members appointed to a special AIDS advisory council in 2000 had signed Internet petitions contesting the 'hypothesis' that HIV causes AIDS. According to his spokesman, Parks Mankahlana, who was later to die of what was widely believed to be AIDS, the panel was to review 'everything about AIDS' including 'whether HIV leads to AIDS'.[21] The dissidents' opposition to ARVs bolstered Mbeki's contention that they were poisonous. A desire to exploit Africa for profit and to use Africans as guinea pigs for testing potentially toxic drugs had led Western scientists, governments and drug companies to collude to misrepresent the AIDS crisis in Africa, he argued. Rather, poverty was the primary issue.

Doctors had long acknowledged that ARVs did not help a minority of people with AIDS, that poverty and a poor diet exacerbated its ravages, and that ARVS could have debilitating side effects, especially if started long after the onset of the disease. But equally the overwhelming scientific consensus was that ARVs were the best way of keeping HIV at bay. So while Mbeki publicly touted the idea that they were toxic, that was not the main impulse behind his policy. Far more important was his hankering to outdo the West and to stand up for Africa. Nozizwe Madlala-Routledge, who was to serve as Mbeki's deputy health minister before falling out with him over AIDS, believes he was fired up by the desire to find an African remedy and by a fury at the West's negative perceptions of Africa. It was not just about going on to the Internet and stumbling on the denialists' websites, she said. Rather, he was determined to prove the West wrong about AIDS in Africa. The denialists offered what he hoped would be his long-sought alternative answer.

This obsession with finding an African solution first became apparent when he was still deputy president and he hailed a supposedly new home-grown cure for AIDS as a miracle drug. Zackie remembers feeling briefly euphoric on reading newspaper headlines on his way to work, proclaiming a breakthrough.

'It's amazing – there might be a God!' Zackie recalls shouting. Then he read the reports and saw that it was a long way from being true. In his enthusiasm to proclaim an African scientific breakthrough, Mbeki went so far as to parade before the cabinet eleven supposed beneficiaries of the supposed 'wonder drug' called Virodene, even though it had not been given the most basic scientific tests. To the embarrassment of Mbeki, its active ingredient was soon revealed as an industrial solvent used for freezing animal organs, with no effect on HIV. But Mbeki would not take his setback lightly. When South Africa's Medicines Control Council (MCC) called for an immediate halt to tests on humans, Mbeki accused it of sacrificing lives by holding up a 'miracle cure' amid 'the pressing crisis of an escalating pandemic of HIV/AIDS'.[22] The MCC's chairman, Peter Folb, was later fired after refusing to allow human testing of the drug, and the council was stripped of much of its authority. It was the first sign that Mbeki was prepared to give primacy to politics over science, although there may also have been another factor in the saga. There have been persistent allegations that the ANC may have been promised a share of the profits for party funds.

In questioning the orthodoxy on AIDS, Mbeki also challenged a more conventional villain in the developing world, the Western pharmaceutical industry. Africa, he argued, was the victim of a cynical drive by the major drug companies to maximise profits at the expense of poor Africans, a charge at the heart of a rancorous dispute with the US pharmaceutical companies and the Clinton administration over intellectual property rights. In the late nineties South Africa fought for the right to reduce the cost of medicines by importing replicas of patented drugs. In an uneasy alliance with Zackie's TAC, the government eventually secured a famous victory when the major drug companies withdrew a court challenge to a South African law enacted in 1997 that had reduced the price of medicines by allowing for the import of 'parallel' medicines. It was a triumph for the developing world over big business. The cost of importing ARVs for South Africa was sharply reduced. On paper this cleared one of the biggest obstacles in the way of a comprehensive ARV programme, as the main plank of the government's formal opposition to the drugs had long been their cost. But the cost had only ever been one element of Mbeki's increasingly outlandish approach – and a disingenuous one too. Just as it had been clear to the mining companies, officials in the finance ministry agreed in private that a comprehensive treatment programme, while expensive, would in the long run be far cheaper than the ruinous costs to the economy of losing a swathe of the most economically active part of the population. In 2001 average life expectancy was fifty-four; by 2008 it was down to forty-seven.[23] Even when the costs were reduced after the landmark victory in the courts, Mbeki still did not endorse ARVs. Rather, the government continued to drag its feet even as every year thousands more babies were born infected with HIV.

The clearest and most devastating insight into his thinking came in an address to the ANC parliamentary caucus in 2000. Madlala-Routledge, then the deputy defence minister, was among those present. She recalls listening in disbelief as he stated that 90 per cent of the deaths in Africa attributed to AIDS were caused by poverty and other illnesses, not AIDS; suggested that critics of his views on AIDS were sympathetic with apartheid; and said that the CIA was involved in a Western plot to help the big pharmaceutical companies by ensuring that Africa took loans from the United States to pay for American drugs. 'There was a hush,' she said. This was the 'hugely respected' president speaking. Some MPs were shocked to hear him utter such a controversial view. But others who did not know much about AIDS listened and believed. 'They were desperately searching for a reason not to believe the nightmarish scenario unfolding. They had seen people die. They were looking for someone to give us good news.'[24]

Mbeki was clearly infuriated by the scientific consensus that the rapid spread of AIDS in Africa was linked to promiscuity, in particular the practice of multiple concurrent sexual partners. This too easily, he thought, fed into old stereotypes of African primitiveness and played down the role of poverty and poor diet in the spread of the virus. It also undermined the very vision that he was seeking to promote, of a new, confident and responsible Africa. He vented his anger in an impassioned address to students at the University of Fort Hare, the alma mater of many of southern Africa's leaders. While he did not mention AIDS by name, he laced his speech with sarcasm over what he saw as a traditional Western condescension towards Africa over AIDS. 'Convinced that we are but natural-born, promiscuous carriers of germs, unique in the world,' he said, 'they proclaim that our continent is doomed to an inevitable mortal end because of our unconquerable devotion to the sin of lust.'[25]

In public he only obliquely denied a link between HIV and AIDS. Nor did he formally endorse the AIDS dissidents. Speaking to me in 2007, he seemed upset that he was still being accused of AIDS-denialism. He rightly pointed out, as he had so many times before, that poverty, poor diet and sexually transmitted diseases, such as syphilis, can contribute to the breakdown of immune systems. 'So I say, "All right, let's respond comprehensively to everything that causes immune deficiency." That's where you get the story that I have denied a connection. No one has ever shown me where I did. They say it. But you say where, when – they can't. It was never said.'[26]

But that is sophistry. It is true that he is not on the record formally denying the link between HIV and AIDS. So too his arguments that poverty was a factor and that ARVs were sometimes toxic and could have worrying side effects were accurate. But it was his responsibility to lead. In this case, by sowing seeds of doubt about the pandemic and ARVs, and by entertaining the views of the dissident scientists, he led South Africans down a dangerous blind alley.

In private, Mbeki was more Stalinist than Socratic, colleagues recall. He imposed a rigid orthodoxy on the government over AIDS policy. Cabinet ministers were too intimidated by his apparent grasp of detail and too craven in the face of his zealotry to question him. One cabinet minister confessed to me that he became quite convinced by Mbeki's arguments until AIDS activists took him to one side and explained the science. Even then the minister did not speak out, either in public or in the cabinet. 'Members of the executive seemed to be very reluctant to question him,' Madlala-Routledge recalled. 'He became quite irritated about the use of the word "pandemic". He spent a lot of time on this. Ministers had to watch out which term they used . . . He believed it was an epidemic.'

The only leader in the ANC who dared to challenge Mbeki was Mandela. Loyal party man, he had held his tongue as the controversy developed under Mbeki rather than breaking with the ANC's tradition of conformity and pushing formally for a change of policy. But a year into Mbeki's presidency he became increasingly outspoken. The turning point was watching several of his relations die and then seeing the child of a cousin recover after taking ARVs. In 2000 he infuriated Mbeki by saying publicly that HIV definitely causes AIDS. Two years later he took his concerns to the ANC's national executive committee and spoke out against Mbeki's AIDS policy. Only two members defended his right to speak out, including Cyril Ramaphosa, Mbeki's old rival.

'I was very shocked,' Ramaphosa said. 'People in the NEC were speaking in defence of Thabo, and in doing so Madiba became fair game. They thought Madiba was still trying to be president.'[27]

ANC members vied with each other to curry favour with Mbeki by deriding the 'old man'. One of the most vicious attacks on Mandela came from Peter Mokaba, the former ANC Youth League leader whom Mandela had berated many times in the early and mid-nineties. After his 'vicious mauling Madiba looked twice his age, old and ashen', a senior ANC leader later recalled.[28] His critics were 'wild, aggressive and merciless', like 'a pack of wild dogs tearing apart their prey'. The NEC went on to decide not to provide ARVs to pregnant women, rape victims or health workers because they 'remained unproven'.

Mandela was distressed and appalled, he made clear to friends. To see ANC leaders slavishly following a policy that was condemning thousands to an early death was a betrayal of all that the ANC had represented. Undaunted by the barbs of Mbeki's backers in the media, he intensified his campaign. In the closing speech at the biennial UN AIDS conference, held in 2002 in Barcelona, he called for leaders to do more to reduce the stigma of HIV. Soon after his return, he visited Zackie, who had pledged not to take ARVs until the government made them freely available and was then weakening from AIDS.

He told Zackie that before going to see him he had telephoned Mbeki's office, checked that the president was at home, and then been driven around to his door. Mandela told Mbeki that he, too, should come, and that if Zackie died, it would be a terrible blow for South Africa and for the country's reputation. 'Madiba then told me, "I don't want to tell you how quickly I had to leave,"' Zackie recalled.

The following year the government finally agreed to abide by court rulings to make ARVs available, and Zackie, who was then weakening fast from AIDS, started to take them. Zackie's health quickly improved, but he was rightly sceptical of the change of policy. Despite the public change of heart, for the next five years many in the government and many provincial health ministers would continue to drag their feet about implementing the policy.

In 2007 the South African government endorsed a national programme that won the approval of international AIDS experts. It was by then implementing the largest ARV programme in the world, largely funded by donors and business. Yet the government continued to send out mixed messages over treatment, and Mbeki shrank from giving an unambiguous endorsement of ARVs.

Even after the 2003 decision to provide ARVs, Mbeki's minister of health, Manto Tshabalala-Msimang, continued to imply that people had a choice between nutrition and medicine. Her interventions were all the more inexcusable, as she was a trained doctor, and yet she did not stand up for science but rather stayed staunchly loyal to Mbeki, with whom she had fled into exile as part of a group of young ANC members back in 1963. She even invited AIDS dissidents to address officials in the ministry, Madlala-Routledge recalls. 'She fought with all the scientists and started to support anything that was not science.' She also allowed alternative practitioners and *sangomas* (traditional healers) to tour South Africa offering quack remedies and denouncing ARVs. The most notorious was a German doctor named Matthias Rath, who marketed multivitamins as the solution to AIDS. He preached against ARVs without sanction from the government. Zackie's movement, the TAC, finally gained a court order to stop him, after it had documented people dying of AIDS who refused to take ARVs, saying they had been told by the distributors of Rath's tablets to rely on his vitamins.

Then there was the case of a former long-distance truck driver called Zeblon Gwala, who had a healthy business hawking a home-brewed anti-AIDS potion he called uBhejane (Zulu for 'rhinoceros'). The ingredients, he said, had been 'revealed to him in a dream' by his dead grandfather. They boosted the immune system and suppressed HIV, he said. But before people took it, he advised them to stop taking ARVs. Tshabalala-Msimang dismissed his critics as 'colonialist'.[29]

She became a figure of derision internationally and was nicknamed 'Dr Beetroot' for her espousal of vegetables as an alternative to ARVs. Her reputation reached its nadir at the 2006 UN AIDS conference in Toronto, where she championed an exhibit dominated by garlic, lemon and beetroot as treatment for AIDS. The UN envoy on AIDS, Stephen Lewis, said that South Africa was 'obtuse, dilatory, and negligent about rolling out treatment' and its policies were 'wrong, immoral, [and] indefensible'. The theories were 'more worthy of a lunatic fringe than of a concerned and compassionate state'.[30] The minister liked to argue that the West was guilty of cultural imperialism in its attitude towards traditional medicine. She received a tart put-down from Barack Obama, then a US senator, when he visited South Africa in 2006. 'It's not an issue of Western science versus African science,' he said. 'It's just science.'[31]

Yet even after all this opprobrium she continued to wield a pernicious influence. When she took time off for a liver transplant operation, her deputy, Madlala-Routledge, championed a credible AIDS policy, raising hopes that the age of denialism in the ministry of health was over. But as soon as Tshabalala-Msimang returned, she reasserted the old views. Within a few months of her superior's return, Madlala-Routledge was sacked. She was the first government minister to be fired by Mbeki. Formally her offence was having flown to a conference in Spain without securing the president's permission. But the real reason for her dismissal, it was clear, was her opposition to Tshabalala-Msimang. After months of opposing the government's AIDS policy, the final trigger for her sacking was her visit in July 2007 to a hospital in the Eastern Cape where a number of babies had died, apparently of neglect. She arrived at the hospital unannounced, berated the hospital staff, and assured patients that the deaths would be investigated. Mbeki and Tshabalala-Msimang later came out in support of the hospital. Months after her dismissal, Madlala-Routledge was still distraught about the repercussions of Mbeki's failings on AIDS.

'The people look up to us in government so much. People should be told: "This is a very serious epidemic. You must know your status. There is no cure, but there are drugs that you can take."'

People in villages needed to know that in America people had been living with AIDS for twenty years by taking ARVs and that they too had once been afraid and were now thriving. And yet the government had at best vacillated in public and at worst supported dissident approaches. 'A senior leader in KwaZulu-Natal recently pulled me aside and started telling me weird theories, saying, "AIDS doesn't kill sheep. So why does it kill humans?" I thought, "Here is a man in denial. He must be scared of the truth."'

Any doubts over whether Mbeki harboured sympathy for the AIDS-denialists disappeared when he had couriered to a biographer an update of a hundred-page denialist monograph about AIDS.[32] This had first been circulated to the cabinet in 2002. A blend of AIDS dissident views and African nationalism, it claimed that Parks Mankahlana, the former presidential spokesperson who is thought to have died of AIDS in 2001, died because he was persuaded to take ARVs. The paper was co-authored by Peter Mokaba, the firebrand who had lambasted Mandela over AIDS. Within a year of the document's release, Mokaba died of what is widely assumed to have been an AIDS-related disease. There are strong suspicions that Mbeki was also a co-author of the document, as it contains quotes from some of his favourite authors and an early emailed version was traced to his computer in the presidency.

The latest version had three new quotations. The first was from Giordano Bruno, the fourteenth-century scientist burned at the stake: 'He who desires to philosophise must first doubt all things.' The second was from George Bernard Shaw: 'All great truths begin as blasphemies.' The implication was clear, his biographer wrote: Mbeki still shared the dissidents' views.

Makgoba, the scientist who fell out with Mbeki over AIDS, believes that to understand his denialism one has to appreciate the shock the disease posed to the ANC when it was unbanned: it threatened the very dream the party had long nurtured. He highlights that before 1990, the year of the party's unbanning, antenatal surveys showed a prevalence of about 0.2 per cent and that thereafter it rose rapidly at a time when ANC members were returning from exile. The dream, he said, became a nightmare.

In those circumstances it was not unreasonable that someone would go into denial, he said. Other governments had had a period of denial and disbelief before then confronting the disease. 'Unfortunately for South Africa, Mbeki's denialism was not a temporary response but rather became a state of mind. When Mbeki is confronted with things, his first instinct is to deny,' he said.

'Everything of national interest he's been confronted with, his instinct is to deny. And it has cost us a lot, in terms of the reputation of the country and the many who could have been saved. The denialism has complicated the simple message that could have been given to the people. It's made it many times harder. Some people say privately that, "If the president says so, why should I believe the science?"'[33]

On the desk in the principal's office in Qondokuhle elementary school is the picture of a little schoolgirl who died of AIDS in August 2007. The child's mother died of AIDS eight months later. In the deep red earth of the school courtyard a newly planted sapling is named after the girl. 'She was a short one like this tree,' explained Mantombi Nala-Preusker, the head teacher. 'At least we could tell her granny this is a reminder of her.'[34] There was something of Mary Poppins about Nala-Preusker. As she strode through the school dispensing instructions to fellow teachers, advice to pupils and guidance to parents signing up for her AIDS programme, her feet barely seemed to touch the ground in her haste.

Her school was in the township of Umlazi, a settlement of lower-middle-class corrugated-iron-roofed bungalows mixed in with shacks and shanty dwellings that sprawl over rolling hills a few miles from the Indian Ocean. In the early 1990s it was one of the many front lines in the political turf war between the ANC and the Inkatha Freedom Party. A decade later it was at the heart of South Africa's fight against AIDS. It was in overcrowded townships such as Umlazi that the virus spread at devastating speed. Of the 560 children in her school, Nala-Preusker knew that at least ten were on ARVs, having in most cases contracted HIV from their mothers during childbirth. Many more of her charges were HIV-positive.

The numbers in her school were dropping dramatically because of AIDS, she confided. This was not just because of infections in her school roll. It was also because more and more children were staying at home to look after parents weakening with AIDS.

Sixteen mothers and a father had come to hear about her plans to teach children about HIV. She had just come back from two months at New York's Columbia University, where she had been sponsored by a cosmetics company to learn about community AIDS projects. She handed out a sheet with ten

AIDS-related questions. Then, treating them like pupils, she quizzed them for answers.

'So you just grab one virgin, and then AIDS is cured: no more AIDS, no more ARVs. Who believes that?' she asked, highlighting a myth in remote parts of rural southern Africa that having sex with a virgin cures AIDS. She nodded approvingly as it emerged everyone had ticked the 'no' box. She then launched into a debate about the merits of having condoms freely available at her school where children in the older classes were sexually active. 'It is such a dirty thing to have in my school!' she said provocatively. While she believed having a condom machine was essential, she knew that many parents disagreed.

After one mother suggested condom machines would encourage casual sex, a heated debate ensued. Nala-Preusker had the final word. 'We know kids are involved in sex,' she said. A recent report in the local newspaper, she said, had found that 41 per cent of fourteen-year-old girls had regular sex.

Private sector initiatives had for several years been promoting safe sex in high-profile advertising on radio, television and billboards on the main transport routes into townships and villages. Yet for some reason the infection rates in Umlazi and other townships had stayed high. Parents said that their daughters, cousins, nieces and nephews engaged in multiple concurrent sexual partnerships. It was this trend, even more than random encounters with prostitutes, that experts believed was at the heart of South Africa's AIDS epidemic.

Three of the parents at the meeting told heart-rending stories of trying and failing to convince relations and friends to use condoms and to get tested.

'Teenagers just won't listen,' said one of the mothers. 'Once they are HIV-positive they say, "Why should I bother with a condom?" There are some I know who say, "I want to infect others."' When her sister found out she was HIV-positive, she gave up all hope of surviving, the woman said. 'I told her to take care of herself. She said she didn't care if she died, as everyone dies.' Her sister died after two months in a coma. She was just twenty-three. 'Now I am the mother of five children, two of hers and three of mine,' the woman said. 'One of my sister's children is infected. I told my sister, "Why should you live a wild life? Who will look after your children?" But with these teenagers it is getting worse and worse. They say, "Mind your own business."'

Nala-Preusker had developed the no-nonsense pragmatism of one who was wearily accustomed to imparting grim news. Some girls were becoming pregnant to be eligible for the child-support grant, she said. Some just did not want to listen to her advice because of the stigma. Others who had HIV 'sleep with people, saying, "I don't want to die by myself."' Many still preferred to go to a *sangoma* and believed that you could not use condoms when taking *muti,* traditional medicine. 'It is a challenge,' she said simply.

In the mines, too, despite the huge investment in ARVs, progress was slow. In 2008 James Steele, the doctor in charge of AngloGold's HIV policy, intimated that step by step the picture was improving. About 65 per cent of employees had taken an HIV test in the previous year, up from 3 or 4 per cent in 2002–2003. Nearly all the employees had been tested at one time or another, but Dr Steele conceded it was rather harder to answer whether they had changed people's sexual behaviour. Also it remained a challenge to persuade people to keep taking ARVs.

In August 2008 Morake, the miner who had made the Lazarus-like recovery, failed to turn up for treatment. A week later I heard he resigned from the company. I recalled the last time I had seen him when I had asked him about his wife, Janey. Was she HIV-positive? I had asked. Had she been tested? And the most sensitive question of all, did they use a condom when they slept together? He had shaken his head to the question about whether she had been tested.

'Even now when we sleep, we don't use condoms,' he told me. 'We just do it person to person. She says she is still strong. I can always say, "Come here," and put her in the mine's clinic, and she will get better.'

The fatalism surrounding discussion of AIDS cannot all be blamed on Mbeki. He was preaching his denialist message to a receptive audience. The stigma over HIV is deeply entrenched in society, particularly in rural areas. In neighbouring Botswana, where the government has shown far more dynamic leadership in combating AIDS, swathes of the population continue to resist the idea of being tested. In 2001, the then president of Botswana, Festus Mogae, announced that his government would give ARVs to anyone with AIDS. Yet more than two years later, barely fifteen thousand people had come forward to accept this offer, less than one-sixth of those believed to be in urgent need of the drugs. Six years later, new rates of infection remained catastrophically high, although the overall prevalence rate was starting to fall.[35]

Jacob Zuma's early unfortunate role in the scandal that is South Africa's official response to AIDS reflects how the spread of the disease is linked to the patriarchal and macho view of sexual relations that still holds sway in many parts of Africa. When he was deputy president from 1999 to 2005, he had special responsibilities for overseeing AIDS policies. Yet the following year, when he was on trial for raping an HIV-positive family friend, he told the court that after having sexual intercourse he took a shower to wash away the virus. He was acquitted, but it was never in dispute that the man who had been in charge of the country's AIDS policy had knowingly had unprotected sex with a woman who was HIV-positive. He later apologised for the 'shower' remark. But it was an appalling statement to have made, as had been his testimony to the court that his accuser had signalled she wanted to have sex with him by wearing a *kanga* (a knee-length skirt) and that in Zulu culture it was the equivalent of rape not to have sex with a woman who was aroused.[36]

Zuma also initially made no attempt to rein in his supporters when they demonstrated outside the trial, saying that the complainant had 'asked for it'. In a country with one of the highest rates of recorded rape in the world, such a stance could only encourage rape and contribute to the spread of AIDS. More than fifty thousand cases of rape are reported annually, and surveys suggest that many others go unreported. Mbeki, however, was incandescent when asked in Parliament about a possible link between the high incidence of rape and the spread of AIDS. His questioner, a white opposition MP, was, he suggested, 'corrupted by the disease of racism'.[37]

Nine years after Mbeki started his engagement with the dissident scientists, the South African government finally showed genuine commitment to confront the disease. After Mbeki was forced from office in 2008, his interim successor, Kgalema Motlanthe, appointed a new health minister, Barbara Hogan, a veteran ANC activist who had spent eight years in prison under apartheid and was known for her opposition to Mbeki's views on AIDS. She swiftly declared that there was no doubt that HIV caused AIDS, and she promised in particular to focus on preventing mother to child transmission of the virus.[38] This was an attainable target that AIDS activists believed if realised could save the lives of over forty thousand children a year. She also talked of the need to transform public health care from top to bottom. But this will require extraordinary commitment and funding. The vicious battles over AIDS policy have further debilitated an already weak health service that in many provinces is all but broken.

As an acknowledged polygamist, Zuma is hardly the ideal role model. He did at least, however, make clear that he would be far more forthright than Mbeki in confronting AIDS. He led by example when he took an HIV test and called on all South Africans to know their status and also to abstain from premarital sex. On taking office he drew a line under the past controversies, promoted ARVs and endorsed an orthodox policy.[39] And yet however dynamic the ANC may be in the future in confronting the stigma, a catastrophe is unfolding that will claim thousands more unnecessary lives as the consequence of fourteen wasted years in which the party failed its people on the most important challenge to confront it.

Chapter 10

THE 100 PER CENT ZULU BOY

This man is our messiah. He will save us.

— GEOFFREY MOTOAWAGAE,
A ZUMA SUPPORTER, 2008

*People think Zuma will make changes, but nothing
will change. 'Mshini Wami' [Zuma's song, 'Bring
Me My Machine Gun'] will end up on the dustbin
heap. What kind of president sings 'Mshini Wami'?*

— BRA BRICKS,
TOWNSHIP ACTIVIST, 2007

The sixty-fifth-birthday party of Jacob Zuma was a splendid affair. Hundreds of the political and business elite of Durban, a humid old British colonial city on the Indian Ocean coast, had gathered in a convention centre decorated as a star-filled night sky. A Zulu praise-singer called Past Four roared a tribute. In bodice-hugging ballgowns five of Zuma's daughters performed a sketch to the tune of 'Happy Birthday' warbling from a cuckoo clock. Everyone sang 'For He's a Jolly Good Fellow'. As a small army of waiters wheeled in a two-metre-long cake, JZ presided gracefully in a black-and-gold Nehru suit.

It was April 2007, and Mbeki and Zuma were caught up in the closing stages of their battle for control of the ANC. The smart money on my table was still just on Mbeki's emerging victorious, notwithstanding the worshipful references to Msholozi (Zuma's clan name), which adorned every conversation.

A young Zulu management consultant on my right was deftly saluting the talents of both men when my mobile phone rang. It was Mahlambandlopfu[1] (the president's residence), a voice told me. Moments later I heard Mbeki's distinctive, deep, mellifluous voice. He had just returned from the Sudan. He wanted to send me an email to follow up on a conversation we had had the previous week.

Even as his enemy was celebrating, surrounded by friends and supplicants, I pictured the president catching up on his correspondence after his latest foray as an African statesman. The contrast pandered to all the stereotypes of the two men: the man of the people and the more formal and reclusive professorial president. Mbeki had long been mocked by his critics for his penchant for surfing the Internet at night. There he was at 9 p.m. on a Saturday catching up on his emails.

'God moves in mysterious ways,' he said in conclusion, although to what I could not quite hear. Back in the ballroom, on the prompting of his guests, Zuma was taking to the dance floor for a solo performance. Most of the stage was occupied by a scarlet-uniformed school choir. He inserted himself effortlessly into the front rank and swayed back and forth. It was close to midnight when he finally spoke. He was self-effacing and pleasingly brief. He would like to open a school to teach people how to propose love, he joked. His large family testified, he added with a beam, to how he was procreating to increase the party's voter base. There was a gentle rebuke to his political opponents and critics. Then he stood down, knowing instinctively, like all good hosts, when his audience had had enough.

I read Mbeki's email late that night. He had wanted to draw my attention to recent cases of supposedly inaccurate reporting of his government. He passed on a friendly message to my family. He concluded with a flourish, that to understand the media I needed to know a Xhosa expression: 'alitshoni lingenandaba.' This he explained could be translated as 'each day brings its fresh baggage of news'.

I wrote back vowing to bear it in mind. Within hours back came another email. To help me to understand the Xhosa saying, he had composed a mock news item.

Last night, while on routine patrol at about midnight, a unit of the Police
Service found President Mbeki riding a goat on the grounds of the Union
Buildings [the government headquarters] stark naked. Scared out of their
wits that they might fall victim to witchcraft, the Police Unit immediately
drove away at high speed and smashed their vehicle into the Sunnyside
Police Station, damaging both the car and the Police Station beyond repair. Miraculously, the two police officers only suffered minor cuts. They
were however admitted into the Intensive Care Ward of the Pretoria Academic Hospital where they were treated throughout the night by Rev
Sam Nkosi, who specialises in exorcising ghosts and other evil spirits.

'One might then respond to this news,' concluded the president, 'by ex-
claiming *alitshoni lingenandaba*! This usage would be akin to the meaning that
the ancient Romans attached to the expression *Ex Africa semper aliquid novi*
[Africa always brings something new]!'[2]

It was vintage Mbeki. This email encapsulated the thoughtful, inquisitive man
who had been groomed from his youth as a future leader and yet whose
hypersensitivity was to destroy his reputation. It also highlighted the contrast
between the party intellectual and his ebullient successor. Quoting Latin is not
Zuma's style. He learned to read and write only as an adult. A genuine man of the
people, he is as comfortable sitting with clansmen in his home village in rural
Zululand, telling stories and, teetotaller as he is, passing round a vat of sorghum
beer, as discussing policy.

Mbeki agonised over what it meant to be an authentic African leader. Zuma
did not suffer from such self-doubt. He was the ultimate modern tribal chief, a
man who would listen to his people, who understood their concerns, and who
would not necessarily let the niceties of Western political convention impede
his plans.

On a balmy night in August 2008 a noisy crowd of some two thousand people
gathered in Freedom Park, a scraggy patch of grass opposite the High Court in
the city of Pietermaritzburg, the capital of KwaZulu-Natal, Zuma's home
province. They had come to drink, to sing, and to show their support for JZ in

his latest appearance in court. Their exuberant rendition of old struggle songs
stirred memories of marches in the early nineties. The echo was deliberate.
Zuma's long-running trial for corruption, the latest chapter of which was to unfold in the court the following morning, was, the demonstrators argued, no less
wicked than the legendary political trials under apartheid.

There were two striking differences from the days when the struggle an-
thems were last sung with such fervour. First, the denunciations were not of
the race-based tyranny of apartheid but of a key prop of a democratic state, the
judiciary. The rally was the latest instalment of a cynical campaign by Zuma's
supporters to undermine the credibility of the judiciary by demonising it as
compromised and tainted with apartheid. The judges from the Constitutional
Court had, a few days earlier, found against Zuma and ruled that tens of thousands of potentially incriminating documents seized from his home and his
lawyer's office in raids in 2005 were admissible in court. They were, Zuma's allies, said 'counter-revolutionaries'. The fact that seven of the ten judges on the
Constitutional Court were black and two of the other three were traditionally
sympathetic to the ANC was brushed aside.

The second change was the assertive and proud display of Zuluness. In the
apartheid era the ANC had insisted it was a non-tribal party. To talk of tribal
differences was to play the game of the Afrikaner Nationalists, it argued, and to
harp back to a feudal past. Rather, it was its rival in the Zulu heartland, the Inkatha
Freedom Party, that stressed its links to Zulu tradition and culture. The murderous
battles between Inkatha and ANC supporters were often as much a matter of
differences between town and country, modernity and tradition, detribalised Zulus
and traditional Zulus, as between rival political parties. The ANC liked to argue
that, unlike many other African states, South Africa had moved beyond the ties of
ethnicity and clan and that Chief Mangosuthu Buthelezi, the Inkatha leader who
attended rallies dressed in traditional garb, was a throwback to the past. Such
protestations were, however, simplistic. Many Zulus, particularly in rural areas,
retained a strong sense of tribal identity. When Zuma's fortunes plummeted in
2005, and he was fired as the country's deputy president following the conviction
of his financial adviser for procuring a bribe for him from an arms company, he fell
back on his Zulu roots to resurrect his political career.

To be a Zulu has a particular emotional and political heft. Zulus are the
most populous tribe in South Africa, and elders have long prided themselves

on their imperial past under Shaka, their Napoleonic king who carved out a vast empire in the early nineteenth century. Urbanised South Africans from other tribes have long mocked rural Zulus as hicks, but many Zulus maintained a residual pride in their warrior tradition. In 1879, a Zulu army equipped with just spears and shields annihilated a 1,100-strong British expeditionary force in one of the most humiliating defeats ever suffered by the British imperial forces before the Zulu kingdom was finally conquered and dismembered.

While the Zulus had garnered military triumphs largely at the expense of other African tribes, the Xhosas, South Africa's second largest tribe, had traditionally dominated anti-colonial politics. The Xhosas waged a series of brutal frontier wars in the mid-nineteenth century against the settlers encroaching on their homeland, the Eastern Cape. In the first half of the twentieth century the Xhosas' elite tended to be better educated than other tribes', as they had benefited from earlier and more frequent contact with missionaries, who founded schools and colleges. For much of the twentieth century the ANC and other liberation movements were dominated by Xhosas. Oliver Tambo, who led the ANC from 1967, and his two successors, Nelson Mandela and Thabo Mbeki, were Xhosas, as was Steve Biko, the leader of the black consciousness movement. So the idea that it was a Zulu's turn to lead the ANC had appeal even among ANC-supporting Zulus who in the apartheid era had regarded talk of ethnicity as retrogressive.

When in 2006 Zuma went on trial for the rape of the thirty-one-year-old HIV-positive daughter of a family friend, he used the courtroom as a political stage, stressing his Zulu roots. He spoke isiZulu in court. He cited Zulu custom as a main plank of his defence. On his acquittal he enthused the mainly Zulu crowd that had gathered outside the courtroom with an impassioned rendition of the old anti-apartheid song 'Lethu Mshini Wami' (Bring Me My Machine Gun). Relying on the ethnic politics that had worked so well for leaders elsewhere in the world – not just Africa – Zuma established KwaZulu-Natal as his electoral stronghold. When he was voted in as ANC president in December 2007, the Zulu delegates voted for him en masse. In a sign of how the old non-tribal ethos had broken down under the stress of the disputed succession, the majority of the Xhosas voted as a bloc for Mbeki. The day after Zuma's victory I spoke to the leader of an ANC branch heading home to the Eastern Cape with a busload of dejected colleagues. They would, he said, in time exact their revenge. Zuma had led the ANC into a new era of politics in which tribal identity was no longer to be a taboo.

There was, however, a less insidious and more inclusive side to his proud and open assertion of his traditional Zulu upbringing. He understood, unlike, it appeared, many in the ANC's urban elite, that traditional values and beliefs still mattered to millions of South Africans. His was a country, after all, in which the majority of the population still believed in consulting traditional healers, and where for many a belief in witchcraft did not contradict the logical certainties of a Western liberal education. Mandela, with his upbringing in a chief's household and his memories of herding livestock in the hills of the Eastern Cape, had bridged the divide in a way that Mbeki neither was able to nor seemed to want to. In the early nineties many in the ANC made no attempt to understand Buthelezi and were keen to use force to supplant him and overthrow the parallel system of government led by tribal chiefs that he backed. Mandela sounded a far more sympathetic note. He understood that chiefs were part of the fabric of rural society and could not just be ousted.

Zuma too, while not of chiefly stock, understood the need to accommodate tradition with modernity. He did not despise Inkatha's nurturing of Zulu culture, which urbanised ANC-supporting blacks regarded as old-fashioned malarkey. Rather, he appreciated it as just as integral a part of South Africa's heritage and day-to-day life in the rural areas as the progressive beliefs of the doctors, lawyers and graduates who had dominated the ANC's leadership. Willies Mchunu, one of his oldest allies, a courteous ANC veteran with an immaculate silver beard and a love of elegant Old World diction, goes so far as to suggest that Zuma and Buthelezi have a lot in common. Zuma, he says, has helped to reinstate tradition to its rightful place in society after it was rejected in the days of the struggle.

'If I may be a little tribalistic, among Zulu people traditional respect has been one of the cardinal ways of life,' he said. 'We are brought up with such discipline and respect for elders that at times in the struggle we didn't know if we were not trampling on our old rites. Vilification of the old values was the order of the day. First Mandela and then Zuma brought us back from that culture.'[3]

Zuma's support base did in time span the country, and he even gained the support of a breakaway faction in the Eastern Cape, as he easily won over ANC members wearied by Mbeki's chilly style. A centrepiece of his appeal was his authentic working-class story as the son of a domestic worker and a rural policeman. The herd boy to president line had been a successful staple in post-colonial African politics. Daniel arap Moi, the second president of Kenya, was one of several leaders who touted their humble upbringings to enhance their appeal. Mobutu sese Seko, the Big Man leader of Zaire, liked to make much of being the son of a cook and the great-nephew of a tribal warrior and magician. With his easy-going manner, his record as a hero of the struggle and his Zulu roots, Zuma was swiftly able to build up a mass following. This was all too apparent outside the Pietermaritzburg High Court, where a toxic undercurrent of Zulu nationalism, bellicosity, prejudice and macho pride swirled through the crowd.

'I am prepared to die for Zuma – to die for Zuma,' announced Sdu Mdluli, a well-built young man with Zuma's face adorning his T-shirt. He had driven 280 kilometres from the town of Dundee. An activist turned businessman, he was determined to prevent the 'counter-revolutionaries' of the Constitutional Court from undermining the ideals of the ANC. The investigation into Zuma and the case against him were part of a 'smear campaign' designed to stop him from taking power. Mdluli had come to the court to denounce an injustice.

But why should people talk of dying for Zuma? And was it not absurd to compare his indictment on corruption charges to the anti-apartheid struggle? 'People were prepared to die for liberation,' he said. 'Why can't they be prepared to die for Zuma? JZ is not only our hope; he is the hope of the whole continent.'[4] Mdluli disappeared into the night. Another Zuma diehard with a '100 Per cent Zulu Boy' T-shirt and a fresh stock of slogans took his place.

Shortly before proceedings began, senior leaders of the ANC, along with their allies in the unions and Communist Party, made their way into a VIP enclosure in front of the court dancing the *toyi toyi*, the high-stepping liberation dance. The purple-robed bishop of an evangelical church and two imams took their seats alongside the ANC hierarchs in an open marquee. Then the rhetoric started. One by one, politicians stood under a giant poster proclaiming 'Innocent until proven guilty' to denounce the Scorpions, the elite unit that investigated and brought charges against Zuma, and to lambaste the Constitutional Court.

A few minutes later, a twenty-strong delegation from the ANC's national executive committee, rose to their feet and strode across to the courtroom, with the bishop and imams trailing in their wake. The last to enter the courtroom was JZ himself. His face was impassive, but he gave an impish wave as he walked through the antechamber. Half a dozen court clerks and cleaners ululated with delight. Then his lawyer set to work addressing Zuma's bid for his corruption case to be struck from the roll on the grounds that the prosecution had acted improperly and unfairly.

Zuma emerged from court flanked by eight security men in dark suits and sunglasses. They walked him through a cordon of khaki-clad veterans of Umkhonto we Sizwe (the ANC's armed wing), several of whom looked barely old enough to remember apartheid, let alone to have fought against it. Zuma skipped on to the stage wearing his warm and easy smile and started flirting with the crowd. He greeted them in four African languages, and then gave a deep belly laugh. He could not say much. The case was sub judice of course. In fact he was not going to say anything. He would say more the next day, so they did not have to rely on 'those who love telling stories about things which they don't know', a dig at the scores of journalists crouching at his feet.

A man with his silky political skills was not, however, going to stop there. Once again came a flash of that bountiful smile, and he was dancing across the stage leading the crowd in 'Lethu Mshini Wami.'

An old woman in traditional tribal dress and clutching a plastic shopping bag danced in front of him. Another appeared twirling an umbrella. The crowd swayed as they chanted his hallowed song. There was a religious – even sexual – fervour to their passion, not unlike that of charismatic evangelists in Brazil. Zuma had become far more than a politician. Briefly it was if he were a revivalist preacher or the leader of a cult.

I had last seen Zuma dancing in January 2008, at the Pretoria township of Atteridgeville at the celebration marking the ANC's birthday. After the speeches and toasts Zuma had been enveloped by a throng of brightly clad traditional healers. For half a minute he could barely be seen amid clouds of smoke and incense from their ritual herbal fires as they inducted him into their order. One Zuma fan sporting an English football shirt had driven 140 miles from the town of Zeerust, on the border with Botswana, the opposite end of the country from the ancestral land of the Zulus. He was star-struck. 'This man is our messiah,' he said. 'He will save us.'[5]

Zuma's life, far more than Mbeki's or indeed Mandela's, encompasses what the struggle meant to most black South Africans. His predecessors in the ANC came from the party's university-educated, middle-class elite. In marked contrast he was very much a rough diamond. There was a second important difference between his experiences and those of his predecessors as ANC leader. He was almost unique in the ANC in having been involved in the three strands of the movement – Robben Island, exile and the internal resistance wing. He had indeed, as he said in his sixty-fifth-birthday speech, 'lived a lot'.

Zuma grew up in a remote Zulu village, where he herded livestock and fought other youths with sticks just as Zulus had done since the days of Shaka. But while he liked to recall his early carefree years lovingly, as time spent hunting birds with catapults and fighting with his fellow herd boys with traditional sticks, it was a difficult and broken upbringing. His was the disjointed childhood experienced by so many growing up under apartheid. His father, a policeman, died when he was young. His mother was away for months on end in Durban working as a domestic servant. There was no school at Nkandla. Years later he recalled that he started to learn to read and write by asking other children in the area who were going to school to share their books with him. He also paid a local woman two shillings and sixpence a month for evening classes, which his uncles allowed him to attend once he had put the cattle in the *kraal* for the night.[6] But this was only the most rudimentary education. In his teens he moved to one of the rougher townships outside Durban, a violent environment where all too many of his contemporaries joined gangs and met an early death.

'Trace his history of not living with his family, and you'd think he'd have become a township *tsotsi* [gangster],' says his old ally, Willies Mchunu. 'His was one of the worst townships, one of the initial squatter camps around Durban. As a young boy he may have been a *tsotsi*, I don't know, but in politics he soon learned the discipline of the organisation.'

It was in the years of early adulthood as a trade union organiser and then member of Umkhonto we Sizwe (or MK) that Zuma's abilities as a leader first became recognised by both the ANC and the apartheid security forces. When preparing to cross the border into the then Bechuanaland (now Botswana) for military training in exile, he was arrested and, in August 1963, sentenced to ten years in prison on Robben Island for conspiring to overthrow the government. Despite his humble origins, Zuma did not seem overawed by his many intellectual superiors in the famous prison. Rather, he charmed them with his unassuming ways. He sang on the boat out to the island to keep up his fellow prisoners' spirits, recalls Ebrahim Ebrahim, a fellow MK activist, who travelled with him in a windowless police van from Pretoria to Cape Town en route to Robben Island. Indeed, he always seemed to be singing, whether in a Zulu choral group that he organised or when he broke out into singing freedom songs in the limestone quarries. He soon became a popular figure on the island, where, under the tutorship of Harry Gwala, the diehard Marxist, one of the many with whom he shared a communal cell, he learned to read and write.

'He was always very cheerful,' Ebrahim says. 'He kept morale very high.' Zuma was captain of a Robben Island football team called the Rangers. Ebrahim remembers Zuma keeping everyone entertained with stories about the Zulu king and about growing up wearing traditional clothing and fighting with sticks. 'He was both a rural person and a modern person, and this rural nature remains with him. He combines Zulu culture with modern life; that is his brilliance.'[7]

The crux of the Zuma legend was forged while he lived, beginning in December 1975, in exile in the 'frontline states', as South Africa's neighbours were known, those initially responsible for receiving the exiles fleeing from South Africa. He progressed swiftly through the ranks of Umkhonto we Sizwe. As head of intelligence from 1987, he was responsible for deploying agents back into South Africa, a risky mission that led to the imprisonment, torture and death of some of his young protégés. He had to make his share of ruthless decisions. In August 1993, Mandela and senior ANC leaders held a press conference in Shell House, the party's headquarters, to mark the release of an internal report into human rights abuses committed in its detention camps in exile. The Motsuenyane Commission gave a scathing indictment of conditions in the camps. 'The camps became dumping grounds for all who fell foul of the security department, whether they were loyal supporters accused of being enemy agents, suspected spies or convicts,' ran one passage. Among the senior officials rebuked, was Jacob Zuma, for 'failing to supervise adequately the supervision of a prisoner'.[8]

Zuma was under a particular cloud over the party's treatment of Thami Zulu, the *nom de guerre* of a commander of ANC guerrilla forces in the late eighties. Zulu was detained in mid-1988 on suspicion of being an enemy agent, after one of his units was ambushed and nine members of it killed by South African security forces. He died within a few days of his release in November 1989. He is thought to have had advanced AIDS, but traces of a poison were found in his bloodstream. It remained a matter of conjecture whether the apartheid special forces or the ANC's security department was responsible for silencing him. According to the ANC inquiry into his death, he had entered detention as a 'large, well-built, slightly overweight person' but left 'gaunt, frail and almost unrecognisable'. As head of intelligence, Zuma would have authorised the detention of Zulu. His father, Philemon Ngwenya, a teacher in Soweto, later testified to the Truth and Reconciliation Commission that he flew twice to Lusaka after hearing he had been detained. On the first visit Zuma and Mbeki were among a number of top leaders who denied his son was detained. On his second visit he spent eighteen days waiting to see Zuma. Zuma was away at first, Ngwenya testified. On his return to Lusaka he refused to see him. 'Why was I not allowed by Mr Zuma to see my son for eighteen days?' Ngwenya asked the hearing. 'Even under the most cruel regime, apartheid regime, people were allowed visitors.'[9] The findings of the commission served as a reminder that behind Zuma's cheery facade there was a hardened revolutionary who had had to make his share of unpalatable decisions.

In these years, however, he was also burnishing his reputation as an inspiring leader. Thoko Msimang, a former colonel in MK who worked under him in exile, says he was adored by his subordinates. She was close to tears when I asked her about her years working under Zuma in exile. 'He was unlike other leaders, who were touting their fancy clothes, their wedding suits,' she said. 'He wore khaki, which he would wash at night and then wear in the morning. He was so down to earth you couldn't think he was a leader.'[10]

Moe Shaik, one of his closest friends, whose younger brother, Schabir, was Zuma's financial adviser and was to be convicted for securing a bribe for him from a French arms company, was part of a clandestine ANC mission that infiltrated agents into South Africa in 1990 as an insurance policy in case the talks with the white government collapsed. Zuma, he said, was the perfect leader. He was always the last to see the agents before they headed off on their perilous mission.

'His words were not those of an uncaring commander hugging an idiot soldier going off to die in battle. When Zuma spoke, you sensed he meant it.' Shaik was on the run for about a year after his mission was uncovered by the security forces. He felt abandoned by the ANC and wrote a 'bitterly complaining' letter to the ANC leaders about his commander, Zuma. Later, when the dust had settled, he went to Zuma to apologise. Zuma just laughed the incident away, telling him the letter was perfectly understandable because he had been very angry. 'There was no bitterness in him,' Shaik says. 'There was no anger at a junior having argued with him in a letter, in a formal way.'

In hindsight those were the glory days for Zuma. In the late 1980s he and Mbeki helped to run a series of secret talks with prominent Afrikaners in a country house in rural Britain. When he returned home in 1990, he cut a very different figure from the raw and poorly educated activist who had gone to Robben Island in 1963. He came home as one of the most valued figures in the exile movement. He was initially smuggled back in early 1990, in collusion with the apartheid authorities following the unbanning of the ANC, to arrange for the return of the exiles. He swiftly charmed his opposite numbers, who only a few months earlier had been sworn to try to kill him. Mandela then gave him a vital task, to try to negotiate peace with Inkatha. At a time of bellicose rhetoric and bloody raids and counter-raids by both Inkatha and ANC supporters, his was a rare voice of moderation. While most ANC leaders were advocating a strategy of crushing Inkatha, Zuma urged a more conciliatory approach.

Frank Mdlalose, a dignified, silver-haired medical doctor, was Zuma's opposite number in the negotiations with Inkatha. He, like Zuma, is as at home wearing the *beshu*, a traditional skin apron that is roughly the Zulu equivalent of a Scotsman's kilt, as a grey suit. He, like Zuma, faced huge opposition from his own party to the idea of talking to the enemy. At that time the valleys and townships around Pietermaritzburg and Durban were divided by multiple front lines, with villages, as in Bosnia and so many other civil wars, riven on a host of issues – social, economic and generational – and with political affiliation often proving only the most overt factor in the fighting.

Mdlalose was hugely impressed that Zuma ignored all the rhetorical sniping from his own side. They met once at the community hall in Mpumalanga, at a time of acute tensions in the township. Zuma calmed everyone and made the Inkatha delegates feel at ease, 'even though just outside the meeting someone might have been shot dead or a home burned down'.[11]

'I found the man very steady and easy, and quick to bring about a joke and a laugh to break the ice,' Mdlalose recalled. 'He was quite firm on his search for peace.' On one occasion the old Marxist Harry Gwala told an ANC meeting that Zuma was making a profound mistake talking to Mdlalose and that he was like Neville Chamberlain appeasing the Nazis. Zuma stood up and said, 'I am afraid I shall continue talking to Mdlalose.'

Mandela valued these qualities and also their worth in trying to salve the pride of Buthelezi. Mandela had known and respected Buthelezi in the early sixties and indeed had in the seventies encouraged him to form Inkatha as a proxy opponent to the apartheid regime. In 1994, rather than giving Zuma, the ANC's senior Zulu, a national cabinet post, as might have been his due given his seniority in the party, Mandela appointed him to the provincial cabinet in KwaZulu-Natal, which was governed by an Inkatha-led coalition. His mission was to broker a lasting peace among the Zulus and end a decade of turmoil in the region. This Zuma helped to negotiate, as probably the finest achievement of his long and varied career. It was also a mark of his qualities as a good party man that he had accepted the relatively junior post without evident disgruntlement.

Three years into the new order, with peace restored to KwaZulu-Natal, the post-apartheid province comprising the old province of Natal and the homeland of KwaZulu, he was elected deputy president of the ANC under Mbeki. He was popular and successful and was the front-runner to be the country's deputy president after the next election in 1999. There was just one cloud on his horizon. It was one that was familiar to politicians the world over but particularly to

members of revolutionary movements who had given their lives to a struggle
and had not thought of earning a wage: money.

When the ANC was unbanned in 1990, thousands of exiles were finally able to
return to their homeland. For many it was a bittersweet homecoming. For long
years they had lived off ANC stipends. Now they had somehow to create a new
life from nothing. Even the most senior officials received only around 2,000
rand a month from the movement, enough for living expenses possibly but not
to support a household, still less buy a home. Mbeki was put up in a hotel suite
in central Johannesburg by Anglo American for a few months, before a businessman gave him and his wife the use of a flat. Kader Asmal, the veteran anti-
apartheid activist who served in Mandela's and Mbeki's cabinets, recalls that
on his return from over three decades in exile he had accumulated enough capital in his years as a university lecturer in Dublin to buy an unassuming house
in Cape Town. But most were not so fortunate. Many comrades returned pen-
niless, he said, and struggled to make ends meet.[12]

When, shortly after the April 1994 election, Archbishop Tutu levelled his
sights at the salaries and perks of MPs, and accused them of riding a 'gravy
train', the party indignantly pointed to the record of many of its members, who
had fought for years in exile and then returned with barely a rand to their
name. A few months later, Makhenkesi Stofile, the party's chief whip, bridled
at talk of a gravy train and suggested returning 'strugglers' deserved to be given
a little slack as they sought to establish their finances.

'It's more like a gravy ox wagon than a train, and I still have to be told where
the stations are,' he said. 'I have not been able to meet the train. I have not been
able to taste the gravy.' It was monstrous to talk of 'fat cats'. He alluded to the
example of Thomas Nkobi, the ANC's treasurer in exile. 'For his whole life he
lived on ANC allowances,' Stofile said of Nkobi. 'He never worked, only struggled. And yet ANC MPs have been scandalised as parasites living on public
funds while doing nothing. The average ANC MP takes home 8,000 rand a
month. Yes, some are buying cars but in many cases not for their usage. These
are for their families. These are the sorts of things that are not understood.'[13]

In the transition years from 1990 to 1994, Zuma relied, as he had in exile, on the party and friends to fund him, as he did his bit to negotiate the end of apartheid. But in 1994 the era of 'struggle accounting' came to an end. In his first post after the 1994 elections as the minister for economic affairs in the provincial government of KwaZulu-Natal, he earned about 20,000 rand a month, a handsome salary by South African standards. When Mbeki made him deputy president in 1999, his salary, including allowances, increased to about 870,000 rand a year. It appears, however, this was not enough for his needs.

He had a large family. A proud believer in the polygamous tradition of rural Zululand, by 1990 he had three wives, including Dr Nkosazana Dlamini-Zuma, who would become Mandela's health minister and Mbeki's foreign minister, and at least ten children.[14] He also faced a flood of expectations in his home village, Nkandla, which was in one of the most impoverished parts of the country. Zuma was expected to step into the traditional role in African villages of the local boy made good and to deploy his influence and money to help the community. As the local 'Big Man', he would also be expected to have a household and lifestyle that fitted his status.

Badly in need of money he turned increasingly to an old comrade from the struggle, Schabir Shaik, an ANC wheeler-dealer who set himself up as Zuma's financial adviser and gave him a series of interest-free loans. Moe Shaik, Schabir's older brother, depicts Zuma as something of a father figure to Schabir. The two had known each other in exile, when Schabir helped to raise money for the ANC. His speciality was channelling a flow of hard currency into South Africa and then getting it converted into rand for disbursement to the underground. He was also involved in trying to launder ANC funds by buying companies in the United States and Europe. Zuma's relationship with Schabir was 'intense' and 'founded in revolution', Moe says. It was only natural that Schabir would want to thank Zuma by helping with his finances when he returned to South Africa. Zuma was just one of many exiles in a temporary 'debt trap'.

'You had to get a car, a house . . . The immediate outlay of capital for an individual was enormous. The question was how to navigate the debt trap. The answer was either by borrowing or by assistance from comrades or from anyone who could help. This is what happened to many people, and this is what happened to Zuma.'[15]

Zuma was indeed one of many senior ANC leaders beholden to friends and business people after the party was unbanned. Mandela himself lived in the Johannesburg mansion of a flamboyant white businessman while he finished his memoirs. But after 1994, even as the ANC was consolidating itself in government and the era of struggle accounting was brought to an end, Zuma was embarking on a dependency on an extraordinary scale. Between 25 October 1995 and 1 July 2005, Shaik gave him 4,072,499 rand in 783 payments, according to Zuma's 2007 indictment on multiple charges of corruption. The question of what exactly Zuma thought Shaik expected in return for this colossal investment was to dominate the most explosive trial of the post-apartheid era and ultimately to precipitate the greatest split in the ANC for forty years. At the very least Zuma's behaviour in accepting the money betrays a lack of judgement that marked him out as a controversial role model for a young country struggling to find its way and to avoid slipping into the corrupt ways of so many post-independence African states.

Billy Downer, the state prosecutor, began the corruption trial of Schabir Shaik in 2004 by rather portentously invoking the first line of Virgil's *Aeneid*: 'I tell of arms and a man.' Shaik was accused of procuring a bribe for Zuma from Thint, a subsidiary of the French arms company Thomson (later known as Thales), and of paying off Zuma's household debts in return for political favours. In 1996 Shaik's company, Nkobi Holdings, was made Thomson's joint venture partner in South Africa. Shaik was specifically accused of seeking Zuma's support in the bidding process in the controversial multibillion-dollar arms procurement package of the late 1990s, and then subsequently seeking his protection from investigations into the deal. While Shaik – not Zuma – was in the dock, the trial amounted to the first round of the judiciary's long-running probe into Zuma's messy finances. In June 2005, Shaik was found guilty of corruption for soliciting in 2000 an annual bribe of 500,000 rand for Zuma from Thint and for giving him more than a million rand in expectation of political favours. He was also found guilty of fraud for writing off more than one million rand that he owed to his own companies, including Zuma's unpaid debts. He was sentenced to fifteen years in prison.

In his conclusion to the sentencing proceedings Judge Hilary Squires gave a stark warning to South Africa: 'I do not think I am overstating anything when I say that this phenomenon [of corruption] can truly be likened to a cancer eating away remorselessly at the fabric of corporate privacy ... If it is not checked, it becomes systemic.' Two weeks later Mbeki fired Zuma as deputy president. A week later Zuma himself was charged with corruption.

As well as triggering a political crisis, the Shaik case cast a much-needed light into the murky recesses of the arms deal of the late 1990s. The transaction, which cost about 50 billion rand, infected the upper reaches of the party with corruption and fuelled a scandal that was to gnaw at the heart of South Africa's young democracy. The deal seemed incomprehensible to many, even when it was being negotiated in the mid-nineties. At the same time that the ANC was embarking on the huge challenge of trying to redress the wrongs of apartheid, it was envisaging spending billions of dollars on fighter jets, submarines and ships. This was to be South Africa's largest arms procurement package ever, at a time when it faced no conceivable military threat. Government officials suggest they needed to keep the Afrikaner security establishment happy by backing their requests for the new arms. The government also responded to critics that the contracts would lead to the creation of many jobs via what are known in the arms trade as 'industrial offsets'. It is a cynical defence that is often delivered by governments and arms companies in support of arms deals. In most cases the offsets deliver only a fraction of the promised investment and job opportunities, as happened in South Africa in the wake of this arms deal.

The most scandalous element of the deal was a decision to pay £1.6 billion to buy Gripen jet fighters and Hawk jet trainers from BAe Systems, the British defence and aerospace company. The Hawks cost twice as much as the Italian jets favoured by the South African Air Force in another rival bid, and the military had no need of the Gripen jets. But Joe Modise, the then defence minister, removed cost as a criterion, and the deal was signed. Modise, a former head of Umkhonto we Sizwe who died in 2001, was one of several officials accused of taking huge bribes from some of the bidders. Among the other people alleged to have profited was Chippy Shaik, brother of Moe and Schabir. He was the director of procurement in the defence force, a post that laid him open to a conflict of interest, given that Schabir was bidding for a subcontract in the arms procurement package. He was later suspended from his post and was censured in a government report, which rejected his claims to have recused himself from the discussions involving his brother's bid. A number of senior politicians were involved in overseeing the arms deal, including Mbeki, who headed the cabinet committee responsible for arms procurement. Zuma himself was not implicated in the big decisions. He was ensnared in the scandal at a much lower level via his old comrade Schabir Shaik, who aspired to have a cut of this mega deal by touting his proximity to the government. This, Shaik thought, would help him land a contract for his company to provide navigation consoles for the French frigates that were part of the arms package.

If the Shaik trial was the story of 'arms and a man', the Zuma case was to be a rather more mundane and un-Virgilian story of 'mortgages and a man'. Like Virgil's warrior hero, Aeneas, Zuma spent long years roaming the world in exile before helping to found a new nation. But Zuma's judgement – in particular his choice of friends – was rather more flawed than the Trojan hero's. Testimony in the Shaik trial revealed how his network of companies helped Zuma to fund a handsome new residence in Nkandla. Hilary Squires, the judge in the Shaik trial, damningly dubbed Zuma's relationship with Shaik as a 'mutually beneficial symbiosis'. When, in 2007, Zuma was charged with fraud and corruption for a second time, the indictment included the new charges of racketeering, money laundering and tax evasion. The indictment highlighted in stark detail Zuma's alleged reliance on Shaik. Shaik's companies are alleged to have paid money to Zuma's wives and ex-wives, pocket money for his children, car repayments, rent, and even on one occasion 10 rand for the 'wash and vacuum' of his car. Shaik had testified in his trial that he had helped to pay for school fees for Zuma's children, airfares and car repairs but had done this out of friendship.

The question at the heart of this saga is what – if anything – Zuma agreed to do in return for this phenomenal support. Zuma's supporters do not deny the payments but say they were loans and insist that he made no undertaking to help Shaik's business arrangements. They argue that his was merely the behaviour of a traditional African leader, who has neither the time nor inclination to bother with petty finances. Asked if it was not a problem that Shaik had subsidised his life, Zuma once said, 'If I thought there was anything wrong with it, I'm sure I would have asked myself: What is wrong with it?'[16]

At the very best the relationship shows an astonishing naivety and lack of judgement, given his official standing. In his memoir of his attempts to investigate the arms deal, the former ANC MP Andrew Feinstein mused, 'Was he [Zuma] a man who out of legitimate and material need while in exile had got involved with Schabir Shaik who in turn had used and abused Zuma's name for his own nefarious ends? Or was he corrupt?'[17] Feinstein left the question unanswered, but he also noted that Zuma's attitude towards his investigation changed from apparent benevolence to hostility after the critical meeting between Shaik, Zuma and a representative of Thint, when Shaik solicited the bribe.

'From that moment his support for me stopped. He'd have no contact,' Feinstein said.[18] It was also around this time that an architect had drawn up the first plan for his spacious residential complex in Nkandla, on the lines of a traditional Zulu chief's home.

Facing such damning charges, Zuma and his supporters cried foul, insisting that the investigation was not a matter of justice but rather of political skullduggery and that the prosecution service had been politicised and was pursuing Mbeki's vendettas. Mbeki certainly had a motive to see Zuma's political position undermined. By 2005 relations between the two old allies had deteriorated markedly. Mbeki's enemies on the left and in the unions had coalesced around Zuma, and some in Mbeki's circle clearly feared that Zuma was lining himself up as a successor.

While Mbeki and the Scorpions vigorously denied any complicity in prosecution, there seems little doubt that the state prosecution service did face intermittent political interference. In 2003 Bulelani Ngcuka, then director of national prosecutions, announced that there was a prima facie case of corruption against Zuma but that he would not be taking it to court. By acting effectively as judge and prosecutor, he was exceeding his powers, and Zuma's allies argued that he was stigmatising him without giving him a chance to defend himself in court. Yet ironically, given Zuma's subsequent accusations of a conspiracy, he initially benefited from this intervention. When Ngcuka made his decision not to prosecute Zuma, he was shielding him from the scrutiny of the law. Zuma was originally a co-accused on Shaik's original charge sheet, but his name was later taken off it. He was formally charged only after Shaik was sentenced and it became all but impossible for Mbeki not to act.

The rape trial of 2006 was overshadowed with claims of political malice. Zuma's supporters suggested his accuser was taking part in a 'honey trap' orchestrated by his enemies in the government. Her best friend worked in the office of Ronnie Kasrils, the minister of intelligence and a close ally of Mbeki's. In the feverish atmosphere in the ANC, this link was seen by Zuma's allies as proof of a conspiracy. But it was never disputed in court that Zuma had had unprotected sex with an HIV-positive family friend, an act that cast further doubt on his judgement and fitness for office.

Then there was the curious timing of Zuma's indictment. A first corruption case against him collapsed in 2005, when the judge struck it off the roll after the prosecution service said it needed more time to pursue its case. For the next two years speculation over when a second indictment would be brought dominated the political debate. In the countdown to the ANC's leadership election in December 2007, Mbeki's advisers were divided on whether to press charges before the vote to try to scupper Zuma's campaign, or whether that would serve only to enrage his supporters, a businessman close to Mbeki told me. Then, on the very morning that Zuma celebrated his victory in the ANC leadership, the lustre of his victory was dulled when prosecutors announced they would be seeking to press charges. Ten days later they laid the charges, just as Mbeki was licking his wounds from his defeat.

Finally, Zuma's allies argued that given the many allegations of impropriety over the arms deal, he should not be alone in the dock. Clearly there were other senior officials who potentially faced charges of corruption on a far larger scale. At the end of 2008 the British and Swedish authorities were separately investigating allegations that several of the successful arms companies gave vast bribes to South African officials. In this context Zuma's friends pleaded that he was the victim of a selective prosecution and also argued that his loan from Shaik was trifling compared to the allegations around the arms deal. But the Scorpions contended that they could only prosecute cases when they had enough evidence. In September 2008 Zuma's supporters claimed that their long argument that he was facing a trumped-up charge had been vindicated when a judge dismissed the corruption charges against him for a second time, saying he had not been granted his due rights when the indictment had been served. In comments that were seized on by Zuma's allies as proof of his innocence, Judge Chris Nicholson said Zuma might have been right to claim political interference. He was satisfied that 'political meddling cannot be excluded.' It had been 'bizarre to say the least' that Zuma had not been charged alongside Shaik, he said, a decision that had brought 'the justice system into disrepute'.[19] There was an echo of the works of Kafka to the case, he concluded.

The ruling paved the way for the final act in the downfall of Mbeki. A week after the ruling, the ANC formally 'recalled' him from the presidency, and he had to stand down, humiliated. But the judge did not state, as Zuma's supporters claimed, that there had definitely been meddling. He also stressed that his decision to dismiss the charges had 'nothing to do with the guilt or otherwise' of Zuma in what was a clear-cut criminal trial. The testimony in the Shaik trial had left no doubt that Zuma had a case to answer. In his judgement, Judge Hilary Squires said it was clear that Zuma had intervened to help Shaik. Since then, the prosecution had worked their way through ninety-three thousand documents seized from Zuma's home and his lawyer's office to compile a detailed forensic report into Zuma's financial affairs. The fact that other senior politicians were facing unsubstantiated allegations of taking far larger amounts of money, and that Mbeki had an interest in seeing the conviction of Zuma, his main rival, did not alter that this was a straightforward commercial criminal case.

Many business people construed the Nicholson judgement as an elegant solution to the crisis confronting South Africa over the trial. In the countdown to the judgement, Zuma's supporters had been alarming investors by making increasingly apocalyptic threats. Zuma's senior lieutenants had made clear they would not accept a conviction, lambasting the judges as counter-revolutionaries. So the collapse of the case spared the country a blatant drive to undermine the judiciary.

While the Supreme Court of Appeal later overturned the Nicholson judgment, saying the judge had 'overstepped' the limits of his authority, on the eve of the 2009 election the case collapsed. State prosecutors dropped all charges after tape-recordings were released in court suggesting the timing of the prosecution had been influenced by politics.

Zuma's supporters celebrated that their idol could take up the presidency free from the shadow of a trial, but the saga had raised troubling questions about the ruling party's attitude towards supposedly independent institutions.

The way that Zuma's supporters and the ANC's senior leaders had treated the judiciary potentially set a worrying precedent, giving the impression that politics could be expected at the last resort to take primacy over the law. Helen Zille, the leader of the opposition Democratic Alliance, said that in dropping the charges the prosecutors had 'not taken a decision based in law but [instead had] buckled to political pressure'. A senior member of the Scorpions, the elite unit that investigated and brought charges against Zuma, said they had faced 'a sinister lobbying campaign' to try to persuade them to drop the case against Zuma in the interest of national harmony. One of the most respected members of the government approached the Scorpions suggesting the case be dropped.

'We met for lunch,' the Scorpions investigator recalled. 'When it was over, he excused everyone else and asked for a quiet word. He said, "Why are you pursuing JZ?" I said to him, "Why are you asking this?" He said, "Zuma is small fry." I can't tell you how disappointed I was to hear those words coming from someone with such a reputation.'[20]

Influential commentators and editors promoted holding a public inquiry into the arms deal followed by a general amnesty. The parallel cited was the Truth Commission. The idea was very dangerous. The Truth Commission had been convened to try to bind the wounds of decades of injustice. An amnesty for a corrupt and tainted arms deal would merely reward the crooked and set a precedent from which South Africa's institutions might never recover.

The prosecutors gamely insisted that the withdrawal of charges against Zuma did not amount to an acquittal. Ahead of the April 2009 national election there was some speculation that Mr Zuma would push a bill through parliament giving the president immunity from prosecution. His supporters cited the example of Silvio Berlusconi, the Italian prime minister, who used his large parliamentary majority to pass a law giving immunity to the country's four largest office-bearers. But as Zuma consolidated his position after his election victory, so talk of a retrial, and the need for such an unedifying step, receded.

Remarkably, despite all the embarrassing revelations and his excoriation in the press, Zuma never seemed to lose his cool. Indeed, if anything, he enhanced his reputation as a true man-of-the-people and reinforced his claim to be just the sort of consultative leader the country might want after nearly a decade under a cerebral and prickly president.

Zuma is in many ways Mbeki's antithesis. He was a brilliant foil as his number two. They had worked closely together in exile. They were collaborators in one of the critical meetings of the transition from apartheid when, in 1989, they flew together from London to a hotel in Lucerne, Switzerland, to meet senior agents from the National Intelligence Service, the intelligence arm of the apartheid government. Zuma was one of the ANC hierarchs who in the mid-1990s advised Mandela to choose Mbeki over Ramaphosa as his successor. When Mbeki picked him as his deputy, ANC insiders assumed that the choice was partly because Zuma posed no threat to his position in an organisation that had traditionally been led by one of South Africa's small, black, educated elite. He was indeed a loyal party man. While he gained a reputation when running against Mbeki for the party presidency for being more outspoken on critical issues, when in office he never publicly condemned the AIDS policy or the stance towards Zimbabwe.

Pallo Jordan, the veteran ANC intellectual, says the key to understanding the difference between the two is their approach to the written word. Mbeki would read policy documents however long from start to finish. Zuma relies on someone to tell him what is in them and would not even read an executive summary. Rather, he would ask someone to paraphrase the document and then tease out the finer points for him.

'Throughout his life he has had to rely more on the spoken word than on the written word. The skills he has had to develop are the person-to-person skills. That's what he is reliant on. He would be a political non-starter if he was not open to people talking to him.'[21]

Engaging he certainly he is. He is one of those politicians who can embrace all comers when he is in a room. He likes to address interlocutors as 'brother' or 'sister'. It was Zuma whom the union and Communist Party leaders turned to when Mbeki refused to take their calls. 'They used to phone pleading for a hearing, and it was Zuma who replied,' one of Mbeki's close aides recalled.[22] When I interviewed Zuma after his election as ANC leader, he was wearing a flowing African shirt, in marked contrast to the grey suits favoured by Mbeki.

He spoke without prompts or advice from his one aide. In an hour he answered thirty questions,[23] five times as many as Mbeki had dispatched in more than an hour and a half in an interview a year earlier. This was the confident self-depre-cating Zuma who, when asked about education at a policy summit, had said that he of all people appreciated the need for a formal education, given that he had not had one himself. The only time he became animated was when asked about his corruption trial, but his approach even then was one of a pastor re-sponding to a misguided congregant than a politician on the defensive.

The contrast between him and Mbeki became all the more apparent once he was cast into the wilderness in 2005, with his dismissal from the govern-ment. While careful to avoid making full-frontal attacks on Mbeki's policies and thus risking the taint of disloyalty to the ANC, he positioned himself as a caring alternative to the president. He courted minorities, in particular Afrikaners. His frankness about the troubles plaguing South Africa, and also the problems in Zimbabwe, was refreshing after the intellectualism of Mbeki. He visited and comforted victims of crime. His task was all the easier as he clearly empathised with the ordinary people. He had even been mugged. He recalled walking towards the ANC headquarters after dark in central Johannes-burg with a lady friend one night, when he became aware they were being fol-lowed by a group of young men. Two of the pursuers dawdled in front of them. He sensed trouble, and suddenly the youths were demanding his money. 'I thought now is a time to fight,' he recalled. 'And then suddenly there were four or five blades at my stomach and my back. And I thought, no. Now is the time to talk.'[24]

The pace of his schedule was reminiscent of US presidential candidates. It was a brilliant insurgency, as it was utterly unlike anything the ANC had expe-rienced before. Traditionally party elections were fixed in advance by party elders in a consensual decision in advance of the vote, as had happened in 1991, when Mbeki and Chris Hani were persuaded to step aside and not com-pete for the party's deputy presidency. The idea of courting voters was seen as distinctly un-ANC. Party officials liked to regard themselves as high priests of some venerable cult and to pretend that the party never engaged in competi-tive internal politics. Mbeki, in particular, regarded electioneering as beneath his dignity, his aides said. Not for the first time he underestimated Zuma.

Mbeki's aides were imbued with intellectual and class snobbery towards Zuma. They saw him as an ignoramus. He did not, after all, have a high school education, still less a degree. 'He's a country bumpkin. He has no idea of policy,' one cabinet minister told me in mid-2007. 'I have known him for a long time. None of us ever thought of him as a president.'[25]

One of the few in Mbeki's inner circle who did appreciate the threat he posed, at least at the end, was Saki Macozoma, the ANC politician turned multimillionaire businessman and a confidant of Mbeki's.

'We have been a bit naive,' he said, speaking on the eve of the vote. The middle classes had not taken Zuma seriously and had seen his rise as 'something that would fizzle'.[26] They hadn't taken into account that for two years it was the only show in town. They had underestimated the careful strategy that lay behind his campaign. They had also underestimated the toughness beneath the jolly exterior, a misjudgement that had been made throughout his career, dating back to his arrival on Robben Island, when he was originally seen as a merry country lad with a good singing voice and a taste for dancing but not much else.

'They thought we were coming to play marbles,' Don Mkhwanazi, a Zulu businessman who was one of his main financial backers, said on the eve of his election victory. 'They did not realise we were playing to win.'[27]

Inside Zuma's office on the tenth floor of the ANC headquarters is a large picture of Oliver Tambo, the reflective, intuitive and understated man who kept the liberation movement alive for long years in exile. There were times in the exile years when the ANC was so divided and demoralised that many of its members wondered if they would ever return home. It is a tribute to Tambo, who led the movement from 1967 until he had a debilitating stroke in 1991, that the ANC managed to surmount these difficulties. So it was an astute move by Zuma on his assumption of the party's presidency to have Tambo's portrait hanging in his office, while pictures of Mandela and Mbeki hang in the foyer. Tambo is unsullied by the post-1994 arguments over the party's direction. By sitting under his portrait, Zuma, the ultimate party man and ever-sensitive to party protocol, had positioned himself in a continuum of ANC leaders.

But refreshing as his mellowness was in contrast with Mbeki's chilly public persona, there is another side to his charming equivocating ways. He has the populist's trait of tending to say what his audiences want to hear. In an interview with me in March 2008 Zuma gently demurred when asked if he was a populist: 'I haven't said things because I want people to be happy. I speak my mind on the issues always.' His record is rather less constant. Soon after his election as ANC leader he promised in an interview with a prominent financial magazine to reconsider labour regulations, including the minimum wage. Then he backtracked a few days later and promised the unions that he would 'lay down his life' for the workers. Bankers publicly applauded his pledge to maintain the party's orthodox macroeconomic policy, but privately feared he might not mean what he said. When speaking to audiences about crime, he suggested he would allow a referendum on the death penalty. When there was an outcry from ANC traditionalists, he insisted he stood by the party line of opposition to capital punishment. He spoke at length once about the failings of Mugabe, but in his first year as ANC leader did not force the South African government, as he could have, to take a less supine stance to the crisis. When Julius Malema, the leader of the ANC Youth League, said he was willing to kill for his leader, Zuma gave him the most gentle of rebukes, suggesting that this was the language of youthful exuberance. ANC veterans found the contrast with Mandela, who had repeatedly torn a strip off one of Malema's predecessors for chanting the slogan 'Kill the Boer' at rallies, deeply dispiriting.

Zuma inherited a delicate political position. No sooner had he won than he faced a challenge to keep the party and his winning alliance together. 'It has no real ideological underpinning,' said Saki Macozoma, the Mbeki confidant. 'They are together in opposition to something, not in promotion of something. All experience of political science suggests that, unless you are together for something, you stand the risk of being pulled in all directions at once.' But fifteen years after white rule, South Africa badly needed strong leadership rather than the equivocation that was Zuma's trademark. It faced wrenching decisions in particular over economic policy, as the unions and the Communist Party, which resurrected his career, pushed for an end to Mbeki's business-friendly policies and a marked shift to the left.

There is a steely fist under the velvet glove. Zuma has a street fighter's instincts born of growing up in a broken and impoverished background. Many of his main allies are from an intelligence or underground background. He knows when to jettison diplomacy. When he was appointed as the chief negotiator in

Burundi between 2002 and 2005, in an attempt to mediate in its civil war, he deployed the full Zuma charm routine on the participants in nights of round-the-clock talks. 'But when he needed to push, he sure pushed,' recalled a senior former State Department official.[28]

At a critical moment in the talks Zuma held a meeting with half a dozen re-calcitrant rebels. They were dressed in fatigues and had shown little interest in heeding the pleas for them to sign the agreement. Then Zuma stepped for-ward. The twinkly-eyed mediator had vanished. This was the man of war. He had hundreds of highly trained white South African soldiers in Burundi, he said. They were old-school conservative Afrikaners – tough, mean and highly trained. If the rebels did not sign the agreement, he would set the Boers loose on them. With that warning the deal was done.[29]

But the question remained whether the Zulu Mr Everyman would be strong enough to say no, whether he would lead – indeed, whether he could lead at all – on issues of good governance in the light of the embarrassments over his relationship with his financial adviser.

Thabani Khumalo, the young management consultant at Zuma's sixty-fifth-birthday dinner, was one of many in the ANC who appreciated Zuma's genius in inspiring people. He was also, however, aware that the world might have misgivings about his leadership. Khumalo had grown up, like Zuma, in an im-poverished Zulu community. His father, too, had died while he was a child, he had been killed by Inkatha supporters in a township outside Durban. Since then, the young Khumalo had emerged from poverty and violence, gained a scholarship to university and, after a stint as an ANC activist in the early nineties, had become a management consultant. In his pink-and-white-striped shirt and designer suit, and with his insightful questions about the state of the international liquid fuel industry, he could have been sitting in an office on Wall Street. He had just driven down from the port of Richards Bay, where he had inspected a business opportunity. He admired both Mbeki and Zuma. As a young Zulu he was proud of the rise of Zuma, but Mbeki had put Africa on the world map by speaking on podiums around the world, a routine it was hard to see Zuma maintaining.

ANC leaders had always been men of letters and even wordsmiths, he mused. 'Now you get this uneducated Zulu country man. One day he can talk to Thabo Mbeki, the next day to people like my mother, who is also a Zulu peasant. Whenever I go back, I find it extremely difficult to engage with my old classmates, but he can.' People appreciated Zuma's tendency to speak in public in Zulu. When he addressed South Africans in Zulu, he was behaving not as a tribalist but as a true African leader. Yet Khumalo predicted a very short honeymoon.

'People will say, "This man knows us. He comes to our *kraal* and eats with us," but they will soon start to ask questions. It will put the new administration in a difficult dilemma.' People would expect him to deliver on his promises of a better life and would not accept the argument that there was no more money for education. Whenever he travelled abroad, he would have the 'huge alba-tross' of the corruption allegations around his neck. 'When Thabo Mbeki takes to the podium, hate him or love him, I sit down and listen because I know here is a man who knows the future about Africa. Jacob Zuma will have to convince a lot of people he is worth his salt.'[30]

If South Africa is lucky, Zuma will be its Ronald Reagan. He will make the country feel good about itself after the awkward questions that Mbeki had asked of it, and leave the business of governing to technocrats. He is in many ways ideally suited to reassure South Africa's disparate citizens, in the way that Reagan's folksy charm heartened Middle America after the uncertainties of the Nixon and Carter years. He is a blend of rural and urban, traditional and pro-gressive, old and new. When he repairs to Nkandla, he dons the *beshu* and holds court, listening to locals' grievances like an old-fashioned tribal chief. He apologised in 2006, after recalling how as a youth he and his friends would set upon gays and beat them with staves.[31] His comments outraged urbanised South Africans, but they struck a chord with as many in the rural areas, where prejudice runs deep. A senior Western diplomat who has known the leaders of the ANC for several decades says that, whenever he has raised the subject of Zuma with Mandela, the 'old man' has replied, 'Zuma is really an African leader.' Mandela never says that of Mbeki, the official added. 'It's a sense of the true nature of the man [Zuma]. He is a true African man with all the strengths and weaknesses that come with it.'[32]

At Nkandla and at his home in suburban Johannesburg, there is always a line of people waiting to see him, whether businessmen, friends or fellow members of his clan passing through town. None are turned away. He likes to maintain the same tradition when he is travelling, a businessman close to him says. When the ANC leader was visiting London in April 2008, marking his formal coming out onto the world stage with a visit to see Gordon Brown, the British prime minister, he stayed at the Dorchester. Leading business people flocked to meet him, including Lakshmi Mittal, the billionaire Indian industrialist. When he arrived for his appointment, the ANC leader was running late. Someone was dispatched to Zuma's suite. It was assumed that he was negotiating the unfolding crisis in Zimbabwe. Instead, he was chatting away to two members of his clan who happened to be in London and wanted to come to pay their respects.

It is a charming image. After several years of trading nightmare scenarios about the implications of Zuma becoming president, business people competed with each other to tell such endearing stories about his calmness and his willingness to listen to their concerns. After Zuma took over the presidency following the ANC's victory in the April 2009 elections, his supporters eagerly talked of a change of approach, of a more vigorous leadership focused more on the mechanics of helping the poor than on the theories.

There is, however, a less reassuring scenario than that of the latter-day Reagan: the growth of a Big Man personality cult designed to mask South Africa's growing social and economic problems against the backdrop of a government making ever grander promises, and a steady implosion of the ANC's sense of purpose.

Moe Shaik, his close ally, says that Zuma will be all the more determined to be 'squeaky clean' to prove the sceptics wrong. His government's left-wing impulses, he adds, will not turn the country back to doctrinaire socialism but will merely lead to a greater role of the state in trying to reduce the inequalities between rich and poor. But whatever Zuma's intentions may have been, the chances of his being able to slow, let alone stop, the steady growth of crony capitalism under Mbeki's government seemed slim. To secure first his comeback and then his election, Zuma had to make extravagant promises to people inside and outside the party. He was indebted both politically and financially.

South Africa had had the liberation 'saint'. It had then had the Africanist intellectual. In 2009 it embarked on rule by charismatic populist. Bra Bricks, the activist running the recycling plant in Orange Farm, was not convinced.

'People think Zuma will make changes, but nothing will change,' he said. 'To go around the townships doesn't mean you are on the side of the poor. It will be as bad. He and Mbeki are under the same ANC umbrella. I don't think Zuma is any different from Mbeki. "Mshini Wami" will end up on the dustbin heap. What kind of president sings "Mshini Wami"?'[33]

His comments went to the heart of the debate over Zuma. No one disputed that he was a canny politician with a popular touch. He had fought long and bravely against apartheid. But it was hard to argue that he was the best man for the job of leading South Africa as it faced the difficult challenges of the second chapter of the post-apartheid era. The greatest danger under Zuma was not of sudden ideological lurch but of a vacuum of leadership and authority. The ideal solution to the power struggle in the ANC would have been for both Zuma and Mbeki to have stepped aside, paving the way for someone from the next generation to take over, someone less scarred by the battles of the past. Instead, South Africa was to enter a new age of uncertainty.

Chapter 11

THE SHADOW OF ZIMBABWE

*After climbing a great hill one only finds that there
are many more hills to climb.*

— NELSON MANDELA,
1994

*We thought we were different ... We've been
brought very firmly to the ground.*

— DESMOND TUTU,
2008

Almost from that very first triumphant day of the new era, when Nelson Mandela
was sworn in as president before an adoring crowd, South Africa's post-apartheid
journey was overshadowed by the depressing events across its northern border
in Zimbabwe. There, another septuagenarian ex-liberation leader was in charge,
but he was imposing an increasingly tyrannical regime. Within a decade of
Mandela's inauguration, hundreds of thousands of Zimbabweans had fled into
South Africa seeking to escape President Robert Mugabe's autocratic rule and
the implosion of the economy. Zimbabwe's collapse compounded the stress on
South Africa's resources, intensifying the challenge for the ANC in trying to
reverse apartheid's injustices. It also posed something of an existential crisis for

South Africans, in particular whites. To the fury of many in the ANC, it became seen in the outside world as a possible case study for the fate of South Africa if they failed: both countries had, after all, started out with much promise but were hobbled by the shortcomings of rule by a hegemonic party, the difficulties of overcoming a fractured past, and the challenge of tackling stark inequalities that broadly split down racial lines.

President Robert Mugabe was lauded as a statesman at independence in 1980, when he took over what had been white-run Rhodesia after a brutal civil war. His reconciliatory speech on winning the country's first election fuelled hopes that he might not be a Marxist tyrant-in-the-making as his opponents feared. To set the right tone he jettisoned his then standard Maoist tunic for a suit. Pledging 'fair and just' rule, he said there was a place 'for everyone' in Zimbabwe.[1] In the eighties he was a vital player in the regional game of geopolitical chess aimed at brokering a peaceful end to apartheid. When his North Korean-trained soldiers massacred up to twenty thousand supporters of his principal rival, Joshua Nkomo, in the early eighties, the West conveniently turned a blind eye. In a reflection of his standing, in 1993 Mandela named Mugabe as one of a trio of world leaders, including John Major, the then British prime minister, and Helmut Kohl, the then German chancellor, he had consulted to find a way of persuading Chief Mangosuthu Buthelezi, the proud leader of the Inkatha Freedom Party, to drop his threats of secession and take part in the election.

By 1994, the logic of Mugabe's misrule was clearly taking its toll. He had inherited one of the most diversified economies in sub-Saharan Africa – founded on a highly efficient commercial farming sector with potential in manufacturing, mining and tourism – but the economy was disintegrating after years of mismanagement. An initial investment in education and health had stalled. His ruling ZANU-PF faced no credible opposition and had become slothful and corrupt. State television and radio were its mouthpieces. Yet still Zimbabwe was thought to have some positive lessons for South Africa as it embarked on majority rule. The country was stable. Mugabe had not tampered with the 4,500 white commercial farmers whose enterprises were the backbone of the economy. Most in the tiny white minority of about 70,000 maintained that race relations were excellent. Many were rather irritated by an article that had appeared in a

British magazine in 1995 asserting that black and white Zimbabweans lived in two separate worlds and that trouble was brewing between the two races.

Sitting on the veranda of his farm just north of Harare in April 1995 sipping freshly squeezed juice from his orange grove, Micky Townsend argued that the thesis was exaggerated. His family had worked Lowdale Farm for three generations. An immaculate green lawn stretched down from a colonial homestead. They had 2,800 acres supporting about a hundred black Zimbabwean families. It was a mixed farm of arable land and cattle. His family had been there since 1903, when settlers were pouring into the country and staking out prime agricultural land. He was confident that they would be there another hundred years.

Whites were much better off than in 1980, when the outlook had been terribly bleak, he said. 'If you stop beating your head against a wall, it gets much better.' He had heard that some forty thousand whites wanted to come back to Zimbabwe. He had relatives coming back. 'Their predictions of disaster just did not materialise. In 1980 there was a feeling that Mugabe was an evil monster. Now there is a feeling that far from that, he is very competent. If people work their farms, they should feel no threat. You get stuck in and help, or get out.' Townsend was choosing his words carefully, but his argument reflected a fuzzy consensus among many whites in Zimbabwe that if they kept their heads down and continued to boost the national economy, they would be OK. Even as Mugabe's rule became more authoritarian and the erosion of democratic institutions accelerated, many whites continued to prosper, particularly in business and in farming, the mainstay of the economy. They were, however, living in a fool's paradise. Bobby Godsell, one of South Africa's most prominent businessmen, a former chief executive of the giant mining company Anglo Gold Ashanti (formerly AngloGold) and a tireless promoter of multiracial ventures in South Africa, argued that white Zimbabweans' retreat into a *laager* contributed to the disaster that unfolded under Mugabe. 'They said, "We've given them freedom, and let's retire to our tents and get rich." There was a retreat from public responsibility,' he said. White South Africans needed to bear that in mind. 'Thank God we haven't done that,' he concluded, although many would argue that most white South Africans had done exactly that.[2] To suggest white Zimbabweans were heterogenous in their mindset was unfair. White Zimbabweans' bitter riposte is that as soon as they did engage in politics, the government turned on them.

As the economy shrivelled, Mugabe turned to populist measures. In 1997 he bowed to the pressure of thousands of veterans demanding compensation for the war of independence and ordered unbudgeted payments of 50,000 Zimbabwean dollars (then about £5,500) to every registered veteran and also recurring monthly stipends. The payments set the Reserve Bank on a ruinous course of printing money. Two years later, facing the first serious political challenge to his authority since taking power, following the formation of the Movement for Democratic Change, Mugabe launched a brutal crackdown to nullify the threat. The campaign for the 2000 parliamentary elections was marked by vicious state-sponsored violence. Mugabe also turned on the white farmers, some of whom had been backing the MDC, and sanctioned the invasion of their farms by state-backed gangs ostensibly to redistribute land, but in reality to reward his allies and punish his foes. Among the victims driven from their land by mobs was Townsend, the farmer who in 1995 had hosted me at his homestead with freshly squeezed juice from his orange grove.

Mugabe portrayed the invasions as the righting of an old wrong. Landownership in Zimbabwe *was* rooted in the injustice of the colonial era. Many of the white settlers in the early years of the twentieth century would ride out for a day from a point designated by colonial officials. They would then mark out the boundary of their future farm, while the Africans were crowded into native reserves, much as in South Africa. Unfortunately, since taking office, Mugabe had made no serious attempt to reform landownership. At independence, Britain, the former colonial power, pledged to help land reform by offering compensation to farmers on the basis of 'willing buyer, willing seller'. But Whitehall halted the payments in 1990, after it emerged that far from helping the poor, land reform was primarily benefiting the elite. Most of the farms handed over in the eighties went to government bigwigs rather than the poor.

The same cynical pattern emerged in the second, enforced round of land reform after 2000. Many of the so-called war veterans who led the invasions were ZANU-PF lackeys and thugs who were far too young to have fought in the liberation war. Many of the confiscated farms ended up in the control of government and ZANU-PF officials. Percy Gombakomba, a stocky former hero of the anti-colonial fight, was among the thousands who enthusiastically took part in the invasions. He had been shot in the arm and lost countless friends in the liberation war and twenty years after independence believed that a reward was long overdue. He was one of a dozen who ejected a white farmer and his family from their 150-hectare spread in Banket, north of Harare, but their dream did not last long. The farmer took most of his equipment. The squatters were given no government support. Two years later ZANU-PF officials drove up to the farm. 'They said there was a new white owner, and we had to go,' he said. 'But we knew they were lying. The farm was given to a cousin of a senior party official. We were just chased away.'³ Within a few years commercial agriculture had collapsed. By 2007, commercial agriculture's share of exports, which overall had declined 55 per cent, had fallen from 40 per cent to 25 per cent. Its share of GDP, which had declined 40 per cent overall, had fallen from 18 per cent to 10 per cent. Its share of formal employment, which had halved overall, had fallen from 25 per cent to 10 per cent.

The redistribution was not a genuine attempt to help the poor. Rather, it was a bid by an ageing autocrat to stay in power. The real target of the crackdown was the MDC, the new opposition party led by a bluff former trade unionist, Morgan Tsvangirai. When campaigning in the 1995 parliamentary election, Mugabe insisted there was a free and fair vote. 'No one is forcing anyone to vote in any direction, so yes, it will be democracy,' he told me as he bounded out of a stadium where he had just addressed thousands of supporters dutifully clad in Mugabe T-shirts. In a telling caveat he added that there was no chance of people voting for anyone else. ZANU-PF was the party of the struggle, he said. Zimbabweans would not consider voting for another party lacking that revolutionary record.⁴

Mugabe saw himself as the personification of Zimbabwe, one of his former cabinet ministers said.⁵ He had founded the country. He could not conceive of ceding power. The idea of being supplanted by Tsvangirai, a man who had stayed at home to support his family during the liberation, was out of the question. As Mugabe's supporters occupied hundreds of farms in the countdown to the 2000 parliamentary election, ZANU-PF militias attacked and tortured MDC activists in outlying rural constituencies, guaranteeing him victory at the polls. Mugabe hailed the election as the new round in the anti-colonial struggle, even though his opponent was a black Zimbabwean trade unionist who had long campaigned for the rights and interests of the poor.

For Mbeki this posed a major test. The violence erupted shortly after he assumed power. As leader of the regional powerhouse, he was seen by Western diplomats as the obvious person to mediate in the crisis and, they hoped, to persuade Mugabe to leave office. It was an awkward assignment. Although in the seventies the ANC had backed the rival Zimbabwe liberation movement led by Joshua Nkomo, the ANC and ZANU-PF had strong historical ties as fellow liberation movements. Mbeki told me he was euphoric on hearing the news in 1980 that Zimbabwe was independent.[6] He knew he had to avoid appearing like the West's messenger if he was to have any influence on Mugabe. There was little doubt the Zimbabwean president was never going to take kindly to advice, still less admonition, from Pretoria.

Archbishop Tutu, who once knew Mugabe well, says that the Zimbabwean president's pride was badly dented when Mandela came out of prison and Mugabe ceased to be the focus of attention in the region. 'Mr Mugabe used to be the blue-eyed boy of everybody,' Tutu said. 'The media used to flock to him at meetings. Then here comes this old man out of prison, and journalists dump Mugabe like a hot potato. He would probably be able to rationalise that and say, "Madiba is old. He has been in prison for so long." But Thabo is younger than Mugabe. He was not in jail. Mugabe despised him, and so Mbeki faced a huge, huge problem.'[7]

In Mugabe's eyes Mbeki was a pipsqueak. In the 1980s he had been Oliver Tambo's aide at meetings between the ANC leader and Mugabe. 'He was the young subordinate at a meeting of two grand old men,' a senior former US State Department official said. 'Mugabe always treated him as the bag carrier, and Mbeki let him keep him there.'[8]

Mbeki's aides argued that the international outrage over Zimbabwe was tinged with racism. They were right that there were far worse crises in Africa that went all but unnoticed in the West. Many British newspapers did initially focus more attention on the plight of the white farmers who were thrown off their land than on Mugabe's beleaguered black political foes. For many South African whites, the plight of Zimbabwe's white farmers and their families marked the first time they had paid much attention to the dramas further north in the continent. But that was no reason for Pretoria to turn a blind eye to the despotism across its border. The ANC endorsed three fraudulent elections in

2000, 2002 and 2005, ignoring widespread abuses and intimidation by supporters of ZANU-PF. It also all but ignored one of Mugabe's most dictatorial abuses, Operation Murambatsvina ('Clear Out the Trash'), the forced removal of thousands of shack dwellers from the two opposition strongholds, the capital, Harare, and the second city, Bulawayo.

I once suggested to Mbeki that he take a page from the book of Theodore Roosevelt, who famously advocated talking softly and carrying a big stick. Mbeki murmured that he did not have a 'big stick'.[9] There were no easy policies for South Africa to pursue. Yet there was a precedent from the late 1970s, when the South African prime minister John Vorster forced Ian Smith, the prime minister of Rhodesia, to look for a settlement after he threatened to cut off Rhodesia's electricity, most of which came from South Africa.

By 2008, the situation was deteriorating ever more rapidly. In April, the opposition briefly celebrated after initial returns showed they had won the first round of presidential and parliamentary elections. In the forty-eight hours after the vote, members of ZANU-PF started to come to terms with the idea of losing power. Ishmael Dube, a former diplomat and intelligence officer, who broke with Mugabe in the nineties, was sitting at home the day after the election, when a director from the feared Central Intelligence Organisation and a presidential aide drove up to his front door. 'They said they came as friends and colleagues,' he said. 'They wanted to know how to get in touch with the opposition.'[10] For three days, in a sign of the government's panic, the state-appointed election commission stalled in releasing results. State television ran endless reruns of old films and footage of Zimbabwean dancing. Then one night a dismal sequel of the children's classic *Treasure Island* was suddenly interrupted. The unsmiling face of the head of the election commission came on the screen. A decision had been made not to concede. The commanders of the security forces, it became clear later, had backed Mugabe not to leave office. Results were drip-fed to the public over a month while Mugabe enforced a new crackdown and the downward spiral continued. Inflation reached 2 million per cent. A cholera outbreak at the end of 2008 claimed more than 1,200 lives.

In February an agreement finally paved the way for the MDC to join the Zimbabwean government but this was only after wasted years of silence from Pretoria. When asked about South Africa's failure to speak out about

Zimbabwe, Tutu's eyes blazed with fury. Mbeki's stance was a repudiation of all that the ANC had fought for in the struggle, he said. His despair over what was a bleak cautionary tale for the consequences of rule by a hegemonic party was absolute.

As the crisis worsened in the early years of the twenty-first century, many ANC officials adopted a rather patronising attitude towards Zimbabwe. It was as if the tales of desperation, of people lining up with plastic bags full of bank notes to do their shopping, reinforced a superiority, a confidence that South Africa with all its relative wealth and development could never go down that route. The ANC was particularly disdainful of the Zimbabwean opposition, the MDC, arguing that South Africans had taken to the streets to challenge apartheid and that if the Zimbabweans wanted to bring down Mugabe they might have to do the same. Talk of potential parallels between Zimbabwe and South Africa was lambasted as reactionary, if not racist. In 2001 Jeremy Cronin, a senior member of the Communist Party, suggested that the ANC had become intolerant of internal dissent and was behaving like ZANU-PF. Comrades in the Communist Party and unions believed that they were 'living through a kind of tragedy' reminiscent of the 'Stalin era . . . or what's happened in Africa with ZANU', he said. He had to make a rapid retraction.[11]

The Zimbabwean analogies were simplistic, not to say insulting. South Africa's independent institutions were far stronger that Zimbabwe's had been at independence. South Africa's newspapers, increasingly led by fiery non-white editors, held the ANC to account. The courts forced Mbeki to back down on his controversial AIDS policies. More important was the difference of political context. By winning freedom after the end of the Cold War, the ANC took power in a post-ideological age, when it was far harder to pursue ruinous economic policies. There was also no totemic Mugabe figure in South Africa holding the country in his thrall; one of Mandela's many gifts to South Africa was to step down after one term.

But the ANC, while stemming from a far richer tradition and blessed with many more talented members than ZANU-PF, shared the same flaws and weaknesses of other liberation movements. It had not shaken off a revolutionary mindset. It was prone to thinking in authoritarian Marxist ways. It deployed 'cadres' to government positions. As the ANC lurched from crisis to crisis in

2008, with its senior officials berating top judges as 'counter-revolutionaries' and splits emerging on lines of ethnicity, class and personality, many ANC elders started to despair of their beloved party's future. Fighting erupted between factions at a meeting in the North West Province. A party official was stabbed in a scuffle in a party branch in the Western Cape. A conference of the ANC Youth League, the very body that Mandela had founded to force the ANC to confront the National Party, degenerated into drunken scuffles. One faction carried mock coffins with the names of their rivals through the conference hall before the meeting ended in disarray. When a follow-up conference was called two months later, the Youth League officials attracted fresh controversy and newspaper headlines, but not for their policies or ideology – for the scale of their business interests and the flashiness of their cars.

Cheryl Carolus, the activist turned businesswoman, was one of the veterans deeply worried about developments. Aghast by the attacks on the judiciary, she was also perturbed by the resurgence of old revolutionary rhetoric about the need for 'life and death' loyalty. Such sentiments had been understandable in the days of the struggle but were outdated and needed to be discarded, she said.

'I expect more of the ANC, and the public expects more, and it is right to,' she said. 'The ANC is going to govern this country for a long time. It places a huge responsibility on us. We are at a crossroads where the cost is very high. I think we will be OK . . . or we can go down a slippery slope like Zimbabwe, and say, "Oh my God! Everything I've laid down my life for is on the line."'[12]

December 16 has long been a momentous day for South Africans. On 16 December 1838, a few hundred well-armed Boers entrenched behind wagons and backed up by native servants annihilated a far larger force of Zulus armed with spears, rawhide shields and extraordinary courage. The Afrikaners seized on their victory on the banks of Blood River as a message from God that gave divine blessing on their race. In time this legend became one of the founding props of Afrikaner Nationalism. The Day of the Covenant, as 16 December became known, was to be the holy of holies under apartheid, when Afrikaners would give thanks to God for their great victory. For the ANC the date also had huge meaning. Umkhonto we Sizwe, the ANC's armed wing, announced itself to South Africa on 16 December 1961, by detonating a series of bombs outside post office buildings and government offices. The acts of sabotage caused little damage, but they marked a decisive moment in the fight against white rule, as the ANC abandoned its philosophy of non-violence. In 1994 the date was named the Day of Reconciliation. Then on 16 December 2008, the date laid claim to be another turning point in South Africa's history, as a group of senior ANC leaders met to launch a new party to challenge the ANC.

It was the most significant split in nearly fifty years. The previous rupture of this magnitude came in 1959, when a group of Africanists who opposed collaboration with whites and Asians broke away from the ANC to form a rival liberation movement, the Pan-Africanist Congress, which earned a tragic place in history for organising the demonstration at Sharpeville in March 1960, when police shot dead sixty-nine unarmed protesters. The origins of the new party dated back to the tumultuous party conference in December 2007, when Mbeki was denied a third term as leader of the ANC and was voted out in favour of Jacob Zuma. By stopping Mbeki's drive to maintain his dominance over the party, the vote was the most concrete sign since the ANC took power that its leadership would be held accountable by its members. It also set in motion a chain of events that was to lead to speculation that the monolith had finally cracked. As Zuma and his allies in the Communist Party and the unions cemented their control of the party, a group of senior ANC members loyal to Mbeki agonised over whether to leave the movement to which they had devoted most of their lives. Their thinking crystallised in September 2008, when the party ousted Mbeki as the country's president after a judge threw out Zuma's corruption trial, suggesting there might have been political interference in the case. Mbeki's summary and enforced departure from office was the final straw for the would-be rebels. They renounced their ANC membership, rejected attempts by Zuma's faction to broker reconciliation, and declared they would set up a centrist alternative to the ANC.

The breakaway party sought to drape itself in ANC history. It was launched in Bloemfontein, where the ANC had been founded in 1912. It called itself the Congress of the People (COPE) in a deliberate echo of the 1955 Congress of the People in Kliptown, Soweto, where several thousand delegates of the ANC and allied parties met to launch the Freedom Charter, the ANC's blueprint for a democratic, non-racial and – as it was then assumed – socialist future. The police broke up the original Congress of the People on the second day, and Mandela, who was then under a 'banning' order that restricted his movements, evaded arrest by sitting and watching from a distance. There was no need for such subterfuge in 2008. The only question was whether COPE would suffer the same fate of other ANC breakaway wings, which had ultimately foundered in the shadow of the great movement.

COPE appealed to members of the black middle class who were disillusioned by the left-wing rhetoric of Zuma's allies. It drew on the support of the dispirited Mbekiite factions in the party, several of which had been ousted from regional governments since his defeat. Powerful voting blocs in the Xhosa heartland of the Eastern Cape were promising sources of electoral support. The party also hoped to draw inspiration from the impeccable anti-apartheid records of its two leaders. Neither leader could be dismissed as a throwback to the era of white minority rule, the badge that the white leaders of the Democratic Alliance found it so hard to shed. Mosiuoa 'Terror' Lekota was a legendary student activist in the seventies and spent eight years on Robben Island, from 1974 to 1982, before serving another term in prison in the late eighties. On his release he was one of the party's more popular figures. He led the party's first ever canvassing drive on a bright August Saturday morning in 1993, bounding from matchbox house to matchbox house with the enthusiasm of a teenager. His co-founder was Mbhazima Shilowa, a former founder and leader of Cosatu, the main union federation, who in the early nineties had led marches through Johannesburg chanting workers' slogans and denouncing a free-market economic policy.

The precedents for splits, however, were not encouraging. In exile the PAC had styled itself as a rival to the ANC. On being unbanned in 1990 it briefly aspired to outflank the ANC on the left, but lacking funding and with a listless leader, it never posed a serious threat. After winning less than 2 per cent of the vote in the April 1994 election, it faded from view. In 1996 Bantu Holomisa, a rambunctious former leader of the Transkei homeland in the Eastern Cape, was expelled from the ANC after accusing one of its leaders of corruption and founded a new party with Roelf Meyer, the reformist Afrikaner, Nationalist who had been the principal constitutional negotiator of the last white government. Led by an African and an Afrikaner, the United Democratic Movement presented itself as South Africa's first truly multiracial opposition party. But the UDM never managed to expand its support base outside Holomisa's home region in the Eastern Cape, where loyalty to the old leader remained strong. Meyer concedes that such was the aura of the ANC as a liberation movement that the development had come far too soon to succeed.

'The ideals were perfect, but it was just too early to launch such an initiative,' Meyer said. He was speaking a few weeks before the launch of COPE, but he thought it was still too soon for a competitive rival to the ANC. A viable opposition party competing for power would not be 'feasible' for quite a time. ANC voters were not ready to abandon the party that was so intrinsic to South Africa's liberation. Rather, the best hope for democracy would have to come from within the ANC. The party had shown it had a democratic spirit when Mbeki was rejected. South Africa had to ask, he said provocatively, if Westminster-style democracy, with parties opposing each other in Parliament, was exactly what South Africa required.[13]

In the fifty years since the start of decolonisation in Africa, the debate over the merits of multiparty democracy in the continent has ebbed and flowed. Many of the early leaders declared that Africa was not ready for contested elections and imposed one-party states. Hastings Banda, the eccentric tyrant of Malawi, liked to argue that Africa was entitled to its own brand of democracy. 'Democracy did not come to Britain on a platter from the Angel Gabriel in heaven,' he once told his party. 'There are varieties of cow, varieties of sheep and goat, varieties of chicken – so why should there not be varieties of democracy? We have to have our own kind of democracy based on African institutions.'[14] Self-serving as such an argument was, many experiments with multiparty democracy in Africa were disastrous, with parties splitting down tribal lines and elections leading to chaos and civil war.

The outbreak of inter-ethnic violence in Kenya in January 2008 in the wake of disputed elections led once again to commentators posing the question whether multiparty democracy was right for Africa. The question was flawed. What was at issue was not the readiness of the voters, who in Kenya were itching to cast their ballots, but of the rulers to cede power. In the last decade of the twentieth century, Western donors put a new emphasis on tying loans to democracy. A series of long-standing leaders, including Daniel arap Moi in Kenya and Kenneth Kaunda in Zambia, reluctantly submitted to holding elections and were voted out of office. The carrot and stick approach did not always work. In Zimbabwe, Western diplomatic and economic pressure failed to make any impression on Mugabe as he blatantly stole election after election. But if his peers had been prepared to apply meaningful pressure, he might have given ground. More important, there was never any doubt that most Zimbabweans were desperate for the chance to vote Mugabe and ZANU-PF out of office.

If the ANC is to avoid becoming entrenched in power and defiant of the electorate's wishes, at some stage its hegemony will have to end, and it will have to leave office. A spell in opposition would be healthy for the party and for South Africa's democracy. India's Congress Party revitalised itself after losing power and later returned reinvigorated to government. Mexico's once dominant party, the PRI, also showed signs of starting to revive itself after being voted out of office. But the question is how soon – and indeed how – the ANC will leave power.

COPE certainly rattled the ANC ahead of the elections scheduled for the first half of 2009. The ANC tried and failed to secure a court ruling to deny it the right to use the name Congress of the People. It denounced the leaders as traitors and turncoats. Party radicals reverted to more chilling rhetoric. Jason Mkhwane, the chairperson of the ANC Youth League branch in the township of Sedibeng, was quoted as saying that its leaders were seeking to destroy the history of the ANC and behaving 'like cockroaches and . . . must be destroyed'.[15] The language was a grim echo of the poisonous rhetoric of Rwanda at the time of the genocide in 1994, when radio stations urged members of the Hutu majority to kill the 'Tutsi cockroaches'. There was no danger of genocide in South Africa, but the heated rhetoric traded between supporters of COPE and the ANC was a reminder of the country's history of political intolerance between rival parties feuding for black support, and of the dangers inherent in the opening up of politics. In the eighties, supporters of AZAPO, the black consciousness movement, fought and lost a bloody feud with the ANC. In the far more widespread and deadly violence between the ANC and the Inkatha Freedom Party, townships and villages became divided between supporters of the two parties, with followers of each risking death if they strayed into the other's territory.

But COPE did not expect to mount a serious challenge for power. Its most realistic ambition was to bring the ANC's majority down below 60 per cent, a level the party had surpassed in all three multiracial elections, but it failed to meet even that objective. While the ANC may not have the mesmeric hold on the electorate's affections it had in 1994, when it campaigned under the banner of Mandela, it is the party synonymous with the struggle and for which many South Africans have dedicated their lives. COPE's denunciations of the ANC's records and calls for it to revolutionise its approach rang a little hollow, given its leaders' close connection to Mbeki, the very man who had been leading the party for the previous decade. When the results were tallied the ANC's share of the vote had dropped by 3.79 per cent to just under 66 per cent, the mildest of rebukes. The Democratic Alliance won nearly 17 per cent, an increase of nearly five per cent of the votes cast over 2004, but still not enough for its leaders to claim it had become a genuinely viable alternative. COPE came third with 7.4 per cent. Most of its votes had been taken from the ANC. The ruling party masked its losses to COPE by absorbing large numbers of votes traditionally going to the Zulu-dominated Inkatha Freedom Party. But still, despite all the controversies, Zuma's share of the vote was higher than Mandela's ANC in 1994, and the ANC remained the overwhelming dominant force.

South Africa has to hope that the formation of COPE is a harbinger of a future non-racial party, aligning supporters of the Democratic Alliance with centrist members of the ANC in a viable multiracial opposition to a left-leaning ANC. But that is just an aspiration. The ANC remains the country's engine room. It is the ANC that will continue to form policy. It is the ANC that will control all state appointments. It is the ANC that will decide on the future of black economic empowerment. If South Africa is to correct the corrosive drift of the first fifteen years of democracy, it is the ANC that has to change.

There is a small landlocked country north of South Africa that offers a happier analogy than Zimbabwe's. Since independence, Botswana has had a stable society and a thriving economy. The World Bank found in 2008 that Botswana's was one of only thirteen economies that grew at an average rate of 7 per cent a year or more for twenty-five years or longer in the postwar period. While it did not suffer the agonies of apartheid, its attainments should not be beyond South Africa, but only if a new generation of leaders can step forward and guide the ANC out of its morass.

Chapter 12

BEIJING AND BEYOND

I hope we will be able to rediscover our bearings.
— ARCHBISHOP TUTU,
2008

*The new South Africa, warts and all, is a much
better place.*
— F.W. DE KLERK, 2010, 20TH ANNIVERSARY
OF THE RELEASE OF MANDELA

*Unfortunately, some government officials regard
money and political power as more important than
principle. And that is sad.*
— DALAI LAMA, ON THE EVE OF ZUMA'S
ELECTION, MARCH 2009

The delegates from the giant Chinese steel company were clearly nonplussed.
They had flown thousands of miles from north-west China to a mine in the
expanse of *veld*, north-west of Pretoria, for the launch of a blast furnace in which
they had a major share. On arrival they had been whisked to a marquee, arranged
with immaculately laid tables for a celebratory lunch. Their dark suits made them
look all the more incongruous against the dusty backdrop of the African bush.
They also appeared to be suffering from chronic jet lag. As they surveyed their
reception, a group of South African and Chinese miners mounted a makeshift
stage and launched into Elvis Presley's 'You were always on my mind'. The other

attendant dignitaries, South African mining managers, courtiers of the Queen Mother of the Royal Bafokeng, looked equally bemused. Watching from the back of the tent, a twinkling-eyed Chinese diplomat, however, was beaming with delight.

Zhou Yuxiao, then the deputy head of China's mission in Pretoria, was one of China's most experienced diplomats in Africa. One of his responsibilities was to try to counter the perception in the West and parts of Africa that China was engaged in a neo-colonial race for the continent's minerals. The symbolism of the song's lyrics – and the harmonious imagery of the hulking Afrikaners and black African miners standing alongside the more diminutive Chinese – was clearly not lost on him. 'China is always regarded as an elephant,' he said. 'And when that elephant comes people tend to be scared. Actually the Chinese are just ordinary business people.'[1] His assessment was a little disingenuous. But it is a view that many in the ANC are broadly happy to accept: namely that the West is too reflexively suspicious of Beijing's engagement with Africa. Against the backdrop of a new 'scramble' for Africa's resources, with Chinese and Indian companies muscling in to the territory dominated since the nineteenth century by Westerners, Zuma made very clear from his earliest days in power his belief in the benefits of being close to Beijing. As China's economic and political might expand, it is a relationship which will shape South Africa's future.

The dramatic re-engagement of China with Africa in the first decade of the twenty-first century was the most significant development on the continent after the end of the Cold War. Previously the attention China paid to Africa had been, at best, sporadic. In the fifteenth century Zheng He, the Chinese admiral and explorer, had famously displayed a giraffe at the imperial court after leading a naval expedition down the east African coast but thereafter interest waned. In the 1960s and 1970s Mao Zedong provided aid to Africa, but as Moscow and Washington fought for supremacy on the continent, Beijing kept its distance. Then early in the twenty-first century, to the consternation of the West, China pursued a concerted drive to extend commercial links across the continent. This was driven by China's need for raw materials to fuel its economy, and the business arrangements were often crude. In many of the deals China offered cheap loans and infrastructure in return for minerals. The West was especially critical of the ties with repressive regimes, in particular Beijing's relationship with the Sudan and Zimbabwe's President Robert Mugabe. In Zambia the Chinese ties became a sensitive political issue as locals complained of mistreatment by Chinese overseers and also that much of the work was being done by imported Chinese labour and not Africans. Yet for many African countries China was filling an important gap. In Angola five years after the end of its civil war in 2002, Chinese construction companies were building hospitals, schools, roads and railways across the country. Also, as many African officials pointed out, the West's criticism was deeply hypocritical. After all, in the Cold War it had had no compunction about backing tyrants such as Mobutu Sese Seko of Zaire.

In South Africa in the first decade of the twenty-first century the relationship was more nuanced than in most other African countries. South Africa needed neither cheap credit nor the infrastructure. It also feared that Chinese-manufactured garments would destroy the local textile industry. In 2006, after angry protests by trade unions, the government negotiated a limited system of quotas for Chinese textile imports. The Elvis performance at the ferrochrome mine in the *veld* reflected the nuance. One line of the song regretfully refers to 'little things I should have said and done'. It is tempting to see that as reflecting the prevailing Western view of China's burgeoning relationship with Africa: the behemoth trampling over the interests of smaller countries. But the ferrochrome project was symptomatic of a new and subtler phase of Chinese engagement. There were just five Chinese in the 1,000-strong workforce, and all at a senior level. Rather than injecting human capital, the Jiuquan Iron and Steel Company (Jisco) from northwest China invested over US $30 million in the mine in a joint venture with the Australian-based International Ferro Metals. Crucially for IFM, Jisco also guaranteed to buy half the product. Ferrochrome is a key ingredient of stainless steel, for which China has a colossal appetite.

The singers finished 'You were always on my mind' to sustained applause. Mike Horn, the South African general manager of the site, and a member of the bi-national 'choir', later ruminated that it was not just the Chinese who were learning from these partnerships. It was, he suggested, very much a two-way trade. 'Their outlook is totally different than ours. They have long-term plans. We are working on five-year, ten-year, twenty-year plans. These people will go forty and fifty years or longer. That opens your eyes.'[2]

For President Thabo Mbeki the pursuit of the 'south-south' partnership with other influential developing nations *was* a priority. He was still president when in late 2007 the tall and understated Afrikaner chief executive of Standard Bank, South Africa's largest bank, startled the financial markets by announcing that China was to make the largest single foreign investment in South Africa since the end of apartheid. Jacko Maree had clinched a deal for the Industrial and Commercial Bank of China, the biggest lending bank in Asia, to take a 20 per cent stake in Standard Bank. It was a dramatic sign of China's expanding ambitions for Africa. It was also a reminder of how South Africa, with its sophisticated banking sector, is the obvious launch-pad for the rest of the world to move into Africa.

Yet Mbeki appreciated and even warned of the potential for the relationship to shift into dependency if not servitude. His bond with Beijing was, officials suggested, driven as much by a desire to present a counter-balance to the power of the United States as by a desire to fashion closer ties to China. He infuriated Washington and its allies – and human rights advocates, including Archbishop Tutu – by siding with China at the UN Security Council in opposing a resolution censuring the Burmese junta. Yet he was one of the very few African leaders to sound a note of caution about Beijing. Towards the end of his presidency he cautioned that Africa needed to guard against falling into a 'colonial relationship' with China.[3]

His successor, however, appeared to have fewer qualms.

Towards the end of the international climate change summit in Copenhagen in December 2009 a sudden wintery blast of weather temporarily grounded the South African presidential plane. Jacob Zuma had intended to leave the conference early. But with his plane's windshield iced over he postponed his departure and returned to the talks. They were then reaching a critical stage as the nations of the developed and developing world faced off over their obligations to confront global warming. One of Zuma's confidants believes that this chance event influenced both the outcome of the summit and South Africa's future standing in the world.[4] The former claim may be a bit of an exaggeration, but the delay certainly enabled Zuma to make his first mark on the international stage. At the very least he can claim to have been present at one of the more telling moments of global diplomacy in the 21st twenty-first century.

With the talks close to collapse, on the last night of the summit President Barack Obama paid a final call on the Chinese premier, Wen Jiabao. When he arrived, however, he found that the Chinese leader was already meeting three other leaders of the developing world: India's prime minister Manmohan Singh, Brazil's president Luiz Inacio Lula da Silva – and Zuma. The European diplomats who were, to their frustration, excluded from the meeting speculate whether, as American officials have insinuated, Mr Obama was genuinely startled to find the other three there ahead of him or whether he feigned surprise to reduce the wrath of the Europeans. But whatever the truth behind the diplomatic platitudes, the encounter was a clear reflection of the shifting balance of global power. For South Africa there was an added symbolism.

For Brazil and India to be engaged in the last stage of the talks was unsurprising. They, alongside China, are the emerging powerhouses whose markets are playing an ever larger role in the global economy, and whose economies helped to move the world out of recession after the financial crisis of 2007–2008. They are also integral elements of one of the more striking economists' concepts of the decade: the Brics. Economists and analysts have seized excitedly on the coinage of Jim O'Neill, chief economist for Goldman Sachs, linking Brazil, Russia, India and China as the coming economic behemoths. His bold prediction in 2001 was that in three or four decades they would overtake the six largest Western economies in economic might. In such company South Africa was very much the odd one out. Its economy was far smaller and less dynamic, and, given its dependence on minerals, its potential was rather less sparkling. But politically South Africa at Copenhagen sensed an opportunity.

Since the end of apartheid South African officials had long dreamt of being a global player. On that deadlocked night in the Danish capital Zuma saw his chance. In the early sessions of the summit European officials believed that he was amenable to their perspective as they pushed for hard commitments from all big polluters. Instead, they found he was firmly with China. South African officials liked to think that that gathering marked the launch of a new international grouping and one which entrenched their presence at the top table: Basic, or Brazil, South Africa, India and China.

A month later, one of Zuma's closest advisers sketched out an expansive vision of South Africa's future as one with increasingly close ties to Beijing.[5] He was speaking in the shadow of the Union Buildings in Pretoria, where the Afrikaner Nationalists had planned so many foreign policy initiatives in the previous era. Then, the objective had been to cleave as close as possible to the West by presenting South Africa as a bulwark against communism. Two decades after the fall of the Berlin Wall, Pretoria's priorities were very different. China was not only the coming world power and an increasingly important player in Africa, the adviser said. Its belief in state-run capitalism as opposed to the free-market ideology of the West also offered, he said, invaluable lessons for Zuma's ANC as it rethought its policies in the wake of the financial crisis. In short, the relationship entailed not just a closer diplomatic alliance but even, he hoped, a meeting of minds.

In late 2009 the strength of the relationship was formalised when China emerged as South Africa's largest trading partner. It was a striking turnaround. Only a year or so earlier China had been the fifth largest destination for South Africa's exports. In part, the change reflected the decline of Western demand in the wake of the credit crisis. But it also reflected an attempt by Beijing to resolve Pretoria's frustrations over the previous trade deficit. For Zuma it was tangible proof of the advantages of the relationship. He had already made very clear his views, in a diplomatic rumpus over South Africa's refusal in March 2009 to give the Dalai Lama a visa to attend a conference in Cape Town. The Dalai Lama deftly brushed aside the controversy, joking that he had had far more publicity by being denied a visa than if he had been granted one. But he was distressed by the ANC's move and echoed Tutu's misgivings about the character of the party. Too many in the party had become more interested in business than public service, he said. 'Unfortunately, some government officials regard money and political power as more important than principle,' he said. 'And that is sad.'[6]

The government formally denied they had succumbed to pressure from Beijing. But few doubted South Africa had acted to do Beijing's bidding. One government adviser said Zuma had stepped in when the cabinet was arguing over the issue. Of course they had to take Beijing's side, Zuma ruled. That is where, he judged, South Africa's interests lay.[7]

Zuma's decisiveness over China belied his domestic reputation as a man who is all things to all people.

Many of his early appointments and policy statements were praised at home and abroad. On taking office he moved rapidly to distance himself from the controversies under Mbeki. On World AIDS Day in 2009 he announced a major shift in policy. South Africa would treat all HIV-positive babies and rapidly expand testing for the virus. His rhetoric made a striking contrast with the equivocal stance of his predecessor. 'At another moment in our history, in another context, the liberation movement observed that the time comes in the life of any nation when there remain only two choices: submit or fight,' he said. 'That time has now come in our struggle to overcome AIDS. Let us declare now, as we declared then, that we shall not submit.'[8]

Amid expectation that he might shift economic policy to the Left, he reassured the financial markets with his retention of Trevor Manuel, the long-serving finance minister, in the cabinet, albeit in an amorphous post as a policy co-ordinator. He courted whites, in particular Afrikaners, urging them to stay loyal to their country. He also frequently acknowledged the shortcomings of the ANC's record. After the years under Mbeki, when criticism of the government was frequently dismissed as disloyalty or racism, his candour was refreshing. Ministers acknowledged that the ANC's record on education was poor, that they urgently needed new initiatives to combat crime and that people in townships were right to complain about 'delivery'.

Collins Chabane, a boyish party member known for his dedication to public service, was appointed to a new post charged with monitoring the performance of ministers and progress in delivering basic services. 'Delivery' would be the primary focus of the Zuma presidency, he insisted.[9] Another senior official even lambasted one of the pillars of the party's strategy: the system of deploying 'cadres' into government. Under the headline 'We can serve our people better', Malusi Gigaba, the deputy housing minister, wrote an article in the ANC's online newsletter denouncing elected ANC councillors who had abused their positions. 'It is clear in some municipalities that the issue of deployment has been thoroughly abused . . . Comrades have distorted the deployment strategy and perverted it to suit ignoble ends.'[10]

Such rhetoric suggested a rekindled and welcome spirit of self-criticism, but inside the ANC and the ruling alliance the politics were increasingly sulphurous. Mbeki had been accused of centralising power but he had at least given a clear lead and left little doubt over policy. Under Zuma, fierce and public battles were fought within the alliance over control of economic policy. South Africa deserved such a debate in the aftermath of the global financial crisis. In 2008 the economy plunged into recession for the first time in over a decade as demand, in particular for its minerals, plunged. Some of the rows were between centrists and the Left, pitching those in favour of maintaining the business-friendly policies of the Mbeki era against those seeking greater state intervention. Others were more personal and virulent and potentially destructive. Julius Malema, the splenetic leader of the party's Youth League, who had infamously offered to kill for Zuma, toured the country delivering inflammatory speeches, including calls to nationalise the mines. It fell counter-intuitively to senior figures in the Communist Party to reject the call. The bickering underpinned a concern before Zuma's election, that he might not be the man to take the wrenching decisions South Africa badly needed.

All the while Zuma maintained his familiar man-of-the-people routine. At the politically sensitive memorial service for Mbeki's health minister, Manto Tshabalala-Msimang, he burst into song to put mourners at their ease. His instinctive style of politics was for many comforting and infectious. Yet his colourful personal life, which was repeatedly on the front pages of the newspapers, was acutely embarrassing to many of the old guard in the ANC, and also to the country's ambassadors abroad, underlining the pitfalls of a populist president. Just two months after he unveiled the new AIDS policies it emerged that he had had a child – his twentieth – in an extra-marital relationship with the daughter of an old family friend. The furore was all the greater as it came just a few weeks after he married for the fifth time in a proud and public display of polygamy. It also revived memories of the embarrassing revelations in his rape trial. Helen Zille, the leader of the Democratic Alliance, said it set an appalling example. Zuma's conduct was, she argued, as damaging to the struggle against HIV and AIDS as the 'denialist' approach of Mbeki.[11]

In such a climate white critics were inevitably dubbed as diehard racists nostalgic for the past. It was an easy rhetorical device, but lazy and dangerous. Too often the past is just a convenient distraction from the present. The ANC needs to stop dwelling on the villainy of the apartheid past and the glory of the transition, and concentrate on the future.

The Reverend Frank Chikane, one of Mbeki's closest advisers, knows as much as anyone about the awfulness of apartheid and the incongruities and bizarreness of the negotiated settlement. In 1989, when he was one of the foremost clerics in the anti-apartheid movement, he had to be rushed to the hospital several times after suffering a series of mysterious collapses. Apartheid agents, it later emerged, had attempted to assassinate him by lacing his clothes with poison. More than a decade and a half later, Adriaan Vlok, the law and order minister at the time of his poisoning, came to him to beg forgiveness. Vlok ended up on his hands and knees washing Chikane's feet in a symbolic bid for atonement.

By the end of Mbeki's presidency Chikane's reputation had plummeted. The former anti-apartheid hero was seen as a yes-man compliant in Mbeki's follies. In July 2008 he was pacing up and down his office in the West Wing of the Union Buildings, deeply distressed. The previous day, South Africa's leading Sunday newspaper had branded him a liar on the front page over comments he had made on Zimbabwe.[12] 'How can they write that? It is unfair and untrue,' he kept saying.[13]

For half an hour he gave an anguished defence of Mbeki's policy on Zimbabwe. Then, unprompted, he digressed into memories of happier times. He recalled how, soon after he took up his post as director general of the presidency, he was going over his department's records and saw that they were paying for an office and secretary in Bloemfontein. Assuming this was a scam he looked into it and found to his surprise that this was for the former state president, P.W. Botha, the very man whose agents had tried to kill him. Among the responsibilities of his department, Chikane ascertained, was to fund an office for all former state presidents. He also had to take charge of their funeral arrangements and was obliged to visit the family of a dead president within twenty-four hours of his death. So when Botha died in 2006, Chikane had had to fly down to the old diehard's house to express the state's condolences.

'What a wonderful country this is,' he exclaimed. 'P.W. gave the order to kill me, and yet I took care of him until he went to his grave. I paid for his secretary and an office of 120 square metres, paper and computers. And then I was in P. W.'s house within twenty-four hours of his death to say, "How can we help you?"' He chuckled before launching into further reminiscences, clearly delighted to escape from thinking about his political misfortunes.

South Africa *did* defy all predictions in reaching an agreement between Africans and Afrikaners. In January 2010, just before the twentieth anniversary of his unbanning of the ANC on 2 February 1990, F.W. de Klerk recalled how there was nothing inevitable about that momentous decision.[14] There were many in the security forces, he remembered, who were arguing that they should hold out. While the apartheid regime was under siege economically and diplomatically it was, after all, far from defeated on the battlefield. At 73, the stocky, balding Afrikaner seemed little changed from the dramatic days in the early 90s when his clipped English and Afrikaans accent dominated international news bulletins. Seated at his favourite restaurant in Cape Town, he smiled to recall how he became the first Nationalist leader to master political 'spin', by keeping the news of his intentions from leaking to the media ahead of his dramatic speech to parliament.

After briefing his senior ministers he kept his counsel, knowing his announcement would seem all the more dramatic and draw all the more international attention if it was unexpected. His hapless spokesman was dispatched to brief journalists to expect nothing special. Even his then wife, Marike, his childhood sweetheart, was in the dark. The first inkling she had that anything was up was when he told her as he took the salute outside parliament: 'After today South Africa will never be the same again.'

De Klerk says he looked into the future and realised there was only disaster if the Afrikaner Nationalists dug in their heels. While he shares the concerns of many Afrikaners over affirmative action and warns that the ANC is trying to erode some of the principles of the constitution, he says the deal had to be struck and quickly if the country was not to disintegrate. He plays down the accusations of Afrikaners that he ceded too much and should have enshrined minority rights in the constitution.

'How would South Africa have looked today if we had not signed the agreements which were reached? We would not have exported one case of wine this year. [Wine is one of South Africa's healthiest exports.] South Africa would have been on a downward slope towards calamity and catastrophe. So the new South Africa, warts and all, is a much better place.'

To his credit, in his retirement de Klerk has remained a loyal ambassador for his country's new masters. As the years pass, the magnitude of his decision to unban the ANC and release Mandela is all the more striking. He was not an inspirational politician. Long after he left politics in 1997 many in the ANC argued he had been too evasive over responsibility for apartheid and did not do enough when in power to curb the abuses of the security forces. And yet at a critical moment in his country's history he conquered his fear of the unknown and acted in the best interests of his country and not his party – and that marks him out with greatness. Lord Renwick, who was British ambassador at the time of the speech, argues that de Klerk deserved the Nobel Peace Prize twice over for handing over power.[15] 'The hardest thing in politics is not to receive power but to give it up,' he said. 'He changed the history of South Africa.'

But that is the past. As Mandela wrote, ending apartheid was only the first of many hills South Africa had to climb.[16] Since then, some have been conquered, but rather too many others have been skirted. If the ANC is to stop atrophying, it needs to focus squarely on the future and remember the clarion call of the first election campaign: 'A better life for all.' Fifteen years after the end of white rule, several commentators pondered whether the world's rapture with the wonderful story of the Afrikaners ceding power and Mandela's subsequent magnanimity to his oppressors had done South Africa a disservice. By enveloping post-apartheid South Africa in such majesty and mystique, did the world set the country up to be a disappointment once Mandela stepped aside?

Building a new society out of the rubble of an unjust system is invariably an ugly and harsh process. But Archbishop Tutu rightly draws no comfort from the observation that the ANC has become another compromised political party.

'It doesn't help when I have a toothache to say these other guys have a toothache too. It doesn't relieve my anguish,' he said. 'Maybe we were arrogant and have come with a bang to terra firma to realise that, after all, we are actually human. But you know, when we were involved in the struggle, we were quite extraordinary.'[17]

Tutu was looking out over the Atlantic rollers at Robben Island, sporting the same black workman's cap that had adorned his head during countless anti-apartheid rallies in the 1980s. His nostalgia for the Mandela era was unmistakable. Many in the struggle had been intent on helping the people, not themselves, he said. He had imagined that 'the idealism, the altruism, the high moral ground' of the anti-apartheid era would endure once freedom had been won, but South Africans had been brought 'very firmly to the ground'.

'I hope we will be able to rediscover our bearings,' he said. He did not sound truly convinced.

ANC politicians justifiably complain that an engrained Afro-pessimism informs international perceptions of the country. Beyond the lurid headlines about the appalling rates of crime and its tragic record on AIDS, there are heartening developments in communities across the country, underlining how South Africa is changing. For every comrade hungry to exploit political power for riches, there are others committed to improving the lives of their compatriots. Non-governmental groups and the opposition are constantly keeping the ANC in check, relying on the courts and the constitution to curb its excesses.

Yet many of the positive developments come despite rather than because of the ANC. The party has to impose tight limits on the business arrangements of government officials, civil servants and MPs. It needs to stop making grandiose promises that have inflated expectations way beyond what is possible. It should stop thinking about lucrative business deals and refocus on governing. It needs to go beyond talking of the crises of education and crime and confront them. Most important of all, it must shed its revolutionary ambitions to take control of every aspect of the state. Unlike so many newly liberated states in Africa, South Africa has a large educated class that should be able to oversee such reforms, although Zimbabwe's population was far better educated and that did not spare it from disaster. It also has the wealth to fund many of the necessary policies, and a sophisticated business class able to take advantage of shifts in the global economy. The question is whether the ANC has the will to change its ways. One of the most haunting anti-apartheid poems, written in the dire late years of the eighties, when the townships were in flames, talked of how South Africa was 'drinking too deeply from poisoned wells'.[18] Somehow it has to stop drinking from them and look to the future before it is too late.

South Africa has defied the odds many times before and its leaders have a history of making the right decision at the last minute. As it realigns itself towards

Asia and intensifies links with China, it can draw inspiration from other developing countries that have also at one stage appeared destined to stagnate and then recovered. Government and business in India are corrupt but democracy has not only survived but matured in the decades since independence, and the country's economy has flourished. Yet to follow India's lead, the reformists in the ANC have to keep the more avaricious populists in check. Otherwise the fate of so many other liberation movements awaits the party, and South Africa will – in a decade or so – find itself led by an ossified ruling party overseen by bickering apparatchiks presiding over a sclerotic dysfunctional state. It will easily be exploited by unsentimental Chinese companies who will no longer need to treat it with the respect shown by the miners of Jisco in their joint choir in the bush.

The dreams of its becoming a beacon for the continent – and of the anti-apartheid struggle – will lie in the dust.

ACKNOWLEDGEMENTS

South Africans have been wonderfully generous to me with their time, thoughts, and hospitality over the years. Some I quote in these pages. Others would rather remain anonymous. A list of the plucky and devoted ANC activists who have helped me over the years would fill more than a page. I owe a special debt to South Africa's journalists. Mondli Makhanya and his fellow musketeer Justice Malala, Abbey Makoe, Peter Bruce, Barney Mthombothi, Karima Brown, Tim Cohen and Caroline Southey were particularly free with their advice and insights during the frenetic eighteen months of my second stint. It is a golden age for South African non-fiction writers. Mark Gevisser's biography of Mbeki, Andrew Feinstein's insider account of the ANC, Allister Sparks's trilogy on South African politics, William Mervin Gumede's account of the politics in the ANC, Anthony Butler's biography of Cyril Ramaphosa, Jonny Steinberg's books on the police and AIDS, Jeremy Gordin's biography of Jacob Zuma and John Carlin's account of the Mandela magic are treasure troves for anyone seeking to understand South Africa, as are the memoirs of Mac Maharaj and Tony Leon. I have relied heavily on them.

As a foreign correspondent I owe much to my colleagues at the *Financial Times* in London who allowed me to roam around South Africa and the region. Lionel Barber plucked me from Washington, gave me the privilege of a second chapter in one of the world's more compelling sagas, and then gave me time off to write the book, even as the news from southern Africa was bubbling. He also brought a rare smile to Thabo Mbeki's lips at a difficult time for the then president with his tale of a Botswanan white elephant. William Wallis, the *Financial Times*'s irrepressible Africa Editor, repaid a sweaty dinner in Mobutu's Zaire many times over. James Lamont, World News Editor, and Tom O'Sullivan, Middle East and Africa News Editor, masters of encouragement to distant correspondents, appreciated the importance of the crisis in the ANC long before most other international newspapers were paying attention. Mike Skapinker and Andy Davis championed ideas that helped to generate this book. Shawn Donnan and the World News Desk held the fort with brio while I sprinted to the finish. In a previous era, Max Hastings and Nigel Wade, two of the great correspondents, posted me to Johannesburg in the last days of white rule, and Charles Moore kept me there for the Mandela years. Without their and Pat Prentice's patronage, and the support of Paul Hill and Patsy Dryden, this book could never have happened.

Bill McPherson, sage of Bucharest and so much more, received the first outline of my book in DC over a faltering Internet connection from Angola. His enthusiastic response fired me up to press ahead. Patrick Bishop did me yet another favour and steered me towards Annabel Merullo, the sparkiest of literary agents. She and Zoe Pagnamenta found it excellent homes with two brilliant editors, Clive Priddle and Caroline Gascoigne. Clive and Niki Papadopoulos have proved that the art of editing is far from dead with some inspired – and rightly unremitting – advice. Stephanie Sweeney picked up the baton with infectious energy and drive. Beth Wright's copy-editing was invaluable and done at top speed. Melissa Raymond worked through Christmas and the New Year to keep me – just – on schedule. Tess Callaway was splendidly unflagging in the face of a miasma of editing tweaks and requests. Tom Williams never lost patience in trying to find me in Zimbabwe for transcontinental telephone calls. Liz Faunce drew a fine map. Colossal thanks too are due to Richard Foreman for his tireless and inspired efforts to keep *After Mandela* in the public eye.

Stephen Robinson is making a habit of taking on the burden of *Financial Times* correspondents' manuscripts on South Africa. Now I understand why Patti Waldmeir, a predecessor of mine in Johannesburg, hailed him for his forensic and insightful editing. He has done the same again, brilliantly. Robin Gorna steered me through the thickets of the debate on AIDS and urged me to keep writing with the same drive that she has brought to combating that terrible disease. My indomitable eleventh-hour readers, Lourens Ackermann, Barney Mthombothi, Tim Cohen and Greg Marinovich, rightly nudged me on to my soapbox. Ann Bernstein cannily steered me away from some infelicities over land reform. I take full responsibility for the views expressed. Joy Brady conquered officialdom and traced obscure references with the spirit that should see her running a large company. Peter Nkomo guided me to so many scenes of heartache in the old and new South Africa. Gigi Mafifi splendidly kept speaking truth to power. The evergreen Professor Tony Hawkins unlocked the secrets of Zimbabwe's economy and much more. Richard Stovin-Bradford, Jenifer Cohen, Michael Bleby, Sven Lunsche, that intellectual dynamo Michael Power of Investec Asset Management, Jeff Gable of ABSA and a valued DC confidant Andrew Webb guided me through Johannesburg business and South Africa's economy. Greg Marinovich and the *Guardian*'s Chris McGreal, the brightest stars in the foreign-correspondent corps, were co-conspirators in so many dramas, as were Greg's outstanding 'substitutes', Leonie and Luke Marinovich. Michael Hill of the *Baltimore Sun*, Hugh Dellios of the *Chicago Tribune*, Robyn Dixon and Bob Drogin of the *LA Times*, and so many other colleagues enriched so many stories as did the great Michael Holman over the years. Will MacNamara and Tom Burgis, two stars of the future, were the best of colleagues.

Caroline Russell and Roly Keating provided a wonderful port in a storm. They and the most stalwart of counsellors, Jonathan Rugman and Francis Harris, gave astute advice on how to find calmer waters, as did John Kampfner, Robert Peston and Anton La Guardia. Mark Stephenson's enduring axioms kept sentences on a tight leash. Lourens Ackermann and Liesa Jossel, Sally and Lyndon Burt, Abbey and Mpine Makoe, Jamie and Polly Carr, Christopher and Denise Munnion, Robert Legh and Kathryn Gawith, and Joy Brady and her family received us back into their homes as if we had never left. The Pridwin parents gave the warmest of welcomes. Rainhill Farm, Rex and the Hartleys gave me critical space and freedom to think. Dorah Mafifi and her family reminded me constantly of the greatness of South Africa: its heart. John Battersby, a fine journalist charged with the, at times awkward, task of selling the ANC to the world, has dispensed endless timely advice.

As ever, I owe a huge debt to my parents and my sisters, Caroline and Lucy, for all their support and counsel and love, but my greatest debt of all is to my wife, Sophie. Yet again through her own experiences she saw and understood so much in South Africa that I missed. Yet again she read chapters in early miscued drafts and then set them on a better course. Yet again she endured having a husband doing two jobs simultaneously. She and those irrepressible companions, Mungo and Ned, have my pledge not to embark on another book just yet.

NOTES

Introduction: The New Struggle

1. Robert Van Tonder, interview with the author, Muldersdrift, June 1993.
2. Quoted in article by Marida Fitzpatrick, Beeld, 18 April 2009.
3. Michael Wines, 'South African Is Acquitted of Rape Charges', *New York Times*, 9 May 2006.

Chapter 1: Succeeding a Saint

1. Author's notes from rally, Katlehong, August 1993.
2. All quotations from Mandela's January 1994 speech and his comments are from the author's notes.
3. Nelson Mandela, speech (author's notes), Johannesburg, November 1997.
4. Mokaba chanted the slogan at rallies in the countdown to the end of white rule. It appalled whites, since it came at a time of mounting attacks on white farmers on their homesteads.
5. Carl Niehaus, Mandela's spokesman before the 1994 election, interview with the author, Johannesburg, July 2008.
6. Desmond Tutu, speech to Foreign Correspondents' Association, Johannesburg, 13 November 1995.
7. Raymond Mhlaba, interview with the author, Bisho, November 1994.
8. Nelson Mandela, *Long Walk to Freedom: The Autobiography of Nelson Mandela* (Boston: Little, Brown, 1994), 559.
9. Author's notes, December 1997.
10. Anthony Sampson, *Mandela: The Authorized Biography* (New York: Knopf, 1999), 9.
11. Nelson Mandela, inauguration address, 10 May 1994.
12. Alec Russell, 'Understudy Steps Out of Mandela Shadow', *Daily Telegraph*, 22 July 1996. 'Starry-eyed rainbowism' is a reference to the 'rainbow nation', Desmond Tutu's magnificent coinage for the post-apartheid nation.
13. Patrick FitzGerald, interview with the author, Johannesburg, July 2008.
14. Edwin Cameron, interview with the author, London, September 2008.

15. Thabo Mbeki, address to ANC conference, December 2007.

16. Thabo Mbeki, interview with the author, Pretoria, July 1996.

17. Ibid.

18. Senior Western official, interview with the author, Johannesburg, 29 July 2008.

19. Nkosazana Dlamini-Zuma, conversation with the author, Windsor Castle, June 2001.

20. Sydney Mufamadi, briefing in Pretoria, 15 April 2008, http://www.dfa.gov.za/docs/speeches/2008/mufa0416.html.

21. Desmond Tutu, interview with the author, Cape Town, 30 April 2008.

22. Allister Sparks, *Beyond the Miracle: Inside the New South Africa* (Chicago: University of Chicago Press, 2003), 273.

23. Dali Tambo, interview with the author, February 1996.

24. Thabo Mbeki, epigraph to Ronald Suresh Roberts, *Fit to Govern: The Native Intelligence of Thabo Mbeki* (Johannesburg: STE, 2007).

25. Nelson Mandela, speech to Foreign Correspondents' Association, Johannesburg, December 1997.

26. Nelson Mandela, closing address to ANC conference, Mafikeng, December 1997.

27. All quotes from Cyril Ramaphosa in this chapter are from an interview with the author, London, 9 September 2008.

28. Interviews with the author, August 2008.

29. Mark Gevisser, *Thabo Mbeki: A Dream Deferred* (Johannesburg: Jonathan Ball, 2007), 718.

30. Interview with Saki Macozoma by the author and William Wallis, Africa Editor of the *Financial Times*, 18 December 2007.

31. Senior diplomat, telephone interview with the author, 2007.

32. Presidential adviser, message to the author, 10 June 2008.

Chapter 2: The Other Side of the Rainbow

1. Charl van der Merwe, interview with the author, Koppies, 28 June 1993.

2. Johannes Tladi, interview with the author, Koppies, April 1995.

3. Charl van der Merwe, interview with the author, Koppies, October 1995.

4. All quotations from *Tannie* Joan in this chapter are from an interview with the author, Koppies, July 1994.

5. An old word for unbeliever, it is the equivalent of 'nigger' in the United States.

6. Interview with the author, Johannesburg, November 1995.

7. Peter De Ionno, 'New Police Chief Puts Clamp on Racist Tape', *Sunday Times* (Johannesburg), 5 February 2005.

8. Wilhelm Verwoerd, interview with the author, Stellenbosch, June 1995.

9. Author's notes from interview on Radio 702, Johannesburg talk-radio station, June 1995.

10. François Pienaar, interview with the author, London, September 2008.

11. Gigi Mafifi, interview with the author, Johannesburg, July 1995.

12. Desmond Tutu, interview with the author, Cape Town, June 1996.

13. Ibid.

14. Padraig O'Malley, *Shades of Difference: Mac Maharaj and the Struggle for South Africa* (New York: Viking, 2007), 401.

15. Dirk Coetzee, interview with the author, Vlakplaas, October 1996.

16. Jacques Pauw, *Into the Heart of Darkness: Confessions of Apartheid's Assassins* (Johannesburg: Jonathan Ball, 1997), 51.

17. Opening hearing of Truth and Reconciliation Commission, from the author's notes; see also http://www.doj.gov.za/trc/hrvtrans/index.htm.

18. Joel Netshitenzhe, 'Search for Closure Continues', *Sunday Times*, 20 April 2003.

19. Thabo Mbeki, interview with the author, Pretoria, July 1996.

20. Thabo Mbeki, 'Letter from the President', *ANC Today* 7, no. 10, 16–22 March 2007, http://www.anc.org.za/ancdocs/anctoday/2007/text/at10.txt.

21. Thabo Mbeki, interview with the author, Pretoria, April 2007.

22. Thabo Mbeki, 'Letter from the President', *ANC Today* 1, no. 43, November 16–22, 2001, http://www.anc.org.za/ancdocs/anctoday/2001/text/at43.txt.

23. Desmond Tutu, interview with the author, Cape Town, April 2008.

24. Anonymous businessman, interview with the author, July 2008.

25. Malegapuru Makgoba, interview with the author, Durban, August 2008.

26. Du Wet Potgieter, *White Poverty: A Solidarity Report*, September 2008.

27. Desmond Tutu, interview with the author, April 2008.

28. Survey by Bureau of Market Research, University of South Africa, *The Times* (Johannesburg), 18 August 2008.

29. United Association of South Africa, *Seventh Employment Report*, June 2008.

30. '2008 Development Indicators', 17 July 2008, http://www.thepresidency.gov.za.

31. Simon Kuper, 'Team Colours', *Financial Times*, 21 July 2007.

32. Interview with Padraig O'Malley cited in Anthony Butler, *Cyril Ramaphosa* (Johannesburg: Jacana Media, 2008), 380.

33. Jacob Zuma, conversation with the author, Johannesburg, June 2008.

34. Shadrack Gutto, interview with the author, Johannesburg, October 2007.

35. Christo van Greunen, interview with the author, Koppies, August 2008.

36. Koos du Plooy, interview with the author, Koppies, August 2008.

Chapter 3: Liberation Movements
Have a Habit of Not Ageing Gracefully

1. Joao Domingos, interview with the author, Luanda, September 2007.

2. Aguinaldo Jaime, interview with the author, Luanda, September 2007.

3. Nelson Mandela, address to ANC conference. Bloemfontein, December 1994, http://www.anc.org.za/ancdocs/history/mandela/1994/sp941222.html.

4. All quotations from Harry Gwala in this chapter are from an interview with the author, Pietermaritzburg, July 1993.

5. William Mervin Gumede, *Thabo Mbeki and the Battle for the Soul of the ANC* (Cape Town: Zebra Press, 2005), 2.

6. Nelson Mandela, closing speech to ANC conference, Bloemfontein, December 1994, http://www.anc.org.za/ancdocs/history/mandela/1994/sp941222.html.

7. Mandela, closing speech to ANC conference, December 1994, and author's notes.

8. Cheryl Carolus, interview with the author, Johannesburg, August 2008.

9. All quotations from Blade Nzimande in this chapter are from an interview with the author, Cape Town, November 1994.

10. Johnny de Lange, interview with the author, Cape Town, November 1994.

11. Cheryl Carolus, speech to Foreign Correspondents' Association, Johannesburg, July 1997.

12. Nelson Mandela, speech to Foreign Correspondents' Association, Johannesburg, December 1997.

13. Manne Dipico, interview with the author, Kimberley, September 1995.

14. Desmond Tutu, interview with the author, Cape Town April 2008.

15. Carol Paton, 'Soul for Sale', *Financial Mail*, 19 January 2007.

16. Andrew Feinstein, *After the Party: A Personal and Political Journey Inside the ANC* (Johannesburg: Jonathan Ball, 2007), 242.

17. Smuts Ngonyama, interview with the author, Johannesburg, June 2007.

18. Gumede, *Thabo Mbeki*, 289.

19. Anthony Butler, *Cyril Ramaphosa* (Johannesburg: Jacana Media, 2008), 353.

20. Nelson Mandela Lecture, July 2006.

21. 'Where Are Your Voices Now?', *Sunday Times* (Johannesburg), 1 June 2008.

22. S'Thembiso Msomi, 'ANC Incorporated Takes Over', *City Press*, 27 November 2005.

23. Jeremy Cronin, interview with the author, Johannesburg, July 1996.

24. Thabo Mbeki, conversation with the author, Cape Town, April 2007.

25. Abbey Witbooi, interview with the author, Cape Town, June 2007.

26. Kader Asmal, interview with the author, Cape Town, June 2007.

27. Justice Malala, 'There's No Stopping ANC Yet', *Times* (Johannesburg), 21 July 2008.

28. In 1994 the ANC won 62.6 per cent of the vote. Ten years later it increased its share to 69.7 per cent, above the two-thirds threshold required to change the constitution. The next nearest party in 2004 won 12.3 per cent.

29. Carolus, speech to Foreign Correspondents' Association, July 1997.

30. Feinstein, *After the Party*, 123.

31. 'The State and Transformation: A Discussion Paper towards the Alliance Summit', *Umrabulo* 5 (July–September 1998), http://www.anc.org.za/ancdocs/pubs/umrabulo/articles/sprst.html.

32. Two cabinet ministers, interviews with the author, November 1994.

33. Feinstein, *After the Party*, 175–6.

34. Tony Leon, interview with the author, Johannesburg, May 2007.

35. Friend of Mbeki's, interview with the author, London, March 1998.

36. Senior government official, interview with the author, Johannesburg, June 2008.

37. Party veteran, interview with the author, Polokwane, December 2007.

38. All quotations from Pallo Jordan in this chapter are from an interview with the author, Pretoria, April 2008.

39. Padraig O'Malley, *Shades of Difference: Mac Maharaj and the Struggle for South Africa* (New York: Viking, 2007).

40. Adriaan Basson, 'ANC Rogues' Gallery', *Mail & Guardian* (Johannesburg), 18–24 January 2008.

41. Kader Asmal, interview with the author, Cape Town, April 2008.

42. Jacob Zuma, address to sixty-fifth-birthday party (author's notes), Durban, April 2007.

Chapter 4: The Difficulties of Delivery

1. Nkululeko Ncana and Thabo Mkhize, 'Winnie: Violence Born of Desperation', *Times* (Johannesburg), 16 May 2008.

2. From notes by the author, who witnessed the exchange, Diepslootve, May 2008.

3. Isaac Maela, interview with the author, Diepsloot, May 2008.

4. Clinic nurse, interview with the author, Diepsloot, May 2008.

5. Nelson Mandela, address to victory celebration, Johannesburg, 2 May 1994.

6. Anthony Sampson, *Mandela: The Authorized Biography* (New York: Knopf, 1999), 435.

7. Sam Shilowa, interview with the author, Johannesburg, July 1994.

8. Julian Ogilvie Thompson, interview with the author, November 2008.

9. Ibid.

10. All quotations from Trevor Manuel in this chapter are from interviews with the author, Pretoria, April 2007 and May 2008.

11. Rebecca Sebolecwe, interview with the author, Soweto, March 2007.

12. Sam Makgoka, interview with the author, Orange Farm, December 2007.

13. Bricks Mokolo, interview with the author, Orange Farm, December 2007.

14. Moeletsi Mbeki, interview with the author, Johannesburg, April 2007.

15. Mokolo, interview, December 2007.

16. Ernest Rambau, interview with the author, Orange Farm, December 2007.

17. Dudo Mazibuko, interview with the author, Ladysmith, April 2007.

18. Moses Moshelane, interview with the author, Lichtenburg, February 2007.

19. State employee, interview with the author, Boikhutso, February 2007.

20. Moshelane, interview, February 2007.

21. Christo van Greunen, interview with the author, Koppies, August 2008.

22. Cheryl Carolus, interview with the author, Johannesburg, August 2008.

23. All quotations from Thamsanqa Kambule in this chapter are from an interview with the author, Johannesburg, June 1996.

24. Institute of Race Relations, *Race Relations Survey 1988–89*.

25. Clarence Mlokoti, interview with the author, Soweto, June 1996.

26. Wendy Luhabe, addressing forum sponsored by *Sunday Times* of Johannesburg, published 17 August 2008; transcript: http://www.thetimes.co.za/News/Article.aspx?id=823624.

27. Malcolm Ray, 'Educashen Crysis – Wanted: 68,000 Engineers/Artisans', *Finance Week*, 7 February 2008; Barloworld Logistics, *Annual Survey of South African Logistics*, 2007.

28. South African Institute of Race Relations, *2007 Survey*. South Africa spent 18.5 per cent on education, in comparison with Brazil (12 per cent), India (12.7 per cent), and Poland (12.2 per cent).

29. Mosiuoa Lekota, speech to dinner for opposition leader, Tony Leon, Johannesburg, May 2007.

30. Renier Schoeman, interview with the author, Cape Town, November 1994.

31. Carolus, interview, August 2008.

Chapter 5: A City Under Siege

1. Robert Müller, interview with the author, Johannesburg, December 1994.

2. Antony Altbeker, *A Country at War with Itself: South Africa's Crisis of Crime* (Johannesburg: Jonathan Ball, 2007), 45.

3. Roelf Meyer, interview with the author, London, September 2008.

4. Candice Bailey, 'ATMS Under Siege', *Saturday Star* (Johannesburg), 12 July 2008.

5. Borrie La Grange, '600: That's How Many Times Restaurants Have Been Hit in Only One Year', *Times* (Johannesburg), 8 July 2008.

6. Lionel Barber and Alec Russell, 'Softly Softly: Mbeki Seeks Ways to Limit Chaos to the North and Tensions Within', *Financial Times*, 3 April 2007, http://www.ft.com/cms/s/0/c5b97158-e12f-11db-bd73-000b5df10621.html.

7. Charles Nqakula, cited in Wendy Jasson Da Costa, 'Crime Whingers Can Leave', *Cape Argus*, 2 June 2006.

8. Mosiuoa Lekoa, minister of defence, quoted in Angela Quintal, 'Fleeing Whites Feared Black Rule', *Cape Times*, 15 April 2007.

9. Misha Glenny, *McMafia: A Journey through the Global Criminal Underworld* (New York: Knopf, 2008), 225–28.

10. Gomolemo Mokae, interview with the author, Pretoria, October 1994.

11. According to Section 49 of the Criminal Procedure Act, under apartheid it had been justifiable homicide to kill suspects if it was impossible to stop them fleeing in any other way. This had led to many cases of suspects being killed when trying to escape after committing minor offences. But this was amended in 1998 to accord with the new constitution, which enshrined the presumption of innocence and the right to a fair trial.

12. Susan Shabangu, address to conference on security, Pretoria West, 9 April 2008, cited in 'Kill the Criminal Bastards, Deputy Minister Urges Cops', *Star*, 10 April 2008.

13. Jacob Zuma, speech to gala dinner, KwaZulu-Natal, April 12, 2008, reported in *Business Day*, 14 April 2008.

14. Edwin Cameron, with Nathan Geffen, *Edwin Cameron: Witness to AIDS* (London: I. B. Tauris, 2005), 24.

15. Edwin Cameron, interview with the author, London, September 2008.

16. Helen Suzman, *In No Uncertain Terms: A South African Memoir* (New York: Knopf, 1993), 228.

17. Police officer, interview with the author, Thokoza township, February 1994.

18. All quotations from Leonie Wagner are from an interview with the author, Pretoria, September 1995.

19. He was sentenced to death in 1989, but the government imposed a moratorium on capital punishment in 1990, and he was set free in 1992 in a tit-for-tat release of 'political prisoners'. He was later granted amnesty by the Truth and Reconciliation Commission.

20. All quotations from Johan Nothnagel are from an interview with the author, Pretoria, November 1995.

21. Mlondi Nhlangulela, interview with the author, Atteridgeville, November 1995.

22. Lazarus Mosesi, interview with the author, Atteridgeville, November 1995.

23. Jackie Selebi, quoted in Sam Sole, Stefaans Brümmer and Nic Dawes, 'Selebi: Here's the Evidence, Minister', *Mail & Guardian*, 24 November 2006.

24. Mark Lamberti, remarks given at the World Economic Forum for Africa, Cape Town, 5 June 2008, quoted in Chris van Gass, 'Government Out to Lunch on Crime', *Business Day*, 6 June 2008.

25. Boyd Webb, 'Justice System Is a Disgrace: De Lange', *Star*, 14 August 2008.

26. Jonny Steinberg, *Thin Blue: The Unwritten Rules of Policing South Africa* (Johannesburg: Jonathan Ball with Open Society Foundation for South Africa, 2008), 178–9.

27. Millicent Chuene, interview with the author, Johannesburg, February 2007.

28. Ibid.

29. Jerry Marobyane, interview with the author, Soweto, April 1996.

30. Harris Baleaga, interview with the author, Sekororo, April 1996.

31. Mbulelo Musi, interview with the author, Johannesburg, June 1997.

32. Anastasia Mathebula, interview with the author, Soweto, September 1994.

33. Student, interview with the author, Soweto, September 1994.

34. Gerhard van den Bergh, interview with the author, Cape Town, July 2007.

35. Rod Panagos, interview with the author, Cape Town, July 2007.

36. Glenny, *McMafia*, 216–41.

37. All quotations from Leonard McCarthy are from an interview with the author, London, September 2008.

Chapter 6: The White Africans

1. 'South Africa's Party of Apartheid Takes Final Bow', Associated Press, 11 April 2005.

2. F. W. de Klerk, speech in London, January 1997, cited in 'Surrender without Defeat: Afrikaners and the South African Miracle', *Spotlight* magazine (South African Institute of Race Relations), 1997.

3. Author's notes from Terre'Blanche's speech at Voortrekker Monument, 15 December 1993.

4. Eugene Terre'Blanche, interview with the author, Klerksdorp, December 1995.

5. Tim du Plessis, interview with the author, Johannesburg, November 1997.

6. Interview with the author, Cape Town, February 1997.

7. Tony Leon, *On the Contrary* (Johannesburg: Jonathan Ball, 2008), 571.

8. Ibid., 286.

9. Renier Schoeman, interview with the author, Johannesburg, July 2008.

10. Koos Botha, interview with the author, Pretoria, November 1994.

11. J. C. van der Walt, interview with the author, Johannesburg, November 1997.

12. Richard Stovin-Bradford, 'Van Zyl All Smiles about Sanlam's New Smile', *Business Times*, 11 March 2007.

13. Bok van Blerk (Louis Pepler), interview with the author, Johannesburg, February 2007.

14. All quotations from Pallo Jordan in this chapter are from an interview with the author, Pretoria, April 2008.

15. All quotations from Carl Niehaus in this chapter are from an interview with the author, Johannesburg, July 2008.

16. *Saturday Star* (Johannesburg), 28 June 2008.

17. All quotations from Hermann Giliomee are from an interview with the author, Stellenbosch, March 2008.

18. Kyle Esterhuyse, interview with the author, Klerksdorp, February 2007.

19. South Africa Institute of Race Relations, *Fast Facts,* August–September 2006.

20. Statistic from the Engineering Council of South Africa, quoted in *Mail & Guardian* (Johannesburg), 18–24 April 2008.

21. Heidi Holland, interview with the author, March 2008.

22. Helen Suzman, *In No Uncertain Terms: A South African Memoir* (New York: Knopf, 1993), 114.

23. Confirmed by Helen Suzman in an interview with the author, Johannesburg, March 2008.

24. Ronald Suresh Roberts, *Fit to Govern: The Native Intelligence of Thabo Mbeki* (Johannesburg: STE, 2007).

25. *ANC Today,* 3–9 November 2006, http://www.anc.org.za/ancdocs/anctoday/2006/text/at43.txt.

26. Ibid.

27. Tony Leon, interview with the author, Johannesburg, May 2007.

28. Pallo Jordan, interview with the author, Pretoria, May 2008.

29. Leon, interview, May 2007. To put someone in Coventry is an old British saying meaning to ostracise someone.

30. Leon, *On the Contrary,* 94.

31. Leon, interview, May 2007.

32. Leon, *On the Contrary,* 551.

33. Helen Zille, interview with the author, Johannesburg, May 2007.

Chapter 7: The New Randlords

1. All quotations from Mmemogolo (the Queen Mother) are from an interview with the author, Phokeng, April 2008.

2. Tokyo Sexwale, interview with the Foreign Correspondents' Association, Johannesburg, April 1993.

3. Tokyo Sexwale, interview with the author, Johannesburg, August 1997.

4. Tokyo Sexwale, interview with the author, Johannesburg, June 2008.

5. Anglo American manager, interview with the author, February 2007.

6. Nkobi's regular travelling companion to Malaysia was Schabir Shaik, who in 2005 was jailed for soliciting a bribe for Zuma. Shaik abused his position on the trips to Malaysia by claiming to be the ANC's representative and then pocketing fees from Malaysian companies.

7. Jeffrey Herbst, 'Mbeki's South Africa', *Foreign Affairs,* November/December 2005, 102.

8. All quotations from Moeletsi Mbeki in this chapter are from an interview with the author, Johannesburg, April 2007.

9. The investment company had been set up with the support of Sanlam, the very financial house that was set up by the Afrikaner empowerment scheme and that Moeletsi Mbeki argued was behind the original BEE policies.

10. Anthony Sampson, *Mandela: The Authorized Biography* (New York: Knopf, 1999), 570

11. 'First Black Broker Feeling Bullish', *Daily Telegraph*, 17 September 1996.

12. Conversation with the author at ANC dinner in Johannesburg, June 2008.

13. In 2002 a new law made the state the custodian of existing mineral rights. Mining houses could apply for 'new order' rights on proving their BEE credentials, including the transfer of a 26.1 per centage equity stake.

14. Tokyo Sexwale, interview with the author, Johannesburg, June 2007.

15. Friends of Macozoma in conversations with the author, April 2007.

16. Conversations with Cyril Ramaphosa, Johannesburg, April 2007, June and August, 2008.

17. Trevor Manuel, interview with the author, Johannesburg, April 2007.

18. Kevin Wakeford, 'Empowerment Must Be an Investment Not a Cost', *Business Day*, 9 September 2004.

19. Heribert Adam, Van Zyl Slabbert and Kogila Moodle, *Comrades in Business: Post-Liberation Politics in South Africa* (Cape Town: Tafelberg, 1997), 201.

20. Simon Robinson, 'Welcome to the Club', *Time*, May 2005.

21. All quotes from Happy Ntshingila are from an interview with the author, Johannesburg, 1996.

22. Unilever Institute/University of Cape Town survey on Black Diamonds, cited by Clare Bisseker, 'Black Magic', *Financial Mail*, 6 July 2007.

23. Patience Bogatsu, interview with the author, Madikwe, April 2008.

24. Mark Wilcox, business partner of Tokyo Sexwale, interview with the author, August 2008.

25. Sexwale, interview, June 2007.

26. John Burton, 'Malaysia to Ease Affirmative Action Policy', *Financial Times*, 23 September 2004.

27. Simphiwe Piliso, 'Gravy Train on Track', *Business Times*, 13 July 2008.

28. Eugene Tsitsi, interview with the author, Phokeng, April 2008.

29. Kgosi Leruo, interview with the author, Phokeng, April 2008.

30. Ibid.

Chapter 8: The Graves of the Ancestors

1. Nelson Mandela, *Long Walk to Freedom: The Autobiography of Nelson Mandela* (Boston: Little, Brown, 1994), 143.

2. Bheki Kubheka, interview with the author, Charlestown, October 2007.

3. Peter Nkomo in conversation with the author, Charlestown, March 1994.

4. Jotham Dube, interview with the author, Charlestown, March 1994.

5. Halban Sangweni, interview with the author, Charlestown, March 1994.

6. Stephen Ngwenya, interview with the author, Charlestown, October 2007.

7. Zimbabwe statistics from Tony Hawkins, professor of economics at University of Harare.

8. Sol Plaatje, 'Native Life in South Africa', quoted in William Mervin Gumede, *Thabo Mbeki: The Battle for the Soul of the ANC* (Cape Town: Zebra, 2007), 6.

9. Tozi Gwanya, interview with the author, Pretoria, November 2007. All statistics cited in this paragraph were provided in the interview.

10. Gwanya, interview, November 2007.

11. Ann Bernstein and Jeff McCarthy, *Land Reform in South Africa: Getting Back on Track*, Centre for Development and Enterprise, Johannesburg, May 2008.

12. Theo de Jager, interview with the author, Johannesburg, November 2007.

13. Ann Bernstein, interview with the author, Johannesburg, May 2008.

14. All quotations from Friedl von Maltitz are from an interview with the author, Saxon Park Farm, October 2007.

15. *Sunday Times* (Johannesburg), 20 January 2008.

16. Ephraim Semahla, interview with the author, Saxon Park Farm, October 2007.

17. Koos Mosae, interview with the author, Catarina Farm, October 2007.

18. De Jager, interview, November 2007.

19. Conversation with Zuma, Rand Club, Johannesburg, June 2008.

20. Shadrack Gutto, interview with the author, Johannesburg, November 2007.

21. All quotations from Mangaliso Kubheka are from an interview with the author, Johannesburg, November 2007.

22. Frans Fourie, interview with the author, Charlestown, October 2007.

23. Bheki Kubheka, interview, October 2007.

Chapter 9: The AIDS Betrayal

1. All quotations from Eric Morake are from an interview with the author, Gt Noligwa, August 2003.

2. UN AIDS, *2008 Report on the Global AIDS Epidemic,* http://www.unaids.org/en/KnowledgeCentre/HIVData/GlobalReport/2008/2008_Global_report.asp.

3. Edwin Cameron, with Nathan Geffen, *Edwin Cameron: Witness to AIDS* (London: I. B. Tauris, 2005), 52.

4. Pride Chigwedere, George R. Seage, Sofia Gruskin, Tun-Hou Lee and M. Essex, 'Estimating the Lost Benefits of Anti-Retroviral Drug Use in South Africa', *Journal of*

AIDS 49, no. 4 (1 December 2008): 410–15, http://www.aids.harvard.edu/Lost_Benefits.pdf.

5. All quotations from Peter Piot are from a briefing to the Foreign Correspondents' Association, Johannesburg, March 1995.

6. All quotations from Zackie Achmat are from an interview with the author, Cape Town, August 2008.

7. Edwin Cameron, interview with the author, London, September 2008.

8. M. W. Makgoba, 'The Perils of Pseudo-Science', *Science*, 19 May 2000.

9. Barton Gellman, 'South African President Escalates AIDS Feud: Mbeki Challenges Western Remedies', *Washington Post*, 19 April 2000.

10. Interview with Debra Patta, 'On the Record', E.TV, 24 April 2001.

11. Dorah Mafifi, interview with the author, June 2007.

12. Peter Slevin, 'Mbeki Says Diplomacy Needed for Zimbabwe', *Washington Post*, 25 September 2003.

13. All quotations from Nigel Trevarthen are from an interview with the author, Gt Noligwa, August 2003.

14. Anton van Hoek, interview with the author, Gt Noligwa, August 2003.

15. Christo Viljoen, interview with the author, Gt Noligwa, August 2003.

16. All quotations from Bobby Godsell are from an interview with the author, Johannesburg, August 2003.

17. Mark Gevisser, *Thabo Mbeki: A Dream Deferred* (Johannesburg: Jonathan Ball, 2007), xxxix.

18. Frank Chikane, interview with the author, Pretoria, June 2008.

19. Jacob Zuma in conversation with the author, Johannesburg, June 2008.

20. Thabo Mbeki, interview with the author, Pretoria, April 2007.

21. Tony Karon, 'Why South Africa Questions the Link between HIV and AIDS', *Time*, 21 April 2000.

22. Chris McGreal, 'Thabo Mbeki's Catastrophe', *Prospect Magazine*, March 2002.

23. UN AIDS, *2008 Report on the Global AIDS Epidemic*.

24. All quotations from Nozizwe Madlala-Routledge are from an interview with the author, Cape Town, August 2008.

25. Address at the inaugural Z. K. Matthews Memorial Lecture, Fort Hare University, 12 October 2001.

26. Thabo Mbeki, interview with the author, Pretoria, April 2007.

27. Cyril Ramaphosa, interview with the author, London, September 2008.

28. Ngoako Ramatlhodi, 'The Mauling of Mandela, and How to Catch a Tsotsi', *Sunday Times* (Johannesburg), 19 October 2008.

29. Anso Thom, 'Manto's Cavalier Policy on Muti', *Star*, 20 August 2008.

30. Lawrence K. Altman, 'UN Official Assails South Africa on Its Response to AIDS', *New York Times*, 19 August 2006.

31. Jeff Zeleny and Laurie Goering, 'Obama Challenges South Africa to Face AIDS Crisis', *Chicago Tribune*, 22 August 2006.

32. Gevisser, *Mbeki*, 736.

33. Malegapuru Makgoba, interview with the author, Durban, August 2008.

34. All quotations from Mantombi Nala-Preusker in this chapter are from an interview with the author, Umlazi, May 2008.

35. For statistics on AIDS in Botswana, see the website of UN AIDS, http://www.unaids.org/en/CountryResponses/Countries/botswana.asp.

36. Michael Wines, 'South African Is Acquitted of Rape Charges', *New York Times*, 9 May 2006.

37. Thabo Mbeki, speech to Parliament, 21 October 2004, http://www.thepresidency.gov.za/main.asp?include=president/pqa/q1021–04.htm.

38. Barbara Hogan, speech to HIV scientists, clinicians, and activists, Cape Town, 13 October 2008, http://www.tac.org.za/community/node/2421.

39. Zuma took an AIDS test in March 2007. Chris Makhaye, 'Zuma Takes AIDS Test', *Sunday Independent of South Africa*, 4 March 2007.

Chapter 10: *The 100 Per Cent Zulu Boy*

1. In English this means 'where the elephants bathe'.

2. Thabo Mbeki, email message to author, April 2008.

3. All quotes from Willies Mchunu are from an interview with the author, Pietermaritzburg, August 2008.

4. Sdu Mdluli, interview with the author, Pietermaritzburg, August 2008.

5. Geoffrey Motoawagae, interview with the author, Pretoria, January 2008.

6. Jeremy Gordin, *Zuma: A Biography* (Johannesburg: Jonathan Ball, 2008), 5.

7. Ebrahim Ebrahim, interview with the author, Johannesburg, December 2007.

8. 'Human Rights Violations Submissions: Questions and Answers' (transcript), Truth and Reconciliation Commission, 26 July 1996, http://www.justice.gov.za/trc/hrvtrans/soweto/ngwenya.htm.

9. Thoko Msimang, interview with the author, Pietermaritzburg, August 2008.

10. Moe Shaik, interview with the author, Johannesburg, December 2007.

11. All quotes from Frank Mdlalose are from an interview with the author, Johannesburg, August 2008.

12. Kader Asmal, interview with the author, Cape Town, April 2008.

13. Makhenkesi Stofile, interview with the author, Cape Town, November 1994.

14. By 2008 he had at least eighteen children and two new wives. Of his first three wives, Dr Nkosazana Dlamini-Zuma, with whom he had four children, divorced him in 1998, citing 'irreconcilable differences', and Kate, with whom he had five children, committed suicide in 2000.

15. Moe Shaik, interview with the author, Pretoria, December 2007.

16. Carol Paton and Stuart Theobold, 'Talking Cure', *Financial Mail*, 22 February 2008.

17. Andrew Feinstein, *After the Party: A Personal and Political Journey Inside the ANC* (Johannesburg: Jonathan Ball, 2007), 220.

18. Andrew Feinstein, interview with the author, Johannesburg, November 2007.

19. Chris Nicholson, transcript of judgement, Pietermaritzburg, 12 September 2008, http://www.dispatch.co.za/pdfs/nicholsonjudgment.pdf.

20. Scorpions investigator, interview with the author, Johannesburg, May 2008.

21. Pallo Jordan, interview with the author, Pretoria, April 2008.

22. Senior government adviser, interview with the author, Johannesburg, December 2007.

23. Transcript of full interview published 6 March 2008, http://www.ft.com/cms/s/0/40a1dbea-ebab-11dc-9493-0000779fd2ac.html.

24. Jacob Zuma in conversation with the author, Johannesburg, June 2008.

25. Cabinet minister, interview with the author, Cape Town, June 2007.

26. Saki Macozoma, interview with the author, Johannesburg, December 2007.

27. Don Mkhwanazi, interview with the author, Polokwane, December 2007.

28. State Department official, interview with the author, Johannesburg, August 2008.

29. Ibid.

30. Thabani Khumalo, interview with the author, Durban, August 2008.

31. Gordin, *Zuma*, 188.

32. Senior Western diplomat, telephone interview with the author, July 2008.

33. Bra Bricks, interview with the author, Orange Farm, December 2007.

Chapter 11: The Shadow of Zimbabwe

1. David Blair, *Degrees in Violence: Robert Mugabe and the Struggle for Power in Zimbabwe* (London: Continuum, 2002), 14.

2. Bobby Godsell, speech at dinner for Tony Leon, Johannesburg, May 2007.

3. Percy Gombakomba, interview with the author, Harare, April 2008.

4. Robert Mugabe, interview with the author, Harare, April 1995.

5. Author interview with former cabinet minister, February 2007.

6. Interview with the author, Pretoria, April 2007.

7. All quotations from Desmond Tutu in this chapter are from an interview with the author, Cape Town, April 2008.

8. Telephone interview with senior former State Department official, August 2008.

9. Thabo Mbeki, interview with the author, Pretoria, April 2007.

10. Ishmael Dube, interview with the author, Harare, April 2008.

11. Jeremy Cronin, interview with Helena Sheehan, Cape Town, 24 January 2002, http://webpages.dcu.ie/~sheehanh/za/cronin02.htm.

12. Cheryl Carolus, interview with the author, Johannesburg, August 2008.

13. Roelf Meyer, telephone interview with the author, from London to Pretoria, September 2008.

14. Philip Short, *Banda* (London: Routledge and Kegan Paul, 1974), 250.

15. Comments made to al-Jazeera, reported in Janet Smith, 'Hate Speech: It's Just a Metaphor', *Star*, 29 November 2008.

Chapter 12: Beijing and Beyond

1. Interview with the author, Buffelsfontein, 29 May 2007.

2. Interview with the author, Buffelsfontein, 29 May 2007.

3. Address to South African Students Congress in Cape Town, 15 December 2006.

4. Interview with the author, 16 January 2010, Pretoria.

5. Interview with the author, 16 January 2010, Pretoria.

6. Conversation with the author, March 2009, New Delhi.

7. Conversation with the author, London, May 2009.

8. Zuma speech on World AIDS Day, 1 December 2009.

9. Interview with the author, Pretoria, January 2010.

10. *ANC Today* 23 to 29 October 2009, http://www.anc.org.za/ancdocs/anctoday/2009/text/at42.txt.

11. Helen Zille, SA TODAY, 4 February 2010, http://www.politicsweb.co.za/politicsweb/view/politicsweb/en/page71654?oid=159017&sn=Detail.

12. Wally Mbhele, Dominic Mahlangu and Mpumelelo Mkhabela, 'Frank Chikane's Lie Is Exposed', *Sunday Times* (Johannesburg), 8 June 2008.

13. All quotations from Frank Chikane in this chapter are from an interview with the author, Pretoria, 9 June 2008.

14. De Klerk, interview with the author, Cape Town, 14 January 2010.

15. Lord Renwick, interview with the author, London, 7 January 2010.

16. Nelson Mandela, *Long Walk to Freedom: The Autobiography of Nelson Mandela* (Boston: Little Brown, 1994), 617.

17. All quotations from Desmond Tutu in this chapter are from an interview with the author, Cape Town, April 2008.

SELECT BIBLIOGRAPHY

Adam, Heribert, Van Zyl Slabbert and Kogila Moodle. *Comrades in Business: Post-Liberation Politics in South Africa.* Cape Town: Tafelberg, 1997.

Alagiah, George. *A Passage to Africa.* London: Little, Brown, 2001.

Allen, John. *Rabble Rouser for Peace, The Authorized Biography of Desmond Tutu.* Markham, Ontario: The Free Press, Simon & Schuster, 2006.

Altbeker, Antony. *A Country at War with Itself: South Africa's Crisis of Crime.* Johannesburg: Jonathan Ball, 2007.

Ayittey, George B. N. *Africa Unchained: The Blueprint for Africa's Future.* New York: Palgrave Macmillan, 2005.

Blair, David. *Degrees in Violence.* London: Continuum International Publishing Group, 2002.

Butler, Anthony. *Cyril Ramaphosa.* Johannesburg: Jacana Media, 2008.

Calland, Richard. *Anatomy of South Africa: Who Holds the Power?* Cape Town: Zebra Press, 2006.

Cameron, Edwin, with Nathan Geffen. *Edwin Cameron: Witness to AIDS.* London: I. B. Tauris, 2005.

Carlin, John. *Playing the Enemy.* London: Atlantic Books, 2008.

de Klerk, F. W. *The Last Trek – A New Beginning: The Autobiography.* London: Macmillan, 1998.

Feinstein, Andrew. *After the Party: A Personal and Political Journey Inside the ANC.* Johannesburg: Jonathan Ball, 2007.

Gevisser, Mark. *Thabo Mbeki: A Dream Deferred.* Johannesburg: Jonathan Ball, 2007.

Glenny, Misha. *McMafia: A Journey through the Global Criminal Underworld.* New York: Knopf, 2008.

Godwin, Peter. *When a Crocodile Eats the Sun.* New York: Picador, 2007.

Gordin, Jeremy. *Zuma: A Biography.* Johannesburg: Jonathan Ball, 2008.

Guest, Robert. *The Shackled Continent: Power, Corruption, and African Lives.* Washington DC: Smithsonian Books, 2004.

Gumede, William Mervin. *Thabo Mbeki and the Battle for the Soul of the ANC.* Cape Town: Zebra Press, 2005.

Holland, Heidi. *Dinner with Mugabe: The Untold Story of a Freedom Fighter Who Became a Tyrant.* New York: Penguin, 2008.

Krog, Antjie. *Country of My Skull.* London: Jonathan Cape, 1998.

Leon, Tony. *On the Contrary.* Johannesburg: Jonathan Ball, 2008.

Mandela, Nelson. *Long Walk to Freedom: The Autobiography of Nelson Mandela.* Boston: Little, Brown, 1994.

Marinovich, Greg, and João Silva. *The Bang-Bang Club.* Port Melbourne: William Heinemann Australia, 2000.

Meredith, Martin. *Nelson Mandela: A Biography.* New York: St. Martin's Press, 1998.

_____. *The State of Africa.* London: Simon & Schuster, 2005.

O'Malley, Padraig. *Shades of Difference: Mac Maharaj and the Struggle for South Africa.* New York: Viking, 2007.

Pakenham, Thomas. *The Boer War.* London: Weidenfeld & Nicholson, 1979.

Roberts, Ronald Suresh. *Fit to Govern: The Native Intelligence of Thabo Mbeki.* Johannesburg: STE, 2007.

Sampson, Anthony. *Mandela: The Authorized Biography.* New York: Knopf, 1999.

Sparks, Allister. *Beyond the Miracle: Inside the New South Africa.* Chicago: University of Chicago Press, 2003.

_____. *The Mind of South Africa.* New York: Knopf, 1990.

_____. *Tomorrow Is Another Country: The Inside Story of South Africa's Road to Change.* Chicago: University of Chicago Press, 1996.

Steinberg, Jonny. *Thin Blue: The Unwritten Rules of Policing South Africa.* Johannesburg: Jonathan Ball with Open Society Foundation for South Africa, 2008.

_____. *Three Letter Plague: A Young Man's Journey through a Great Epidemic.* Johannesburg: Jonathan Ball, 2008.

Suzman, Helen. *In No Uncertain Terms: A South African Memoir.* New York: Knopf, 1993.

Waldmeir, Patti. *Anatomy of a Miracle.* New York: Viking, 1997.

INDEX

Achmat, Zackie, 218, 221–222
  as AIDS activist, 206–207
  creates Treatment Action Campaign
    (TAC), 205
Affirmative action
  in BEE as disincentive for investors,
    178
  criticisms called racist slurs, 173
  as factor in Eskom power cuts, 104
  issues in local government, 97–99
African National Congress (ANC), 2,
    221, 274–5
  analogies with Zimbabwe's
    degeneration, 268–274, 285–288
  change crucial to be successful
    democracy, 274–275, 287–289
  coalesces under Mandela, 62–63
  extends influence over the state,
    73–75
  faces corruption trend of liberation
    movements, 56, 58
  fails to implement policies, 104, 121,
    122, 189, 288
  and hostility towards white
    members, 154–155
  and land reform, 197–199
  new party breaks away: COPE, 270
  officials focus more on money than
    governing, 66–69
  paramilitaries, 125
  party history, background, 58–61
  perceived as repudiating the left, 70
  and South African Police Service,
    121

unity eroded by exile–inzile conflict,
    63–66
African Rainbow Minerals, 170, 171
Afrikaans language, 145, 146–147
  imposed as schools' medium of
    instruction (1976), 100
Afrikaner Weerstandsbeweging (AWB),
    136, 137
Afrikaners
  as adaptable to new order, 138, 141
  culture, ethnic identity, 141–148
  exploit post-apartheid businesses,
    markets, 142
  post-apartheid negotiations, 27
  threaten to secede, 60, 136
AIDS
  antiretroviral drugs (ARVs), 202,
    215
  death rate statistics, 203–204
  Mbeki denies science, impedes
    treatment, 14, 203, 205–209,
    216–225
  in mining industry, 210–214
  neglected by Mandela, 7–8, 206
  quack healers denounce ARVs,
    222–225
  stigma attached, 227, 229
  in Umlazi township, 225–227
Alexandra township, 83, 113
Amajuba Berries project, 186, 200
Amantombazana [the Girls] Security
    Services, 123
Amnesty promise to human rights
    abusers, 36

ANC. *See* African National Congress (ANC)

Anglo American Corporation, 71, 88, 163
    and BEE deal with Johnnic, 167

AngloGold mining company, 210–214, 227
    distributes ARVs to work force, 202, 204, 215–216

Angola's MPLA party. *See* MPLA (Popular Movement for the Liberation of Angola)

Anti-crime initiatives, 110, 116, 128–132

Apartheid
    economic legacy/crisis of, 61, 86
    as explanation for violent crime, 115–117
    fears of crime feed white prejudices, 112–113
    homeland borders as integral policy, 188
    police function to protect whites, 117–119

arap Moi, Daniel, 7, 149, 237, 272–273

Arms deals
    government procurement package, 247–252
    inquiry, 74–75
    Shaik's bribe from Thint for Zuma, 246

Asmal, Kader, 72, 78, 244

AZAPO, 39, 235
    brutally targeted by ANC, 115, 273
    organises Soweto Uprising, 59

Bafokeng, 158–160, 179–180

Baloyi, Martin, 76–77

Banda, Hastings, 76, 272

Bantu schooling, 99–101
    Bantu Education Act of 1953, 99

BEE. *See* Black Economic Empowerment (BEE)

Big Man personality
    exemplified by Daniel arap Moi, 7, 237

liberation rhetoric justifies misdeeds, 9
    masks social, economic problems, 259
    Mobutu sese Seko as, 237
    Zuma as, 245

Biko, Steve, 39, 117, 235

Black consciousness movement. *See* AZAPO

Black Economic Empowerment (BEE), 160, 161
    considered a disincentive by bankers, 178
    millionaires trade political contacts for shareholdings, 169–173
    reforms called for, 176–179
    relies on asset transfers, 162, 164, 166–168

Black Management Forum, 173

Black spots, 182–183

Blair, Tony, 22, 75, 208

Blood River battle (1838), 31, 136, 269

Bogatsu, Patience, 176–177

Bophuthatswana homeland, 136–137, 188

Botha, Louis, 43

Botha, P. W., 134, 151

Botswana, 274–5
    AIDS policies, 227
    as successful democracy, 274–5

Brown, Gordon, 22, 259

Burundi, 256–257

Business, 69–70
    Afrikaners' corporations prosper, 142
    free-market macroeconomic policy, 88–89
    MPs' conflicts of interest with state contracts, 66–68
    perceived by poor people as selling out, 92
    political contacts traded for shareholdings (BEE), 169–173
    revolving door with politics, 68, 171

Sexwale's enterprises through BEE, 161–162

substandard education as disincentive for investments, 102

Buthelezi, Mangosuthu, 163, 234, 236

Cameron, Edwin, 13, 116–117

Carjackings/hijackings
coordinated by syndicates, 114
near people's homes, 124
statistics, 110, 111, 143

Carolus, Cheryl, 60, 106, 269
on affirmative action vs service delivery, 99
as inzile, 63, 65
on pitfalls of ANC's electoral dominance, 73

Carroll, Cynthia, 71

Chancellor House, 67

Chikane, Frank, 65, 100, 216, 285–6
poisoned by apartheid agents, 285

China, 16, 91, 142, 277–283, 289
demands minerals, 171
invests in South African bank, 280
re-engages with Africa 278–9

Chuene, Millicent, 123

City Press newspaper, 69

Civil service jobs
affirmative action issues, 97–99
dominated by Afrikaners under apartheid, 87, 97–98
inefficiency of workers, 195
skills crises in, 97

Clinton, Bill, 207, 208, 218

Coetzee, Dirk, 37, 38

Communist Party/communism
criticises ANC intolerance, 268
global collapse removes Nationalists' fear of takeover, 135
and overthrow of apartheid, 18
push to end Mbeki's business-friendly policies, 256

South African Communist Party (SACP), 69–71
supports, allied with, Zuma, 106, 253–4, 270

Congress of the People (COPE) political party, 270–272
connected to Mbeki, 270, 271, 274

Corruption
criticisms called racist slurs by Mbeki, 68
government arms deal, 74–75, 247–252
Madikizela fired as Mandela's deputy minister, 83
MPs' conflicts of interest with state contracts, 67
of Mugabe's Zimbabwe, 169, 262
scandals of Brett Kebble, 68, 167
Shaik solicits bribe, expects political favours, 246–247
throughout post-apartheid police, 121
as trend of African liberation movements, 53–56
Zuma's indictments, trials, 234, 238, 247–252

Cosatu trade union federation, 166, 271

Crime, criminals. *See* Violent crime

Cronin, Jeremy, 70–71, 268

de Klerk, F. W., 40, 135, 139, 286–7

de Kock, Eugene, 37

de la Rey song, 142–148

de Lange, Johnny, 61–62
fails to support arms deal investigation, 74
on lack of criminal justice accountability, 122

Death penalty, 116, 256

Democracy in South Africa
Mbeki's perception of centralised leadership, 73
merits of multiparty government questioned, 272

Democracy in South Africa *(continued)*
   and pitfalls of ANC's lack of
      opposition, 62, 73
   renewed by ousting Mbeki as leader,
      77–78
   with violent crime increases, 110
Democratic Alliance (DA), 139,
   153–155
Democratic Party, 138, 139, 150–153
Dingaan, Zulu king, 112
Dipico, Manne, 64–65, 69
du Plessis, Tim, 138

Eastern Europe after fall of communism,
   35, 67, 139
Economy
   AIDS treatment costs vs loss of
      population, 219
   ANC inherits financial crisis of
      apartheid, 61, 86
   Botswana as analogy for South
      Africa, 274–5
   buoyed by China's demand for
      minerals, 171
   China's growth vs South Africa's
      unemployment, 91
   free-market macroeconomic policy,
      12, 66, 88–89
   inflation, food, fuel prices lead to
      violence, 84
   mismanaged throughout post-
      colonial Africa, 86
   nationalisation renounced by
      Mandela, 86–87
   policies shift away from left, 70
   under Trevor Manuel, 87, 89–94
Education
   Bantu schooling bankrupts system,
      adults, 99–100
   funds mismanaged at local level,
      102–103
Elections
   loans tied to, 272–273
   Mbeki's victories, 22

   merits of multiparty government
      questioned, 272–273
   of National Party (1948), 58
   1994 results, 138
Emigration of whites from South Africa,
   148–149
English-speaking white South Africans,
   33
   compared to Afrikaners, 138,
      150–151, 165
   dominate civil service, government,
      business, 98, 134
   and Natives' Land Act (1913), 187
   support National Party, 135
Eskom electricity provider, 69, 104
Ethnic cleansing in South Africa, 82
Executions. *See* Murders; Necklacing
Exiles, 18–19
   Asmal as, 72
   autocratic leadership style, 63
   challenge the ANC, 59, 255
   Mbeki as, 20, 244
   meet with Anglo American in
      Zambia, 163
   rivalry with inziles, 63–64
   Tambo as, 255
   Zuma as, 240–242

Feinstein, Andrew
   criticises ANC, 73–74
   queries Telkom-Ngonyama-Ngcaba
      deal, 67
   tries to expose ANC members' arms
      deal, 74, 249
Financial Times newspaper, 48, 89,
   110–111
Freedom Charter, 59, 86, 270
Free-market macroeconomic policy, 12,
   66, 88–89

Gautrain, 68
GEAR. *See* Growth, Employment, and
   Redistribution programme
   (GEAR)

Gevisser, Mark, 23
Ghana, 14–15, 86
Gigaba, Malusi, 283–4
Giliomee, Hermann, 146–147
Gini coefficient, 46
Gorbachev, Mikhail, 12, 135
Gordhan, Pravin, 91
Government
    builds substandard housing, 94–95, 97
    fails to provide basic services at local level, 96, 97
    initiative ignored by corrupt teachers, 103
    lacks accountability, 122
    See also African National Congress (ANC)
Growth, Employment, and Redistribution programme (GEAR), 88, 89, 94
Gwala, Harry, 58, 240
    as communist, 70
    as warlord against Inkatha Freedom Party, 57
Gwanya, Tozi, 189–191

Hani, Chris, 161
Herdbuoys, 174, 175
Hogan, Barbara, 228–229
Holland, Heidi, 149
Holomisa, Bantu, 8, 271
Homelands (Bantustans), 136–137, 138, 188
Horn, Mike 279
Housing
    ANC reneges on promises, 87
    statistics on homes, 93
    substandard from incompetent local government, 94–95, 97
Human rights abuses, 36, 117, 240
Human Rights Watch, 55

Immigrants/foreigners

attacked, killed in pogroms, 82–84, 106, 113
resented because of poverty, inflation, housing, 84
sale of land to (land invasions), 198, 199
Immorality Act and Mixed Marriages Act, 42
Impala Platinum, 158, 180
India's Congress Party, 56, 78, 273
Inequality gap between rich and poor. *See* Wealth–poverty gap
Inkatha Freedom Party
    battles ANC, 57, 113, 115
    nurtures Zulu culture, 235
    threatens to secede, 60, 163, 262
    Zulus attack ANC headquarters, 60
    Zuma advises conciliatory approach, 242
International Ferro Metals (IFM), 279
Intokozo [Joy] vigilante group, 125
Inziles, 63–64, 65
Itsoseng [Stand Up on Your Own] recycling project, 92

Jaime, Aguinaldo, 55–56
Jinquan Iron and Steel Company (Jisco), 279, 289
Johannesburg, South Africa
    crime rate compared to Luanda, Angola, 114
    as murder capital of the world, 108
    residents use armed private militias, 123–124
Johnnic of the Anglo American Corporation, 167–168
Jordan, Pallo, 77–78, 144–145, 153, 253

Kambule, Thamsanqa, 100–101
Kangaroo courts resulting in lynch mob killings, 115, 125–128
Kaunda, Kenneth, 76, 272–273
Kebble, Brett, 68, 121, 167

Kenya, 149, 186, 272
Kerry, John, 22
Kerzner, Sol, 8, 128
Khumalo, Thabani, 257–258
'Kill the Boer' slogan, 5, 256
Koppies, siege of Kwakwatsi, 25–28, 47, 49–51, 60, 74, 86
Korumbi, 115
Kubheka, Bheki, 182–186, 200

Land Act of 1913, 182, 187, 189
Land Bank, 194–195
Land reform, 195–200
    Amajuba Berries as success story, 186, 200
    and Bantustans ethnic homelands, 188–189
    disastrous consequences in Zimbabwe, 186–187, 197, 198, 264
    private sector funding affects land transactions, 199
    redistribution of land to black farmers, 190–192, 194
    statistics of people forced off land, 198
    tenants evicted by farmers, 185, 197–198
Leadership in post-colonial Africa. See Big Man personality
Leakey, Richard, 149
Left
    alienated by free-market macroeconomic policy, 88
    becomes marginalised after April 1994 election, 70, 71–72
Lekota, Mosiuoa 'Terror,' 103–104
    leads COPE breakaway party, 271
Leon, Tony
    criticises ANC, exposes scandals, 152–154
    as leader of Democratic Party, 74, 139, 150

Leruo, *kgosi* of Bafokeng, 179–180
Liberation movements
    to be won by negotiations, not military action, 12
    brutal violent crime emerges in South Africa, 110–111
    Mbeki groomed as leader, 11, 16–17
    with parties failing to adapt to governments, 55
    unbanning announced, Mandela released, 135, 244
Luanda, Angola, 53–55, 114
Luhabe, Wendy, 102
Luthuli, Albert, 66, 72

Macozoma, Saki, 22, 171, 255, 256
Madikizela-Mandela, Winnie, 31, 83
Madlala-Routledge, Nozizwe, 217, 219, 220, 223
Maela, Isaac, 84–85
Mafifi, Gigi, 34, 84
Mahlatsi, Solomon, 28
Major, John, 107
Makgoba, Malegapuru, 43–45, 207, 224
Makgoka, 'Comrade Sam', 91–92, 93
Malan, Magnus, 9
Malawi, 76, 272
Malaysia, 164–165, 178
Mamoepa, Ronnie, 67
Mandela, Nelson
    brokers lasting peace among Zulus, 243
    encourages belief in reconciliation between races, 31–32
    fails to make AIDS a priority initially, 7–8, 206
    personal characteristics, 6–7, 8, 9, 21
    political failings, 7–9
    as symbol of moral authority, 2
    in 2002 challenges Mbeki's anti-ARV AIDS policy, 220–221
Mandela United Football Club, 83
Mangope, Lucas, 136–137

Manuel, Trevor, 65, 105
    designs post-apartheid economic
        recovery, 87, 89–94
Maponya, Japie, 37–38
Marxism. *See* Communist
        Party/communism
Mashinini, Tsietsi, 101
Mathebula, Masilo, 128
Mbeki, Govan, 18, 70, 165
Mbeki, Moeletsi, 93
    critical of disincentives of BEE,
        165–166, 179
Mbeki, Thabo
    as autocratic, 65, 73, 75
    believes whites should not be
        involved in politics, 154–155
    and China, 280
    compared to Zuma, 232–233,
        252–259, 283–5
    demonises white and black critics,
        150, 151–152
    denies AIDS science, impedes
        treatment, 14, 205–209,
        216–225
    denies violent crime crisis, 111–112
    fails to condemn Mugabe's
        repression in Zimbabwe, 14–17,
        285
    government lacks accountability,
        122
    indicts all whites as being racist,
        40–41
    ousted as ANC leader, 77, 270
    political weaknesses, 9–10, 19–23
    revolutionary new approach on
        macroeconomic policy, 88–89
    shifts away from Mandela's
        reconciliation, 10–13, 23
McCarthy, Leonard, 131–132
Media
    attacked by ANC for exposing
        corruption, 68

blame immigrant killings on
    xenophobia, 83
Mandela supports independence of,
    9
Mexico's Institutional Revolutionary
    Party (PRI), 56, 273
Meyer, Roelf, 272
    and anti-crime initiative, 109–110
Middle class (black)
    appealed to by COPE, 271
    dilutes apartheid, 51
    emerges under BEE, 176–178
    expansion of, 42
    Mbeki promotes, 14, 46
Militias, private, 123–124
Minimum wage mandated by ANC, 185,
    197–198
Mining houses
    and AIDS epidemic, 210–214
    platinum, 158
Mlambo-Ngcuka, Phumzile, 173
Mlokoti, Clarence, 101
Mobutu sese Seko, 237, 279
Moeketsi, Stompie, 83
Mohapi, Mapetla, 38–39
Mohapi, Nohle, 38–39
Mokaba, Peter, 4–5, 221, 224
Mokolo, Bricks, 92, 94–95, 259–260
Moosa, Valli, 69
Mosesi, Lazarus, 120
Moshelane, Moses, 96–97
Motlana, Nthato, 167
Motlanthe, Kgalema, 228
Motsepe, Patrice, 171
    as South Africa's first black
        billionaire, 170, 172
Movement for Democratic Change
    (MDC) of Zimbabwe, 139, 149,
    264
Mozambican immigrants attacked,
    81–82, 106
MPLA (Popular Movement for the
    Liberation of Angola), 53, 54, 55

Mugabe, Robert, 15, 76, 279
  background, 262–265
  brutalises MDC opposition party,
    149, 265
  co-opts Nkomo, 139
  drives white farmers off land, 149
  steals elections from opposition,
    265, 273
Müller, Robert, 108–109
Murders
  of Chris Hani, 161
  of Korumbi, beheaded by children,
    115
  lynch-mob killings, 125–128
  man attacked with a shovel, 108
  of Maponya by de Kock, 38
  of Mathebula, 128
  of Mxenge by Coetzee, 38
  of Ndeleni, stoned to death by
    children, 127
  post-apartheid statistics, 110–111,
    117
  of Steve Biko, 39
  See also Violent crime
Mvelaphanda Group, 164

Naspers company, 142
National Party
  and affirmative action for Afrikaners,
    97–98
  collapses, 134, 138–139
  compared to ANC, 104–105
  early background of white
    supremacy, 133–134
  early leaders, 134
  hands over government in debt, 87
  merges into ANC, 139
  responsible for education crisis, 99
  and Truth and Reconciliation
    Commission, 36
Nationalisation, 86–87, 165–166
Ndeleni, Eric, 127
Necklacing, 82–83, 106, 126

Neighbourhood watch, Hout Bay,
    128–130
Neto, Agostinho, 53
Netshitenzhe, Joel, 39, 74, 154
Ngcaba, Andile, 67
Ngonyama, Smuts, 67
Nhlangulela, Mlondi, 120
Niehaus, Carl, 145–146
  sidelined by Mbeki, 154–155
Nkobi, Thomas, 164, 244
Nkomo, Joshua, 139
  backed by ANC in 70s, 266
  supporters massacred by Mugabe,
    262
'Nkosi Sikelel' i-Afrika' liberation hymn,
    33, 58
Nkrumah, Kwame, 14–15, 86
Nothnagel, Johan, 119–120
Ntshingila, Happy, 174–176
Nzimande, Blade, 60–61

Obama, Barack, 20, 223
Ogilvie Thompson, Julian, 88, 89, 175
O'Neill, Jim, 281
Oppenheimer, Harry, 163, 164
Opposition parties
  and health of ANC, 272, 273
  Mugabe's brutal responses in
    Zimbabwe, 149
  multiracial South African, 154, 271

Pahad, Essop, 46, 68, 83
Pan-Africanist Congress (PAC), 59, 270,
    271
Paramilitaries
  of ANC, 125
  right-wing, 193
  Terre'Blanche's Ystergarde, 136
Parliament, post-apartheid
  and ANC participative democracy,
    62
  becomes rubber stamp for Mbeki,
    74

challenged by transfer of govenment, 60–61

opposition MPs challenge ANC, 74

Pharmaceutical industry, US, 218

Pienaar, François, 34

Pieterson, Hector, 100

Piot, Peter, 204–205, 207

Plaatje, Sol, 187

Police

of Angola act as deterrents to criminals, 114

and anti-crime initiatives, 128–132

under apartheid, 117–119

black officers strike against racism in force, 31

cooperate with vigilantes, 125

failure met with private security services, 122–124

with high suicide rates, 120

Police and Prisons Civil Rights Union (POPCRU), 71

Poverty

as explanation for violent crime, 114

increases due to local government mismanagement, 95

linked to anti-immigrant riots, executions, 82, 84 85

social welfare benefits statistics, 93

Pretoria, South Africa, 117–120

Progressive Business Forum of ANC, 140

Public service unions strike, 71

Queen Mother of Royal Bafokeng Nation, 157–160, 278

Race relations, post-apartheid

in Koppies and Kwakwatsi, 49–51

Tutu's perspective, 42–43

in universities, 43–45

Zuma's perspective, 48

Rainbow nation, 30, 43, 47

Ramaphosa, Cyril

accused of conspiracy against Mbeki, 20

and anti-crime initiative, 109–110

as BEE tycoon, 167–169, 174

and exile–inzile split, 63–64

on Mbeki's political failings, 19, 21

on whites' indifference to apartheid abuses, 46

Ramphele, Mamphela, 102

Rape

post-apartheid statistics, 110, 111, 228

South Africa as high recorded rate, 228

Zulu custom regarding, 228, 235

Zuma's trial, 228, 235, 250

See also Violent crime

Reagan, Ronald, 12, 258, 259

Reconciliation

intended to shift to transformation, 11

as Mandela's planned scheme, 2, 6, 33–34

struggles in outlying towns, 29, 30

undone by Mbeki, 41

Reconstruction and Development Programme (RDP), 87, 88

Retief, Piet, 112

Robben Island prisoners

ANC leaders imprisoned, released, 18, 59, 162, 240

communists, 56–57

realise apartheid will eventually collapse, 6, 18

Roberts, Ronald Suresh, 150

Romania, 35, 127

Rugby World Cup finals (1995), 33–34

Rwanda genocide, 31, 273

SACP (South African Communist Party). *See* Communist Party/communism

Sanlam financial house, 166

Saro-Wiwa, Ken, 15

Sasol energy company, 173

Scandals. *See* Corruption

Schoeman, Renier, 104, 140

Scorpions anti-corruption force
    denounced by ANC politicians, 155, 237
    investigates, brings charges against Zuma, 237, 250, 252
    investigates ANC, 130–132

Sebolecwe, Rebecca, 90

Security businesses (private), 123
    armed private militias, 123–124

Selebi, Jackie, 121, 130, 131

Self-defence units, 115, 118

Sexwale, Tokyo, 160–163, 164, 170–171
    on BEE, 177–178
    deals with mining companies, 167

Shabangu, Susan, 116

Shaik, Schabir, 245–247

Shaik, Moe, 242, 245, 259

Sharpeville Massacre, 32, 59, 116–117, 270

Shilowa, Mbhazima 'Sam', 87
    leads COPE breakaway party, 271

Sisulu, Walter, 9, 18

Slovo, Joe, 74

Smith, Ian, 149

Solidarity trade union, 45, 104

South African Broadcasting Corporation (SABC), 30, 74

South African Police Museum, 117–118

South African Police Service, 121, 122

Soweto township
    imbizo community gathering, 76
    Jabulani Mall, 90
    and Mandela United Football Club, 83

Soweto Uprising (1976), 59, 100–102

Spaza shops versus supermarkets, 90

The Star newspaper, 61

Steinberg, Jonny, 122

Strijdom, Hans, 134

Strydom, Barend, 118–119

Suburban Bliss television programme, 30

Suzman, Helen, 135, 150

Suzman, Mark, 108

Tambo, Dali, 18–19

Tambo, Oliver, 9, 151, 255
    in exile, 60, 255
    with Mbeki as aide-de-camp, 11
    as an Xhosa, 235

Tax revenue, 91

Teachers unions, 103

Telkom national telephone provider, 67

Terre'Blanche, Eugene, 136–137
    addresses rallies, 144

Thabo Mbeki: A Dream Deferred (Gevisser), 23

Thailand, and AIDS epidemic, 207

Thatcher, Margaret, 12, 75

Thin Blue (Steinberg), 122

Tladi, Johannes, 27–28, 47, 49, 209

Torture
    of opponents of apartheid, 37, 62, 92, 152
    by police, 115
    victims argue against amnesty, 36
    wet-bag treatment, 39
    in Zimbabwe, 265

Tripartite alliance in post-apartheid government, 61, 69–70

Truth and Reconciliation Commission, 35–40, 241, 252

Tshabalala-Msimang, Manto, 209, 223, 284
    espouses nutrition over ARVs to cure AIDS, 222

Tsvangirai, Morgan, 265

Tutu, Desmond
    on death penalty, 116
    on domination of exiles in ANC, 65
    on improved race relations, 42–43
    leads Truth and Reconciliation Commission, 35–36
    on Mandela, 5, 288
    on Mbeki, 17–18, 266, 268, 280, 282
    on wealth and poverty disparities, 45

Ubuntu as moral corrective, 36

Ugandan AIDS epidemic, 208

Umkhonto we Sizwe (MK), 12, 36, 269–270
Umlazi township, and AIDS epidemic, 225–227
Unemployment/employment, 91–94
    and shortage of skilled workers, 96, 173
    tied to anti-immigrant riots, executions, 82, 84–85
Unions/union movement
    Cosatu, 166
    expect rewards for alliance with ANC, 87
    needed by ANC, 71–72
    as part of tripartite alliance, 61, 69–70
    pressure mines to reform hostels, 211
United Nations Programme on HIV and AIDS, 204–205, 207, 221
Usual suspects, 170

van Blerk, Bok (Louis Pepler), 142–148
van der Merwe, Charl, 27, 28, 50
van Schalkwyk, Marthinus, 133–134, 138, 139
Vendas evicted from clinic, 85
Verwoerd, Hendrik, 32, 134
Verwoerd, Wilhelm, 33
Vigilantes. *See* Paramilitaries
Violent crime
    apartheid/resistance to apartheid as explanations, 115–117
    compared to other African nations, 114
    increases in last years of Mandela's presidency, 11
    inequality gap as partial explanation, 113–114
    Johannesburg as murder capital of world, 108
    and lack of police accountability, 122
    lynch-mob killings, 125–126
    Mbeki's failed positions against, 14

poverty as explanation, 114
private security, militias seen as solution, 122
shootings, hold-ups, 110
statistics, 109–113, 114, 124
and vigilantes, paramilitaries, 125
See also Murders; Rape
von Maltitz, Friedl, 192–195
Vorster, John, 134

Wade, Abdoulaye, 71
Wagner, Leonie, 118
Wakeford, Kevin, 173
Wealth–poverty gap
    BEE developed to solve, 164–165
    despite growth of black middle-class, 46
    exacerbates rift between whites and blacks, 45, 173
    and Malaysia indigenisation programme, 164–165
    relates to violent crime, 113–114
White South Africans
    extremists, 60, 135–137
    view Zimbabwe possible warning, 261–262
    See also Afrikaners; English-speaking white South Africans
Williams, Chester, 33–34
Wit Wolf (Barend Strydom), 118
Witbooi, Abbey, 71
Witch 'trial', 126
World Economic Forum, 71, 86

Xenophobia, 83
Xhosas
    as voting bloc, 235, 271

Yeltsin, Boris, 71
Youth League of ANC, 59, 269
    hears Mandela's speech about AIDS, 2–5
    as supporters of Zuma, 72–73

Ystergarde [Iron Guard] paramilitary of
    Terre'Blanche, 136
Yutar, Percy, 32
Yuxiao, Zhou, 278

Zambia, 11–12, 75–76, 163, 272–273
Zille, Helen, 155, 252, 284–5
Zimbabwe
    compared to South Africa, 114, 262,
      268–269
Zimbabwe *(continued)*
    crony capitalism of, 169
    disastrous land reform, farm invasions,
      186–187, 197, 198, 264–265
    economy collapses, 262–264
    and immigration crisis in South
      Africa, 84–85, 113
    Mbeki does not stand up to
      Mugabe's tyranny, 14–17,
      265–268
    Mugabe co-opts Nkomo, 139
    skilled emigrants get jobs in South
      Africa, 102
    stresses South Africa's resources, 261
    as warning to South Africa, 155,
      261–262
    whites become regime's scapegoats,
      149, 155

Zulu culture, ethnicity
    tribal identity as warriors, customs,
      60, 234–235
    as voting bloc, 235
    of Zuma, 236, 240, 257–258
Zulu nationalist movement. *See* Inkatha
    Freedom Party
Zuma, Jacob
    battles for control, revenge in
      Mbeki's ouster, 72–73, 77–78
    as charismatic populist leader,
      258–260
    compared to Mbeki, 232–233,
      252–259, 283–5
    at Copenhagen climate change
      summit, 280–2
    corruption trial, 130, 131, 238,
      245–252, 270
    personal history, 236–237, 239–244
    political equivocation of, 255–256
    on post-apartheid race relations, 48
    rape trial, 228, 235, 250, 284–5
    and referendum for death penalty,
      116, 256
    reinstated as ANC deputy president,
      76
    Zulu tribal identity of, 234–239

DAVID LOYN

Butcher & Bolt

'Excellent'
MAX HASTINGS, SUNDAY TIMES

'Gripping ...A timely and important book'
JOHN CROSSLAND, DAILY MAIL

Afghanistan has been a strategic prize for more than 200 years.
Foreign invaders have continually fought across its beautiful
and inhospitable terrain, in conflicts variously ruthless, misguided and bloody. A century ago, the common sneer about
how British soldiers treated Afghan tribesmen was that they
would 'butcher' them, then 'bolt'.

Butcher & Bolt recounts this violent history, beginning in 1809
with the very first British mission – an encounter that ushered
in two centuries of conflict littered with misunderstandings
and broken promises, in which the British, the Russians and
later the Americans repeatedly underestimated the ability of
the Afghans and the power of the Frontier tribes.

In a new final chapter, Loyn examines the emerging threat of
the Pakistani Taliban and the challenges faced by those fighting
on the most dangerous frontier in the world.

'Superb ...Few Western journalists know Afghanistan better than Loyn'
SAUL DAVID, DAILY TELEGRAPH

'Impressive ...Should be required reading for everyone in the Foreign Office'
JOAN BAKEWELL, SUNDAY TELEGRAPH

LIAQUAT AHAMED

Lords of Finance
1929, The Great Depression, and the Bankers who Broke the World

Shortlisted for the BBC Samuel Johnson Prize for
Non-fiction and winner of the Financial Times/
Goldman Sachs Business Book of the Year Award

'Compelling and convincing ... humanises the world's descent into economic chaos'
ROBERT PESTON

The current economic crisis has only one parallel: the Wall
Street Crash of 1929 and subsequent Great Depression of the
1930s, which crippled the future of an entire generation and
set the stage for the horrors of the Second World War. Yet this
financial meltdown could have been avoided, had it not been
for the decisions taken by a small number of central bankers.

In Lords of Finance, we meet these men – the four bankers who
truly broke the world. Their names were lost to history, their
lives and actions forgotten, until now. Ahamed tells their story
in vivid and gripping detail, in a timely and arresting reminder
that individuals – their ambitions, limitations and human
nature – lie at the very heart of global catastrophe.

'Highly readable ... he cannot have foreseen how timely his book would be'
NIALL FERGUSON

'Has immense importance to modern policymaking ... a fascinating and even
a great book'
THE TIMES

'Brilliant and Timely'
GUARDIAN

RACHEL HEATH

The Finest Type of English Womanhood

'Heath combines imaginative, fast-paced storytelling with an unerring sense of
period, place and mood ... an exceptionally well-written, suspenseful novel'
GUARDIAN

It is 1946, and seventeen-year-old Laura Trelling is stagnating in
her dilapidated Sussex family home, while her eccentric parents
slip further into isolation. A chance encounter with Paul Lovell
offers her the opportunity to alter the course of her destiny –
and to embark on a new life in South Africa.

Many miles north, sixteen-year-old Gay Gibson is desperate to
escape Birkenhead. When the girls' paths cross in Johannesburg,
Laura is exposed to Gay's wild life of parties and inappropriate
liaisons. Each in her own world, but thrown together, the girls find
their lives inextricably entangled, with fatal consequences ...

'Excellent on the atmosphere of post-war Britain and the lure of South Africa ...
compellingly told, reminiscent of early Doris Lessing ... the twists keep the
reader glued to the novel'
INDEPENDENT

'The writing is strong and when the girls' paths become entwined it is
thrillingly macabre'
DAILY TELEGRAPH

THE POWER OF READING

Visit the Random House website and get connected with information on all our books and authors

EXTRACTS from our recently published books and selected backlist titles

COMPETITIONS AND PRIZE DRAWS Win signed books, audiobooks and more

AUTHOR EVENTS Find out which of our authors are on tour and where you can meet them

LATEST NEWS on bestsellers, awards and new publications

MINISITES with exclusive special features dedicated to our authors and their titles

READING GROUPS Reading guides, special features and all the information you need for your reading group

LISTEN to extracts from the latest audiobook publications

WATCH video clips of interviews and readings with our authors

RANDOM HOUSE INFORMATION including advice for writers, job vacancies and all your general queries answered

Come home to Random House

www.rbooks.co.uk